Resurrection After Rape

By

Matt Atkinson

RAR Publishing, Oklahoma City, OK

RESURRECTION AFTER RAPE: A GUIDE FOR TRANSFORMING FROM VICTIM TO SURVIVOR. Copyright © 2016 by Matt Atkinson. All rights reserved. All material quoted from other sources is cited and used in accordance with Fair Use for educational/commentary purposes. Portions of this book may be excerpted and quoted for the purpose of classroom education, facilitation of support groups, critical articles, reviews, and correspondence with the author. Permission is not granted for multiple copies of any section of this book to be made and/or distributed. All excerpts from journals, artwork, or individuals' statements contributed by former clients and friends (including their names) are used with the express permission (and proud enthusiasm) of the donors.

ISBN 978-0-615-20966-1   **Fourth Edition (Updated 2016)**

Covert art ("The World Tree") by Teresa Moorhouse Howley, used with permission. www.teresahowley.com

Artist's statement: "We would be the hand, out of which is growing the world tree, which would represent our hopes and dreams for this future that we have chosen. We stand ready at the gates of this new experience. As soon as we say, "I do", we enter the gates and right on the other side of those gates are lions and they must be fed, now. No one ever tells us this part of the story. If we feed the lions meaning, then we get to walk consciously into our lives...and we are after the water of life way up in the background, which is the very best that we can make out of our experience. If we ignore the lions, they will devour us. If we feed them something that has no substance, then we turn to stone and are unable to feel. The first room in any experience is loaded with stone statues."

More Praise for Resurrection After Rape:

"I had been to numerous therapists throughout my life and they all seemed to treat my outward 'symptoms,' without ever attempting to get to the root of the underlying causes. Talking about my abuse was never of importance as far as they were concerned. I firmly believe that this book offers the true help that others in my situation could greatly benefit from. It contains a wealth of information that would be an incredible tool to any survivor who feels hopeless or wonders why her previous efforts to cope haven't worked. In addition, I think that this book can especially benefit other women out there who are struggling to even come to terms with realizing that what they experienced was, in fact, abuse."
- Katie W., Survivor

"Thank you! So many times I have thought that no one cared and the only way out of the pain was to commit suicide. I am slowly beginning to have some hope for my life and it is people like Matt that are like a light breaking through a crack in the wall of pain. So many people don't realize that these little words of encouragement help so much."

- Sue Jacobs, survivor

"I would definitely recommend this book to anyone I know who has had similar difficulties in life. I let my doctor read some of these journal exercises (along with my responses to them) and he was very interested as well. Honestly, I don't think anyone should have to endure this without reading this book."

- Martine M., survivor

"Matt brings his years of experience working in the sexual violence field to a new audience. His understanding of the intricacies of working with those affected by sexual violence as well as his therapeutic knowledge will be helpful to counselors and anyone who wants to support victims and survivors of sexual violence."

- Jennifer McLaughlin, Sexual Assault Specialist
 for the Oklahoma Coalition Against Domestic
 Violence and Sexual Assault

"*Resurrection After Rape* is one of the best workbooks/sourcebooks I have come across. It is well written, easy to understand, and has a support group on Dailystrength.org. I have recommended it to my counselor and therapy groups I attend."
- Nadine, survivor

"Fantastic tool both as a survivor of rape and one that I will keep close at hand professionally as well. What a book."
- Deb, survivor

"When I started treatment, I thought I was already a rape survivor. After all, it had been over fourteen since I was raped. In that time, I had graduated from both college and law school and become a successful attorney. The problems that brought me to treatment were work related, or so I thought. Fortunately, I ended up in group therapy with Matt as my therapist. I think he saw right through the veneer of "survivorhood" within which I had barricaded myself. I had been able to convince my mind that I had dealt with what happened to me and that I had come out unscathed on the other side. But, my heart wasn't buying it. So I ignored my heart. As Matt rightly pointed out, I had co-opted the language of a survivor as a means of avoiding the pain and anguish of what had happened to me.

"Looking back, I think I had convinced myself that if I spoke the way a survivor speaks and acted the way a survivor acts, then I must *be* a survivor. What Matt taught me was that there is no specific survivor-speak and that the process of transforming oneself from victim to survivor is unique to each person – just as each of our traumas are unique to us. Transforming oneself from victim to survivor is neither simple nor painless. By ignoring my pain and refusing to grieve for what had been taken from me, the part of me that could feel love and respect for myself had died. But by doing the work and telling my story, that part of me has come back to life and is stronger than ever. In Matt, I found someone who taught me how to bring my heart back from the dead.

"Matt is one of those rare individuals who brings to his work not only a tremendous intellect and vast knowledge of this subject matter, but more importantly a depth of compassion for and understanding of the experiences of rape survivors, the likes of which exist in no other individual I have ever encountered. This community is lucky to have Matt serving as an advocate and therapist for those who have often felt forgotten, betrayed, weak, misunderstood, or even worthless. I know this because I have felt each of those and more. However, it is by way of Matt's patience and unwavering kindness that I am now able to see myself not as any of those things, but as a survivor. I will know this now for the rest of my life.

"My hope for those of you who have the courage to start your journey by reading this book is that you will find as much compassion, wisdom, and strength from Matt as I have."

Shalom,
Victoria Bailey

"Have you ever wished, more than anything, you had a hand to hold? *Resurrection After Rape* has been that for me. This journey was thrust upon me - I did not choose it. Rape found me.

"There is no way to describe how much this book has meant to me. I am trying to gather and absorb as much as I can. I have struggled many years with what happened to me, and sometimes I feel like I have gone nowhere. I have truly been suicidal only once in my life and that was just prior to responding to this book. I literally poured about 80 Effexor XR 150mg BACK in the bottle because what I was reading gave me hope for the first time... I know Matt is personally aware of many lives he's impacted over 10 years time...Mine, he saved.

"For a very long time, I believed rape killed a part of me, and was slowly claiming the remainder of whatever life I had left. Then, in the lowest minute of my life, I found *Resurrection After Rape*. This book didn't take away the rape - it didn't erase it, make it not matter anymore. None of that is possible - or even healthy. No, what I found in the pages of this book has been life-changing...life-saving. The most effective tool towards recovery from rape I have ever read, and I have shelves full of rape recovery materials.

"But this one handles the issues of rape differently. It isn't full of platitudes, or even promises. It is full of information. In applying the truths found in it's pages, this book has transformed the way I see myself. I read through it in two days. Then, I began feverishly working through the journaling assignments. I found a keen insight, coupled with a fierce compassion, multiplied by a pure desire to aid victims through their darkest hours. I found hard work. I found understanding. I found my voice, and the ability to use the hard work of this book to remind me that I was forever changed by rape, but not forever marred by it. Today, I am working through it again, and in so doing, I see what I have learned - I see change. I see hope. I see transformation. I see resurrection. I found a hand to hold."

- Leitha Brogan, survivor

Dear Reader,

Thank you for choosing *Resurrection After Rape* as your guide through the healing process. This book was a labor of love, and was written not to make money or gain status, but with a sincere desire to help and uplift others. This book has been endorsed by several State Coalitions Against Sexual Assault, by several psychologists, treatment centers, and by some universities which now use this as a course textbook.

A word of caution: this is a very challenging, difficult book to work through. I am often affectionately teased by my readers about the times they have hurled the book in frustration, calling it "that damned book" and referring to me as "the jerk who wrote it!" They tell me this with fondness, though, to humorously describe their own initial response to the work. Without exception, the feedback continues: "...but when I started to work hard at it, this *really worked!*" My online discussion group has over 350 members, and almost daily one of them shares the same testimonial: "this was the hardest book of all the ones I tried, but it was the one that helped me the most" and, "the parts that made me the angriest at first are now my favorite parts." So in other words, don't give up when it gets hard.

Do not rely on *any* book or website as the sole source of support if you are in crisis; trained and qualified in-person support is essential in some circumstances.

Work through this with your therapist, and don't give up. Recovery is not a straight course, but a zig-zag pattern of success, relapse, despair, and more success. If sometimes you struggle, if you falter, you are normal. *More than you know.*

Sincerely,
Matt

I love to get feedback from readers!
Don't forget to visit **www.resurrectionafterrape.org** for extra materials, and a free online discussion with other survivors!

What makes a therapist proud during rape trauma counseling:

*The moment a survivor begins to argue back against a critic in her life, and demand respect;

*The moment a survivor ditches a bad boyfriend because she will no longer tolerate power and control disguised as love;

*The moment a survivor tells me she listens to Ani Difranco and Tori Amos for strength, rather than ICP and Eminem;

*The moment a survivor reads her trauma story and finally weeps for her loss;

*The moment a survivor realizes that this issue is bigger than her, and that part of her recovery is to take on activism to change things for future survivors;

*The moment a survivor, who had refused to ever be touched by anyone, gives me a hug goodbye when she's done with me;

*The moment a survivor realizes I've been helpful, but she's outgrown the need of me;

*The moment a survivor stops asking me (or anyone else) to tell her how she feels and why, and begins to identify her OWN feelings and reasons;

*The moment a survivor has the courage to state her disagreement with me, her father, her sister, her mom, ANYONE she has been told all her life she has to submit to;

*The moment a survivor realizes that cutting herself is not a form of fighting back, but journaling and telling her story IS;

*The moment a survivor realizes that abuse and love are very different (and so are rape and sex);

*The moment a survivor stops giving me all the credit for her recovery--as complimentary as that is--and finally says with pride, "you know what? *I* did this! I worked damned hard, and I made it!"

Sigh. And to think, people actually ask me, "How can you do this work? Doesn't it depress you?"

You can do all of these things. But they won't happen by just waiting for yourself to get better, and they won't happen if you are destroying yourself in the meantime. Prepare for the hardest work you will ever do, but with the greatest reward you could ever achieve.

Recipe for Recovery

A group of survivors had a conversation about what they felt were the necessary ingredients for recovery. Each of them offered her own insight:

Leitha said, "Determination. I think being determined to heal is important to this journey. I think we have to have determination in order to seek out the painful issues that we shrink away from - in order to conquer them. Yup, my first ingredient would definitely be determination."

A teen girl suggested, "Recognizing what you yourself have done! Recognizing the little steps and big steps alike, and seeing yourself grow from a victim into a survivor. I feel like we all need this, because many of us forget how far we have come, we forget the obstacles we have overcome, when we should be realizing them and bubbling over with pride about them!"

Judy: "Honesty. Honesty with yourself. Sitting back and recognizing progress and honestly seeing it for yourself. Writing the facts as they present themselves....not just the ones we are willing to disclose because we are afraid of having to hash them out in session…And patience with ourselves...that sometimes we progress with ease and some times sessions are just awful. Patience with our progress...it goes no faster or slower than it has to. Patience with the person trying to help guide us, they don't know what's in our heads...unless we tell them. Patience with our significant others when they are unable to be what we need them to be at a moment, but take stock in them as a whole. Mine is worth it! Oh and they don't know what's in our heads either...unless we tell them, they can't do any different than they do."

Leitha: "Nurturing. I know this MUST be an ingredient that is important, because my therapist is pressing so hard for me to find the ability to nurture myself. He tells me that I am so hard on myself, that I need to treat myself kinder, to use my nurturing tools when dealing with myself."

Andrea added, "Hope for brighter days, especially when you are in the depth of depression each and every day. Hope that you will truly love who you are as a person. Hope that you can see your worth as a human being. Hope that you can make others lives better, because of who you are."

She also included, "Learning to love the person that we are now. Loving ourselves enough to realize that we are just as important as any other person in this world. And knowing that we deserve to be loved with respect! We deserve to be loved, unconditionally. Being able to love someone unconditionally, realizing that they have faults. Loving what we can accomplish as a survivor of rape or sexual abuse. Loving who we were at the time. Because, that girl or guy deserves love despite the circumstances."

I suggested, "Mercy. Remember to be merciful to yourself, rather than sifting through the mistakes of your past and condemning yourself for them. You are not wicked, and you are not without value. You may find it hard to believe at times, but there are people who will know your story and yet look you in the eyes with pure respect and acceptance. Do not forget to do that for yourself, AND for others you meet along the way who may have also stumbled. Survivorhood is built from a never-ending process of forming linkages between merciful people who see one another as humans, not as person-shaped collections of flaws."

Stephanie said, "I think positive music has been a huge part of recovery for me. It calms me down when I'm upset. Lifts me up when I'm down. And it's something I can blast in my car and sing along to on the highway to both drive away my fears of 18 wheelers and chase away tiredness. Music is something that has gotten me through a lot of hard times in my life. I don't know what I would do without it."

"We need to admit when it is we need help, when we are struggling, when it gets too big for us. We need to take action when this happens, because depression is never far away, and it can swoop down on us, and swallow us up if we fail to admit our feelings, to ourselves, and to others who want to help us - if they only knew when we need them most."

Graffiti spotted on urban sidewalk

All this time you thought I was weak
When I was just pretending
All this time you made me believe that I should be sorry
You should be sorry for making me fall
Gradually I will get wiser
I will get stronger
I will be bolder
I will not settle
                                        -Rosie Thomas

"I just think you should know, I have real trust issues with men."

This has become one of the most common statements that rape survivors make to me on Day One. And frankly, many of them take one look at me and are scared to death: I'm 6'5", I have long hair, I wear the traditional beadwork and jewelry of my Native American tribe, and I often wear large leather boots. To a rape victim, I can be an early test of her courage. The day Danée met me was one such day, except that her reaction wasn't quite as polite as "I just think you should know that I have trust issues."

It was more like, "I'm not telling this man $%&*!!"

Danée is tiny in contrast to me, a slim young woman with straight reddish hair, freckles, and glasses. She wears exotic charms on multiple silver bracelets around her tattooed wrists. She sits slumped over and her eyes are glassy, with the dazed look I recognize in someone who feels empty, exhausted, hopeless, and worthless. She offers no eye contact, and only short staccato murmurs to my questions.

I learn only basic biographical facts at first, but nothing that gives me insight into her story. Danée works as a social worker investigating child abuse and neglect cases. She is currently living apart from her own four daughters and husband, because her emotional life has become too difficult and too sorrowful for her children to see. She feels she is incapable of loving or being loved, and has diagnosed herself with "Reactive Attachment Disorder", a complex condition arising from lack of bonding in childhood and resulting in inability to form emotional connections with significant others.

She tells me that she has seen previous therapists, including one colleague of mine who suggested she join my group when Danée's depression became critical. But truthfully, she doesn't expect to ever be any different. Danée is a multiple rape victim from as early as age four into adulthood, and has been binge drinking, cutting herself, and harming herself with compulsive sex acts with strangers in an effort to either prove to herself that she is worthless, or to distract herself from the pain of believing she has been proven worthless.

But her face shows a flash of surprise and puzzlement at the answer I give her: "Of *course* you have issues with men," I reply. "I wouldn't expect you to feel any other way. If you're here saying that today, it's probably because men have done a good job justifying you not trusting them, and I'm not going to try to talk you out of that!"

Danée explains to me that whenever she has divulged her "trust issues," other men have tended to initiate the same script: "Well, you know *all* men aren't bad" and "that's an irrational belief we'll need to work on" and "Okay, but you can trust *me*" and "That could block your therapy." Consequently, Danée's first experience in nearly any attempt at deeper contemplation of her pain is to have the very core effects of her rape invalidated. She is used to being told her feelings are wrong, irrational, or exaggerated. She is used to being treated as a defective woman, needing to be *fixed*.

Danée tells me, "I've spent my whole life being raped by one guy or another, to the point I can't even count how many times it happened growing up." No eye contact. Leg vibrating wildly now.

Instead of asking her the questions she expects—"What happened? Who was it? Did you report to the police? Why not?"—I ask a new question: "What things have you tried using to help you cope?"

She says, "Mostly, doing things I regret. Cutting myself. Having affairs."

Danée spends every day in my therapy group curled up in a blanket, head down, eyes hidden from the view of any other person. She almost makes a camping tent from the blanket, and hides from us—worlds away from the people beside her. Listening. She doesn't speak, and she doesn't cry; she just listens. Danée said to me once on the way out the door to go home, "I don't want to say anything because I'm not important. Other people matter more than I do. If I opened up, it would let something evil out of me and damage he ones around me who deserve help. I don't. I'm nobody."

Danée wrote in her journal,

> I FEEL ~~CONFUSED~~ ALONE
> BECAUSE I CONTINUE
> TO PUSH PEOPLE AWAY.
> I'LL LEAVE THEM SO
> THEY DONT LEAVE ME
> FIRST.
> I FEEL BROKEN. I FEEL
> DISCONNECTED. I FEEL
> ABANDONED. I FEEL
> LONELY. I FEEL SCARED.
> UNSURE. LOST. UNSTEADY.
> ANGRY. WRONG. I FEEL
> WRONG.

Victoria is an attorney, and one of the most intelligent women I have ever seen in therapy. She's also become completely convinced of her worthlessness. She is doubled over in agony, actually shaking in spasms of despair, her face tear-stained as she confesses to me, "I just hate myself so much! And I keep waiting for you to show me your disgust at me, and it never comes."

I tell her that there isn't a molecule in my body that could feel disgust for her, and not one flicker of a thought in my mind that I would ever give up. She says, "I know. And I don't know why." But in truth, she *does* know why my disgust never comes. She knows that this work is more than a paycheck, more than a career path; she knows that for those of us who do this, it is *always* personal, despite all the pious talk about "professional distance" and the proper "Customer-Provider" dynamic (an obscene hierarchy I have rejected as heartless).

I tell Victoria that many, many women have sat alone with me, ready to finally uncover what they feel is the worst shame of their lives—the thing that will finally cause me to reject and abandon them, or even hospitalize them. And with eyes brimming with tears, these women open up those painful secrets and brace for the rebuke they expect. But no rebuke ever comes. I remind her that I am flawed too, that I am imperfect, that I would never want my "feet of clay" to become the sole measure of *my* worth or character, and neither would I punish any other human being for her struggles or secrets either. I tell Victoria what my guiding principle is: I will not work harder at this than you will, but if you are willing to work hard I will never abandon your effort.

Victoria describes coming through some of the most excruciating violence any patient of mine has ever described in all my years in rape crisis work. At times she will nearly vomit during therapy as she feels waves of sadness and despair. She, like Danée, wonders if there really is any way through this, yet she trusts me to continue anyway: "I know if I don't finish this, I *will* be dead soon."

Both of these women, and so many others, have struggled with the same troubling questions: "Is there actually any hope that I can get past this? Can I get my life back? Is there such thing as resurrection after rape?"

Thank God the answer is yes.

The world is full of suffering;
It is also full of the overcoming of it.
-Helen Keller

Is recovery even possible?

The great lie of sexual assault is that it causes a permanent emotional wound, a stain, that can never heal. Sometimes for years, the victim of a rape may feel empty, valueless, unlovable, and frightened. It can feel like a contradictory entrapment: you may wish desperately that someone would accept and know you, and yet you fear that someone *might* truly know you now, and then at other times it also feels like *everyone* can tell you've been raped by merely looking at you.

"I'm afraid nobody will ever know me, and I'm afraid anybody might ever know me."

In the beginning of coping and recovery, you may find yourself using very stark, dreadful words when you describe yourself:

- Scarred for life
- Worthless
- Damaged
- Filthy
- Unknowable

You may notice yourself using extreme and permanent-sounding terms to describe yourself, your pain, and your life, such as "always, never, forever, nobody, everybody, nothing," etc.

These kinds of words describe a rape *victim*. But the recovery process is one of transforming from a *victim* into a *survivor*.

- **Journal activity: What is the difference between a Victim and a Survivor?**
- **How do you think you will recognize the point when you have transformed from victim to survivor?**

A victim is not less than a survivor; this is not about moving from something of less worth to more worth. They are simply different states of being, defined by different sets of reactions to pain. A victim tends to feel defined by pain, as if every aspect of her life, spirit, and future are now corrupted by rape.

During the period of life in which you are still a rape victim rather than a survivor, it is likely that you will repeat the same ineffective patterns of coping. Many rape victims turn to alcohol or marijuana to numb their emotions; they take up smoking; some begin injuring themselves; and still others begin to use sex as a form of self-harm. During your "victim" phase, you may become more and more frustrated with yourself because nothing you try seems to work for longer than a moment. You exhaust yourself in a scavenger hunt for new ways to feel, or new ways *not* to feel; new ways to struggle with your rape, and new ways to *avoid* struggling with your rape. And you criticize yourself for how long the process is taking because you say to yourself (and other people say to you), "Aren't you over this yet? It's time to let it go!"

You're not sure how to try *different*, so you just keep trying the same things *harder*.

You may be feeling guilty and depressed. You may have trouble eating and sleeping. You may feel empty and grey inside, confused even about who you are. You may find yourself becoming angry at people who do not correctly guess how to respond to your needs, and wind up driving other away (and perhaps even feeling even *more* victimized by the loneliness that results).

These should not be the feelings you carry for the rest of your life, but for right *now*, at this point, these are the logical and reasonable emotions that trauma will stir. Don't deny your emotions because you have guilt or pressure telling you not to feel them; women who are unable to genuinely accept what they feel during this process have much more difficulty getting through it. Being depressed is not the same as being suicidal; as long as you are not suicidal, assure others in your life that you are safe and not to be afraid of what you are experiencing.

Emotions are forms of communication within yourself and they have some important things to say. If you shove them away, ignore them, suppress them, blur them with alcohol, or find other ways to counterfeit how you truly feel, your emotions will not be able to finish their task of expressing data to you, which will cause those emotions to persist in more confusing forms. Allowing our emotions to be heard and understood will not result in being "drowned" in a tidal wave. In fact, the opposite happens: they are able to release their data, then finally withdraw and fade into vapor. This is not an easy process, so it is important that you not squander your relationships with allies.

What I'm going to do in this book is show you how to fully express the emotions of your rape, learn from those emotions, reprogram your understanding of the data they send to you, and allow those compressed voices of hurt to finally rest. It won't involve any trendy buzzwords or hocus-pocus, and I'm not promising the newly-discovered "easy trick" to this. It will be the hardest thing you have ever done, I promise you. Women have even written to me that at times they have thrown this book across bedrooms! But I will explain exactly what the research says about how brain science (neurology), psychiatry (medication), psychology, sociology, and even spiritual faith all become your tools. This will not be easy, because it will ask you to do the opposite of your instinct: to face your rape, rather than fleeing from it. To accept yourself as a Survivor, rather than hiding the truth.

My intention is that you will use this book in conjunction with guidance from a skilled therapist, and it is written with that context in mind. If you do not have access to a therapist, it is still possible to benefit from this book's activities, but I do suggest seeking some type of interactive support system to help you with the difficult parts. The website www.dailystrength.org has a group of over 280 women (as of this writing) who have voluntarily come together to use *Resurrection After Rape* in their daily recovery. Many of their journals are included throughout this book. Here is my friend Leitha's journal about "Victims and Survivors":

My definition:
A VICTIM is a survivor who hasn't grasped their full potential in healing.

That is MY definition, and I am sure it rubs against the grain of the traditional answers for this. But, to have been raped, since it is a violent crime committed against someone, we all are victims.

LIKEWISE, since we are all currently breathing, we survived our attacks. So, in the simplest terms, we all are on the path to survivorhood. We just haven't arrived, each of us, to a point where we don't victimize ourselves. So, we live, but at different points on the trek to survivorhood.

Unfortunately, some will never get there. Victims just give in to the negative ways of dealing with the pain of the violence and what it left them with. They stop short on the journey up the mountain, and fail to claim the prize. They may exist on the side of the mountain, may even figure out ways to keep air in their lungs and food in their stomachs, but exist and nothing more. Victims see others climbing, and they watch as those pursuing survivorhood pass by.

But the survivors, well, you can tell them right off. The survivors keep their hiking boots laced, and their canteens full, and we carry with us everything we need on our journey. The greatest difference? We carry enough for our journey, access it when we need to, AND WE SHARE WITH OTHERS along the way. We stop, and we minister to the victims who have stalled, or feel defeated, and we encourage them. And we lift them up with our words and our strength. Strength we sometimes fail to recognize in ourselves. We aren't heroes. We aren't saviors. We are survivors, and a true survivor may stumble on the rocks, or get bogged down in the snow on the mountainside. But a true survivor recognizes their plight, and reaches out for help. And likewise, that same survivor, reaches back, and lifts out of the depths of despair, another weary from the journey.

We aren't survivors just because we lived through a horrific experience, we are survivors because we continue the fight to live....everyday.

Danée wrote:

> Victim: Says it's her own fault.
> Survivor: says "hell no, it's not my fault! He *chose* to rape me. *He* made the decision." She puts the blame where it belongs.
>
> Victim: says "I'm dirty."
> Survivor: Says "What happened to me was dirty. He was dirty."
>
> Victim: says "I'm unlovable."
> Survivor: says "My rapist tried to convince me I'm unlovable, but I'm worthy of love. I'm full of love. I'm love. He can't take love away from me."
>
> Victim: Keeps the secret.
> Survivor: Breaks the silence, be it talking about it with a therapist, trusted friend, writing about the rape and reading it aloud, attending a support group…
>
> Victim: Self-injures, be it cutting, bingeing, purging, drugs, alcohol, or sex.
> Survivor: Confronts her rape with great courage, instead of numbing the memories that haunt her by injuring herself over and over. She realizes that the rapist still has the power if she chooses to destroy herself. A survivor chooses against these behaviors.
>
> Victim: says "I'm powerless."
> Survivor: Takes her power back, by talking about the rape. Writing about it. Encouraging other survivors. Attending support groups. She begins to speak out about this crime.

If you truly want to do the work to transform into a survivor, one of the fundamental first steps is to forgive yourself for how long you have already struggled, and to preemptively forgive yourself for however long the process will take. This isn't like getting over a cold, and well-meaning people may heap pressure on you to "hurry up and get over it." Rape is a life-changing experience—the most severe form of physical assault short of homicide—and it is perfectly acceptable for you to work at your own pace. The United Nations considers rape to be a form of terrorism, so try not to be rough on yourself for the time it's taken to arrive at today.

If you wish to successfully transform into a survivor, you must take care of yourself. You cannot succeed at this work if you are skipping therapy sessions, avoiding homework, using drugs (including alcohol and marijuana) during the process, or ignoring medical self-care (including responsible and consistent use of psychiatric medications). If you are not willing to form a personal covenant to manage your physical, emotional, and even *spiritual* health during this process, this transformation will be more painful than healing. Every week, I see women begin this process who have not committed to taking care of themselves, and then become overwhelmed. Those who do commit to self-care tend to do very well, through.

If you truly want to transform from a victim into a survivor, you must, must, *must* start with a committed decision that you will live. I mean that as plainly as I can say it:

you must *decide* that your life is worth saving. If you have been suicidal, you must *decide* that this is no longer an option. That means no more threats, no more veiled comments about "wanting to sleep and never wake up," no more fate-testing by overdrinking, driving with eyes closed, abusing medications, etc. To some readers this may sound startlingly unusual to read, while others may know exactly what I am describing and relate to it. Ashley, a 20-year-old survivor, put it this way:

> I do want to live. I just get so tired of being depressed and constantly feeling like I have to lie to others. I'm tired of keeping everything bottled up inside about what happened. I'm tired of driving past the complex he lived/lives in and crying, tired of falling asleep and startling awake at the slightest thing. I fell asleep on my mom's bed yesterday and she touched my back to wake me up and I was startled so bad I came up off the bed at her before I even know what happened.
>
> Do you know what its like to not even want to go back to see your parents because you're 5 minutes from him? Do you know what its like to be afraid in your own bed, in your own apartment? Do you know what its like to be afraid for your life every day?

This doesn't mean you are failing if you have slip-ups. From time to time, *every* rape victim I've counseled has lapsed and relapsed in some form: a night of binge-drinking, an episode of cutting, a regretted sexual experience with an unloved person. I cannot give any permission or approval of any of these things, but I can *understand* them. If you slip up, make a pledge that you will immediately divulge the incident to your therapist, rather than hiding it. You can use these lapses to learn more about recovery by identifying triggers and stressors, and tracking down the inner thoughts ("self-talk") you sometimes have that promote relapses. There is a Buddhist teaching that no experience is a failure if it promotes new learning.

The goal of each day is progress, not perfection. I've had clients who are reluctant to even do journaling because they are afraid the writing will be imperfect or that they "won't say it right." Other clients of mine have hidden the fact that on weekends they may have become intoxicated or had compulsive sex with someone they didn't even care about. They are afraid I will judge them (because they are already telling themselves that these incidents make them worthless, failures, or freaks). The progress in therapy halts, and I can sense it, but until they come clean we cannot cope with the issue.

Remember, if you do slip up or relapse, it does *not* mean that every sign of progress before is suddenly erased. It does *not* mean that you start again at "square one," with no strengths and no victories. You still get to keep and draw on all your previous successes, and relapses do not suck them away from you like a tidal wave. If you slip up, acknowledge it and explore what triggered it. One 21-year-old woman wrote this in her journal in response to her choice to succeed at rape recovery:

> I think I can finally make you a promise. One that I can keep, one that involves something more than just trying, one that is spoken with confidence rather than whispered in hesitance.

I will not leave you.

I don't care what happens in the future. I can leave a situation or a belief or an emotion behind. But I will not be forced to lose my life. If I genuinely want you to be happy, to feel loved, or accomplished in your life, then it's time for me to live up to my word. I've always wanted to give back the love you've given me. I have to be alive in order to do that. So I promise you - come whatever may - I will never leave you or my life behind. Please don't let me forget.

There is, however, one experience that will absolutely prevent your successful transformation from a victim into a survivor. If you are currently in a relationship where you are being emotionally, physically, or sexually abused, by definition you cannot recover from trauma because the abuse continues to add traumatic experiences. Yet clinical research—and my own observations as a therapist—have shown that survivors of sexual abuse and rape are more at risk for later involvement in abusive relationships! In fact, prior sexual trauma is the *number one* predictor of a woman's risk of being abused by a partner later. And the reverse is also true: women in abusive relationships are far more likely to be sexually assaulted.[1]

It is a fantasy that a victim can somehow muster enough personal strength to rescue a dysfunctional relationship, because there is no such thing as a victim who can rehabilitate a person who is hurting her. How can a woman rebuild her confidence, spirit, and hopefulness, if someone in her life is sending her ongoing messages of being faulty, inferior, and defective? If you are in a relationship where abuse occurs, my advice is to change agendas and address that situation first, before attempting the difficult and painful work of this book. Rape recovery cannot be done alone; it requires a reliable support system. I have had many women join therapy because they hope to "fix" themselves so that an abusive person in their lives will finally stop hurting them. But that isn't how it works.

Part of the recovery process is to finally make connections between the rape itself and your current feelings that affect your behaviors and relationships now. The connection may seem self-evident at first, but until you really examine it, write about it, and learn to successfully challenge it, the belief that you are worthless or damaged will continue to drive a constellation of other symptoms such as anxiety, panic attacks, substance abuse, self-injury, and sexual dysfunction. Alice Sebold, in her book *Lucky*, describes her recovery as the struggle *after* her struggle, meaning that "I was about to begin my real fight, a fight of words and lies and the brain."

In your recovery, it is important to change the *language* of rape that you might use. I have found that rape victims can be very cruel to themselves and recycle awful self-criticisms in their own minds. For example, "I'm scarred for life." A person in

---

[1] Lauren R. Taylor with Nicole Gaskin-Laniyan. "Sexual assault in abusive relationships." National institute of Justice, January 2002, no. 256, http://www.ojp.usdoj.gov/nij/journals/256/sexual-assault.html Two-thirds of women in physically abusive relationships had also been sexually assaulted.

recovery will reconsider what "scarred" truly means: a scar is a *healed* place, a marker and reminder of what was formerly a wound but is now a protected and useful (and even useable) growth. While we cannot lose our memories of the wound that caused the scar, we carry the evidence of our healing *as* the scar.

Examine the self-talk you use:

- Do you continually degrade yourself, criticize yourself, and expect rejection?
- Have you begun to believe that because of your rape, you no longer have anything worthy inside to contribute to another person's life?
- Does it feel like you have "hurt me" printed right on your forehead?
- Do you find yourself accepting all of peoples' criticisms, but none of their praise?
- Do you continually produce art or writing obsessed with images of defeat, injury, or despair?
- Do you pick fights with people, or have a "chip on your shoulder," and then criticize others for failing *you* when the conflict starts?
- Do you behave in ways that you think will *cause* people to reject you because you believe "they'll reject me anyway, so let's get it over with"?
- Do you tell yourself that nobody can love you now?
- Do you warn people who love you that you are no good, and suggest that they abandon you?
- Do you deliberately provoke people who love you in an effort to drive them away to "save" them from you?
- Do you find yourself asking permission to speak, apologizing for seeking help, or feeling undeserving of time?
- Do you make comments like, "you would be better off without me" or "I'm sorry to be such a burden on you" to people who try to support you?

Recovery is absolutely possible—many people *do* recover from this trauma. The ones who do not recover are women who commit suicide, who remain in abusive relationships, who continually choose alcohol or self-injury over the difficult work of recovery, or cannot find competent support and help from others. I simply can't imagine how anyone would recover from this if, at the same time, she were also beating herself up with negativity.

Be not the slave of your own past. Plunge into the sublime seas, dive deep and swim far, so you shall come back with self-respect, with new power, with an advanced experience that shall explain and overlook the old.
-Ralph Waldo Emerson

What is trauma?

When I analyze myself I realize that I've spent a large portion of my life being "on guard". I've been on guard with people I don't know and trust. I've been on guard that another family member will become ill and die. I've been on guard that someone I love will be injured/killed in an accident. I've simply been on guard about any lousy possibility that can potentially happen... and I have to fight that in me consistently. Most of the time, I win... but I absolutely HATE it when I lose. When I feel overwhelmed by fear and uncertainty. When I want to wrap my family in bubble wrap and set them in a safe place.
                                                                               -Kaye

The conventional psychological understanding of trauma is that it is any safety-threatening event that 1) is sudden, unexpected, or not normal in a person's experiences; 2) exceeds the individual's perceived ability to cope; and 3) disrupts the individual's mental and emotional functioning in a way that interferes with activities of daily living.[1] Trauma can include natural disasters, war and combat, intentional human violence, or life-threatening accidents.

After a trauma, you may have access to whole memories of the incident, or parts of those memories may be suppressed. Fragmented memories are common and normal responses to trauma, and it is also common for memories to change over time. Neither you nor your supporters and loved ones should begin to doubt your claims of having been raped simply because your memories, and therefore your accounts, change over time. The

---

[1] I. Lisa McCann, Laurie Anne Pearlman. (1990) *Psychological Trauma and the Adult Survivor*. Psychology Press, p. 10.

fragments that seem to be missing will often later return to "haunt" you as they are triggered by some seemingly-insignificant reminder.

Post Traumatic Stress Disorder (PTSD) is the clinical term for the collected symptoms a person may experience after surviving a trauma. It includes:

- Recurring and intrusive recollections of the event. This can include memories, flashbacks, nightmares, etc.
- Inner distress when you are exposed to cues that relate to the initial trauma. For example, talking about rape causes you to feel nausea, gagging reflexes, or anxiety. Triggers for these reactions can include sights, smells, certain music, anniversaries of trauma, scenes in movies or TV shows, dental and OB/GYN exams, being grabbed, sexual intercourse, etc.
- Physical symptoms of stress when you encounter triggers related to the trauma: pounding heart, adrenaline, shakiness, tunnel vision.
- Efforts to avoid anything associated with the trauma. For example, avoiding certain places, skipping or dropping out of therapy, using self-injury or drugs to suppress feelings, being unable to talk about the trauma.
- Heightened fear of danger, and increased arousal of the senses for the purpose of remaining on "high alert." You may experience irritability, anger outbursts, difficulty concentrating and remembering, exaggerated startle/flinch responses, and sleep difficulties.
- Changes in emotion: numbness, loss of pleasure, depression
- The symptoms last for more than a month, and interfere with your daily life.

Research finds that nearly *all* rape survivors meet criteria for PTSD in the first month after the rape, and the PTSD rates are highest among women who were raped before age 18.[2] After one year, the rate of PTSD symptoms drops to around 60% of all victims. It does not appear to continue to decline after that without therapy, which means that in the big picture just over half of all rape victims carry long-term PTSD symptoms. They will continue until some deliberate, effective effort is made to address the trauma and recover.[3]

That is exactly what you are doing by reading this book and facing your past.

What is Rape Trauma Syndrome (RTS)?

When post-traumatic stress is caused by rape, the specific term for the symptoms of depression, flashbacks, avoidance, and anxiety you feel is Rape Trauma Syndrome.[4] It is very similar to PTSD, but with a few key differences:

---

[2] Saba W. Masho, Gasmelseed Ahmed. "Age at Sexual Assault And Posttraumatic Stress Disorder among Women: Prevalence, Correlates, And Implications for Prevention." Journal of Women's Health. 2007, 16(2): 262-271.
[3] *Treating the Trauma of Rape: Cognitive-behavioral therapy for PTSD*. p14-17.
[4] Patricia Searles, Ronald J. Berger, editors (1995). *Rape and society: Readings on the problem of sexual assault.* Westview press, pp239-245. "Rape Trauma Syndrome" is not used as commonly today as it once was, but is still a useful term for the purposes of this book.

- Exaggerated startle response, or hyper-alertness. Have you noticed that since the rape, you become more alert and uncomfortable when someone walks behind you? Or that you suddenly stiffen up when you are hugged, even by someone you love? Or that footsteps now cause waves of fear? These are "startle responses."

- Guilt and self-blame about surviving behaviors used during the rape. Rape victims, with no exception I've ever found, struggle with some degree of self-blame for the rape. Sometimes the self-blame is related to actions the victim did during the rape itself, such as walking to a place where she was told to go by the rapist, or removing her own underpants, or remaining silent, or not reporting the rape afterward. In a court case in Texas, a woman's rape case was dismissed because she had asked her knife-wielding attacker to wear a condom, which the defense attorney portrayed as a sign of consent from her. In reality, all of these things were done for the sake of *survival*, in order to minimize the rapist's use of force as much as possible.

- Impairment of memory and concentration. Countless clients of mine were frustrated by their own inability to remember key details about the rape itself. The most common example of this is, "I can remember the rape, but I can't remember what happened before, and I can't remember what I did afterward." You may be unable to recall how you got to a certain place, or who else was there, or what you said during the rape, or what happened the rest of the day afterward. Even months later, concentration may be difficult; literally dozens of young women were admitted to therapy with me for "anxiety disorders" due to poor work performance or dropping grades and missed classes at college, when the real reason they could not concentrate is because of rape trauma.

- Avoidance of activities that arouse memories of the rape. One in three clients who begins therapy will drop out when the issue of rape is meaningfully introduced. Clients will "forget" or postpone assigned homework about the rape. Victims may use complex rituals of self-injury, meaningless sex, and substance abuse to numb or distract their feelings about the rape. On online web forums, victims will refer to "r*pe" or "the incident" or "when it happened," but avoid the word "rape" itself.

Rape Trauma Syndrome is not a clinical diagnosis; it is a term used to explain the nature of a person's PTSD. Survivors of rape constitute the largest group of victims of violence or crime (including war) affected by PTSD.[5] The term "Rape Trauma Syndrome" is not used in medical documents, where the term "PTSD" is preferred.

One particularly strong trait of PTSD is the state of dissociation, a temporary flatness of mood in which a person's mental and emotional attention to a painful issue is briefly blocked.[6] The purpose of dissociation is to "vacate" (or literally, to "take a

---

[5] Petrak, Jenny. "Rape: History, myths and reality." *The Trauma of Sexual Assault.* 2002. p4.

[6] Anderson, G., et al. "Dissociative experiences and disorders among women who identify themselves as sexual abuse survivors." 1993 Child Abuse Negl 17;5:677-86. This study found an incidence of dissociation in 88% of sexual trauma survivors.

vacation from") an experience of stress related to the memory of trauma so that it can be kept locked away in a compartment while other parts of the mind drape a blanket of numbness over the memory. The end result is a feeling of emptiness and emotional vacancy, floating passively in an imaginary world. It is as if the person sends their conscious mind outside of their own bodies so that the sensations within their bodies are not felt. The younger we are when trauma occurs, the more likely we are to use dissociation.[7]

Survivors of trauma often create a mental "wall" between their conscious thoughts and the memories of the trauma. But this isn't a solid wall; it leaks. Triggers such as sounds, smells, touches, and images that remind you of the trauma drill little "holes" into that wall, allowing suppressed memories to burst through into conscious thought. Dissociation is an attempt to patch the cracks in the wall again. You may have noticed that memories and triggers that cause you to dissociate are highly emotional, and usually nonverbal; that is, they are not logical thoughts that are easily managed. They feel powerful and unchallengeable, which convinces many trauma survivors "I just can't deal with this."

Dissociation is a short-term solution to emotional pain, but at the same time that it soothes immediate discomfort it also prolongs the total duration of trauma by postponing the re-emergence of those painful feelings.[8] It's not a form of erasing emotions; it's a form of compressing them into a mental box. Imagine stuffing more and more laundry into a drawer until it's full; it takes more pressure, more effort to keep the drawer shut, and each time you have to stuff more into it, the risk of the contents overflowing is increased. Dissociation is shutting a drawer on increasingly-compressed contents within it. From a journal:

I used to rely on dissociation because I thought it was the only way to be safe. I eventually realized I could do it by choice: find myself in a harmful situation, or feeling awful, and just turn my mind off. Just like that, and I'm floating and blank. It was my dream world, and people thought I was just thoughtful or imaginative. But I was really the classic lost child.

Then I discovered that dissociation wasn't just going blank. Sometimes it was an experience of spinning randomly through different fantasy feelings, one after the other, none of which were part of my real life. But I did this inside my mind, while the physical part of me sat there, unaware, on "standby" mode. It was like staring blankly at a TV screen while flipping channels without purpose—just "click, click, click," and let's see where I end up.

The trouble was that sometimes I was lucky—I only ended up forgetting entire lectures in class, but sometimes I was very unlucky. I returned to my conscious mind to find guys I didn't even know all over me. And that meant that my dream world became more important than my real one, and I got too far lost.

---

[7] Schiraldi, Glenn, Ph.D. *Post-Traumatic Stress Disorder Sourcebook*, McGraw-Hill, 1999, p20.
[8] Gilboa-Schechtman, E. and Foa, E. B. "Patterns of recovery from trauma: the use of intraindividual analysis." 2001 J Abnorm Psychol 110;3:392-400. "Sexual assault victims experienced more severe peak reactions and had slower recovery rates from their assault than non-sexual assault victims."

Dissociation isn't entirely good or bad; it's a normal thing that most people do to escape anything from boredom to distress. Dissociation doesn't mean you are "crazy;" on the contrary, for many people it has been a part of their emotional survival. That doesn't mean it's a good choice for a permanent coping skill because it only postpones dealing with memories, it doesn't eradicate them. In time, those memories will continue to intrude more and more until they are processed. There are whole books just on treating dissociative symptoms after trauma, but I have observed that just allowing the suppressed emotions to finally seep forward through the gauzy bandages of mental avoidance and be cleansed is usually enough to reduce dissociative symptoms. After all, why keep using a trick to hide from something you've faced and overcome?

During Danée's dissociation in therapy, she would fill entire pages with sequences of numbers and patterns, without meaning

During your therapy for rape trauma, you and your therapist will address three ways in which you were victimized by your rape in addition to the obvious physical injuries from the rape itself. This may not happen in a formal manner—"let's look at Level One in today's session"—but all three will be addressed.

The first way in which your trauma victimized you was to demolish your beliefs and assumptions about yourself and the world. Your sense of safety, trust, and invulnerability have been shattered, and that can make the world seem very chaotic and confusing. It can also drain your previous self-image, causing you to feel stupid, weak, childish, ugly, and alone. This will make it difficult to accept help from others, to trust, and even to see yourself as a good and worthy person.

The second way you have been hurt is one of the most difficult to overcome. This is what I call the "second trauma," and it describes the daily re-injuring you receive from peoples' insensitivity, lack of support, and flat-out rudeness about your trauma. If you reported your rape to a hospital or police, you may have experienced this secondary wounding during a rape evidence exam, or by having to constantly repeat your story to a detective (who is deliberately trained to challenge you about details of your story). People may be telling you that your rape wasn't "real" rape because your perpetrator was a boyfriend and not a psycho in an alley. They may tell you to "get over it." They may even scold you for being raped, suggesting that it was *your* fault (when it wasn't). Ridicule at school, smirks on the face of your rapist if you see him again, rumors and gossip, and jokes are all forms of re-injury. "An individual becomes a victim in the primary experience of the rape act, but can be further victimized by negative and judgmental reactions following the rape incident," write Irina Anderson and Kathy Doherty, "which may prompt feelings of guilt or shame *on the part of victims* about their conduct in relation to the crime perpetrated against them."[9]

These secondary traumas are caused by peoples' ignorance, cruelty, burnout, misunderstanding, and personal issues with the subject of rape. In response to these traumas, you may even find yourself doubting your own memory ("Did I imagine that? Did I misunderstand? Am I crazy?"), joining with your critics against yourself ("I know, I was stupid!" and "It was my fault. I put myself in that position." and "It's no big deal.").

The third way in which your trauma will affect you is by planting a type of "I'm a victim and nothing more!" style of thinking. This is the self-rejection and self-hatred that rape victims universally experience: "I'm damaged goods," or "nobody will want to marry someone like me" or "I can't take the pain anymore. God has even forgotten me." While you have little control over the first two kinds of victimization, you can learn how to overcome this part, which is good news because it is this level of harm that is most damaging and potentially fatal (through suicide, eating disorders, self-injury and addiction).

---

[9] Anderson, Irina and Doherty, Kathy. *Accounting for Rape: Psychology, Feminism and discourse Analysis in the Study of Sexual Violence*, 2008, p9-10.

Please   please seek and find a safe person and start talking.
Don't let the poison continue to spread through your life.
There is freedom. There is hope. There is joy.

Is therapy necessary for recovery?

I am often questioned by women who are skeptical about the need for therapy and ask me, "Can't I just do this work on my own? Can't I just use my own methods and get through it? I don't see the value in 'spilling my guts' to someone I don't even know, which would make me feel worse, not better."

This is certainly a valid question, and I do not doubt that there are some who can successfully recover from rape independently of counseling. But several points need to be made to fully answer the question. First, we need to clarify just what "recovery" is, or else we have no way to accurately recognize that a person has "recovered" either with or without therapy. I have known more than a few rape victims who insist, "I'm over that— I've recovered!" while still engaging in self-harm, self-hating thoughts, and substance abuse.

Research finds that 94% of all rape victims meet criteria for *post-traumatic stress disorder* within the first week[1] after a rape; PTSD is a very serious, life-altering, debilitating condition that does *not* tend to vanish simply with the passing of time. Its symptoms diminish gradually, so that three months later the percentage of women with

---

[1] With one exception: a full diagnosis of PTSD requires that the symptoms last for one month or longer. Technically, the diagnosis for these symptoms prior to the one-month marker is "Acute traumatic stress disorder," but other than the length of duration the symptoms are the same.

PTSD drops to about half, but this is where the improvements stall.[2] In other words, nearly *all* rape victims experience PTSD at some point, and about *half* still will even months and years later, with "no further recovery" occurring without therapy.[3] Some researchers even argue that these rates may be low because victims in younger ages may cope with rape through denial, rather than re-experiencing phenomena, and thus may lack the criteria for diagnosis of PTSD while still exhibiting a full spectrum of signs of trauma.[4]

And this is just for starters. Ninety-five percent of rape victims meet conditions for a diagnosis of "major depressive disorder" following rape, leading to a suicide attempt rate of one in three women per year, *each* year, following rape, adding up to a *50%* overall suicide ideation or attempt rate among rape victims. The level of a stress hormone called cortisol remains elevated;[5] cortisol is a "survival hormone" that saps emergency calories from body tissues. Although short-term bursts of cortisol are necessary for daily life, extended elevation can cause chronic aches and pains, joint soreness, and even weight gain as metabolism slows due to loss of lean muscle. The lifestyle effects of depression with PTSD after rape include:

- Increased substance abuse
- Eating disorders, including overeating, food refusal, and bingeing,[6]
- Deliberate self-injury behaviors
- Onset or increase of smoking habits
- Fatigue and loss of energy
- "Anhedonia" – the loss of sensations of pleasure
- Exaggerated startle responses
- Loss of relationship quality
- Anger outbursts
- Retarded motor skills/response times
- Diminished ability to concentrate

As we will see, these symptoms are not caused by personal weakness, but by internal biological functions within certain regions of the brain and nervous system. And if these symptoms are not caused by personal weakness, personality, or mental frailty, they cannot be *undone* by personal toughness, determination, or intentions.

A therapist's job is to understand the research into why the brain develops certain patterns of thought and emotion after trauma, and which techniques can be used to diminish those symptoms. This is *not* the same thing as the stereotypical "spill your guts to someone you don't even know" image of therapy from a couch while a psychologist scrawls in a notebook. One thing a good therapist will do is to provide research-based,

---

[2] "A prospective examination of post-traumatic stress disorder in rape victims." *Journal of Traumatic Stress*, 5:3, (1991), pp455-475.

[3] Patricia A. Resick and Monica Schnicke. *Cognitive Processing Therapy for Rape Victims.* 1996, p5.

[4] Petrak, Jenny. "The psychological impact of sexual assault." *The Trauma of Sexual Assault*, 2002, p29.

[5] Resnick, H. S., Yehuda, R., Pitman, R. K., and Foy, D. W. "Effect of previous trauma on acute plasma cortisol level following rape." 1995 Am J Psychiatry 152;11:1675-7

[6] Zlotnick, C., et al. "The relationship between sexual abuse and eating pathology." 1996 Int J Eat Disord 20;2:129-34

well-developed homework assignments that will challenge your thoughts and beliefs, so that your instinctive responses to stress, sadness, and crisis are altered away from a trauma-based response, toward a more conscious, controlled response. This "thought-challenging" *cannot* happen internally and independently; it takes an external other person who can identify your mind's patterns and apply research-based methods of nudging those patterns into gentle change.

But does it work? The research says yes. One study examined the effects of clinical therapy on the symptoms of trauma and depression among female rape victims, compared to those who did not receive therapy and opted for a "go it alone" approach. The study found that using mental health therapy to explore a victim's rape experience (her "narrative") had three outcomes: their actual spoken narratives increased in length (indicating less need to avoid pain and shame, and an ability to incorporate more details gleaned from her education about rape itself); their thoughts became more organized; and their depression was diminished. Women who completed therapy were more able to consciously manage their thoughts and feelings about their rape, rather than having abrupt, disorganized emotional *reactions* to the trauma. These benefits were not found among the "go it alone" control.[7]

Another study found that the benefits of therapy were lasting. That is, the "good" effects didn't just wear off, whereas trauma survivors who received no such therapy did not even *receive* the benefits of reduced depression, more organized thought, improved relationships, and so on. In an analysis of multiple scientific studies on trauma therapy outcomes, the Department of Psychiatry at the University of Washington found that whether the trauma was caused by war or by assault (including rape), *"the impact of psychotherapy on PTSD and psychiatric symptomatology was significant."* The study found no substantive "decay" in the benefits of therapy at follow-up, "[which] suggests substantial promise for improving psychological health and decreasing related symptoms for those suffering from PTSD."[8] This does not mean that women did not occasionally have lapses and fallbacks after therapy was finished, but they did not return to the same level of crisis, and were better able to overcome the crisis.

The benefits of therapy continue. One of the areas that rape trauma has a particularly crushing impact is on a marriage between a rape survivor and her partner. Research into marriages which include a rape survivor find that the effects of rape include increased risk of divorce, and reduced understanding, communication, sexual intimacy, and even sexual dysfunction (the divorce rate after the rape of one spouse is very high). However, these problems and the overall risk of divorce itself were all reduced if the rape victim received therapy; the beneficial outcomes were even higher if her partner or spouse participated even occasionally in treatment sessions.[9]

I do think that therapy is important to recovery for most rape survivors, for several reasons. It may be possible for some survivors to independently work their way

---

[7] "Change in rape narratives during exposure therapy for posttraumatic stress disorder." *Journal of Traumatic Stress*, 8:4 (1995), pp675-690.
[8] "Effects of Psychotherapeutic Treatments for PTSD: A Meta-Analysis of Controlled Clinical Trials." *Journal of Traumatic Stress,* 11:3 (1998), pp413-435.
[9] "The effects of rape on marital and sexual adjustment." *the American Journal of Family Therapy*, 10:1 (1982), pp51-58

through the trauma of rape, but it's very rare. Perhaps you can. But the majority, if not ALL, of my clients were women who tried to do that for years. They dreaded coming to therapy, but the panic attacks, depression, suicide attempts, self-injury, addictions, divorces, sexual encounters, and sleep disorders had just become too overwhelming. They were often ashamed of even seeking therapy, as if it proved they are "too weak" to handle their rape trauma alone: "I kept insisting I was doing well all by myself, and I wasn't! My mood was awful, I was just barely getting by, I had suicidal thoughts and attempts, I had panic attacks, I kept telling myself what a worthless f--- I was…" (journal entry by one client).

What therapy CAN do is help a survivor understand the physical basis of depression caused by changes in the neurotransmitter system.

It can help someone understand why flashbacks happen, and that they are biologically-based, and how to regulate the brain's crisis response centers so that flashbacks and nightmares diminish.

It can help reduce the use of self-injury by using the newest work of brain scans and neuroscience to understand the role of the endogenous opioid system on the cycle of self-harm.

It can help when women have lost the ability to feel sexual pleasure after a rape, or when a survivor becomes very sexual after a rape, to understand why these happen and how to change them.

It can help diminish self-criticism, guilt, and shame.

It can reduce the damaging effects of rape trauma on your significant relationships.

It can improve your sleep.

This stack of document illustrates the extent of rape trauma in the clients I have worked with in therapy. Each 1-to-3 page document represents a single client, adding up to hundreds of clients just representing the face of sexual assault.

None of these effects are immediate upon starting therapy; these benefits come gradually. In fact, the early stages of therapy can be especially stressful and make some symptoms feel *worse* as you come face-to-face with the pain and shame you struggle so desperately to escape. Like purging a toxin, the process is awful, but the result is life.

> **Online support groups are good sources of inspiration and encouragement, but they are *not* replacements for clinical mental health therapy.**

I will admit this, though: not ONE of my clients, in the hundreds of rape survivors I have worked with, wanted to be in therapy. They dreaded the "spill your guts to someone you don't even know" thing, and they came in as last resort. So I don't discount anyone's reluctance to begin therapy. And besides, there are some awful therapists out there who do little more than reinforce their patients' conclusion, "See? I knew that therapy wouldn't help!" Plenty of my own clients had previously been through that type of unhelpful counseling, and I don't regard it as boasting to say that we often have to begin by undoing the harmful effects of previous therapeutic incompetence.

So what is the difference between the "go it alone" approach that works, and the kind that doesn't work? I asked Dr. Patricia Resick, a noted author of clinical textbooks for therapists on treating PTSD in rape victims. Dr. Resick responded,

> "If personal strength comes from feeling one's emotions, reaching out to others and discussing what happened and what they have been thinking about it, then I would say that personal strength is possible. If personal strength means being stoic and trying to forget or ignore what happened, then it is likely to backfire and the person will not recover."

How will I recognize "Recovery" when it happens?

I surveyed a group of rape survivors to ask this very question. Their answers were complex but had very similar themes:

- When you can face the thoughts of rape rather than having to avoid them;
- When you understand the connection between your current self-concept and your rape, so that when you feel down on yourself you won't accept that as a permanent "truth" of who you are;
- When you no longer engage in self-harming behaviors (including substance abuse) to manage emotions and memories;
- When flashbacks have diminished to the point they either no longer happen, or no longer interfere with your life and emotions;
- When you can appropriately respond to people's ignorant attitudes about rape, rather than withdrawing from them and wilting in lonely shame;
- When you have begun to offer support to other survivors;
- When you have begun to view your body as a valuable thing and not as a betrayer or curse, and you take care of its needs;

- When you learn to recognize the warning signs of dangerous men and avoid them, no matter how charming they appear to be;
- When men no longer have control over your opinions of yourself;
- When you are able to confront, challenge, and speak proudly to men;
- When you make your own choices whether to disclose your rape to someone because of something *you* need to say, not something you need to *hear*, for you to make progress;
- When you no longer feel guilty for asking for help, or for having rough days, or for taking the length of time needed for growth.

This sounds like a difficult list, but you don't have to achieve all of these at once. You will have some breakthrough "a-ha!" moments that bring success to several of these at once, too, like a domino effect. Improvements in one area will tend to bring improvements in many other areas too. If you continue through your therapy, and with this book, you will find yourself accomplishing most (or all) of this list.

Journal Exercise: What is *your* definition of "Recovery," and how will you know when it has happened?

Recovery from rape is perhaps as difficult as surviving the rape itself. You will feel frustrated, you will get angry at yourself, and you will connect with intense pain. Writer and filmmaker Angela Shelton, speaking about her own recovery, said that "it hurts more to pull a sword out of your body than it was for the sword to go in. You need to acknowledge that it's going to be really painful, there are going to be a lot of tears, and it's going to hurt. And guess what? It's so worth it! Because you can actually live your life!"

Kaye, a 47-year-old woman who was assaulted as a teenager and again at age 20, wrote to other women in her journal:

If I could, I would encourage all those who have been raped to find someone and talk! Really talk. Talk to the point of having no more words, wait a minute, and then talk some more.

I waited 25 years to open up and divulge the details of my secrets. Twenty five years I carried around the weight of my guilt, the shame of the abuse, the humiliation and the fears that lurked quietly in the background of my mind, dictating my reactions to various things in life. Twenty five years of the little nagging voice that says; "You say you love me, but if you knew... if you really knew the truth, your love would vanish and you would leave."

Why did I stay silent for so long? When I first shared, I didn't receive the response I needed, so I stuffed it inside. It seemed safer to keep it to myself. I could maintain the charade that I was fine if no one knew. I didn't want to be seen as damaged. I didn't want to step out and trust anyone with something they could turn around and injure me with. I didn't want to trust. I didn't want to be vulnerable.

Eventually, God enabled me to share and I thought I was being incredibly open when I would tell someone that I had been raped. Just saying that one sentence felt as though it was all laid bare. I would pat myself on the back for being so transparent. But it was still there: that nasty place in my heart and mind that knew things that they didn't know; things that if anyone found out, they would know were all my fault, just like I knew it was.

Twenty five years is far too long to carry such secrets. After twenty five years of silence, the build-up of pressure becomes too much. I hit a spot that flipped me backward, straight into the trauma, like it had just happened. I was experiencing multiple triggers on a daily basis. I wasn't able to sleep without enduring nightmares that I would thrash my way out of, crying in anger, fear and frustration. I couldn't eat much. My gag reflex was set on high. Depression carried me though my days and I felt I had really accomplished big stuff if I got dressed and washed the dishes.

I identified every little idiosyncrasy I had that was directly related to being raped, whether little or big things. And I grew angry that it still had any effect on my life. I wanted change and I knew that I had to talk or I would implode.

It was like having poison in me and the only way to get it out was to throw it up. I don't know about you, but I hate throwing up! I started talking--slowly and shaking, but talking. When I couldn't talk, I wrote. I wrote it all down and handed it to a friend to read. She held my secrets carefully and tenderly. She spent many days just being with me. Listening, crying and laughing with me.

I shared all about it with my husband, all but the explicit details of the rapes themselves. (I didn't want those pictures of me in his head.) But I told him the "worst." I told him what I had done that made me feel guilty. I was resigned to it and knew there was nothing he could do but agree with me and forgive me. It was startling to find out that he didn't see it at all the way I did.

I found a rape support group and discovered that others... so many others were experiencing the same things I did. I found out that my reactions were all normal for rape victims.

Twenty five years of guilt, because it was locked in my head with only my thoughts! But [I finally found] amazing, incredible gifts! Gifts that I never would have discovered if I hadn't talked.

Please.... please seek and find a safe person and start talking. Don't let the poison continue to spread through your life. There is freedom. There is hope. There is joy.

How to take care of yourself during rape trauma therapy

The therapy you receive for your rape will test you. At times, you will be furious with your therapist, and you will regard them as cruel and insensitive because they compel you to examine issues that are painful and that you would rather leave in the vague realm of subconscious thought. My patient, Victoria, told me that at times the process felt "more like punishment than therapy; why is Matt doing this to me?"

It is possible to arm yourself to take on this struggle, though. You will be fighting dragons in the weeks ahead, and every battle leaves its bruises. If you go into battle unprepared with weak armor and useless weapons, you will not succeed. But if you regard yourself as a warrior, not a shrinking victim, you can see this process as a form of fighting back against rape itself.

Here is a list of survival tips for managing your health during your treatment process:

- Eat. Do not starve yourself, and do not subsist on junk food and caffeine. Your brain requires protein and healthy fats to function, and foods rich in omega-3 fats (fish, or supplements) do an incredible job of stimulating the parts of the brain that manage stress and conflict. Consume plenty of these healthy sources of fat and protein.
- Sleep. Do not stay up late and wake up early. If you have difficulty sleeping because of stress, speak to a doctor who can prescribe some medical help for this problem. Don't lay in bed and text or surf the internet "one last time" before sleep.
- Manage your hygiene. It's hard to re-conceptualize yourself as a strong, capable woman if you neglect your physical health. Keep up with laundry, clean clothes, and grooming. Lack of care to these details is a common symptom of depression.
- Buy a journal and write as often as possible. Do the homework you are assigned by your therapist and this book. Actually hand-write your entries, rather than typing them at a computer.
- Prepare yourself mentally for therapy sessions. Therapy should not an appointment you cram into your day. Consider what you would like to work on in each session, and rehearse talking about anything you need to reveal to your therapist. Don't wait until the last 10 minutes of therapy to bring up an issue.
- Do not listen to violent or abusive music. Trauma survivors can have an uncanny attraction to aggressive, abusive music because it creates a false sense of power. But this "power" comes from vicariously identifying with the performer, and if your music is abusive and violent you are teaching yourself to regard violence and abuse as forms of strength. This subconsciously reinforces your perception of yourself as weak.
- Listen to triumphant, empowered music. Intelligent singers and songs about positive choices are forms of medicine. When you listen to love songs, you'll notice that they almost always obsess about another person: "I need you, you're my whole world, and I can't live without you." Instead of adopting the "love song" mindset that you need another person to complete you, begin to hear those as love songs to *yourself*.
- Read as much about rape as you can. I'll list suggested books at the end.
- Don't try to take on the whole issue at once. Take on only a small bite of the issue a day. If you feel overwhelmed, slow down. If you experience panic, discuss it with your therapist and work on coping skills related to panic attacks.

- Don't skip sessions, or drop out, just because the work gets hard. A good therapist will understand how difficult this is for you. One of the symptoms of rape trauma is the urge to avoid any stress that is triggered by memories of your rape. If you succumb to the temptation to abandon therapy, recovery will become more difficult when you attempt it the next time. I like to compare this to a bacterial infection: if you partially treat the infection but stop the treatments too soon, the bacteria that survive become stronger and more resistant to medications. Subsequent attempts to treat the infection are less and less effective. This is a good analogy about what happens if you start treatment for this, and then terminate the process too soon.

- Stay sober. If you're working in therapy sessions and then getting drunk or high at night, there's a problem. It actually increases your risk of problem drug use because it teaches you to associate both pain *and* recovery with substances.

- Find the right therapist for you. You are a person, not just a patient, and you have every right to search for the helper who fits. Don't just jump to a new therapist because you're ticked off at something your current therapist is coaxing you to work on, though! But if your therapist shows signs of not being skilled at rape trauma work (and not every therapist is!), feel free to continue services with a different person.

One woman, M.B., wrote in her journal, "There is something that survivors need to know. It would seem simple and, like a 'Duh!' moment, but, I know how hard *honesty* is when you are seeking therapy. Not that I am talking about blatant dishonesty, more like shielding the truth. It is a self-preservation, self-realization thing."

How to tell if your therapist is competent at rape trauma work

Many therapists claim or advertise that they treat rape and abuse issues, but surprisingly few are actually well-trained and skilled (training and skill are not always the same thing!). Therapists have to receive a certain amount of training in core skill areas each year to remain licensed. Too many mental health therapists mistakenly believe that attending a training workshop on a topic qualifies them as skilled in that area. Example: "I went to *a* training on rape trauma, so now I'm trained to treat rape trauma." Becoming skilled at rape trauma therapy has taken me years with countless trainings, consultation with mentors, reading dozens of books and journals, and ongoing experience; I can't imagine any brief training seminar that could have granted the same skill level.

Here are a few guidelines on recognizing a skilled therapist.

First, most rape crisis centers offer free counseling. That alone suggests that the counseling you would receive is by a person specifically experienced in rape trauma therapy.

My personal preference for treating rape trauma is Cognitive Processing Therapy (CPT) in a group setting. Research suggests that CPT is slightly more effective in reducing effects of trauma than simply being in a support group; group-based CPT is the best approach.[10] I would advise you to seek a therapist skilled in CPT who uses group work for the treatment of rape. The best-accepted clinical literature on rape treatment supports a CPT methodology.[11]

I describe my approach as "eclectic", meaning that I draw on several techniques—psychodynamic, Dialectical Behavior Therapy, Transference-Focused Protocol, and narrative therapies—but CPT remains the underpinning. Don't fret if those terms all sound like gobbledygook to you; feel free to research them online if you like, but it's more important that your therapist understands those models and is trained to use one or more of them.

Gender: Conventional wisdom suggests that the therapist ought to be female, but actual-life clients have disagreed with this. Males and females can both be excellent therapists, and either can also be abysmal. Many female clients *prefer* a male therapist, in fact (of the two best therapists for rape trauma I know, one is male and one is female). Still others will refuse a male therapist. One woman I know had a poor experience with her therapist and dropped out of therapy because "when I went to the counseling center they wanted to give me a girl counselor even though I requested a male. They said that it would be easier for me to connect with a female after my 'traumatic experience.' This was wrong." Echoing this statement are the words of activist and author Patricia Yancey Martin in her book *Rape Work*:

> [Another lesson I learned] concerned *gender*. Before entering the field, I assumed that women were better at rape work than men. I shared stereotypical assumptions about women as more caring and supportive and men as more discomfited and judgmental about rape…but I soon discovered that this was a mistake.[12] A risk with some untrained male therapists is that they may tend to emphasize the sexual dimension of rape, rather than the power and control dimension.[13]

Some male therapists overcompensate for gender in an attempt to appear liberal and approachable, with the actual result being that they may treat female clients in a patronizing and superficial style. If your therapist--male or female--seems to approach rape as a sexual issue, it's time to move on. Rape *affects* sexuality, but it is not a sexual behavior.

---

[10] Bryant, Richard A., et al. (1998). "Treatment of Acute Stress Disorder: A comparison of cognitive-behavioral therapy and supportive counseling." *Journal of Consulting and Clinical Psychology*, 66:5, pp962-866.

[11] For example, Patricia A. Resick and Monica Schnicke's 1996 book, *Cognitive Processing Therapy for Rape Victims* and Edna B. Foa and Barbara Olasov Rothbaum's 2001 book *Treating the Trauma of Rape: Cognitive-Behavioral Therapy for PTSD*. Also: Resick, Patricia A., et. Al. (2002). "A Comparison of Cognitive-Processing Therapy with Prolonged Exposure and a Waiting Condition for the Treatment of Chronic Posttraumatic Stress Disorder in Female Rape Victims." *Journal of Consulting and Clinical Psychology,* 70:4, pp867-879.

[12] Martin, Patricia Yancey. *Rape Work*. 2005, Routledge, p6.

[13] Silverman, D. (1977) "First do no more harm: Female rape victims and the male counselor." *American Journal of Orthopsychiatry, 47,* 91-96.

Qualifications: not everyone who calls themselves a "counselor" is actually equipped to provide mental health therapy. There are legal loopholes that allow individuals to get by with calling themselves "counselors" rather than "therapists," and they may have little or no actual training. Some of them are motivated purely by religious zeal and others might be using "therapy" with clients as a way to resolve their own trauma issues. Consulting with clergy is fine, but be clear that this is a way to address spiritual aspects of recovery, not mental health aspects such as depression, panic attacks, self-injury, or PTSD. <u>Beware</u> of charlatans posing as "alternative healers," gurus, shamans, and such; these individuals can cause more harm than help, and tend to offer new-age concepts in place of clinical skill and research-based expertise.

Psychiatrists will be helpful, but you should know that increasingly, psychiatrists attend to medication management far more than providing interactive mental health therapy, with some exceptions of course. In most cases, you would need a psychiatrist to meet with monthly to assist with medications for anxiety, sleep, or depression, while having a second clinician at least weekly to provide the "talking therapy" part.

Having a degree and a license is not synonymous with having skill. I get emails nearly every week from women asking, "is this normal?" after having awful experiences with therapists who are unskilled at rape work. For example, a poor therapist might lack control over a therapy group, allowing competitive members to battle for group dominance, gush out grotesque topics to disturb the group, or wander from topic to topic aimlessly, all concluded with "Let's continue next time." One women told me her therapist had noted her self-injury, bulimia, panic attacks, and migraines, but concluded after a few sessions that she couldn't see any ongoing connection between the woman's sexual abuse and current state of mind!

It is very fair to question a prospective therapist before contracting for services. You are a customer, not a beggar, and a good therapist will not balk or appear threatened by inquiries. If a therapist seems defensive at your questions, that alone is a red flag. No therapist should present themselves as a superior know-it-all who cannot be questioned; I routinely reminded my clients that "you have to teach me how to be a good therapist for you. I *will* mess up sometimes, so stay in touch and keep me informed how you feel about the way we're working."

Some questions that might be asked first:

1. What is the extent and type of training you have received in Rape Trauma Therapy? What books do you consider most helpful for me as a client?
2. What is your approach to "victim-blaming" issues that often arise in processing rape?
3. How frequently do you treat cases of rape trauma?

Additional questions you probably wouldn't open with, but which are important to discuss over time as you work with your therapist:

4. Do you regard rape as a societal and cultural problem, or a problem of individual pathology in rapists?
5. Other than providing treatment services, what forms of social advocacy or activism do you do about the issue of rape?
6. Do you have songs, books, workbooks, or other media available for your clients to use in recovering from rape?
7. Do you see rape as a sexual issue? What is your understanding of the underlying causes of rape?
8. How do you explain that 99% of rape is perpetrated by males? What makes this a men's issue, and why are men the primary perpetrators?
9. How will you define successful recovery?
10. If I have trust issues that cause occasional resistance, how will you handle that?

Now, just to be interesting, here are what MY answers would be if I were asked these questions by a patient:

1. Some of the better books that a therapist ought to be acquainted with would include: "Cognitive processing therapy for rape victims" by Patricia Resick and Monica Schnicke; "Quest for Respect" by Linda Braswell; "Rape Recovery Handbook" by Aphrodite Matsakis; "After Silence" by Nancy Venable Raine; and "Treating the Trauma of Rape" by Edna B. Foa and Barbara Olasov Rothbaum. Give extra credit if the therapist is familiar with Jackson Katz ("The Macho Paradox") or the book "Transforming a Rape Culture."
2. A good therapist will not send even subtle hints of victim-blaming. Too many therapists think it's therapeutic to ask leading questions like these: "Can you change other people's behavior? Whose behaviors can you change? What could *you* change in *this* situation where you were raped?" or "Let's talk about how to not put yourself in that position again." Women don't put themselves in the position to be raped; *rapists* put women in the position to be raped. If it had not been for a rapist in the environment, the same behaviors the woman was doing when she was raped would not have resulted in a rape. A good therapist understands that remnants of self-blame are the driving factor in flashbacks and nightmares!
3. This should not be the therapist's first (or one of a few) instances of treating rape trauma. Too many therapists think that merely having an opinion on the matter, or *caring* about the issue of rape, qualifies them to treat it.
4. Rape is a *social* problem, not individual pathology. If a therapist believes that rapists are isolated cases of sickos, psychos, and deviants, they miss the point. Rape is increasingly *normalized* by cultural values, and rapists are almost always so-called *normal* boys and men who respond to the social attitudes about power, sex, and control in relationships. Anyone who fails to get this point should read Jackson Katz's stunning book, *The Macho Paradox*. A key component to successful rape recovery is social activism, precisely because our society tolerates misogyny. Likewise, if your therapist sees rape as a "women's issue," they are failing to understand the matter. Rape is a men's issue (too), and framing it solely as a women's issue gives men permission not to address it.

5. The therapist should support, if not actually participate in, activism such as Take Back the Night. A well-informed rape therapist would also be aware when Sexual Assault Awareness Month is (it's every April). It would be even more reassuring if they actually carried literature from your local crisis center.

6. A good therapist will understand the role of art in recovery. They should be aware of songs that positively address sexual assault (extra credit if they know Tori Amos, Beth Hart, Plumb, or Ani Difranco). I have collages created by previous clients that I can show to new clients so they can see tangible examples of victory (or progress) by women who have gone before. I also share the book *Letters To Survivors: Words of Comfort for Women Recovering from Rape* to show examples of hope.

7. Rape is not a sexual act. Men don't rape in an effort to get sex; rapists use sex in an effort to get power and control. Sex is the method, not the goal, of rape.

8. See #4. Males receive socialization that endorses the use of power, control, and privilege in relationships with women. If your therapist fails to accept this[14], they cannot accurately address the role of social norms in the creation of rapists. Likewise, your therapist should not excuse rapists as "people who were abused as children (or sexually abused) to make them that way." Hey, *you've* been sexually abused, and so have 1 in 4 other women, but women aren't turning out in droves to become perpetrators. So this crap about "rapists are that way because of abuse" is a phony excuse. Rapists are that way because of their *decisions*.

9. *You* should define recovery. But here are some things to look for: you can begin to think and talk about your rape without feeling shame or fear, and you should be well-informed enough to confront and challenge ignorant comments by others. Nightmares and flashbacks should subside. You should be able to experience moments of conflict or sadness without using self-destructive coping measures. You should be able to accept your innocence in this crime, and not just intellectually—you should *feel* innocent again. You should be inspired to assist other women who are struggling with this issue.

10. A good therapist will accept these issues. Your recovery has *nothing* to do with whether men (or "malekind") are redeemed in your eyes. Recovery is not about getting you to accept malekind. Frankly, it's YOU who have been doing the work here, not malekind, so the ultimate goal is your acceptance of yourself. If, along the way, you begin to notice that good men exist, then great—but that is an eventual outcome, not the goal. If a woman left therapy with me (a male therapist!) and still felt conflicted toward men, that would be perfectly fine. I'd rather you give trust too slowly than too quickly. You are not at fault simply because you recognize that not all men deserve to be partners in your recovery.

But let me acknowledge one thing: although I've done years of work and read nearly every book you can name on the subject of sexual violence, and written and published papers, *none* of that made me necessarily a good therapist--only an educated one. It's little more than bragging, and has nothing to do with skill, to list my academic accomplishments on the issue of rape. If I have any ability to "get it," it's because of the

---

[14] Women do perpetrate rape, but 99.8% of rapes are perpetrated by a male. That means that of every 1000 rapes, 998 of the rapists are male. If this isn't a *male issue*, what is?

hundreds of women (and some men) who have trusted me enough to tell me their stories, and who guide me in "getting it." Whatever I became as a therapist, I became because of the hundreds of survivors who have taught and led me. The highest praise I have received isn't from a plaque or certificate, it's from a woman who says to me, "you get it. You really get it."

When Danée started therapy with me, she barely spoke for two weeks. But that was not two wasted weeks; she was watching carefully to see how I responded to other women in our group. Danée later said to me, "rapport and trust can be built by *not* speaking, too." She was watching to see whether I would blame victims ("Let's talk about how to not put yourself in that position again"), or whether the work was merely a paycheck to me. When another woman told her rape story and Danée saw me become emotionally moved, it was the moment of opening for her to trust me as well.

Likewise, Victoria once told me that what made the most difference in her work was not a collection of clinical methods I threw at her, but "your patients know you love us. Without you having to say it, I knew you loved me. You would accept me. You would never abandon or shame me because I could sense your respect for me." This does not mean we didn't clash—we did all-out battle sometimes, as both Danée's and Victoria's stubborn sides came out—but Danée later recalled, "when we clashed, it was because you were challenging my self-blame. You were refusing to let me settle for shame, and I had tried so hard to hang on to parts of that."

We need to finally see and accept this fact: it is SURVIVORS who create the possibility of success for one another. It is SURVIVORS who produce the hope and understanding in all of this. I wish more survivors saw this and could feel called to cooperate in this genesis, rather than feeling dark, ashamed, and broken forever. Without survivors swimming back upwards to light, no healing would be possible at all for any of us.

Common mistakes that happen in rape trauma therapy

Rape trauma therapy never happens without hitting some bumps and snags, and I have never encountered a client whose recovery progressed flawlessly (in fact, I get concerned when anyone's recovery seems to be going *too* well, with no difficulty). It is essential that you keep in mind that therapists are not flawless people, and that you are the paying client. This means that there will be times when a therapist makes mistakes, just like you do, and will fail to correctly understand some things, just like you will. When that happens, try to resist the impulse to become frustrated, blame the therapist, or feel betrayed.

I have had clients who never spoke up about concerns or insights they wanted to address in sessions. Trying my best to intuitively direct sessions without that feedback meant that I made mistakes and operated under beliefs that were not always correct. I was not aware of these blunders until a client would suddenly drop out of therapy! Clients would assure me that I was helpful and effective, but in my absence complain to others that their needs were not being met. They would praise me in person and then blast me to others a month later (often for the very things they had lauded). In defense of your therapist, it is unfair to withhold concerns from him or her, and yet hold your therapist responsible for ineffectiveness. You and your therapist are a team, and communication, not extra-sensory perception, will keep the process running smoothly. If you become frustrated or concerned, discuss this with your therapist!

Honestly, I cannot claim that I have been a catalyst for full recovery in every client I saw in therapy. I believe that in some way I have *helped* all of my clients, but there are some who simply have not yet achieved full recovery from rape. This does not mean that therapy, or I, or they, failed. It means that the process may not be complete, but it went as far along as it could be at that point.

But I have also seen clients in therapy who came from treatment centers, drug rehab programs, hospitals, and other therapists, and did not receive beneficial therapy because of several common mistakes. You should be watchful for these mistakes and address them if you recognize them.

#1: "It's in the past, so it's no big deal"

Perhaps the most common, and disastrous, mistake I have seen therapists make is to minimize the impact of rape on your functioning. I have seen two ways that this mistake happens. First, a therapist who is misinformed about rape trauma may believe that because your rape may have taken place many years ago, it is no longer a relevant issue. Clients of mine have described being in therapy in which previous therapists failed to connect a rape from a decade ago to *current* symptoms of panic, substance abuse, or depression. Because they were apart in chronological time, the therapist assumed that they are separate matters. After all, the therapist concludes, if the rape were really the core issue, you probably would have been in counseling back then instead of just now. So they regard the rape as a background detail, but not part of the current spectrum of issues.

The second way this mistake happens is that therapists are not the only ones who err in this way. Many clients of mine have come into therapy for addictions, panic attacks, meltdowns at work or school, self-injury, eating disorders, or general depression with sleep disturbances—yet they say "this isn't about my rape. That was so long ago; I've dealt with it, it's in the past!" These are the *classic* symptoms of rape trauma![15] Regardless of how long ago a rape occurred, the symptoms can echo through time until they are addressed.

#2: "It wasn't rape."

I once had a client with a particularly outrageous story of how this disastrous assumption by a (male) therapist caused her immense harm. The client had become very sexually compulsive in the three years after her rape (more on that issue later), and reported to her therapist that she was engaging in self-injury, binge drinking, and drunken sex with random partners. Any therapist with a lick of sense would *immediately* spot these as the telltale signs of prior sexual assault! But instead, the therapist labeled her an alcoholic (which was accurate, but incomplete, as far as her drinking behaviors themselves), and dismissed her sexual conduct with the hurtful comment, "Boy, you must just really like sex, huh?" His conclusion was that the client was simply an experimentally-minded young woman, indulging in decadent pastimes—a "party girl." His astounding ignorance caused him to miss the flashing neon signs and sirens that

---

[15] McCauley, J., et al. "Clinical characteristics of women with a history of childhood abuse: unhealed wounds." 1997 JAMA 277;17:1362-8

would have alerted any other therapist in their sleep, "This person is a *rape survivor!*" Needless to say, the therapy fizzled.

Being well-informed about sexual assault is essential for any therapist doing this work. There is a tendency for some rape victims to earnestly search for any shred of information that redefines their trauma as something other than rape—*anything* but rape! I have had women in therapy question me meticulously about the most specific details of their assault, hoping that some speck of information will suddenly cause me to light up and exclaim, "Oh, *now* I get it! No, that wasn't rape." They want to be saved from the "scarlet letter." I've noticed that the single most often asked question on online forums for rape recovery[16] is "Was I raped?" The narratives that follow the question are nearly always crystal-clear depictions of sexual assault, but one can sense the desperate hope in the writer that she will be assured somehow, in some way, that hers was not a rape experience.

In anticipation of this, I actually keep a file in my desk drawer full of printouts of my state's legal definitions of rape, including age of consent laws. In particular, therapists and clients alike can easily be distracted from the factuality of rape by the issue of alcohol or drug use, as if being drunk or high somehow changes whether an incident is truly rape. For the record, *every* state has laws that clarify that a person who is intoxicated cannot give legal consent to have sex, and this is included among prosecutable definitions of rape. What's more, many rapists deliberately use alcohol or drugs as tools of sexual assault, which is why the term "drug-facilitated rape" has gained use among therapists and lawmakers alike.

For the record, the best simple definition of rape I've ever heard is "sexual penetration without valid consent."

#3: "Rape is only one of your issues, so we'll just spend a small portion of our time on it."

When a woman comes into therapy (or into a hospital or treatment program) with multiple mental health issues, it's tempting for a therapist to see each one of them as a separate matter needing separate attention. For example, consider a client who requests therapy because she is experiencing panic attacks, depression, alcohol abuse, and sleep disorders. During her assessment interview, the therapist learns that she also smokes, hates her body, and has been raped in the past.

Some therapists would create a treatment plan that suggests the issues to be addressed in therapy are, obviously, anxiety, depression, substance abuse, and sexual assault. Not bad, but I propose that this minimizes the point. I would propose that rape, or perhaps childhood sexual abuse, *is* the core treatment issue, and that the rest are likely symptoms of it rather than a collection of other additional issues.[17]

I have had clients (who want to avoid the rape issue altogether) accuse me of being so "rape focused" that I zero-in on that one issue, letting the others fall to the wayside. These same clients, incidentally, later tend to acknowledge the correctness of the trauma-focused approach after all. But here is what I have observed: identifying

---

[16] Dailystrength.org, aftersilence.org, for examples

[17] Briere, J. N. and Elliott, D. M. "Immediate and long-term impacts of child sexual abuse." 1994 Future Child 4;2:54-69. Discusses the adult consequences of childhood sexual abuse, including PTSD, cognitive distortion, emotional pain, avoidance, impaired sense of self and interpersonal difficulties.

sexual assault as the core trigger of the other symptoms *works*. Countless clients of mine have been in drug rehab programs, hospitals, and residential treatment centers, but they say the same thing to me again and again: "they never dealt with this when I was in treatment before!" There may be lip-service in rehab programs that link rape with shame with substance abuse, but the focus remains primarily on the substance abuse. Or a woman with panic attacks is given workbooks about panic attacks, with barely a word about trauma.

I am not suggesting that we ignore those issues and assume that simply processing sexual assault will "cure" the rest too; I am suggesting that *as* we address each of these issues, we deliberately explore connections between them and the rape. For example, how does your rape pertain to your drinking or drug use? Why do you suppose that the number one predictor of cigarette smoking among young women is a prior history of sexual abuse? (that's true!) How does your rape relate to your sleep disturbances and panic attacks? How does your rape pertain to a tendency to form relationships with abusers? How can rape teach a woman to hate her body, and alter her eating patterns? Therapists are taught to collaborate with clients in the development of treatment goals, and no client is forced by the therapist to follow the therapist's dictates about those goals. But incorporating goals that relate to trauma and its effects on other life functions is not only reasonable, but likely necessary.

More and more research is finding that sexual assault is one of the most powerful experiences that will launch substance abuse, smoking, self-injury, panic attacks, sleep disorders, eating disorders, and so on. For a well-trained therapist, a certain cluster of symptoms will reliably hint at undisclosed sexual trauma, and he or she can approach the matter directly and ask. I have seen many women burst into tears when I have asked them about their rape history, not because they were humiliated by my asking but because they were relieved to finally have the opportunity to talk. Therapists who lack such training cannot see the rape in the background of these symptoms, and take the symptoms at face value as if they *are* the whole story. Consequently, women are frequently misdiagnosed with psychotic or personality disorders, when the core of PTSD is overlooked.

Example: I know of a clinician who was seeing a client in inpatient treatment who presented to the hospital emergency room after a suicide attempt, with symptoms of panic, depression, self-injury, and uncontrollable fits of rage. During a treatment team meeting, the psychiatrist suggested that these symptoms strongly suggest the likelihood of sexual abuse or rape. The counselor agreed and said she had already asked her client, and been told yes, the client had been raped a few months earlier. But the clinician concluded with the statement, "…and we've already covered that in a session last week."

#4: "We've already covered that in a previous session."

I don't expect I really need to explain to readers why this is a mistake. Rape, as we know, is not an irritant that disrupts our lives in some annoying way until we have "*a* therapy session" about it. It is life-changing, and takes constant, steady, long-term work.

#5: "I've already gone through rape counseling, so that part is worked out."

Clients of mine frequently assure me that despite their continuing panic attacks, substance abuse, self-injury, depression, and sleep disorders, at least their *rape* has been taken care of already!

The truth is, though, that recovery is never a straight line. And it's not like dropping a rock and moving on, never to carry it again. Rape recovery happens in spurts. If I have a client who has previously received therapy for rape, and now she is re-experiencing these symptoms, it does *not* mean that her therapy failed. Nor does it mean that attention to the rape issue was misguided, and it's time to try something different as a treatment goal. Perhaps her therapy was really, really *good*. But rape trauma syndrome doesn't just vanish, and at times you may need to revisit therapy in the future to reinforce your recovery. Plenty of my own clients have graduated successfully, and then later begun to re-experience similar symptoms again. Does that mean I did a crummy job? Or that she did? No; it means that recovery is like hunger; being filled once does not mean you will never need the energy-providing sustenance of therapeutic "food" again.

If anything, the return of symptoms gives you a head-start on your next counseling. Instead of saying to yourself, "Gee, I thought working on rape would fix all this other stuff. But it didn't, so obviously rape isn't the issue and I should try therapy for something else," you can approach your therapist and say, "I've done counseling for rape issues before, so I know exactly where these symptoms are coming from. This tells me where we need to focus, which saves us both a lot of time exploring."

#6: Clients are assigned to therapists based solely on who has few enough cases to add you, rather than who has expertise in this issue.

I am very fortunate that I worked with a brilliant treatment team who recognized that each of my coworkers and I have varying skills. For example, I'm not particularly good at drug and alcohol counseling. But when a new client came to our office for an assessment, they weren't assigned to a therapist simply because a therapist has fewer cases and the load should be "balanced." I may have had more, or fewer, cases than my coworkers, but if a woman became a patient and needed help for rape trauma, she was likely to be assigned to my group regardless of patient census numbers. We recognized that the emphasis ought to be on the clients' needs for best clinical care, not a "numbers game" so that you are assigned to a therapist based on caseload rather than "fit."

On the other hand, there are settings where the reverse is true. A new patient arrives, and without knowing *anything* about him or her, the treatment team looks at the number of cases each therapist has. "Amy, you only have X cases, so you'll get this young lady. Matt, you'll get the next two who come in." As a result, there is no deliberate effort to fit clients to therapists; women are in a lottery system about the type of care they will receive.

If you are about to become a patient for therapy at a counseling agency, speak up *during* the assessment and clarify that you want to be assigned based on the therapist's clinical fit to your needs, not simply to round off the numbers of cases that any particular therapist happens to have.

#7: "I'm a qualified rape therapist because I care, and I have an opinion."

This is worth reiterating. I conduct trainings and workshops about techniques of sexual assault prevention and treatment, and I find that the room is packed with therapists who are hungry for this information. They recognize that this is a complex issue, and they want to hear from others in this work about what skills and innovations are helping us treat PTSD in rape victims. I am so proud to see my workshop sessions packed to standing-room-only capacity, which indicates that therapists are willing to seek out training from others doing this work.

But it's the ones who *don't* attend that frighten me. I hear stories quite frequently about therapists who have taken on a rape victim for counseling, convinced of their own qualifications to treat rape simply because he or she "cares" about the issue, or feels emboldened by strong views and beliefs about rape itself. In some truly disturbing cases, I am aware of counselors taking on rape work because of their *own* latent rape trauma, and this work becomes a means through which they process their personal rape issues using clients as proxies. You can spot this fairly easily: the therapist relies on expressions of their own emotions as their method of "reaching" you, they make dramatic speeches about rape in an effort to either convince or inspire you out of your trauma, they disclose personal trauma issues to *you* (and quite soon in the process), and they reward you for "success" when you express a point of view in line with their own, as if verifying their beliefs is the measure of your progress.

#8: "I'm the only one who can help you."

Becoming too dependent on a therapist is unhealthy, even if your therapist is gifted and superb. One of the ways I can tell if a patient is becoming too dependent on me is that she will express a very dark, depressed, or hopeless belief, but do little work on her own part to challenge and defeat that belief. Instead, I find myself "bailing her out," working to un-convince her of what she has expressed. I catch myself making this mistake, and I also recognize that this dependency is a natural result of being a caring and supportive person. It's understandable, but still a problem. In a healthy therapeutic relationship, the therapist simply guides the patient through the process of challenging her *own* beliefs, rather than the therapist swooping in to alleviate her pain for her. Otherwise, what strength has she developed when she ends therapy? She can't carry a miniature version of me around with her to rescue her from each bleak thought she has.

In the early stages of trauma therapy, it is perfectly appropriate for me to engage in this form of interaction; it's not "rescuing" at that point, it's support during crisis. But as she progresses, it is necessary for the therapist to gradually detach and *not* take the role of her sole rescuer, "the only one who understands," or the one who plucks her out of the "death row" of her negative self-talk. *You* must learn to do that. I have a phrase that my patients absolutely hate to hear, but they come to understand: "I'm going to help you by not helping you."

For this reason, I am also particularly alert when a patient says to me, "You're the only one who has ever understood me. I went to other therapists, and they didn't get me at all. But *you* get me!" I hear phrases like this and rather than feeling encouraged or flattered, I become alarmed that a client is forming a dependent relationship with me. Ultimately, the success you get from rape work depends on *your* labor.

Goals and contracts

The most helpful way to prepare for successful therapy is to set specific goals you want to accomplish, and develop an understanding with your therapist about how you will work toward them. Otherwise, therapy may continue on and on with no clear measure of success. Therapy for PTSD from rape is a difficult process that will take more than just a couple of sessions. I would like to suggest that you formally write down what your goals are with your therapist.

As your work progresses, you may find that there are new goals you will want to add. Make sure you give your therapist, and this book, a chance; at times the work will be tough and you will be tempted to escape by abandoning your therapist altogether. You may even find yourself instigating conflict with your therapist to test whether *they* will abandon you; this is understandable but inappropriate. Each of you must commit to working through the matters that will arise. No therapist can promise that simply by cooperating and writing in a journal your life will magically get better; it will take deep, insightful examination of your thoughts and beliefs, and a choice to deliberately change certain responses and behaviors of yours.

If you are willing to be challenged, willing to reconsider assumptions and beliefs that seem absolutely true to you right now, willing to change aspects of your life, then proceed with this sample contract.

We, _____ (your name) and _____(therapist's name) agree that we will use individual/group therapy (circle one, or both) in order to learn about PTSD from rape, and work toward recovering from rape.

As the patient, I agree to commit to at least _____ weeks of work with this therapist. I understand that this will involve _____hours a week of time in sessions, plus time on my own to complete homework and reading assignments.

During this period of time, I agree to abstain from substance abuse and any self-harming behaviors. If any of these behaviors does occur, I agree to voluntarily disclose them to my therapist at the very next session, at the beginning of the session.

I will not skip sessions, and I will arrive on-time. My therapist agrees to the same conditions. If either needs to cancel a session, we will notify the other as far in advance as possible.

I have set the following goals for my therapy:

1. _____

2. _____

3. _____

4. _____

5. _____

We will update this contract in _____ weeks on _____ (date).

_____   _____
  Patient's signature/date   Therapist's signature/date

Our doubts are traitors, and make us lose the good
we might oft win by fearing to attempt.
-Shakespeare

What are "Triggers," and what should I do about them?

A trigger is any sensory information you take in that causes an overwhelming emotional and/or physical response that you associate with the rape itself. A trigger is *not* merely anything that reminds you of your rape. Some of the symptoms of rape triggers could include anxiety, panic attacks, rage, intense sadness, the urge to drink or drug, the urge to self-harm, dissociation, and even a strong sexual urge. Triggers are associated with post-traumatic stress disorder in that they represent the "recurring and intrusive thoughts" about the rape.

There is a simple physical basis for having trigger responses. The brain has sensitivity to triggers wired right into it! In the center of your brain is a small structure called the *amygdala*. This bundle of nerves in the limbic system has the job of processing your memories of emotional reactions, for the purpose of keeping you alive. The amygdala is a development of prehistoric survival, when our ancestors needed to fend off constant danger in a wild world. Without the ability to learn and recognize danger, humans would forever be at risk for extinction by predators. The amygdala's job is to analyze any moment of extreme, emotion-producing danger in order to learn new ways to survive. It then continually scans our environment for any cues that it associates with dangers we've experienced, so that it can warn us of such risks again. The association we make between the emotions and physical danger of rape program the amygdala to hyper-respond in the future.

The more emotions you produce in your response to danger, the stronger the imprint of the experience on your amygdala. Consequently, the amygdala of a rape victim will be set on "hyper-alert" to detect any recognizable warnings of danger. Any stimulus, no matter how slight, that can be associated with your rape would trigger your amygdala to sound the alarm.[1] Similar sounds, sights, smells, movements, touches, and even words can be interpreted by the brain as indications of similar danger arising again. Scent in particular is associated with emotional memories.

Once the amygdala has sensed any risk of harm, it "triggers" your brain to "switch" from conscious, carefully-determined responses (of the frontal cortex) into the immediate, emotional, and powerful "survival" responses of the lower regions of the brain (medulla oblongata). This activates the sympathetic nervous system of the body, which increases your reflexes, adrenaline, heart rate, and fight-or-flight responses. Your eyes dilate, your breathing changes to "combat pace," and your facial muscles tighten to express fear or anger. Information that you learn during a time of extreme emotional sensation is retained longer, and in more detail, than information learned unemotionally. The surrounding region of the brain, the Hippocampus, forms new long-term memories and retrieves old ones. People who have PTSD because of rape or other trauma actually have an atrophied—diminished—hippocampus.[2] Your brain physically begins to lose its ability to choose how memories are managed; the result is that your memories manage *you* instead.[3]

Amygdala

This is why abused children have vivid "imprints" of their emotions about the abuse and can recall moments of abuse with strong feelings even years later, but might not be able to recall lectures or statements made by their abuser during less emotionally-intense times. Children learn fewer lessons, not more, when they are being abused in the guise of discipline: it is the *emotion* of the event, rather than the moral lesson of it, that imprints. When a child is terrified of an adult, the learning centers of the brain turn off

---

[1] "Neuroscientists Identify How Trauma Triggers Long-lasting Memories In The Brain," http://www.sciencedaily.com/releases/2005/08/050814175315.htm

[2] "Stress and your brain: War, rape, sexual abuse, and other severe trauma--even a car accident--could make part of your brain disappear." Robert Sapolsky, 3/1/1999, http://discovermagazine.com/1999/mar/stress

[3] Stein, M. B., Koverola, C., Hanna, C., Torchia, M. G., and McClarty, B. "Hippocampal volume in women victimized by childhood sexual abuse." 1997 Psychol Med 27;4:951-9
Also: Bremner, J. D., et al. "Magnetic resonance imaging-based measurement of hippocampal volume in posttraumatic stress disorder related to childhood physical and sexual abuse--a preliminary report." 1997 Biol Psychiatry 41;1:23-32. "Patients with PTSD from childhood abuse had 12% smaller left hippocampal volume than matched controls, even after multiple variables were considered..."

and the emotional centers begin to soak up the feelings of fear and humiliation for long-term storage. This is why more and more parenting experts recommend firm but calmer methods of discipline, which seem to actually imprint lessons, as opposed to harsh and terrifying punishments, which seem to only imprint *fear*.

Your rape "taught" you the same emotional imprinting. Your brain is now programmed to anticipate harm, and so it scans all incoming information like a "security agent" in an effort to filter and detect any recognizable predictions of harm to you. Once the amygdala spots anything it associates with your rape, it will fire a powerful and super-fast alert message through a single channel of nerves that triggers the shift in brain function from logic/reason and into immediate emotional "freak out." This is why you often look back in hindsight at your responses to triggers and feel ashamed, or recognize that how you reacted was inappropriate—these reactions are not part of your normal brain function, but are part of the crisis "fight or flight" response. This is why so many rape victims become enraged toward family members, shrieking and screaming during arguments and conflicts, even years later. It also explains the tendency of triggers to produce sudden tearfulness, panic, anger, or desperation.[4] Fortunately, there is a documented positive effect of antidepressants on amygdala functioning, to reduce its sensitivity (or over-sensitivity) to triggers.[5]

One of the effects of your amygdala being triggered is that it stimulates the adrenal glands, which are small glands above the kidneys. These glands secrete adrenaline, a chemical that supercharges your body with several immediate biological changes: your heart rate increases, your pupils dilate, digestion slows (hence the nausea during some triggers), lungs breathe more quickly, and even your blood thickens. All of your senses are extra-alert to sounds, smells, and sight. You aren't going crazy; this is a biological function. If anything, it proves your body is *healthy*, operating to survive. What we need to do is teach your brain not to go into "survival" mode whenever you see, hear, or smell every little trigger.

So now we know that "triggers" are physiological phenomena, and not the result of being "crazy" or "too sensitive." The reason some rape victims and survivors have stronger trigger responses than others has nothing to do with whether they are personally stronger or weaker as people; it is a result of the way in which their brain encodes emotional memories and then seeks environmental reminders of them. Some researchers are now suggesting that brain scans may, in fact, be the best way to diagnose PTSD.[6]

---

[4] There is research suggesting that people with Borderline Personality Disorder have over-responsive amygdalae, causing them to perceive threats or intentions of harm toward them by others. This results in a persistent fear of being abandoned, mistreated, or harmed by others—even loved ones. People with BPD, for example, tend to perceive hostility in photographs of neutral faces. Donegan et al. (2003). "Amygdala hyperreactivity in borderline personality disorder: implications for emotional dysregulation.". *Biological Psychiatry* 54 (11): 1284-1293. See also: F. Corrigan, "The role of dysregulated amygdalic emotion in borderline personality disorder." *Medical Hypotheses*, 54:4, pp574-579.

[5] Sheline et al. (2001). "Increased amygdala response to masked emotional faces in depressed subjects resolves with antidepressant treatment: an fMRI study.". *Biological Psychiatry* 50 (9): 651-658.

[6] "Brain scan could be better test for PTSD." 1/23/2007, http://www.armytimes.com/news/2007/01/TNSPTSD230107/

To cope with triggers, a trauma survivor must learn how to interrupt this "amygdala hijack" in two ways: by learning to prevent emotions from capturing all of the brain's decision-making processes, and by therapeutically processing your trauma in excruciating detail until the amygdala no longer mistakes minor reminders in everyday environments as indications that another trauma is constantly imminent.[7] This is not easy at first, because our brain is conditioned to accept something as an absolute truth if it merely *feels* true. Consider your rape as an example: you may be convinced, despite all evidence to the contrary, that you are a worthless, degraded, filthy person—simply because you *feel* that way. "Emotional reasoning" is a pattern of thinking in which we assume that our emotions are the only evidence we need to verify a belief. If I feel ugly, that's all the proof I need that I am ugly. If I feel stupid, it is undeniable that I am stupid.

But in addition to the physiological and chemical basis for triggers, there is another way to look at them. Your rapist, through his act of violence and invasion, has tried to create a "map" for you of what your life is. His actions are his efforts to define *you* to himself, to yourself, and to others. You are naturally trying your very best to resist his map of your life, but triggers are those occasional moments when something seems to confirm *his* view rather than yours. The reason they cause so much panic and distress is that for a flicker of a moment, something around you seems to suggest that his world, not yours, is the real one.

There are several ways to teach yourself to reprogram your emotional reasoning so that your triggers do not consistently cause you to explode in panic. Yale psychologist Peter Salovey has identified five steps as the basic path,[8] and I have adapted them here for use by rape survivors:

1. Know your emotions. Work on increasing your self-awareness, the ability to recognize a feeling as it happens. Learn as much vocabulary about emotions as possible, so that you are not limited into narrow understandings of how you feel. Instead of routinely saying "I feel bad/horrible/ashamed," learn more complex *words* that better describe the nuances of your feelings: Fear, Anger, Ambivalence, Disgust, Anticipation, Shock, Disappointment, Envy, Intimidation, Discovery, Loss, Grief, Courage, Cautious, and so on. By expanding the language of your emotions, you will be more capable of expressing your own responses to triggers, rather than having to sort your emotions into basic "Good/Bad," which is hardly ever the accurate choice.[9]

2. Regulate your emotions. Improve your ability to handle feelings and to recover quickly from upsets and distress. Your therapist will assist in this area more than I can do from a book. But the tools for doing this seemingly-impossible task are to use self-talk to challenge your emotions, and to begin compelling you to question whether something really *is* true simply because it *feels* true.

---

[7] The "amygdala hijack" concept was coined by Daniel Goleman, author and researcher on the topic of Emotional Intelligence.
[8] Dianne Schilling, "How's your emotional intelligence?" at
http://www.womensmedia.com/new/emotional-intelligence.shtml
[9] http://simple.wikipedia.org/wiki/List_of_emotions for a list

3. Motivate yourself. Learn to delay the gratification of your desire for instant comfort when distress sets in. Many rape victims are so upset by triggers that they will begin a search for some method of quickly suppressing the anxiety, such as alcohol, marijuana, self-injury, or even sex. Or stashing this book out of sight and avoiding it for the next month. One of the most difficult things you will learn in therapy is to "sit with the feelings," to let them surge and withdraw like a flood, and re-learn the skill of remaining fully aware and controlled during a painful sensation. One way I have helped clients do this is to instruct them to sit alone in their home, with no TV or audio sound, and just listen. Attentively listen to the silence. Familiarize yourself with every tiny sound. Spend three minutes meditating in this way before opening your journal and writing. Add three minutes to the meditation each day. The purpose is to re-experience silence (and even aloneness) as a safe time, a time preceding healing, and a personal time. Another thing I do is to prohibit group members from interfering when someone is experiencing an emotional outburst during a therapy session. It appears cruel to my patients at first, but I do not allow members to touch, move closer to, hug, swarm around, or even interrupt someone who is vocally struggling with an aspect of her rape that brings a flood of grief to her. The reason is that interference will prevent her from fully processing the grief. She must fully pass through her emotional state, so that emotions no longer become enemies.

4. Cultivate empathy. Try to recognize, identify, and feel what others are feeling. Find a person whose approach to crisis impresses you, and begin to model them in similar situations. I can tell when a change from "victim" to "survivor" is happening by the way she responds to other victims' experiences. During the stage of being a victim, it is common for patients of mine to hear other women's stories and respond in these (and other similar) ways:

- "Oh, that's like my story" or "That reminds me of me" or "I'm the same way!" (other women's stories are used to return attention to herself)
- Criticism of other rape victims. Blaming them. Talking tough about how *she* would never put herself in the same situation.
- "Why do we always have to talk about *rape* in group? Can't we talk about something *else*?!"
- "I'm over that. I've dealt with it, and I barely even think about it anymore. I've moved on with my life, so can we work on other stuff, please?"
- "I've been through all that stuff too. Look, here's what you need to do…"

But when a woman transforms from a victim into a survivor, the word "rape" and the stories of other women no longer have so much power to knock her off balance. She is able to hear the word, listen to the stories, and respond in a way that honors the other women who tell them. Gradually, she evolves from thinking that other women's narratives have value (or danger) only to the extent that they remind her of herself, into a new way of thinking where other women's stories become opportunities to relate, to support, to nurture, to encourage, and to uplift. This is not a codependent form of thought where you feel you must take on and heal every other rape victim's burdens, but a sense of personal power and calm that allows you to share together in the struggles and successes without always personalizing them. It's a change from "it's all about me" to "it's all about *us*."

5. Manage relationships. Managing relationships means maintaining the important ones. Never squander a precious friendship or alliance. Do not let a single conflict become the permanent end of a valuable companionship. Develop yourself as a leader who will be able to assist other survivors in the future. It may seem that relationship skills have little to do with triggers and amygdala hijacks, but they are very much intertwined. The more relationship skills you possess, the fewer threats your amygdala will perceive in everyday interactions. And as you become more assertive, your amygdala will be able to relinquish much of its self-protective burden because you will now be better-defended in daily life.

I once had a client who would answer every question I asked her with an inquisitive tone. If I asked her what a successful journal assignment meant to her, she would reply, "um, that I'm strong?" If I asked her what she had learned from a reading assignment, she would answer, "that it's not my fault I was raped?" This was a woman who could not make declarations because she had to seek my approval of her thoughts before she would own them herself. I learned from her pattern of approval-seeking that she was terrified that if she made a mistake or said the wrong thing, she would be punished in some way. As a result, her triggers were constantly flaring and she spent most of her day suffering through anxiety and panic attacks, needing alcohol each night to calm herself. Her progress in treatment screeched to a halt because her alcohol use (and self-harm) prevented her from developing *inner* coping skills, and thus she was never confident of her own beliefs.[10]

Being assertive, demanding respect, and knowing your rights and limits are all ways to alleviate some of the amygdalic triggers that mess up your days and nights. Remember, just because something is a reminder of your rape does not mean it is a "trigger"—the word is woefully over-used on internet rape forums, for example. A trigger is a reminder that specifically activates the physical sensation of panic, dissociation, or other responses beyond your control.

For more detailed information about PTSD and trauma, I suggest Dr. Aphrodite Matsakis's terrific book, *I Can't Get Over It: A Handbook for Trauma Survivors*.

I guess things really began to change when I realized I can't make it all go away,
but if I can recognize what I am feeling and accept that feeling for what it is
I can give value to why it's there.
-Deb, age 34

If you allow yourself to feel the way you really feel,
then maybe you won't be afraid of that feeling anymore...
- Tori Amos

---

[10] A terrific book for this is Beverly Engel's *The Nice Girl Syndrome: Stop Being Manipulated and Absued and Start Standing Up For Yourself.*

If you have panic attacks

Panic attacks begin when the body senses a cue to trigger its stress responses. These responses, such as faster breathing and pounding heart, become worse because our fear of the panic starts a cycle of self-talk that magnifies the fear: "I'm having a heart attack, I'm going to die, I can't deal with this, I'm going crazy." A panic attack is a combination of physical and psychological processes.

Just changing the self-talk you automatically respond with can cut the length and intensity of a panic attack in half. A few basic changes in how you respond, physically, can push that progress even further. For example, when you feel the signs of panic begin do not let yourself run through a list of terrified, catastrophic thoughts. Panic attacks cannot cause heart attacks. They cannot cause you to go insane. They cannot cause you to pass out and fall unconscious to the floor. Our fear of the panic comes from a lack of understanding about panic itself; we have a "fear of the fear."

Start to pay attention to the automatic thoughts you have when you feel panicky. Chances are, you make enormous conclusions right off the bat when you feel panicked, such as that you're having a heart attack, you're going to fall, you're going to die, etc. It is your interpretation of body sensations that causes your fear to magnify. Some doctors have begun referring to panic attacks as "the panic trick," meaning that you are actually tricked into believing that what is happening is dangerous and tricked into doing things that actually make the panic attacks worse, not better (examples of this would be rapid breaths, fighting and resisting the panic, breathing into a paper bag, and engaging in rituals of avoidance or superstition that you think will prevent an attack).

There is a reason your body responds the way it does, and once you understand it you will not be as likely to jump to "I'm having a heart attack and dying" conclusions. The reason we hyperventilate during a panic attack is that the brain makes a mistake in how much carbon dioxide it senses in the blood; we actually have too much oxygen. This is astonishing to learn, since a panic attack makes us think we don't have *enough* oxygen! We start over-breathing to expel carbon dioxide, which prevents our blood from absorbing the oxygen in our lungs, and the pace of the breaths is fast and shallow. This means that we aren't able to restore "normal" carbon dioxide efficiently, which causes the brain to send even *more* signals, rather than fewer, that tell us we're suffocating (when we're not).

When carbon dioxide levels in the blood drop, blood vessels constrict. This limits the amount of blood that reaches the brain, heart, and limbs. This is *not* dangerous—you are not "choking off" your blood flow, and it cannot cause damage. What it does cause is a "fuzzy" feeling: your eyesight becomes tunneled, your legs feel weaker (they're really not weak; they just feel that way!), and you feel like you'll pass out. *You won't.* The second effect of reduced carbon dioxide is that the acidity of the blood changes, which limits the amount of oxygen that reaches the brain. Again, this is *not* dangerous. It is not slow-motion suffocation. The brain continues to work perfectly fine, but it feels like you're "blanking out." The change in blood acidity causes our hands and feet to tingle, and it causes chemical changes in the body that mimic anxiety.

So right away, you can challenge your "I'm having a heart attack and dying" thoughts with medical knowledge. When you feel like you're beginning to panic, say to yourself, "a whole bunch of what I'm feeling is caused by an imbalance of oxygen and carbon dioxide. I just need to restore that balance, and I'll be fine."

One way to do that is to begin "deep breathing." This is not the same thing as desperately gulping for air like a drowning person. Instead, imagine a phone book laying on your belly just below your ribs (or actually practice this with a real phone book while lying down). Your goal is to take breaths that lift the phone book using the muscles underneath it, not the muscles near the top of your chest around your heart. Take your breaths in a rhythm, with as little gap as possible between the "in" and "out" parts. Don't vacuum in the air with a wide mouth; use your nose or a small opening between your lips to slow the rate. Imagine the air rushing down through your body all the way to the toes. Pay attention to your neck in particular, and relax your muscles; a stiff neck compresses the arteries to the brain and will limit blood and oxygen flow. The effect will take 3-4 minutes to kick in, on average, so don't quit after one boring minute and tell yourself, "well, that didn't work!"

This will take practice; don't expect it to work the first time or two and give up. Just using this method and eliminating the catastrophic self-talk helped one patient of mine reduce her panic attacks from an hour in duration to 3 minutes, in 10 days of practice.

The pattern of a panic attack appears to be:

1. Initial trigger (internal or external)

2. Physical sensations begin, such as heart rate increase, shortness of breath, sweating

3. Internal self-talk – "something's going wrong with me!"

4. Catastrophic thoughts and beliefs – "I must be having a heart attack! I can't handle this! I'm going to die! I have to bolt out of here!"

5. Full-blown panic attack.

We can intervene most effectively at steps 3-4, where we interpret the feelings we are having. We can either tell ourselves that we are going through a threatening crisis, or we can use replacement thoughts:

•   My heart rate is increasing to help my body receive oxygen. Therefore, my increased heart rate is a sign that I am about to get better, not worse. It's also proof that I am not going to suffocate; on the contrary, my body is trying to manage a surplus of oxygen. A heart can beat 200 times a minute for several *days* with no damage, so my heart is not going to fail.

•   My chest feels stiff and harder to move, but this doesn't mean I can't breathe. It's happening because my chest muscles are tight because my nervous system is trying to use muscle pressure to help propel blood to my organs. My tightened chest *helps* me, so I shouldn't interpret it as a heart attack or some form of suffocation.

- My head feels dizzy because my blood acidity has changed. It is not because I have no oxygen in my brain, or I'm having a stroke! What I should do next is to drop my shoulders into a loose position, sit upright, and relax my neck as much as I can. I'll start my "phone book breathing" pattern now.

To help you prepare for this, use the following worksheet in therapy sessions to identify your catastrophic thoughts and replacement thoughts. Write as many entries as possible, not just one or two.

My body sensations

Catastrophic thoughts

Replacement thoughts

Perhaps the most critical, harmful catastrophic thought that takes hold during a panic attack is "I have to fight this with every bit of strength I have!" Resisting initial feelings of panic is likely to make them worse, not better. Rather than running from these feelings, "talk" to them in your mind. Accept what you are feeling, float through the feeling, and say things to yourself like,

- "This is annoying, but I can get through it."
- "I can feel this way and still cope with what's going on."
- "I'm not in a crisis. This happens sometimes, and as unpleasant as it is, it's not going to be any bigger deal than I make it."
- "I'll just let my body do its thing, whatever it must to get balanced again."
- "I don't have to push myself. I just need to breathe and take a break from life for a few minutes while my blood oxygen recovers."
- "None of this is going to hurt me, it's just going to irritate me."
- "Okay, dammit, another frakking panic attack. Sheesh. Okay fine, I'll give it a moment to get past, then move on."

- "I'm feeling this way because of tiny (and safe) chemical changes, not because of danger or crisis."
- "Big f---ing deal. So what."

This is crucial. Replacing negative self-talk ("Oh no, here it comes!") with coping statements ("I can handle this; this is just anxiety and I can let it pass") lets us modify how we respond to those first physical sensations of panic.

When you feel the early signs of a panic attack, you can respond to them, but fighting them is not going to be helpful. This does not mean you have to be a passive "victim" to panic either, since doing absolutely nothing is even less helpful. What you can do, however, is to simply exit a situation that triggers panic until you can return (returning to deal with the trigger is the difference between taking a time out and *escaping*). Find someone to talk to, and move around and become active if you can. Stay attentive to the here-and-now environment you are in, and find some simple activity you can do repetitively (such as counting numbers or people, counting ceiling tiles, running your fingertips over beads or keys, putting cold water on your wrists or face, or moving your eyes back and forth without moving your head, like watching a tennis game).

Finally, you can use specific muscle relaxation techniques to calm the symptoms of panic. By compressing your muscles tightly and then releasing them, you help stimulate oxygen flow and lower stress hormones. By tightening your muscles and then releasing them, you open up more blood flow, which allows the panic attack to pass more quickly. Many books have been written that will teach you an in-depth method, and perhaps it's worthwhile to invest in a book specifically about panic attacks. But you can benefit from this much-simplified version of the technique:

- Begin with your hands. Make tight fists and hold for 12-16 seconds. Count the seconds with breaths of 4 seconds each, through the nose if possible. The process should be "in-out-in-out" for 3-4 seconds per breath. Release your muscle pressure during the final "out" breath during the 4 seconds you exhale. Rest for 15 seconds before the next step.
- Move upward through your arms, by tightening your biceps next. Bend your arms so that your fists come to your shoulders, like lifting a dumbbell weight. Make a muscle for the same four cycles (in-out-in-out) of deep breathing, followed by another 15-second rest.
- Tighten and release your neck and head muscles. Lay your head back as far as you can and tense your muscle. Relax the tension during the breathing cycle. Then lay your head forward and do the same thing. Last, keep your head straight and raise your shoulders to your ears. Just like in the other exercises, release the tension during the final "out" breath.
- Pull your shoulder blades together behind your back for four breath cycles.
- The last step is to push the pressure downward and out of your feet. Tighten your legs and hold them still—don't fidget them—and release. Finally, make "fists" with your toes and release. Picture yourself squeezing the panic downward out of your body, like toothpaste out of a tube.

Is dissociation the same thing as a flashback?

Not really. In a dissociative state, you tend to go numb, lose time, and your mind wanders. It's as if you leave your body in order to avoid a certain sensation. It is the separation of mental content that ordinarily would be processed together, in order to separate one's self from the full impact of a thought or emotion. For example, maybe you have sex but you never feel "present" through it because you're sailing in the whiteness and everything is blank. Or during abuse, you send your mind into some other world. Or when you have memories of your traumas, you remember them as if you are watching it happen to someone else. Some victims even begin to wonder whether it was really them who suffered the abuse or whether it happened to someone else, all because in their memories they are watching it happen as if they are in the room, on-looking (this is a form of dissociation called "depersonalization"). An extreme form of dissociation, amnesia, is forgetting all or parts of the trauma, which explains why many rape survivors have gaps in their memories ("what happened next? How did I get from one place to the next? What did I do afterward?"). I've even had clients who were hospitalized after violent assaults, but did not remember that they had also been raped until weeks later, often resulting in rage from loved ones who suspect she is either making up the rape account afterward, or are hurt because they believe she falsely denied the rape to hide it from them. Good law enforcement training teaches detectives to contact a rape victim several times over 2-3 weeks following a rape report, because the traumatized mind often recalls memories over time that had been suppressed during the earlier stages of the crisis.

A flashback is a sudden and intrusive "vomiting" of memory. It's intense and you feel powerful emotions, as opposed to the numb, vacant flatness of dissociation. If dissociation is an attempt to create a false and temporary sense of normalcy, flashbacks are the reverse: a sudden intrusion of *real* memories on an otherwise-normal moment. Flashbacks are not hallucinations; hallucinations are imagined and artificial constructs of your mind, whereas flashbacks are intrusive memories of actual events.

The confusion comes because people having a flashback often appear dissociative to others: they may sit silently and passively, staring blankly. As a result, other people, even therapists, accidentally interchange the two words. One similarity between them, though, is that in each one you temporarily feel "not there." In dissociation, you're "not there" because you're numbly "faded out." In a flashback, you're "not there" because you're mentally back in the trauma. Published research suggests that the presence of flashbacks alone is a sufficient indicator that trauma has occurred.[11] The United Kingdom is currently moving toward acceptance of Rape Trauma Syndrome as admissible evidence of assault in rape cases.[12]

---

[11] LA Duke, DN Allen, PD Rozee, M Bommaritto. "The sensitivity and specificity of flashbacks and nightmares to trauma." Journal of Anxiety Disorders, March 12, 2007.

[12] Keogh, Andrew (May 2007). "Rape Trauma Syndrome—time to open the floodgates?" Journal of Forensic and Legal Medicine, 14:4, pp221-224. And: Patricia A. Frazier and Eugene Borgida. (June 1992) "Rape Trauma Syndrome: A review of case law and psychological research." Law and Human Behavior, 16:3, pp293-311.

Why flashbacks happen, and what to do

Flashbacks feel like hell, but they're not dangerous. A flashback occurs when the subconscious mind is trying to resolve some conflicted or painful detail about your trauma. They happen when the mind is sufficiently at ease that the subconscious can inject the troubling memory into your conscious without the defensive walls of numbness, dissociation, or intoxication holding them back. This is why people who suffer flashbacks often abuse substances: the mind can't retrieve these memories when it is incapacitated. Substance abuse becomes a self-destructive, temporary block to the problem of flashbacks (and may make you more susceptible to flashbacks in the long run—*do not* use alcohol or drugs as a strategy to stave off flashbacks).

The trouble is, unless the conflicted memory is acknowledged, fully expressed in your mind, and resolved, it will continue to percolate as a flashback. Therefore, using substances or self-injury to prevent flashbacks does *not* truly calm the issue; it postpones it in magnified form. The longer you postpone resolution of these memories in these ways, the more difficult it will be to manage them when you can't resist them anymore.

The *good* part of having a flashback is that they indicate you are finally ready to resolve these traumatic memories. Although they feel frightening, they also suggest an unusual form of mental strength—as long as you don't sacrifice that very strength in destructive efforts to suppress the memories! It's like having the "check engine" light come on in your car: it doesn't tell you *what's* wrong under the hood, only that something needs your time, attention, and correction.

The most potent trigger of a flashback is a self-shaming thought about your rape. Merely thinking about the rape, or rape in general, does not trigger flashbacks! No, it's the thought of rape when it's connected to *guilty and self-blaming beliefs* about the rape that triggers them. This is why flashbacks usually present you with the most painful, explicit, or humiliating moments of the rape; those moments tend to the instances when you had the least power over the incident, which triggers the self-blaming talk "*that's* the part I should have prevented!" or "*that's* the part that makes me the dirtiest!" (and consequently, "*that's* the part I have to keep secret from others, so they don't also blame me or know how awful I am!"). One researcher described the origin of flashbacks very vividly:

> Many victims of traumatic events, especially childhood physical and sexual abuse, will suffer long-standing [disturbances]. Severe traumatic experiences disrupt every belief system the victim has had an opportunity to develop. It can profoundly disrupt the victim's beliefs about what is safe, secure, and predictable…Victims are left with a damaged sense of themselves. Likewise, patients lose their sense of control over their bodies and future. Their memories become distorted, distant, and incomplete. Suddenly, the world is no longer safe, and for many it will never be safe again. Finally, many victims see themselves as defective, unwanted, and filthy objects. Their perceptions seem to match the extent of the traumatic experiences or the perpetrator's actions.[13]

---

[13] J. Douglas Bremner, Charles R. Marmar (1998). *Trauma, Memory, and Dissociation*. American Psychiatric Pub, Inc. p64-65.

Overcoming flashbacks requires you to do the exact opposite of what your "comfort instincts" tell you to do: rather than avoiding these memories (with whatever tricks you use to numb them), you have to directly *examine* them. In every detail. Even the yucky ones. *Especially* the yucky ones. (Journaling will be described in the next chapter.)

One other thing can trigger a flashback, and you need to be aware of it. When you verbally tell your story or talk aloud about explicit details of the story you've never expressed before, it is common to have disturbing dreams and sleep problems that same night. This is absolutely normal.

The trouble is that few therapists remember (or even know) to advise you of this. Then if it happens, you might feel like you're going crazy and falling apart. "Well that sucked," you say to yourself. "I guess that was a bad idea. I feel worse instead of better." So many people hide this from their therapist because they think it'll be interpreted as a sign of psychosis, and they'll be hospitalized. Even more drop out at this critical moment, convinced they are losing control…when in fact they were finally on the verge of *finding* it again!

But if you know it's common and normal, it's not as scary if it happens. Telling the worst parts of your story exposes you to others, which forces you to face your worst fear: rejection. Since flashbacks are triggered by self-blaming and shaming thoughts, it's no wonder confronting this fear brings on some strong ones!

A flashback is a confirmation that your pain is real: *This does hurt! This did happen! It is important to me to deal with it!* Many times, rape victims doubt whether they were even raped at all, and try to talk themselves out of that conclusion for years (there is a classic book called "I Never Called it Rape" for this reason). But if it wasn't rape, then why are you going through trauma? If it was normal sex, then why are you going through trauma? A flashback can be used as proof to yourself, and to a doubting world, that you *are* hurt(ing), and that the pain *does* matter. Consider reframing flashbacks as proof that what you know is true: the rape is not a lie you made up, not a false accusation, not an attention-seeking tale, not an excuse. Flashbacks don't prove you are crazy, they prove you *aren't*.

The best immediate response to having a flashback isn't to reach for a bottle, razor blade, or joint. It's to reach for a journal. Write down every detail of the flashback, and examine it from every sense: what you heard, what you felt, what you smelled, what you tasted. Write down even the things that seem bizarre and unrelated ("I remember looking up at my wallpaper and seeing where a corner was torn, and thinking how I'd have to fix that," and "I remember suddenly I was in the floor space between my bed and my wall, and I don't remember how I got there").

In talking, there is freedom.
For everything else that gets taken from you,
Don't let your voice be one of them.

Begin challenging your old beliefs about rape

One of the reasons rape is such a trauma is that it collides with the old beliefs we previously had about ourselves and the world. We want to see ourselves as strong, tough, and clever people, but rape *seems* to prove that we are none of these, and as a result victims often put themselves down as stupid, weak, and disposable. If you are unable to find support after a rape, these messages compound even more. And if you seek support but find *scolding* instead ("You shouldn't have put yourself in that position!" and "Why didn't you use your head?" and so on), the weight of this self-rejection becomes even heavier.

It will be important for you to begin to challenge your own beliefs about rape and how it changes you. You may even have to re-invent the narrative story of your rape and its impact on your beliefs. It sounds impossible, but there is a clever technique that can start this process. I have my clients do a journal activity in which they write a letter to themselves *backwards in time*, to the day just before they will be raped. The letter must begin with this phrase:

"Dear _____,
Tomorrow something is going to happen to you that will change your life. What I want you to know about it is…"

The rape cannot be prevented; it *will* happen. But in this letter you are to say everything to yourself that you wish anyone had been able to say at the time. What would have helped you through it? What kinds of words do you wish you could have heard in your head during the rape to sustain you?

In most cases, women write very compassionate, tender letters to themselves. They begin to rebuild their own thoughts by writing supportive, concerned words. And in writing the letters imaginatively back in time, they are also beginning to budge their *current* beliefs into changing in the here-and-now. Here are some examples of actual letters some women have written:

Dear Andrea,

Tomorrow something is going to happen to you that will change your life. What I want you to know about it is that you will be raped, and your boyfriend will be the rapist. You will find yourself unable to scream because you are so shocked and confused because you really liked this guy, and you had worked so hard to get him to notice you. Because of that, you will not be able to tell anyone about the rape for more than a year.

After the rape, you will begin to feel like cutting yourself to feel better. Please don't! You will tell yourself "this is okay because it calms me down," but you will later realize that cutting isn't calmness; it's deadness. You are taking small pieces of your spirit and tossing them like sacrifices to a monster of fear, to keep it silent for moments at a time.

You will consider telling your sister about the rape, but when you do it she will not respond in a good way. She will criticize you and make you feel worse. This is not your fault; her criticisms do not prove you are bad, they prove she does not understand this issue.

Dad is too busy with the internet and TV to be helpful, so don't feel guilty that you choose not to tell him.

The rape was not your fault, even though you will feel like it was. When you start wondering if you somehow caused it, remember that you fought back and cried—how could he have thought this was okay with you? He knew what he was doing and it's his fault.

A little extra advice: Don't start dating **** the next month. He's an abuser and it'll make you feel worse.

Quit listening to songs by Korn. You keep telling yourself it "helps you" by making you feel good, but it's really dark, dirty music. They scream about hate and rape! Quit putting it into your head and justifying it!

Don't watch the movie the Astronaut's Wife because even tho' it has Johnny Depp in it, there's a rape scene that will upset you.

Please take care, and trust your therapist—it really will help. Tell him about the one detail—you know the one—that you keep most secret. I love you, I love, and I want you to LIVE.

Love, Andrea.

Dear Kayla,

Tomorrow something is going to happen to you that will change your life. What I want you to know about it is that you are still a valuable, important girl. Just because someone hurts you, does not mean you are bad and horrible now. So stop treating yourself bad! You need to understand about this stuff, so that you can work through it. But you will succeed!

When you are raped, you will try everything you can to stop it but it won't work. That doesn't mean you failed or did something bad, so don't spend the next three years blaming yourself—you tried! And just because it was rape doesn't mean you aren't good enough for anyone after that. You are!

At age 17 you will attempt suicide and get put in a hospital. That's where you will meet your therapist, and finally start talking about this. Please tell your story! Everyone will think you're a bad girl because you drink, smoke, and have sex now, but they don't know what happened to you so they can't understand. You will just get blamed for lots of things, and you will start to think you are just bad, too.

You are NOT bad! You need to find yourself again, and love yourself. There is so much good in you! The rape (wow, I really used the word!) will hurt, and you will feel like everyone can know just by looking at you, but you WILL get better again.

Love, Kayla.

Tomorrow something will happen to you that is going to change your life. What I want you to know about is that it will not be your fault. You will struggle with that thought for years, because he will tell you that you caused him to act that way, to do those things. He will blame you for being too pretty. As a result, for years you will hate your own prettiness. When people compliment you, you will feel sick because it will scare you, and you won't even know why.

You will keep it a secret. For years, you will blame yourself for keeping the secret, but you need to forgive yourself. Keeping the secret was not a failure you caused, it was a form of survival that you needed to do. You will be threatened and told that if you tell, it would break the family apart. When you tell your mom at age 13, she won't believe you and she will think you're lying, because he will tell her that. Instead of hating yourself and her, find your aunt and tell her. She will know what to do. Remember, when other people don't help, it's their failure, not yours.

I wish I could say you'll get through it okay. The truth is, though, you won't. You'll start smoking because you feel fat. You'll start flirting with losers. You'll hit walls and scream, and people will take you to the hospital. You'll have to sit there while you listen to people tell a therapist how bad you are, and you won't be able to open your mouth and explain why you're living this way.

You need to talk to your therapist. It won't be as scary as you expect, and you'll feel good. In talking, there is freedom. For everything else that gets taken from you tomorrow, don't let your voice be one of them.

I can't say it will be easy. But I can say there is a way out of hating yourself. Girl, you need to be proud. You need to stop thinking people are bad to you because you're bad. So avoid negative influences, don't feed that kind of hate, and let go of the anger you have against yourself, and find some good anger against the right person. Fight back by talking.

Love, Chelsea

Martine,

Tomorrow something is going to happen to you that will change your life. What I want you to know about it is that it's not your fault. None of this was ever your fault, and you've done your best with what you have. This one instance may not seem like much, but it is. Please don't downplay its significance because you will only internalize destructive habits and then, years later, you'll be unable to figure out why these habits are still a part of your life.

I know how hard it is to love yourself, but please let someone love you. Find the strength to look for a person that can help you, that will love you in both your greatest and most destructive moments.

Maybe this isn't the first time you've been in a situation like this, but it's still not your fault. You did not ask for this pain. You do not deserve this pain. But it's still there so please don't push your emotions away. I know you feel that tears betray you, but if you can, just let them come this time. There are so many years of crying buried deep inside of you, but you don't have to add another burden to the list. I don't know why this instances will stand out to you a few years from now. Maybe it's the only one you can really remember. You need to start healing somewhere, why not start with the moments you remember? Mourn that loss first, and then we can tread into deeper territory - together.

You do not have to do this alone. You are allowed to feel pain that isn't self-inflicted. I know you think that you can control that suffering, but it's not true - you've almost lost your grip a few times before. You are lovable and you are loved, no matter what you do. You have the strength to do this. I will not leave your side. I will never leave you alone with this. Your life is worth it.

- Another self deep within

Dear Sweet Child,

Tomorrow, something will happen to you, something horrible, but this is what you need to know. You have trusted someone who does not deserve your trust. You are not wrong to trust, do not take that message from this day. Trust is a good and wonderful thing, and you will learn how to use it wisely, but tomorrow is not that day.

Tomorrow, your body will be harmed, your mind will be attacked, and your spirit will mourn. But you will not die, you will not lose your mind to this, and your spirit will sustain you. You must not let the events of the day scar your vision of the future. You have a beautiful gift and you must hang on to it. That gift is your meekness. You are a young girl now, and you have a timid spirit because you have been taught that your heart and your thoughts do not matter. But they do. You will make a contribution to this world and you will be a woman who can and should prize her womanhood. You will want to hate the things that make you a woman, but you will not be able to.

Tomorrow, you will begin the lies. Lies to cover a truth that you cannot fathom. You are you know, a sweet child. You are tender, and loving, and you want love that you have not been given, by those who should give it freely. So this mistake was foreseeable. Forgive yourself for being lonely. Forgive yourself for reaching out and finding the wrong hands reaching back. You are without blame in this, but you will not believe that for many, many years.

Tomorrow, you will be frightened and things will happen to your body that you cannot understand. Forgive yourself for seeking to understand that which is deviant and wrong. Be proud you cannot put yourself in a place where what they do to you makes sense. You did not cause this. You could not cause this. Your dreams and girlish imagination could not predict this. Your mind had no knowledge of the path this day would take. Do not be ashamed you do not understand. Do not believe the vile and ugly things they say to you. Listen to the buzzing in your head and follow it to a place where they are not. It will help you feel less of what they are doing.

But my sweet child, you cannot remain there. You cannot stay where your mind says it's safe and comfortable, because that, like their kindness, is an illusion. It is a gift sent to you to help you through this horror. And you must give the gift back, you must come back. You must come to where I am....not in the closet, not in the quiet of unconsciousness, but here. Come to me, and I will join with you...and we will walk the rest of this journey as one. For without you little girl, I cannot be whole, and without me, you can never grow up.

I love you. Did you hear me? I said, I love you, and I do.

Dear Kaye,
Tomorrow something is going to happen to you that will change your life. What I want you to know about it is that it is called rape. You are not bad and what happens isn't something that you merely let 'get out of hand'. It's not something you can prevent from happening because there is no way for you to see into the future. I know that if you could, you wouldn't go to the party. I wish you could know that about yourself.

You're going to have to deal with a lot of memory loss and because of this, you're going to fill-in-the-blanks, aiming the blame at yourself. You're going to take on the sin that was done to you and treat it and yourself as though you are the guilty party. You'll make excuses for the one whose fault it really is and it will take you 31 years to look at the evidence and see it for what it is. You were drugged and you were raped.

You didn't deserve it. No one deserves to be a victim of a crime.

You're a girl. Just a sixteen-year-old girl. You can't understand the evil in the world yet. Being innocent/naive is not a crime. Being unsuspecting is not a crime. It doesn't make you stupid - rather, it makes you pure. That's a lovely and good thing.

You'll think that all is lost - your innocence, your purity, your virginity. You'll consider yourself dirty and unworthy, but you're not. You'll find that out one day.

Hold on. You're going to do alright.
  Love, Kaye.

Notice the sensitivity and encouragement in these letters! By writing "letters to the past," a woman can help begin to change her thinking. Since rape victims often feel like the rape has degraded them, it has become difficult to say kind things to yourself today. But if you write them to yourself in the day *before* your rape, the rape stigma does not obstruct you and you can release a flood of positive, respectful words for yourself. Then when you sit back and read what you've written, it will occur to you that you wrote those things *today*, so maybe—just maybe—the rape *hasn't* emptied you of all goodness after all! If you can generate such insightful and healthy thoughts in this assignment today, it's proof that these qualities are still within you.

I have, however, encountered occasional clients whose letters are *not* kind and supportive. Especially early in the treatment process, many women still feel furious at themselves, ashamed, and degraded. If they are still drinking, cutting, or engaging in abusive sexual relationships, they are more likely to write bitter letters to themselves. Danée wrote,

~Little One~
Tomorrow something will happen to you that will change your life. What I want you to know about it is that Renee will drop you off at your grandma's house. She will drive away. You will be left alone in a house that is large and scary. You'll be forced to sleep alone in your grandma's sewing room, the one with the big red leather chair. Your uncle will –R- you in that room. You will cry yourself to sleep at night. You will hide under the covers.

Little one, it's not your fault. Renee should have never left you. Your grandma should have done something, reported your uncle a long time ago. You'll feel so sad, so alone. You'll find places to escape: closets, trees, bushes. You will stay safe in your imaginary world—you're safe there. You're loved there. You'll wake up the next morning to the smell of breakfast, And that's why you hate that smell.

You feel so alone. You won't say anything, little one, you don't even have the words to describe what happened to you. You'll be numb.

Little one, I'm sorry that this will happen to you. He won 't be able to stop himself. He'll hurt you in terrible ways. You'll feel so confused, you'll be introduced to shame. You'll feel dirty inside your body. You'll wonder for years, why? You'll ask what's wrong with you. You'll feel incredibly lonely. You'll feel like everyone "knows" that you are broken. That you were R. You'll feel alone in this world, and you'll spend many years wondering if more R will occur.

> Somehow, little one, you must find your way out of that sewing room and out of the other dark places where they tried hard to destroy your soul. I need you, little one—I need you to find your way out.
>
> You were hurt deeply in every way. It is time to rest, little one. Try to be kind to yourself. Don't let them win.

Danée's letter reveals the pain and anguish she had felt for decades. Despite the brief glimmer of hope when she beckons her young self to find a way out of her darkness, it is clear that she has accepted the false belief that her rape is proof of her own inner failure as a girl. She tells herself that the rape will forever change her in to a lonely, shamed person who cannot escape this identity. Notice the frequent use of avoidance—"rape" becomes reduced to a single letter. Count how often Danée uses words like "shame, alone, sad, hurt, dirty, dark, broken." Notice how Danée lets her rapist off the hook: "He won't be able to stop himself." This is the language of the hopeless and helpless. Look through your past journaling and highlight these kinds of words, and you will be amazed at how you may have accepted the permanence of feeling ashamed.

The third category of self-writing I see is the kind where the woman tries to soothe herself out of feeling upset by downplaying the rape. Shelby, a 14-year-old client who had been sexually assaulted by her father, produced an example of this:

> Little girl,
> Hey stop crying. It's not your fault. All the things that daddy says aren't true. You're not fat, you're not ugly. Let me see that pretty smile. Daddy is wrong for what he does. You don't deserve it. Daddy doesn't know how bad he hurts you.
>
> Don't be afraid to tell mommy what Daddy does. Oh, by the way, you are loved. There's nothing wrong with being a girl. You don't have to take the blame for everything. Not all things are your fault. Good things will come. You'll get out of this mess someday. I know your pain. Just because you're strong doesn't mean you can handle this; you're just a little girl. You need someone to care for you. Someone loves you out there. Hard times are a part of life but you shouldn't have to keep this painful secret.
>
> Tell mommy. She might stop the painful things daddy does. I'm sorry you can't be like everyone else. You can change this now. I love you, and you should love yourself.

During our individual sessions, Shelby and I processed her letter. She had tended to make excuses for her abusive father: "he doesn't know how bad he hurts you." Shelby also coaxes herself to avoid her deeper emotions by telling herself to smile, be happy, be *nice*. In Shelby's family she was unable to express her emotions without being told to "settle down!" or "mind your manners." As a result, Shelby had learned to discredit her own feelings, except for the limited "candy emotions" of being always nice, sweet, and compliant. But Shelby is able to produce some very important insights, as well: not everything is her fault, and that being hurt is not a result of being weak; she should not have to endure this kind of pain. Shelby's letter is an example of a young teen girl who is still living in a home where assertiveness is not "ladylike," but who is yet beginning to connect with her right to defy these family myths.

When you write your letter to yourself, pay attention to the advice you offer. Do you find yourself suggesting sugar-coated cheery niceness and smiles as a way to cope with rape? Do you allow yourself to feel and express deeper emotions, or do you shame yourself for your emotions? Do you make any excuses for your abuser ("he doesn't mean to" or "he doesn't know how much it's hurting you" or "he couldn't help it")? Are you weepy and frail, or thoughtful and wise?

Another way to begin challenging your older beliefs about rape is to reconsider the language you use about yourself. Try to gradually stop using dark, catastrophic words to describe yourself; many rape victims believe they are broken, unlovable, dirty, wounded for life, etc. In truth, you are none of those things—you are *hurt*. Transform your "rape language" from one of being bad to one of being injured but recovering. Avoid using terms like "Weak" to describe yourself.

I have seen many women's journals, collages, poems, and works of art where they describe themselves in images that are very weak, defeated, distorted, and ugly. Online support forums for rape survivors are full of self-hating statements by women, and many of them use photographs of very sad, morose, helpless figures as avatars to represent themselves. In TV commercials, movies, and advertisements about sexual assault, women are often presented as isolated people, heads down, huddled into a small posture, and with very dark and ominous shadows over the images. YouTube is home to countless videos made by rape victims of slideshows set to music, but which depict image after image of injury, darkness, dread, defeat, blood, shadow, and grief—not a single image of empowerment or hope.

Where are the images of victory? What about the success and triumph? Why aren't women offered those images to serve as icons of identity as well? If rape victims are only shown portrayals of themselves as collapsed figurines, how can we hope to hope? I personally like the aftersilence.org T-shirts that have bold messages on them like,

THIS IS WHAT A SURVIVOR LOOKS LIKE

and,

NOT ASHAMED

and,

I'M FREE—I TOLD!

and,

YOU THOUGHT YOU'D DESTROY ME, BUT YOU ONLY MADE ME STRONGER[1]

---

[1] http://www.cafepress.com/aftersilence/

Don't allow yourself to think of rape victims in dark images or broken, faceless women in shadows. No more poems about blood, holes, and unholy souls. You cannot simultaneously crave the triumph of a sanctified survivor while branding yourself with the imagery of defeat and weakness (I once had a client with the word BROKEN tattooed boldly cross her chest. It was years before she added the word NOT in front of it). Declare an intellectual war against the images of women as targets, objects, tools, things, fallen angels, or broken toys. Remember, you are battling your own *inner* beliefs here: you are fighting against the tendency to see yourself as lost, alone, ripped, and ashamed. You are not hollow straw-filled women with dry voices, quiet and meaningless. This kind of transformation *is* possible, but you have to fight for it to happen, not wait for it to happen.

In your artwork, poems, journaling, and thoughts, give careful attention to the words, ideas, and images you choose to represent yourself. It saddens me to see people-- who for once get to *choose* the emblem of their identity, their "selves" as women and survivors--opt for images of defeat and emptiness. Wouldn't it help future young survivors if they found the role models such as you displaying monuments of fortitude, victory, and unbrokenness? For once, *you* get to choose the face of your survival. Choose wisely. Choose triumphantly.

Grieving for your loss

I didn't realize then just how much I hated myself, how much harm over the years I had inflicted on myself, I didn't deserve to be liked or for anything good to happen to me, I thought I was ugly, boring always wrong and had more or less cast myself in to total isolation. I had lied to myself, made the night I was raped fit a more acceptable story, kept it hidden and never told a soul the whole story.

But I clearly remember one day brushing my hair in the mirror and recognizing I wasn't ugly, it was the first time I years I didn't loathe the face that looked back at me. It was the first step for me to hope I could do this

-Deb

What does it mean to begin to cry/grieve more as you experience memories of your rape during therapy? Should you go ahead and cry, or hold back the tears, when you talk about your rape in therapy?

Some women in therapy avoid crying about their rapes, and they describe these events with stoic detachment: "Yeah, I was gang-raped at college when I was twenty," but in the same tone of voice as "Yeah, I recorded this show on TV last night, but I haven't watched it yet." What I have learned is that women who "flatten" their emotions when they describe their rapes are often doing so because they think this is how a recovered survivor is supposed to sound. They say to themselves, "I should be over this; crying is weakness; if I show emotions, then it means I haven't dealt with this yet and that's bad; this is my way of showing that I am strong." This is called "alexithymia," which is a fancy way to describe the state of being emotionally shut down, robot-like, with little connection between thoughts and feelings.

But let me state this as clearly as I can: women who have recovered and overcome their traumatic rapes *do* still have some tender emotions about their experiences, and they do not bury or deny those feelings. It is possible to transform your emotions from the suffocating, flooding despair you might feel now, to a sadness that reflects the hurt you have suffered which doesn't overcome you, drown you, and terrify you.

By crying for your trauma, you are beginning to accept it as a real loss, and not merely "some disgusting thing done to little-old disgusting me." Grieving, as opposed to merely being moody and weepy, is a sign of change for you because it means you are starting to see yourself as a worthy person who was wronged. You are seeing that you are a hurt person, not a bad person, and that you were hurt by someone who never saw your worth. You will also grieve the lost time when you could not see your own worth, and buried it in whatever lifestyle came after your rape.

By grieving, you are changing your attitude toward rape itself, not as something horrible done to a girl who was somehow damaged, unlovable, and awful, but as a form of THEFT from which you are not only recovering but resurrecting.

By grieving, you are recognizing that as you have grown up the world has honored fewer and fewer of your gifts, and offered you less and less choice about who you will be. As a younger girl, many parts of you could be praised and respected. But as you developed physically and emotionally, the attributes that the world sought from you were gradually reduced to "pretty, cute, and nice." And very little else. And rape compounds this diminishment of who you are allowed to be by stealing away your very sense of power and security in the world. Grieving is a healthy way to recognize that you live in a world that has limited who you, as a woman, can be. Recovering is your way of fighting back against those standards.

Try this for homework and bring it to your therapist (s/he will be amazed with you!). Write journals about these two questions:

1) If rape is a form of theft, what did it steal? (hint: begin a new tradition of avoiding cataclysmic phrases like "all of me/my soul/my worth as a person. Rape took NONE of those things from you; you still have them. Try to write toward a new way of seeing: "It stole my nighttimes. It stole the dreams I used to look forward to at night. It stole the safety I once felt of hearing footsteps. It stole the excitement and pleasure I felt in the touch of another person. It stole countless hundreds of hugs I would have given my family if I had not loathed my own body instead.")

2) If rape steals something from you, what parts of you are NOT gone? Which parts of you do you REFUSE to give away, no matter what? What do you hold for yourself as a treasure within?

Notice how the point of these journal ideas is to begin to change the language we use when we talk about rape. You need to see it as a hurt done to you, not a permanent source of filth and badness *about* you. The first part – "what did rape steal?" – does invite a darker way of thinking because it asks you to focus on losses. It is common that this part of the two-part journal can bring up anger and grief. Danée wrote a page before having to stop because of her rage:

> It stole my mother. It stole my true, deep intimate relationship with my family of origin. It stole my restful sleep. It stole my ability to form healthy relationships. It stole my childhood. It stole the child who wanted to pick flowers, play in the dirt, go on dates with her parents. The peace and quiet of a restful night's sleep. Stole the smell of morning breakfast and my mother's touch sending me off to school. It stole being greeted at the door with a kiss and hug. It stole homework time, dinner at the table with laughter and talking. It stole activities and passions, consistency and stillness. It stole school plays, softball games, and the support a child so desperately needed. It stole hugs, kisses, back scratches, and someone laying in bed to rub my tummy when it hurt. My ability to tell the truth. It stole healthy sexuality, a close relationship with my brother, my nights, my holidays, my birthdays. It stole family trips, parent nights at school, and my ability to be friends with girls, or boys without it being based on sex. God, it f---ing stole a lot.
>
> Stop right now.

But the work does not stop there. You are to take one more step toward reclaiming some of these stolen gifts, first by remembering what you have *not* lost. A survivor must avoid "all-or-none" words when she thinks about herself, such as "always, never, everything, nothing" and begin to realize that her entire self-worth is not lost. Again, here is Danée, considering what she has not lost:

> What parts of me am I not giving to you—
>
> You'll never have the joy I feel when I look at my little girls, knowing that they will never be hurt by you, or a man like you. The peace I feel at night when I lay my head on my pillow, knowing I've made the world a better place. It gives me great joy to know that you don't have that peace.
>
> You'll never be able to see the love and compassion that I have for humanity. I would never want you to think I'd give up either one.
>
> There is the amazing person I've become. Smart, funny, caring, loving – that, you'll never see. You will never have the woman that I've become.
>
> You can never touch my healed woman. Never hear her words, live in her world – a world that still hopes, that is committed to keeping children safe from people like you.
>
> You found me when I was alone and abandoned. You should be ashamed. My pride for all I've survived will never be taken by you!

Here is an example from Leitha's journal, which she wrote as if she was speaking to the men who have misused her:

To my rapists...all three;
You could not steal my soul. There was a time I thought you had. I thought I had turned it over to you with a simple invitation for company, but I was wrong, it was in a safe place far out of your reach.

I did not relinquish my person. True, the essence of that person was shattered, but the foundation of my person lived through you attacks. I remained a person, but the rebuilding has been necessary.

I did not release to you my skin. The 'thing' that holds this all together. A carcass to some, but to me, a covering of my most vital parts, you didn't get it. It was torn, and bruised and it hurt, and you never knew how my one wound helped me escape your attack in my mind.

There is a deep love that I have for people in need. Your actions could have made me turn away from others, and be angry that my needs were so overlooked, but, I am different from you, and you couldn't take that from me. You couldn't take away from me that I am NOT like you.

You did not steal my tears. They flow freely, even today, and they let me know that the hurt is still there, that I am not numb. I feel deeply, and you can't take that from me.

You didn't steal my wise-mind, the part of my brain that says all the right things and doesn't put my heart's desire ahead of common sense. Nope, you didn't get that. You took a close look at it, and you toyed with it, and you attempted to leave dirty, vile, unthinkable words to replace my words. But, after all these years, I remember your words, but my words won.

Your attempts at changing a little girl into an instant woman, because of the acts you each forced me to perform, or attempt, they didn't work. The process of me becoming a woman was hindered somewhat, but I am a woman now, and you stole nothing about that but some time. So, you get no credit for your attempt.

If this were scored like a boxing match, you didn't come close to beating me. You knocked me down, but I got back up. Each round you thought you'd won, I came back. I did not fight you, and perhaps that is my greatest victory over this, I won without lifting a fist. Unfair odds, unkind acts, evil.....but you still didn't win. The greatest thing I refused to relinquish was my breath. It flowed in, and eased out, over, and over, and over. My heart, though burdened with fear and sadness, still beat, again, and again, and again.

I went every round, I matched wits, with silence; I matched strength with stillness, you put all your evil on the mat, and I rose above it following the buzzing in my head, and I took my mind where you could not go. So, at the end of the day, I did not relinquish ME! You evil Bastards, I did not relinquish ME!

Leitha's essay is remarkable because it represents a whirlwind of hurt and hope, all together in the same soul. It shows a woman willing to fight back—not in the stereotyped way, but in her mind and soul—for an acknowledgement of honorable parts of her that remain deeply within, despite the rape. If her rape was a form of invasion and theft, even the great burden of pain it left behind does not outweigh her goodness and inner life within, and she names and claims them. She was able to find her life in the parts of her that she could rebuild after her rape, and then she could her voices, her words, rather than her injuries, to speak for her about her pain and resurrection.

Some women have difficulty with this assignment because it causes them to write positive things about themselves—"These are the good things I still have." This is an uncomfortable way for some to think. A person who is accustomed to feeling hollow, worthless, and ugly either resists the assignment, or feels she is being arrogant if she does write about her positives.

But as one client of mine realized in therapy, "There are some pieces of me I just won't ever get back. I have to accept that they are gone. And for years I felt hopeless because of that, as if the core of me was stolen and I had to live out my days like a hollow tin man with no heart inside. But what I realize now is that I don't need those old pieces to re-grow. Those were pieces of a person I'm not like anymore. They were pieces of a hurt and broken me, and they can have 'em. I'm growing someone new."

Transformation Activities

To start successfully transforming from a victim into a survivor, several steps must take place. Therapy is usually the most helpful setting for them to happen. At the very beginning of therapy, your first process will be education and insight-building. The therapist's goal at the start of therapy will be to help you understand the symptoms of PTSD/Rape Trauma Syndrome, and to become familiar with myths and facts about sexual assault itself.

Being raped does not automatically mean that a victim possesses entirely accurate understandings *about* rape; we have already seen that mistaken beliefs can be the root cause of persistent flashbacks, nightmares, and triggers. In order to begin to fully address your rape, you will need to fully inform yourself about the crime and sociology of rape.

It is important that you attend all therapy sessions and complete all assignments for your therapist. If you are unable to complete an assignment for personal reasons, then at least substitute a replacement activity by journaling why you weren't able to proceed. Be on time to groups; one common form of avoidance among women in groups is to arrive a few minutes late so that someone else would have begun talking instead, and she can more comfortably take her seat and listen.

At the onset of therapy, you should be given the opportunity to ask any questions you might have. Your therapist may not have every answer, especially for the larger existential questions like "Why? Why me?" Many rape victims continually replay thoughts of doubt that their experience was actually a rape, and rape discussion/support forums online are *full* of messages by new members asking the same question: "Was this rape? Was I raped?" Having doubts about your own story is *very* common—and normal.

The findlaw.com website states,

> The crime of rape (or "first-degree sexual assault" in some states) generally refers to non-consensual sexual intercourse that is committed by physical force, threat of injury, or other duress. A lack of consent can include the victim's inability to say "no" to intercourse, due to the effects of drugs or alcohol. Rape can occur when the offender and victim have a pre-existing relationship (sometimes called "date rape"), or even when the offender is the victim's spouse.
>
> Under a variation known as "statutory rape," some states make it unlawful for an adult to engage in sexual intercourse with a person who has not reached the age of consent [which varies from state to state].[1]

Notice several key points about this definition. First, it does not limit rape to conventional forms of sexual intercourse. Any form of physical penetration, of any part of the body, can be regarded as rape. This includes penetration of the vagina, anus, or mouth. And it includes forms of assault using the penis, fingers, or objects. All of these are legally regarded as forms of sexual assault or rape.

Also notice that the definition of rape does not require the perpetrator to use pure physical force, weapons, or even threats. The majority of rapes involve no weapons, and rape is not defined by acts or degrees of violence. A rape can occur in a way that is not physically violent (in an injury-causing sense), because legal consent can lack in many circumstances such as a woman being drugged, unconscious/passed out, mentally incapacitated, or not old enough to consent. Many rape victims have difficulty processing their guilt about the rape if they were intoxicated at the time of the crime, but the laws are clear that being intoxicated does not cast doubt on whether she was raped; it *clarifies* that she was raped.

You do not have to expect to discuss your rape in the first session, and many times it takes patients of mine several sessions before they will be ready to talk about it. In a successfully and healthy therapeutic relationship, you should have complete control over the limits of your willingness to discuss rape, and as a rule I always inform my clients—and frequently remind them—that if they ever want to halt the discussion of this at any point, they may. After all, how does a woman heal from having power and control taken from her, if she still has no power and control over her choices during the therapy itself?

The rest of this chapter is divided into Parts. Each Part is a single activity that you will complete and process in therapy. There is no set schedule for how quickly you move from one Part to the next. But do not rush it; speed is not the same thing as progress! You might choose to do one part per week, one per session, or even one per day. You may also decide to only do one part per month—whatever pace keeps you hopeful without overwhelming you. Do therapy the way a dolphin swims: dive down deeply into the darkness, and then surface again to breathe and rest. Repeat.

The process of confronting and overcoming your rape is going to be extremely difficult, and you will be tempted to stop, cancel therapy appointments, or other forms of

---

[1] http://criminal.findlaw.com/crimes/a-z/rape.html

avoidance. I spend several hours a day, every day, leading a women's trauma recovery therapy group and I see first-hand the agony that these woman go through. Many of them have sleepless nights, and during our therapy sessions they feel strung out, weary, tense, and sometimes even physically ill. The most common feedback I get during the first few days of this process is, "I thought this was supposed to make me feel better!"

Think of the recovery process as a hill that becomes more difficult as you ascend. You become exhausted, you feel weak, and you wonder if you will ever make it. And then you begin to notice that this is becoming easier, you're not as stressed, and you don't fear defeat anymore. As a therapist, I *live* for that moment, and it inspires me to see the transformation that my clients make when their rape stops being their "uphill burden" and they cross the summit. This point of transformation from victim to survivor stops being a distant speck on the horizon, and becomes their here-and-now pride, their mountaintop.

At the start of this journey this sounds like a fairy-tale. It seems impossible, and some women even become angry when I describe this possible transformation because they simply cannot imagine it. To them, this doesn't feel like a possible accomplishment, it feels like pie-in-the-sky cheerleading that minimizes their anguish. If you are starting this journey filled with doubt, you are absolutely normal. But at least commit to yourself that no matter how hard the work, you *will* succeed and finally be rid of this emotional poison.

In my therapy session just today, a young 21-year-old woman read and grieved her rape story. She said to the group, "I knew this would be hard, so I read my story several times before I came in. And you know what? You were right! The sting of it does get softer. I actually became excited to do this because I knew I was finally going to win!"

This inspired another of my patients who told me in private that she had been physically nauseated because of so many buried memories resurfacing. But she said, "it's like a viral infection, and I'm so tired of being sick from it. I just want it out so I can be cleansed again. I know I can't undo the past, but I don't want to be defined by it anymore either. I want my life back."

Courage is the price that life exacts for granting peace.
-Amelia Earhart

Part I: Evaluating what you believe about rape

To begin your treatment, you should evaluate what you already know and believe about rape itself. I am providing a simple survey for you to use in the hopes that it may clarify your beliefs.

1. I am embarrassed to discuss or be taught about sexual assault.

       True   False

2. Rape is a primitive instinct in males which makes men's sexual self-control difficult.

       True   False

3. It is up to women to prevent themselves from being raped or sexually assaulted.

       True   False

4. Women should understand that they lose the right to accuse rape when they become drunk, or dress and behave sexy.

       True   False

5. The rapist is 100% to blame, even if his victim is intoxicated.

       True   False

6. The most likely rapist is a stranger who targets a woman at random.

       True   False

7. Rapists have a "type" of victim they look for, based on a woman's appearance and attractiveness.

       True   False

8. If I were sexually assaulted, I would know the right thing to do afterwards.

       True   False

9. I still have questions about sexual assault that I wish I could ask.

       True   False

10. I know where I can go to get honest and private answers to my questions about sexual assault.

       True   False

11. The majority of rapes occur in a relationship where the victim knows her attacker.

       True   False

12. Half of rape victims contemplate suicide after the rape.

       True   False

13. The greatest fear a rape victim usually has afterward is that she will be killed.

       True   False

14. There are few long-term mental health effects from rape.

       True   False

Answers:
1. This answer depends on you. But I doubt you would be reading this, or be in therapy, if it were entirely true. Feeling uncomfortable with the subject is perfectly normal, but the guiding principle of rape recovery therapy is "hate it but do it anyway."
2. FALSE. Rape is a deliberate, conscious choice. There is no biological need for an aroused man to have sex, and rape is not the result of primitive, evolutionary reproductive drives. Rapists tend to anticipate their acts sexual assault, and derive as much sense of power and control from the arrangement of the opportunity to

rape as from the rape itself. You must never excuse or diminish your rapist's guilt by believing he somehow could not help what he did, or that you created an opportunity that he simply "fell into" when he committed rape.

3. FALSE. Rape happens because a man makes a decision to rape, not because a woman somehow failed in her responsibility to prevent rape at every moment. If 99.8% of rapists are male, then it becomes a men's issue to address the problem of rape. Sadly, many self-defense "experts" offer workshops for women about "how to avoid being a victim." Emails constantly circulate among women with so-called "advice" about how to prevent themselves from being raped.

4. FALSE. See the laws above. The age range of rape victims in my state alone (Oklahoma) is from 6 months old to 102 years old. Clearly, these crimes are about power and control, not about the victim's sensual appearances and behaviors.

5. TRUE. And the law agrees.

6. FALSE. Stranger rapes account for only 10-15% of all rapes.

7. FALSE. Rape is more about opportunity, power, and control than anything else. It did not happen because of a victim's appearance.

8. This answer depends on you. We will discuss this more in later sections.

9. Most women answer TRUE. That is a good sign, and your therapist should help.

10. Regardless of your answer, reliable advice is easy to find. I suggest www.rainn.org as a superb resource.

11. True. About 85% of rape victims know their attacker, and on average she has known him a year or more.

12. TRUE. And the first year after a rape is the highest risk.

13. FALSE. Overwhelmingly, the greatest fear most women have after a rape is "Oh my god, nobody will believe me!"

14. FALSE. Tons of research and personal accounts of survivors tell us that some of the after-effects of rape include suicidal thoughts and attempts, eating disorders, self-injury, addictions and substance abuse, smoking, nightmares, depression, difficulty concentrating, risky dieting methods, changes in hygiene and dress, involvement in abusive/battering relationships, and even a lowered immune system.[1] The good news is that each of these can be diminished or overcome through rape trauma recovery.

Which of these myths about rape had you believed before your rape?

- Rapists are strangers who hide in alleys and dark places
- I wouldn't be raped by someone I know
- A woman who is assaulted could probably fight off her attacker if she tried hard enough

[1] Constantino, R. E. et al. "Negative life experiences, depression, and immune function in abused and nonabused women." 2000 Biol Res Nurs 1;3:190-8. "Domestically abused women were significantly more likely to have experienced higher levels of depression, and have impaired T cell function."
Also: Stepakoff, S. "Effects of sexual victimization on suicidal ideation and behavior in U.S. college women." 1998 Suicide Life Threat Behav 28;1:107-26. The attempted suicide rate found in this study was 25%.

- Rape is a rare crime
- Rape happens to certain types of women who are different from me
- Rape happens because men lose control of their emotions
- Rape happens because women entice men
- Most rape reports are false
- Women report rape because they want attention and sympathy
- Women report rape so they can win money from men in court
- You can tell a rapist by how he looks
- Rape is just a form of aggressive sex
- Rape victims usually return to normal in a few weeks
- Family members never commit rape
- A wife cannot be raped by her husband
- Only "bad" women get raped
- Rape happens to women who are weak
- Rape only occurs outside, and at night
- Rapes are "spur of the moment" incidents that weren't planned by the rapist
- Only women are raped. If men are raped, it's a form of homosexuality.
- Rapists are usually psychotic or perverted men with no other stable relationships or access to sex
- If a woman doesn't "fight back," she wasn't really raped
- Women "ask for it" by their looks or actions

Were you surprised to see any of these statements described as untrue myths? Did you ever believe any of them were true? How many of these myths do you think are commonly believed by people today? Where do these myths come from, and why do some people believe them?

These myth and misconceptions are often internalized by survivors of rape, and can be the source of intense self-blame, shame, and anger. Although our social attitudes toward rape are slowly changing for the better, it continues to be important to challenge these old beliefs—not just in courtrooms, but in classrooms, hospitals, churches, police departments, and media.

A wounded deer leaps the highest.
-Emily Dickinson

Part II: Addressing your fears about rape therapy

Professionals will tell you that silence is terribly harmful. They'll tell you that it's vital for rape victims to talk about it in order to heal. They would be right.

Keeping it inside will only give it opportunity to grow worse. Guilt raises up and there's no one there to counter it - no one to declare you *not guilty*. Fear can consume you and there's no one to help bring balance. What you hide and block away will surface in your dreams, demanding your attention.

I was quietly dying inside.

-Kaye, 47

Since it is uncomfortable to jump right in to processing rape, I usually provide my clients with a "preparation journal" that helps them examine their fears and expectations about therapy. Complete the journaling on the next few pages and bring it to your counseling sessions to discuss with your therapist.

Write thoughtful and complete answers.
Do not avoid the questions by writing simplistic, brief responses.

How often do you think about your rape, and do you ever feel like you have thoughts about it that you can't stop?

What kinds of nightmares or memories do you have about your rape?

How does thinking about the rape make you feel, and why?

How hard is it for you to talk about your rape?

What, if anything, makes you afraid to talk to people about your rape?

Who have you told about your rape, and why did you choose to tell them?

What did they do or say about it?

How did your rape make you feel about yourself as a person?

How is your rape affecting you as a person right now?

What thoughts do you sometimes have about yourself because of the rape?

What do you wish people knew or understood about the rape so that they could help you now?

What is the scariest thing about talking or writing about the rape?

If you've ever felt guilty or blamed yourself for the rape, what kinds of self-blaming thoughts have you had?

Why do you think victims of rape tend to blame themselves and feel guilty for rape that someone *else* did to them?

Pcople who have been raped often find ways to prevent or "stuff" their emotions about what happened. Some people use drugs or alcohol, some may cut or hurt themselves, some have sex frequently with persons they don't love, some become violent and "tough." What different behaviors have you used to stop your emotions about rape?

What questions do you wish you could answer to yourself about your rape?

What has prevented you (so far) from fully healing from your rape?

What good things (benefits) will happen for you if you work with your therapist about your rape?

Last question, part 1: are you willing to talk about this more with me (your therapist), even if it's tough?

Last question, part 2: If you want to talk about this with me (your therapist), how should I prepare myself as your therapist? For example, are there any topics you want *me* to do homework on so I'll know how to understand better? Any songs I should listen to that mean a lot to you so I will understand you more? Anything I should pray about? Do you want to give *me* journal homework so I'll be ready to help you? Are there mistakes that other therapists have made with you that I should avoid?

Dr. Schiraldi, in *The Post-Traumatic Stress Disorder Sourcebook*, lists his "seven principles of healing" from PTSD. They are:

1. Healing starts by applying skills to manage PTSD symptoms.
2. Healing occurs when traumatic memory is processed.
3. Healing occurs when confronting replaces avoidance.
4. Healing occurs in a climate of safety and pacing.
5. Healing occurs when boundaries are intact.
6. Kind awareness and acceptance of feelings aid the healing journey
7. Balance in our lives is necessary to heal.[1]

---

[1] Schiraldi, p. 50-53

The best and most beautiful things in the world cannot be seen or even touched.
They must be felt within the heart.
-Helen Keller

Part III: The meaning of the rape

The reason rape causes traumatic symptoms afterwards isn't because of the physical violation only; it is because rape has meaning – significance – to the victim. It changes things, both inwardly and in your relationships. What your rape meant to you will determine what intensity and types of effects it will cause afterward. For example, there seems to be a correlation between the intensity of anger a woman feels about her rape and the severity of PTSD symptoms later. The conflicting thoughts between what you want(ed) to believe about yourself and what rape seems to say, prove, or do to you create painful chasms of confusion: "I wanted to see myself as smart and tough, but the rape seems to prove I am stupid and weak." Or: "I wanted to believe someone would love me, but the rape has made me unlovable."

It is time to begin to put into words what it means to you that you were raped. As one client of mine said, "I thought I knew what it meant, but as long as it was just thoughts I could keep things vague. I didn't have to actually process those thoughts, or think about them; all I had to do was tell myself I *had* those thoughts and that was enough. But once you really look at them, put them on paper, they're real. It makes you deal with them. I don't think I could have truly moved forward if I had skipped this."

Because you will begin to explore and document how your rape has changed you, this step will be difficult. It is at this point that many clients suddenly begin to "forget" their homework, skip sessions, or drop out. All of these are forms of avoidance, and are symptoms of trauma. If you catch yourself doing these, realize that they reinforce the trauma rather than helping you through it.

Our interpretations of events can affect our feelings. The way you think philosophically about rape—*your* rape—can determine how you feel about yourself as a woman. When we are growing up, we are given a view of the world that tends to be black-and-white: things are good or bad. You were a good girl, or you were a bad girl. On TV, good things happen to the good guys, and the bad guys get punished at the end. It's the basic structure of almost every fairy tale. But what happens when those life lessons are no longer accurate?

You will begin to explore the beliefs about life that you had while growing up. What maxims and assumptions about the world were true to you? What did you believe was a guaranteed, always-true rule about how people act?

A woman named Aria wrote this:

> Growing up, I thought that people were fair and that the only time someone would do something mean is if I did something bad. But I never thought of it as mean, I thought of it as punishment. That meant that whenever someone did something to me, I assumed two things: it was fair, and it was because I had broken a rule. Usually, this way of looking at the world was true, and I never had any reason to question it. My parents were never abusive, and they were pretty fair. So it became a truth I lived: I will be treated well unless I do something bad, and then punishment isn't mean, it's just natural.
>
> I also thought that I was tough and strong, and that if anyone ever did try to hurt me I would be able to stop it and make them sorry for what they were doing. I learned this when boys in my neighborhood were picking on my sister, and I went down the street and socked one of them. It was enough to make them stop, and I learned that I can use force to stop mean people. But that also taught me something else: I started to think that "using force" wasn't a way to *be* mean, it was a way to *stop* people who were mean. So since elementary school when I wont hat fight with a boy, I thought it was a permanent truth that I had the power to stop *any* mean boy, *any* bully.
>
> So those were my beliefs. Now [that I have been raped,] I feel like I was completely wrong about everything.

Aria told me that she didn't really have strong emotions about this writing until she got to the last line. In her journal, that line is written in large, jagged letters that cut through the paper from the pressure on the pen she held. In her case, which is unusually clear, her rape's significance has power to apparently crush all of her previous positive beliefs. Her rape seemed to collide with her views of the world, and prove them all wrong. Aria's conclusion, then, was that *she* was all wrong. When I met her, Aria's arms were covered in thick, rope-like scars from intensely-deep self-inflicted gouges.

Aria's story illustrates how her rape changed her: she was no longer able to believe that people were fair, or that she was able to assertively protect herself. Because of her lifelong belief that she would only be hurt (punished) when she had done something bad, her rape also felt like a punishment. Rape, it seemed, was the ultimate condemnation of her as "bad."

Danée had similar belief to Aria's, and she wrote this during her therapy:

What I used to believe… I was so young when it happened, the first time. As a little 4-year-old girl I imagine that I believed that the world was a wonderful place. I believed my parents were superheroes. I believed that they were larger than life, fixers of anything that was wrong. I believed that my parents thought the world of me. They thought I was beautiful, smart, funny, and loving. I thought I was the most wonderful girl on the planet. They'd go to the end of the earth for me. They'd never let anything happen to me. I believed that as long as I had them I'd always be OK. I believed what they said. I believed she'd come back— then the rape happened.

And now I tell myself that the world is a scary place. I tell myself to always keep my guard up. No one can k now the real me. If they saw the real me, the world would see a broken little girl. A scared, afraid, weak little girl. There are no such things as superheroes, no one is gonna come to your rescue. I tell myself the people of the world are too self-absorbed to help rescue a little one. I'm so sorry, little one.

It still seems to me that everyone around me is still larger than life. They're not broken, so why would they want to play with me? I tell myself that no one thinks the world of me. Really, who would want to be around someone that is so messed up like me? There's something wrong with me. I tell myself, "You're alone in this world. Look – you're not even good enough to have parents that love you. Even murderers and rapists have parents that love them and visit them. You're not even good enough to have parents."

I tell myself, "there's no way you were a wonderful little girl, then or now. Your parents never came for you. Your grandma didn't protect you. Your aunts lived right down the road and they never rescued you. You didn't even know where your dad was. Your 'good' uncle lived next door and took in your brother, but not you. They all just left you. They all just left you."

I tell myself now, "I don't need anyone. Get close to no one. One day, they'll drive off and leave you too; they always do. Even when they know you're hurting, they won't come to your rescue. They'll close their eyes and just hope you go away."

Danée's journal describes her intense belief that her abandonment and victimization by her family was proof that Danée was an unlovable, isolated creature. She did not believe her abuse made her bad, she believed her abuse happened *because* she was bad: "All of this makes me feel like I wasn't even worth someone coming back for. I'm not worth someone sticking around, keeping safe, or protecting." When I began to work with Danée, she had developed this self-fulfilling prophecy by moving out of her home, leaving behind a husband and four daughters, because she was convinced she was not the kind of woman anyone would cherish or stick around for anyway.

These conflicts between your prior beliefs (or what you *want* to believe about yourself) and the contrary things that rape seems to teach you are called *stuck points*.[1]

---

[1] Resick and Schnicke, p42.

Stuck points that linger in the mind, unexposed and unchallenged, produce the phenomenon of flashbacks and nightmares as your brain attempts to recreate the rape over and over in search of some way to reconcile your beliefs and the rape's counter-lessons.

Journal activity: Write your own description of the things you once believed about life, fairness, goodness, men and women, and so forth. Then describe the way your rape has changed those beliefs.

As you look at Aria's example, notice that she tends to stick to the level of thoughts rather than feelings. This is very common during rape therapy; as a therapist I will ask a woman how she feels about an issue and she will respond with "I think that…" (This is unusual for women in general, who tend to respond with "I feel" statements. But in coping with trauma, many victims, either male or female, remain in the realm of "I think…")

Aria was a brilliant, high-IQ, emotionally-intelligent young woman who could comprehend the nuances and higher implications of just about any issue, but nudging her from thinking to *feeling* was difficult. Even her last line, "I feel like I was completely wrong about everything" isn't actually a feeling at all, it is a thought—a statement—worded as if it were an emotion.

Pay attention to your writing. Begin by describing your thoughts and beliefs, and then describe how those thoughts affect your emotions.

Journal Activity: Write a counterpart to your last entry. This time, describe how your rape and its effects on your thoughts has impacted your *emotions*.

Again, Aria provides a superb example:

> I feel so confused. I am embarrassed because I think I should have been strong enough to stop him, so now I feel like I am weak. I am afraid that people who claim to support me will reject me if they know more about how I am because of what happened. I am lonely. I used to have high self-esteem, but because of this I have started to feel unworthy of being happy. I yell and scream at [loved ones] as if they are mistreating me, but in reality I don't think I even deserve to be treated well. I feel guilty when I ask for something. I wanted my dad to read a book about rape so he could help me, and when he never picked it up I felt personally rejected, like, Am I not important enough for you to read a book? I told him I was hurt, and as soon as I did I felt guilty for saying it, like I had been selfish. I felt awful, and I cut myself within an hour. Rape has f---ed me up so much I can't even ask someone to be decent to me without feeling like I'm asking for more than I deserve! I feel like the little bad girl who has done something so shameful that she should just be put in a corner for "time out," except that "time out" should last years and years instead of minutes. I feel like I must have done something truly awful for this to have happened. I am so sad, because it's like every good thing in me died that day, and all I have left is shame.

Aria's journaling reveals her true stuck points: she believes she deserved her rape, or at least blame for it, because she had somehow failed to be "good enough." As a result, her rape is a symbolic brand burned into her body and soul, identifying her as "undeserving of love."

If you have difficulty starting this assignment, here is another way to attempt it. Use a three-step flow chart to examine your beliefs. The three steps are:

1. I used to believe…
   [Then the rape happened,]
2. And now I tell myself…
3. …Which makes me feel:

Do not simply write a few words down and consider the work complete. Many women bring this to their session and present it to me:

1. I used to believe…   *I was good*
   [Then the rape happened,]
2. And now I tell myself…   *I am bad*
3. …Which makes me feel: *Sad*

These are insufficient responses. Answers like these are forms of avoidance. Don't cheat yourself with frail, watered-down writings. Make your best effort. And remember, these are not school essays on topics where you will be graded for how well it satisfies some question; *anything* your journaling captures while you write can be of value in your therapy. Don't wait until you have in mind what you want to write so it will seem "good;" just write—don't type—and let your intuition guide the flow.

This is the time to delve into the darkness and truly put into words the beliefs you have because of your rape. Danée was able to finally face the fact that she felt worthless: "I feel like I'm, so messed up that no one could ever love me. I don't even know what love looks like. I feel uncomfortable in the presence of love…I'm scared to say or do the wrong thing, or that someone might know me, and the things that have been done to me, and the things I have done to myself. I feel abandoned by God."

This step has simply exposed the darker, sadder emotions and thoughts you have because of your rape. Therefore it is important you do not stop here, drop out of therapy, or quit this program. We have only begun to unveil some of the inner emotional damage you have endured; we must now identify how you can possibly hope to undo some of that damage when things may seem especially bleak right now.

Engrave this upon your heart:
There isn't anyone you couldn't love once you heard their story.
-Mary Lou Kownacki

Part IV: Your story

The next step is for you to create a detailed written description of your rape. You will recall and describe exactly what happened, through the information gathered by all of your senses during the rape—sight, hearing, smell, taste, and touch. You will then read your story out loud to your therapist and/or group, or other appropriate hearer/supporter.

The paragraph you have just read has likely sent feelings of terror through you. You will not be asked to do anything without preparation and readiness, so continue to read and use some of the steps I'll offer to move yourself toward completion of this goal.

Why should a woman revisit her rape and record it in all of its ugliness? What is the rationale for doing this? To put it simply, it's just not possible to recover from something we have not even named and described. We can say we have "recovered," but from *what*? There is no such thing as a "typical" rape, and nobody's reaction to rape will be exactly the same as another person's. In order to know exactly what you are recovering from, you must *describe* what you are recovering from.

Writing and reading your story also helps with physical recovery, too. Your amygdala has been well-trained to regard every hint of "rape-like" information to be a potential danger, and it continually sounds alarms throughout your life that can make you suffer anxiety, flashbacks, panic, irritability, and pervasive fear. By deeply exploring the rape story itself, you re-program your brain to be less vulnerable to its over-sensitive over-detection of danger. There are actually changes in the way the brain functions during the process of facing your story; rape itself shifts from being a collection of generalized imprints in the amygdalic "alarm center," into a tangible conflict that your controlled, rational, thoughtful brain (the frontal and prefrontal cortex) can manage. It's as if by writing and revealing your story, your brain relocates the problem of rape away from the overly-nervous, traumatized, panicked regions of the brain and hands it over to the parts of the brain that can deflate its power. You engage new regions of the brain in your war against rape, rather than letting the same brave-but-overwhelmed amygdala do all the heavy lifting.

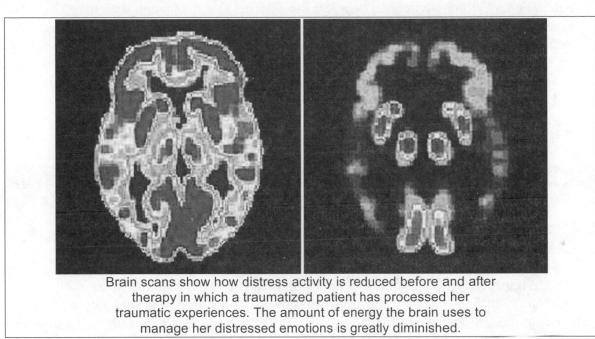

Brain scans show how distress activity is reduced before and after therapy in which a traumatized patient has processed her traumatic experiences. The amount of energy the brain uses to manage her distressed emotions is greatly diminished.

However, your amygdala is still in control at this moment while you read these very words. It (your amygdala) is reading these pages too, and beginning to detect the sensations of danger as you begin just to imagine the act of writing and revealing your story to anyone. It recognizes this as a distressing, upsetting act, and it may have already begun to "hijack" your nerves to steer you away from the very idea. When you contemplate this next step in your recovery, do you feel nervous? Does your anxiety rise? Do you physically feel tense or ill?

If you do, these are not indications that proceeding is a bad idea. On the contrary, they prove that proceeding is absolutely vital: these symptoms show you that rape is still regarded by your survival instincts as a continually-present danger that you must avoid, avoid, avoid, and your sympathetic nervous system actively trying to discourage you from going ahead with this. Your brain thinks it's saving you by warning you not to write or tell your story ("because it'll hurt you," it says), but giving in to this instinct and avoiding your story would actually divert you away from the path of recovery in the end.

The other reason for doing this is that processing your story will begin to dismantle some of the very symptoms of PTSD itself. A central feature of PTSD is the habit of avoiding any hurtful or uncomfortable trigger of the trauma. Consequently, many rape victims engage in denial, memory blocking, self-injury, sex, or substance abuse to avoid these sensations. Abundant research shows amazing results in recovering from PTSD by resisting avoidance instincts and doing the *opposite*: facing the trauma as directly as possible, capturing every awful speck of detail on paper, and stating it aloud to supportive listeners. This act alone can interrupt the mind's need to continually review the trauma through nightmares and flashbacks.[1]

(This is why I strongly advise that you only undertake the complete telling of your story while under the care of a good therapist, and that it be something you do after a long phase of other work first until you've built up strength and have a close bond with the therapist. Writing your rape story on the internet doesn't count, and may even be counter-productive: it exposes the parts of your shame that *most* need compassionate human response, but in a setting that only offers feedback from distant others on a computer screen. Countless times, I have seen people rush to do their "story work" on websites and online forums, and then become angry and frustrated when they found no qualified comrades to help during critical crisis afterward.)

Preparing yourself for the story

> You decide whether to look at your reality or live pretending these feelings don't exist.
>
> -Tori Amos

While writing your story, you may experience a surge of emotions as intensely as you felt them during the rape itself. You will not be harmed or psychologically scarred by these emotions, and they will not re-traumatize you. You will not "go crazy" doing this work, but you need to follow these steps properly. The emotions will recede again, and you will not experience a "permanent doubling of pain," as one of my clients feared.

If the idea of putting pen to paper is too daunting at first, you may opt for some preliminary activities to help you in your struggle. One very interesting way to begin describing your rape recovery is to create a collage about the experience.[2] Many of my clients have done this and reported remarkable insight and self-discovery through the process. Nearly all of them confessed later that they had been skeptical of what they regarded as a condescending "kid's crafts project." But to their surprise, they have produced some magnificent masterpieces of bravery and clarity through their artistic portrayal of hurt and hope.

To create a collage about your recovery, combine words and images cut rapidly from magazines into glued-down arrangements on a large mat board. The images you choose should tell something about thoughts and feelings that are difficult to put into words, and you can create strings of words that form statements. If you cannot find a particular word you need, create it from combined pieces.

Some clients of mine like to divide their collages in half, either down the middle or by using front and back. On one half they use words and images that describe their

---

[1] Brown, E. J. and Heimberg, R. G. "Effects of writing about rape." 2001 J Trauma Stress 14;4:781-90. Women who journaled and then read aloud a description of their rape experience, had decreased traumatic symptoms if they included greater detail and a moderate level of personalization (emotion) in the description.

[2] Bowers, J. J. "Therapy through art: Facilitating treatment of sexual abuse." 1992 J Psychosoc Nurs Ment Health Serv 30;6:15-24; also: Glaister, J. A. and McGuinness, T. "The art of therapeutic drawing. Helping chronic trauma survivors." 1992 J Psychosoc Nurs Ment Health Serv 30;5:9-17.

hurt and sadness from the rape. But on the other, they describe their strengths, hopes, and recovery. This helps create a helpful contrast between the parts of you that are hurt, and the opportunity for recovery that you have. It is also a powerful lesson for a survivor to see that she is not purely impaired, or purely darkened, by her rape; there are living and hopeful parts of her that still speak.

This is the "Hurt" side of Danée's's collage:

Look at the details she describes in her work. The large *4* in the center represents her age when her rapes began. Closed eyes represent the unwillingness of others to recognize the hurt she felt, and the adults who pretended not to see what was happening to her. Danée had a simultaneous fear that "everyone knows my horrible story just by looking at me" versus "nobody can ever truly know me at any level." This explains the image of the child with a mask covering her face, expressionless except for a smile.

She is able to piece together the phrase, "Who Knew? Everyone!" and "I can't stop this!" and "Restrain yourself, men." This is her beginning glimmer of awareness that she is hurt not because of her own failures, but because of the irresponsibility of her rapist in not stopping himself. Other phrases you can see in her collage include:

She Just Left (a reference to her mother abandoning her to a pedophile)
Fending off a grown-up
Inner WAR
Scar, scar away
I feel like I'm always running
Pain becomes a vexing incapacitating burden
I have flashes of a pair of hands
Parent trap
To say there's little recourse for victims would be an understatement
Quit – Stop – Give in

…and more.

By using a collage, some women are able to say things they are not yet ready to write. There is a fantastic process that happens as you gather items for the collage, because your mind begins to recognize words and images on the page that it *wants* to express, and you feel compelled to collect those words and use them. It is an exercise in reclaiming your words and voice back from the rape, taking control of what you express and how. I have collected entire journal notebooks full of collage on every page from clients who were initially unable to write or speak about particularly vicious rapes.

By contrast, here is the flipside of Danée's collage, which depicts her Hope:

The difference is remarkable; replacing *"She Just Left!"* as the image center is now the bold banner, *"SURVIVOR"*. The closed eyes are gone, and on this side the words are:

I Like what I See When I'm Looking at Me
Share the Secret
Guilt-Free
Time to Fight
Promote Woman Power
I Feel Beautiful
Lovely on the Inside – A better mother takes the wheel
Find love, joy and peace of mind after a devastating loss
Quit beating yourself up!

This kind of art is what many women need to do to become ready to tell their story. You have to see yourself produce something of worth and beauty first, almost to convince yourself you even could, so that you will not fear the act of story-writing quite so much. I have been told by many women that they just aren't interested in this step—it feels too "arts and crafts for kids" somehow—but when they try it they find that amazing insights come to them.

Danée was one who initially resisted creating a collage. It felt silly and elementary for her. But it was her, not I, who decided she would undertake this project: "I'm ready to put my story to art. I want to try a collage." I suggested that she not consciously construct the collage in her mind or focus intentional thought on the items she would choose. Instead, she was to flip briskly through magazines and clip out any words or images that caught her attention without second-guessing herself. Then she would begin to arrange them on paper, letting her subconscious control the process.

Other women may need different ways to help prepare for writing their story. The fear may be that the story will be too painful, or that you will not be able to write the actual words. In those cases, it can be helpful to begin by answering questions in a journal until you are comfortable enough with the words and processes of writing to embark on your own. I have had clients work through the following journal as a way to prepare for the act of writing out their story. If it helps, complete these journal questions and bring the work to your therapy sessions.

How much of the rape do I remember? Place a mark beside statements that best fit your experience. If none of them seems to fit, you can write you own answer below.

- ☐ I don't have any memories at all about the rape.
- ☐ I remember some parts, but they are unclear and vague. I am confused because the memories don't seem to fit together.
- ☐ I remember most of the rape, although there are some parts that are still unclear.
- ☐ I remember the rape very clearly.
- ☐ Other:

When I have memories about the rape, how do they usually come to me?

- ☐ In flashbacks
- ☐ Hearing voices in your mind
- ☐ During dreams
- ☐ In memories and thoughts
- ☐ By re-experiencing physical feelings of the rape
- ☐ Other:

When do I most often think about my rape? Try to recall whether there are times of day or night, or times of year, when your thoughts and feelings come to you. What times, days, sounds, songs, smells, or other sensations trigger your memories?

What places, times, or people do I avoid so that I are not reminded of the rape?

What parts of life have I missed out on because of this avoidance?

When I experience memories of my rape, what intensity and amount of strength do the memories have?

- ☐ I feel flooded. The memories take me over and I obsess about them.
- ☐ I feel numb. I suppress my memories and emotions about the rape.
- ☐ I swing back and forth between feeling numb and feeling flooded.

How much energy do I put into avoiding your memories and feelings about the rape?

What are some of the ways I suppress my memories and feelings?

When I am writing my story, I am afraid that I will feel:

If I feel overwhelmed by emotions, I can calm myself and take a break by:

When I am calm and ready to face my emotions and memories, I will begin by:

How many people have I told my story to? Place an X on the line:

●————————————————————————————————————●

Nobody   Two or three   Many people

Some of the thoughts that have kept me from telling my story are:
- ☐ No one will believe me if I tell
- ☐ I will show a lot of emotion, and it will embarrass me
- ☐ The details might not be kept confidential
- ☐ It would tear my family apart
- ☐ Someone might go to prison
- ☐ The therapist might have to report it
- ☐ I will go crazy
- ☐ Someone will stop loving me
- ☐ Maybe it wasn't even rape
- ☐ I don't deserve time and attention for this problem
- ☐ I feel weird about the rape because I liked the guy who did it
- ☐ The rape happened in a relationship that continued afterward
- ☐ The story will change how people think of me
- ☐ Other:

How has my life been affected by having to keep my rape story inside?

Have people ever been hurtful or insensitive when I told them? How?

What responses do I hope to hear from others when I tell them?

How do I think my therapist will respond after I tell?

What positive changes will happen to me when I am able to face and share my story? How could it help others?

To tell your story, go at your own pace.

Who raped you?

How old were you when the rape happened?

Where did the rape happen?

Were other people around? Who was there?

Did anyone else witness the rape?

If you knew your rapist(s), how were you acquainted with him/them?

When you look back in hindsight, do you see any warning signs of a controlling or abusive personality in the rapist?

Begin to describe what happened. Look at each column and circle the words that list each part of your body and his body that were used in the act of rape.

My body	His body
Mouth	Mouth
Hands	Hands
Fingers	Fingers
Thighs	Thighs
Anus	Anus
Vagina	Penis
Breasts	Objects

Next, draw lines that connect the parts of his body you circled with the parts of your body that he attacked with them.

This creates a "map" of your rape that shows you the story of what happened without having to write all the words yourself.

What emotions are you feeling as you do this work?

What is your body doing right now because of this work?

What sounds do you remember hearing during the rape? What did he/they say to you during and afterward?

What do you remember doing after the rape? How did you act? What did you feel at first?

The truth is that most women choose not to tell about their rapes for years afterward. Only about 10-16% of all rapes are reported at the time of the rape. The most common fear women have after a rape is "nobody will believe me about this." Keeping the rape private is very normal, and often very smart; you may have needed time to form trust in others and yourself, and to develop the inner strength to begin facing this. It is *not* a sign of being weak or crazy that your trauma still upsets you after all these years. Nor does it mean that you will feel traumatized forever. As you learn new coping skills, you will begin to feel much better.

Men who rape or abuse may also say things to women that discourage the women from telling anyone. He may use his size, voice, or power to intimidate a woman into being silent. He may threaten to harm her again if she tells. He may say directly to her that nobody would believe her. He may have status in the eyes of others (church, sports team, politics, wealth, celebrity) that gives him an advantage. He may have confused you about the rape by acting very normal afterward, as if what happened was perfectly ordinary, and this can cause women to doubt their own feelings. Rape support forums online are *full* of posts titled "Was this really rape?" and "Was I raped?" because many women have been taught to discount their own perceptions, even about themselves.

Once you have done these journal writings, you have mostly filled in the blanks of your story. But this is not the same thing as actually *writing* the story and sharing it out loud with others. For one thing, circling words and drawing lines between them may be a tough step to take, but it's still a safely distanced, almost mathematic method. It doesn't produce and then expel the burst of emotional energy of actually writing a story. Do not substitute this work for the complete act of sharing your story.

I have several journals in my possession that clients have allowed me to keep and share with others. To show you some of the responses of other girls and women, they are allowing me to publish their answers here:

When do I most often think about my rape? Try to recall whether there are times of day or night, or times of year, when your thoughts and feelings come to you. What times, days, sounds, songs, smells, or other sensations trigger your memories?

At bedtime when I am almost asleep, when my husband wants to have sex and I don't, when I smell the cologne he had on. (-Suzanne)

When I watch cartoons, on the yearly anniversary of the rape. When I eat cake and ice cream. (-Katelynn)

What parts of life have I missed out on because of this avoidance?

I don't enjoy sex. I would rather stay home alone than go out and have fun. I can't hug my family very often. I lost my college financial aid because my grades dropped when I was depressed and drinking. I got mad at God and quit going to church. (Amy)

What are some of the ways I suppress my memories and feelings?

I feel dirty and hopeless. I hate myself easily. I cut myself and I drink. (-Suzanne)

How has my life been affected by having to keep my rape story inside?

I'm scared. I wish I could just simply forget but it's too hard. Why is this so hard to just forget? I'm scared of myself and my memories. Please take it away—I don't want these painful memories. (-Suzanne)

How do you think your therapist will respond to you after you tell?

I still can't believe I'm still reading this. This must be one of those homework assignments where in the beginning I'm gonna hate Matt and in the end I'll thank him. (-Stephanie)

When you look back in hindsight, do you see any warning signs of a controlling or abusive personality in the rapist?

My dad did not show any signs, but Jason showed me signs. He would always talk about sex and stuff, and he would "accidentally" touch me in places. Like he would touch my breast and when he saw I didn't like it, he would say "Oh, sorry, please forgive me," but then when he tried to kiss me and I would walk away he would grab me by the arm. Or scream at me. (-Suzanne)

What is your body doing right now because of this part?

I feel very tired, like I just ran a marathon, which is weird because I'm just sitting here writing. My stomach is tight and feels sick. My throat hurts. My hands are shaking. My mouth tastes like metal. [a metallic taste in the mouth is a sign of increased adrenaline]

What sounds do you remember hearing during the rape? What did he say to you during and afterward?

I remember the sounds of music in the next room, thumping through the wall. That is still a trigger for me. I remember him saying to stop fighting him and it wouldn't hurt so much. I remember him saying things like, "you like this, don't you?" (-Kate)

My memories are always muffled, like I was underwater. But I remember that he kept telling me to "shut up, or we'll get in trouble." I am still angry about that because he was treating it like we were a couple, a team, and WE were doing this. This has been a stuck point for me. (Linda)

"You could have spit." (-Stephanie)

What do you remember doing after the rape? How did you act? What did you feel at first?

I don't remember anything. I don't remember the rest of the day. I feel so stupid, like I might have gone to sleep, when I should have been taking care of myself. I'm mad that I don't remember the rest of the day...I just remember feeling like everyone would be able to tell what had happened by the way I walked or something. (-Shannon)

I told him, "you shouldn't have done that," and I dressed and left. I never said or did anything else about it after that. (-Stacy)

I didn't even know what had happened. I woke up naked, and my roommate started teasing me. She kept telling me I'd had sex with some guy. But I didn't even remember it. I remember things becoming very dizzy, the room spinning, and then waking up and not knowing how I got there and what happened. (-Vanessa)

Those are just a few of the dozens of journals I've been given by clients. It might be helpful to read their answers. It is not unusual for a woman to report feeling numb while doing these assignments; you are being asked to remember and describe an event during which you may have felt dissociated, disconnected, and even paralyzed. It is also not uncommon for women to be unable to remember parts of the rape, which are usually the most frightening parts. But as you resolve some of your conflicts between thoughts and feelings, you may begin to recover some of these memories as well.[3] This is also why it is important to continue and complete this work, and not allow the temptation of avoidance block your progress. If your emotions cannot run their course, they cannot be extinguished. You must, therefore, complete this work to move on, and you must do it without becoming intoxicated or using self-harm to manage the emotions—before, during, or after these exercises.

Here are some tips for writing your rape story:

- Don't write it like a police report. This isn't a basic narrative of what happened ("And then he…And then I…"). Instead, write down the events and the *emotions they caused*.
- Write down memories you have that you had forgotten.
- If you have the same flashback again, write it down every time. Don't tell yourself "I've already written it down, and it's the same flashback anyway, so there's nothing new to write." Big mistake!
- Try to exceed your courage. Write down as much detail as you think you can stand, and then write one or two lines more.

---

[3] Resick and Schnicke, p54.

- Try to identify the worst, nastiest, most painful moments of the story, and write them. These are usually the specks in the story that are most responsible for the flashbacks, so don't let them win by allowing them to return to their burrow in your mind.

Coping with emotions during your writing

Our greatest glory is not in never falling, but in rising each time we fall.
- Confucius

You may begin to feel a flood of emotions as you write, so let's prepare for handling them. Write as much as you feel you can, and when you begin to be overwhelmed just finish your sentence and stop. Draw a line on your paper and write STUCK POINT.

Return to the writing when you can and continue from the same point in the story. Each time you reach a stuck point, mark it on your paper. As your emotions emerge, don't ignore them to try to keep going through the story—add them *into* the story. For example, you can write something like, "this part is making me very angry. I am nauseated." Or, "I am terrified to write this detail because I am so sad about it." Include your here-and-now feelings in your story.

> RECALL THEM + GET THEM OUT. MY MEMORIES ARE TRAPPED SOMEWHERE WHERE I CAN'T REACH THEM. I WANT TO REMEMBER. I WANT TO WRITE THEM. I WANT THEM OUT. I WANT TO MAKE A PICTURE OF THESE PUZZLE PIECES. I WANT TO MAKE SENSE OF IT ALL.

You may also come to points of the story where there are gaps in your memory. If you do, write GAP – STUCK POINT and pause. When you return to your journal, scrawl a note in the margin that asks questions you need answer to in order to fill the gap. "How did I get into the closet?" or "Where did my friend go?" or "What did he say that made me say that back?" Continue writing at the next point of the story you remember. But do not use the "GAP" note just to skip a gruesome or difficult detail; remember, those are the details that most need to be exposed and extinguished.

Any detail that you permit to remain unwritten is a detail you are permitting to remain in nightmares and "thought hauntings." You are giving permission for memories to keep residence in your mind if you allow them to remain concealed; by writing them, you are expelling them and forbidding them from remaining in control.

Think of your memories the way the Wizard of Oz movie portrayed the terrible, frightening wizard. The wizard was scary because it was surrounded by fire, its voice was booming and commanding, and its face sneered in contempt. Nobody had the courage to approach it, question it, or defy it—the wizard *seemed* all-powerful, so people assumed it *was* all-powerful. But in fact, the wizard only had power until its truth was exposed: it was actually a tiny, frail man behind a curtain operating levers and machines. Once its curtain was flung back and its true nature was revealed, its power fell apart and people no longer needed to fear it. The wizard (your terrifying memories) will control you until you pull back the curtain (open your subconscious) and let the truth diminish its power.

If you refuse to "pull back the curtain" and reveal any memory because you fear its power, you are allowing that memory to remain in control. Use your writing as a way to fight against rape: you are weighing your courage against the strength of fear, and insisting on not losing. Research studies found that trauma survivors who included more emotions in their written descriptions had greater physical and mental health gains afterward than those who simply wrote the trauma in a neutral, non-emotional manner.[4]

Trouble getting started

It is not uncommon for a woman to stare at a blank page, and not know how to start her writing. She is afraid it "won't come out right" or that she'll "say the wrong thing" or "not do a good enough job." If you have trouble getting started, here are a few techniques you can use:

- Do not try to mentally arrange the story first before you write it. This is not prose you are writing! Consider the story a form of vomiting up a poison that is inside you so it doesn't kill you; you aren't trying to be graceful and intellectual about it.
- Make sure you have an uninterrupted place to write, with at least an hour of no interruptions. No headphones, no internet, no TV, no music. Cell phones are turned off.
- Try starting with a "lead-off" sentence:
  - "The first thing that comes to mind about my rape is…"
  - "The fear I have about writing about my rape is…"
  - "I have been avoiding this story because…"
  - "I carry my emotions about my rape inside my…[parts of body]"
  - "My emotions are desperately hoping I can do this so they will finally be able to…"

If it helps you, say a prayer before you begin. Light a candle that you pledge will remain lit until you are done. Use a "do not disturb" sign on a door, if needed. Meditate and become calm, and breathe from deeply within your body, not shallow superficial breaths. Have a non-alcoholic beverage near you, but do not eat during your writing (more on that later). Use the style of handwriting to emphasize emotions! Use drawings or sketches on the page to warm up. And if needed, have a supportive friend or loved one available for care afterward.

---

[4] Allard, Carolyn B. et al. "Exploring the Potential of Pennebaker's Writing Paradigm on Betrayal Trauma Sequelae." http://hdl.handle.net/1794/4334

An example of how Danée's handwriting changes as she writes her story from the beginning…   …to the end:

> NOT HOME- SHE SAYS
> SHE FILED A POLICE
> REPORT- ACTUALLY I
> REMEMBER THE DAY
> I TOLD RENEE- I WAS
> LAYING ON THE LIVING
> ROOM FLOOR WATCHING
> TV- I MUST HAVE BEEN

> COUSINS WEEK &
> SUPPOSE TO KEEP
> ME SAFE?!
>
> STUCK PT
>
> I JUST CHECKED OUT.
> I SHOULD HAVE BEEN
> YELLING, SCREAMING-
> I JUST LAID IN MY
> BED- NUMB- STARING

"But writing it makes it too real!"

> It's about realizing, painfully, you've kept that voice inside yourself, locked away from even yourself. And you step back and see that your jailer has changed faces. You realize you've become your own jailer.
>   -Tori Amos

Women have often said they fear writing their stories because it makes it *real*. It's black-and-white fact. They plead with me, "can't I just skip this?" or "can't I just say it instead of writing it?" The "realness" of the writing is, however, exactly why it *should* be written. By writing your story, you are not making anything real that wasn't already real. What happened, happened. You can't recover from something that you refuse to face or pretend was something it wasn't.

Instead of thinking of the written story as a dreadful proof of trauma, try to invent a new way of thinking about it. One woman told me she had imagined that by writing her story, she was purging it out of her mind and trapping it onto a page in a book that can close. The story, she imagined, became trapped and caged somewhere else outside of her. Another woman told me this:

> You know that movie "Ghostbusters?" I used it to help me. When they chase the ghosts, they have to focus their energy on it and control it without flinching or breaking contact. They can then overpower the ghost and pull it down into a box, where they can lock it up and dispose of it. They remember the ghost, but it doesn't haunt them anymore. That's what my journal will be: the locked repository for the ghosts I'm capturing.

Brilliant! She's not describing the "keep it in a box" forms of avoidance and repression; she's describing deliberate, attentive *mastery* over her rape, which comes only by *not* avoiding it.

You can also consider story-writing to be a cleansing. If you were cleaning a contaminated house, you couldn't succeed by just envisioning it differently. You'd have to enter it, find the deepest dirt, and cleanse it. No home can be cleansed if you allow garbage to remain hidden inside. Your writing is a form of throwing open locked doors and tearing open walls with toxic mold inside so you can purge and rebuild. This simply will not work if you halt the work while it's incomplete. You are not contaminated, but the visual image may help you do the "cleansing" work.

Your story is also likely to help other women. Time after time, I have seen women in my groups become inspired by one person's courage to share their story. These stories can trigger memories, but rather than becoming traumatic, they often fill in gaps and answer questions for the women who recover them. One woman journaled,

> I have found that reading other women's accounts of their attacks and recoveries has been extremely healing for me. I thought it would be traumatic, but it has been just the opposite. It is extremely comforting to know others have gone through the same thing and come out the other side thriving.

When you are finished

Once you are finished, it is important to take care of yourself. Give yourself positive strokes and rewards for the work you have done. If you eat after you write, make your first snack a healthy food, not junk food; many women connect their emotions with their bodies and use food as medication for feelings. To create a new habit of health, try to connect your emotional upheaval with healthy self-care rather than sugars and caffeine.

Take a walk and breathe deeply. Go around the block, or up into the mountains, and feel wind and sunlight on your new face. Stretch your body and breathe. Tighten and constrict your muscles for 5-10 seconds and then slowly release them.

Above all, do *not* engage in substance use or self-injury. It is vitally important at this moment—more than at any other—that you resist all these urges and practice self-care and self-respect. You risk making a connection between healing and defeat if you engage in self-harming behaviors, and what is needed most right now is a connection between recovery and courage.

Examples of stories

A few women have allowed me to disclose their stories here in order to help you become inspired to write your own. These stories may contain triggering words and descriptions so proceed with caution; at the same time, though, nearly all of my clients have said that reading previous survivors' narratives—*especially* the emotionally painful ones—gave them a sense of courage and possibility.

If you are easily triggered into depression or self-harm, you may want to skip these stories for now and come back to them with your therapist.

A young client of mine named Suzanne S. wrote in her journal:

> Jason would force his penis into my mouth or vagina, and then tell me that I know I like it and no one will love me like him. And my dad would stick his fingers inside of me or force intercourse. Usually I would be asleep and they would do as they pleased. I'm surprised they never met. For a long time, Jason had me believing that no one else would love me. And my dad had me believing that I was stupid and everything was my fault.
>
> When I ran away I stayed the night at Jason's and when everyone was sleeping he tried to pull my pants down. I kept saying no, and instead he kissed me and said that he was sorry and he loved me, and he was just trying to prove how much he loved me. And then he did it again. I tried to get up but instead he told me to take off my shirt and I asked why, and he said "just do it!" So I did (because I was so scared). He was kissing my stomach and breasts and I was crying (this makes me feel very anxious. My heart is beating. I feel guilty about this part of the story). I was crying, and he told me to stop crying. I asked him why he was telling me to stop and he said "because I think ---'s awake." I said "good," then I tried to get up. But he just held me down and when we heard noise he said "Quick, act like you like it." [STUCK POINT]
>
> And I tried to get up but he held my arm really tight down to the bed so I yelped a little, and --- [sleeping friend nearby] moved again. Then Jason started to hold my hands down and he put my hand down to his penis and got on top of me and started squeezing my breasts (it hurt). He pulled off my pants (I am very upset and embarrassed here because in the story, I was frozen with fear.) [STUCK POINT]----and started touching my vagina.
>
> I asked him to stop and he said no because he said I was his "bitch" and I had to do whatever he wanted me to do because no one else would ever want me and I was worthless without him. And he actually made me believe it. I had sex once with him willingly, but that was only once, and this is what happened. He thought he owned me and could hurt me.
>
> I felt all alone. But when the abuse happened I would freeze. It didn't work, but I couldn't do anything else. I tried to, but it's okay because it was not my fault. I do not know of anything I could have done differently.

Suzanne was a remarkably insightful younger client of mine. She had grown up in DHS custody because of the sexual abuse and rape she experienced by her father and by male peers. Suzanne's story is a good example because she describes the event in detail, and she connects the rape with her emotions as opposed to simply writing a report. Suzanne was also able to identify her "stuck points," which had caused her to feel guilty and ashamed about her rape.

Suzanne's first stuck point was when she was told to pretend like she liked her abuse. This detail caused her a lot of anxiety because she was afraid that she *had* accidentally acted like she liked it. The purpose of being told "act like you like it" was so Jason would not get into trouble, and could succeed at the rape. Since Jason did succeed at rape, Suzanne's guilt for the next two years was that perhaps she had given Jason the impression of her as a willing participant.

But this stuck point was resolved when Suzanne read her story out loud. It was apparent in a much clearer way that ever before that the commandment to "act like you like it" was proof of *Jason's* guilt, not Suzanne's. The very utterance of this command indicates that Jason knew full well that Suzanne disliked it, that it was wrong, and that it would take a lie to play this off as a consensual sexual encounter. Suzanne had never put those thoughts together until she *wrote* her story. Suzanne said about this,

> I'm so glad he said that. As awful as it was, it proves to me that it was rape, and that he knew it all along. And I don't have to feel guilty, because when I read my story all the way through I can see that he was lying and controlling, and still I didn't act like I liked it. I was crying and yelping. Which means I didn't give in to him! I resisted! So my story gives me more than two new ways to see my innocence.

Danée had experienced multiple rapes during her life, as recently as one within the same year that she began to work with me in therapy. But she chose to focus her work on her multiple childhood rapes, beginning at age 4, because she recognized that these had impacted her the most. She wrote her story in feverish scrawl in her journal:

> Who raped me? I remember the first time I was raped, I was between the age 4-5 years old. I lived with my grandmother at the time. Renee (Danée's biological mother) had dropped me off at her house to pursue a job, I think, in St. Petersburg, FL, about 12-15 hours from my grandma's home. I slept in my grandma's sewing room, which is connected to my grandma's room, no door in-between.
>
> The bed I slept on was small, not comfortable. I remember the sheets were some sort of cartoon characters. The sheets smelled old, dusty, like mildew. I hated this room. I was terrified of this room.
>
> [My stomach is in knots thinking about this room. My leg is shaky. It hurts.]
>
> I didn't hear him enter the room. I was hiding under the covers. He just appeared over the bed [I'm now rocking to calm myself – my hands are sweating. My lower brain hurts. Down my spine, below my shoulder blade hurts.]

All I can do is see his shadow. I remember staring out the window. I can see the trees as the lightning flashes. I remember him removing my panties to the side, sliding his gross, disgusting fingers down the inside of my undies. I freeze. My limbs go numb. I just laid there. [Stuck Point]

I remember the pain when he rammed his penis inside me. It burned. I didn't cry out. I laid in silence.

[I'm breathing hard now.]

I laid in silence. Pulled the nasty, smelly sheet back over my head. He disappeared like it was all a bad dream. I remember the sound of thunder, not rain, just thunder. I remember turning my back to the wall and stayed wrapped up.

I think I got out of the bed and just stood at the foot of her bed. I remember being so afraid, terrified. I think my grandmas made me get back in that bed. I laid – awake, I think, till morning. I didn't say anything.

At first, Danée read her story with a detached, emotionless tone. She did not immediately connect her rape with her grief and anger. But there was one detail of her story that just didn't add up, and as she sat with a stern downward glance I cautiously asked her about it: "Did your family know that your uncle (the man who raped Danée at her grandmother's house) was a pedophile?"

"Yes, the whole family knew. I wasn't even the first victim —lots of women in our family were."

"And yet you were left in the home with him?"

"It wasn't even the only time. There were other times when Renee left me in *his* home alone, and even said that she hoped I would learn my lesson from him."

As we talked about this, it became apparent to Danée that her rape had not only been a betrayal by her uncle, but by a family system that had actually conspired to "initiate" her into the family's pedophilic system. Danée suddenly began to sob, and then seethe. She screamed, flinging her journal against the floor in rage, then picked it up and flung it again. Then Danée melted back into her chair and cried and cried like a small child.

"She just *left* me there!"

Victoria found that she was unable to start writing her story until she struck upon the idea of writing it in the form of a letter to a long-lost friend, explaining to him why she had been so upset and angry during their acquaintance (she had abruptly and hurtfully cut off all ties to him without explaining why when her emotional life fell into a shambles). This was not a letter she would actually send, but it was an intelligent way for her to accomplish two tasks at once: she would be able to finally write the details of her story, and she would be able to link the events of her rape and her subsequent rejection of precious friendships because of feelings of shame and rage.

As she wrote, her story took its toll on her. Victoria would scrawl a paragraph, then run to vomit. She could not sleep, and she sobbed for hours. She resisted the urge to binge drink, but she did engage in self-injury by cutting her upper arm—although she noted to me later that it was much less severe than ever before, giving her hope of progress. Victoria was pale and sleepy in my office the next day and I nearly let her off the hook by proposing we wait until another time to read it. But she refused to take the easy way, and insisted on completing the task: "I am just so tired of carrying this for so long. I need to be rid of it."

Victoria began to read, page after page. For sixteen pages she read, pausing to clasp her hand over her mouth with nausea. Her story encompassed not one but two rapes, months apart. Her face and shirt were tear-soaked. When her story was over, she dropped her arms and gazed out the window, expressionless, for several dissociated minutes. Nobody in the room said a word; we just waited. She began to cry again and pleaded to me for answers, "why didn't I just die then? Why did I have to survive it? I don't *want* to be a &%*#ing '*Survivor*', I wish I had just ended. My whole existence should have just ended. Who am I to carry this burden and think I can do anything with it?!"

The truth is, her story brought me to tears as I heard it, too.

After almost 15 minutes of painful crying, the group began to interact with Victoria again. I asked the members to tell Victoria how they were affected by her story, and one by one they each gave her loving and authentic support, telling her they loved her, that they were heartbroken by her pain, that they were proud of her, that they were inspired by her to begin facing their own stories. I asked Victoria to look around the room and describe what she saw on each individual face of the other women looking back at her. She did: "Hope…pride…love…support…love…belief…" I told her to absorb those faces deeply into her mind, because these were now the new memory that her story ends with, not the image of a humiliated and wounded college girl from years ago.

Afterward, I stayed with Victoria for another hour beyond the end of group. We just sat and talked, and she cried more. By the end of the final hour, she was calmer and even able to make jokes with me again, and she asked to give me a hug, "even though I'm all covered in snot and tears and I'm so yucky." And I admit it may have been a bit dramatic, but I confess that I actually answered back, "no, you're the cleanest right now that you've ever been."

When you read your story, emotions may come to you that did not occur during the writing. Occasionally, women will read their story with a numb tone, displaying no emotion. If that is the case, I will interrupt and ask them to describe their feelings as they read. We will discuss the importance of not withholding emotions. Often, women tell me they are afraid their emotions will overwhelm them if they surface. One image that can help soothe this fear is to envision a flood that overcomes the land, but eventually receded and dries up so the land can rebuild and re-grow.[5] Flooded emotions do not remain flooded.

But if a client becomes extremely emotional, I will absolutely not interrupt or attempt to calm her, nor will I permit group members to do so. This can seem cruel to my other clients who want me to console their peer. But interrupting this expression of emotion is a mistake because it interrupts the full release of her compressed feelings.[6] Passing boxes of tissues to her communicates that she should compose herself, regain control, and stop her display of sadness. On occasion, group members have even begun to move closer to her, reach for her hand or arm, or start talking to her in soothing tones. I

---

[5] Taken from Resick and Schnicke, p55.
[6] Ibid, p54.

intervene and direct them back to their places, uttering the simple statement, "let her finish."

In group therapy, members who are uncomfortable with conflict will be the ones who try to interrupt and console you. While their efforts are sincere, they are also misguided; it is their own anxiety about the awkward emotions in the room that they are trying to drive out. When a client is done reading her story, I often let moments of silence continue; sometimes she is crying, sometimes she is staring downward in a daze. I may offer very simple, softly-spoken encouragements for her to continue such as, "let it out. Let yourself finish." Or, "don't hold it back. You're doing well. It's safe for this to come up."

Only once in hundreds of these readings in my sessions has a woman become so distraught that she began to flashback. But even then, many therapists make the anxiety-based mistake of interrupting her "for her own safety," when in fact she would be better served by the full expression and extinction of that flashback. I remained watchful for safety while gently grounding her by reminding her that she is safe, she is not being hurt, these events are not happening again, and she has already come through this. I did not make any physical contact with her whatsoever. Although it sounds trite, the one woman who experienced this later told me that it was extremely helpful to have that voice guide her through (and that my supportive male voice was a positive contrast to the flashed-back voice of her perpetrator), and that the flashback was a burst of suppressed emotions about her rape that helped her release those feelings. She became one of the more successfully-recovered clients I have had.

I have also been known to assign my clients to rewrite their story a second time, if their first narrative is emotionally shallow. Sometimes a woman will read through her journal very quickly, or her story will just be a list of events in sequence. If she does use the words "I felt," it often precedes a thought rather than a feeling ("I felt like it was no use to fight"). Until the *emotions* of the story are expressed, the story cannot serve its purpose in releasing nightmares, flashbacks, and shame from the survivor. Trauma, after all, is not caused by paradoxes and riddles of logic; it is caused by the shattering of beliefs *and* emotions, and each of these must be given the chance to "speak up" in therapy and be released. Using language that is perhaps crude but still very to-the-point, one client wrote it this way:

> I had to realize that it wasn't the biological and anatomical events of my rape that still hurt me. It's not because some jerk's [penis] got rammed in and out of me that I have lived in hell for all these years. It's because of how I *feel* about what that jerk did to me that tortures me. If it was just the physical event itself, my mind would heal as soon as my body did. Just talking about the three or five minutes of rape that I lived through doesn't heal me. It's facing my feelings and shame about it that will heal me, and I haven't done that until now.
> -TyLynne

What you learn from your own story

No one outside ourselves can rule us inwardly.
When we know this, we are truly free.
--Coral Anika Theill

When reading your story, it is important to *hear* your story being said out loud. This may sound like a ridiculous statement because of course you hear your story as you read it. But I am not talking about merely having the sound vibrations of words enter your ear canal; I am suggesting that you actively absorb and consider the voice and the words that come out of you. Almost every time a woman read her narrative in one of my groups, she discovered some hidden gem—some previously-unrecognized truth—about herself and her rape.

The most common discovery women make in their stories is that they are innocent of their guilt. For years, a woman may have told herself that she is somehow at fault; almost always she connects these guilty beliefs to her terrified frozenness at the time of the rape: "I should have resisted; I didn't do enough." These beliefs can lead to other forms of self-doubt: "Is it possible he didn't even know this was rape when he was doing it? If I didn't protest or resist enough, did I fail to somehow *inform* him that he was committing an assault?" Obviously, these beliefs are particularly firm when the perpetrator is a person you have known.

Women may also question whether some inadvertent behavior of hers attracted the rapist to her. The social myth that rape is a sexual act triggered by a woman's sensuous appearance or behaviors continues to influence many peoples' beliefs about rape, including rape victims themselves. Women who believe that their own conduct lured a man into the act of rape are not only excusing their perpetrators, but often try to modify their appearances in efforts to *prevent* future rapes. They may diet or overeat, or change clothing styles.

But in reading their stories, women can be awestruck at how innocent they truly are of these mistaken guilty beliefs. As you listen to yourself describe your painful emotions and physical feelings, the possibility that you (or the rapist) somehow misunderstood the rape melts away.

Often when a woman reads her story out loud, the most immediate insight was that she *had* resisted him. For years, a woman may be punishing herself because she had failed to fight back, say no, or otherwise resist her attacker. Your self-concept may be that you were weak and pathetic for not defying him through this awful experience. Perhaps, you have wondered, *you* are the guilty person in the story, and maybe the guy was just responding to a situation *you* had caused. If this were true, it would validate all of the self-hatred and self-harm you have poured into her life for the next years. And even writing the story down may not be enough to extinguish that belief.

One former patient of mine had forgotten that she had resisted her perpetrator until she actually heard her voice say out loud that she was pushing, trying to say words, and even whispering "stop" repeatedly. She recalled that the man had refused to stop, and had even warned her to stop resisting. She hadn't even remembered writing this. But when she heard herself read the words they astonished her. "I *did* resist!" she gasped, discovering a forgotten truth in her own story. No longer was she the passive, powerless little girl as she had believed for three years; she had done everything she could have. The fact that her strength could not stop the rape wasn't the issue; nobody is guilty because their strength doesn't happen to exceed that of a violent person. But her guilty story that "I didn't resist, so maybe it's my fault" was able to evaporate. She *did* resist, and he *knew* she was resisting, which meant he *knew* he was committing rape, so she was finally able to transfer the blame entirely to him where it belonged.

She also recalled him telling her to stop resisting so "it wouldn't hurt so much." This key point of her story was also vindication for her. It proved to her that he had been aware that he was assaulting and harming, and that he was aware of her resistance. And besides, if her rapist blamed her pain on her resisting him, and the pain was *awful*, then it suggests her resistance must have been spectacular, too.

Laura did not want her story presented here, but she permitted me to share my thoughts. In Laura's case, her story was one that she read quickly with little emotion. When I addressed her lack of emotion as she read, Laura said that she felt afraid of not appearing "tough" if she lost control. But one major stuck point emerged in her story: Laura wrote in sketchy terms that her attacker had forced her head down onto him, and then she leaped to the conclusion of the story immediately after that detail. She did not describe emotions about this, nor did she continue to describe what events caused those emotions from that point. Her traumatic "avoidance" habit had kicked in.

This leap from the most disturbing point of the narrative to "The End" alerted me to a massive stuck point. The lack of emotional resonance from Laura as she read was clue number two. I asked her to describe the significance of that moment in her story, when she was forcibly pushed down. Laura was able to realize that the hand on the back of her head and the gripping of her hair was the moment that confirmed to her that this really was a sexual assault, undeniable by either her or her rapist. Laura's struggle with avoidance had taken the form that "maybe it was just sex, maybe he didn't mean it, maybe I'm interpreting it wrong, maybe I'm being too sensitive." But this part of the story knocked over those forms of avoidances like a wrecking ball.

Marilyn said that she was surprised by the effects of telling her story. "It's like a giant weight lifted off of me. I don't have to carry it around anymore." Marilyn found the experience so empowering that she asked several times in subsequent groups if she could re-tell parts of her story and seek feedback from the group again. A therapist could mistake that as "attention seeking," but when coping with PTSD there is much therapeutic value in reliving the experience again and again in order to diminish its emotional power. Marilyn said, "every time I tell my story, it takes a little more weight out of it." Ashley, a 20-year-old survivor who had been terrified of rape therapy, wrote a message to me in her journal: "I can't believe I'm saying this but I feel a little better right now then I did before. Like a weight's been lifted off of me."

Not all women feel relief after sharing. Often, there is a surge of fear that now the group will judge her or feel differently toward her. I never speak for the group, nor do I ask the group in her behalf; rather, I suggest to her, "Why don't you ask the group about this?" The point is to refocus her onto her relationships with her peers, so that she can hear directly from them how they are affected by her story. Nearly without fail, the consensus is positive and supportive, but I will address the issue of the rare unsympathetic hearer later.

Negative aftermath of telling your story ("Why do my worst nights follow my best days in therapy?")

Although telling your story is regarded as a positive and strong step in your recovery, on occasion there can be problems that go along with it as well. When you tell your story, you are putting yourself in a face-to-face confrontation with your deepest shame and fear; in fact, that's the whole point. But connecting so strongly with these feelings can also trigger self-defeating habits and thoughts that you have linked with shame and fear to this point. Until the sharing of your story *feels* like the victory it is, you may not be able to fully comprehend how it was helpful at all. For some women, the only feeling they have afterward is deeper shame, because their beliefs are screaming at them from inside, "Now I've gone and done it! Now everyone knows! They won't think about me the same way. They'll be imagining the rape when they look at me. They might be nice for now, but it's pretend—they'll really turn on me because now they know how disgusting I am!" Victoria told me much later, "telling my story was the best thing I have ever done. You making me do that literally saved my life. But at the time, it didn't feel like therapy, it felt like punishment. I kept thinking, 'why is Matt doing this to me? Can't he see how much it hurts?'" At one point, Victoria even had a dream that I was attacking her face with a fork, which was vivid symbol of her feeling that I was "putting her through this" to hurt her.

THE FEAR I HAVE ABOUT WRITING ABOUT MY RAPE IS - THAT I'M MAKING ALL OF THIS UP. THAT ITS ALL IN MY MIND. OR THAT I'VE HEARD OTHER PEOPLES STORIES. AND MADE THEM MY OWN.

By definition, your "best days" in recovery are the ones where you accomplish the most work. That means you will have delved deeply into important issues, even when it is uncomfortable. And although you may receive much positive feedback for the work you have done, you may feel very uncomfortable with yourself later that day. This is temporary, but it presents a real risk of lapsing into former unhealthy coping behaviors.

But if you understand why your positive work can sometimes trigger a harrowing night later, it will be easier to get through. During your recovery work that day, you have come face-to-face with your deepest shames and exposed them. You have brought things up into conscious thought and spoken them out loud, taking them out of their hiding places in your mind. These are things you had buried and hidden because you had told yourself that they would cause you to be rejected, scorned, or abandoned if others knew them. That may have even been true in the past. And now they have been revealed.

Ultimately, pulling them out of hiding and revealing them is a very healing thing to do, and it begins the process of ridding yourself of those shameful thoughts. It's like cleansing your house of an infestation. But the positive results aren't immediate outcomes that will affect your *emotional* balance. Before the benefits show up, what impacts your emotions first are those fearful beliefs and self-talk about the shameful, embarrassing truths you have revealed. "I have exposed myself, and that exposure is going to cost me dearly. It is going to change what people think about me now." So the first reaction you have to deep therapy isn't always positive relief, a lifted weight, and freedom; it's terror and disgrace.

The single most common reaction I observe in women after processing their rape narrative is a sudden surge of doubt in the truth of the story at all. They want to pull it all back in, and will begin to fear, "what if it wasn't true? What if I forgot some details? What if I made it all up? What if I just saw this in a movie and thought it was me?" Around two-thirds of women who have worked on their narratives with me have experienced this intense crisis of honesty, and actually begin to doubt their own memories. They feel crazy, or wonder if they have exaggerated a small incident—if it happened at all.

It is vital that you understand that *this is normal.* If you have a tendency toward "emotional reasoning" ("it feels true, so it must be true"), you will likely interpret your distress as proof that you have made a grievous mistake by opening up, and you will toss and turn at night, punish yourself, and obsess over the "badness" of what you have done. The fact that you feel bad does not mean that what you have done is bad—feelings are not facts—and at this point you will have to trust your therapist on two issues: first, that this feeling is temporary, and second, that the work you have done really is beneficial to you.

Until you develop confidence that your revealed story is not going to ruin your relationships, you are at risk for using some of the same mannerisms of coping that you have been trying to change. While it is not universal (or even a majority), *some* women have a powerful relapse of alcohol abuse or self-injury the night of their storytelling therapy.[7] One client spoke up in group therapy to help a peer who was working through her own story. She said, "I didn't take care of myself when I told my story. I knew it felt good to get it out, and I did well in group, and I learned things about myself that were amazing. And the first night was fine. But it was on the second night that I let myself go. I started cutting and doing other things I used to do to hurt myself. I realize now that it was because I felt I had changed so much in therapy, but nobody out there could tell. It was like, 'so what's the point, if nobody else can even see me any differently?' I went back to old behaviors because I wasn't being careful."

Danée told her story on Friday, and on Monday she did not show for group. She did not call, or answer calls.[8] I recognized this as the unmistakable sign of a woman who has crashed hard in the aftermath of telling her story, going back to "visit old friends" (relapse back to cutting, drinking, sex) to numb the shock of the work she has done in therapy. What had happened is that Danée had spent the weekend binge drinking and cruising bars, picking up strangers and having violent sex.

---

[7] Pennebaker, J. W., et al. "Disclosure of traumas and immune function: health implications for psychotherapy." 1988 J Consult Clin Psychol 56;2:239-45. "Healthy undergraduates who wrote about traumatic experiences had significantly increased physical symptoms and negative moods immediately after writing, but at six weeks were happier and had had less health center visits than a control group. Students who wrote about something they had never disclosed before also had significantly enhanced immune response."

[8] This is an important clue for therapists. When clients have deep breakthroughs and then fail to arrive for subsequent appointments, it is often due to lapses into former harmful behaviors. I make efforts to contact such "missing clients" by phone or text messages specifically because of this risk.

On Tuesday, Danée appeared in my office door, staring blankly down at the floor. She was nervous about confessing her weekend secrets to me, expecting to be scolded, rejected, kicked out, or even hospitalized. But before she could say a word, I said as softly as I could, "Danée, you look like a woman who needs a hug." Danée burst into tears, stumbled forward, caught my arms, and sobbed and sobbed.

Months later, Danée told me that it was at that moment that she made a decision to live differently. She had expected my scorn and disgust, and felt that letting me down was a betrayal of her work with me. It wasn't, of course; she was just deeply hurt and frightened of how her life would change after releasing her story. This was no clinical technique, no social worker's method, this was just a brokenhearted woman finding acceptance where she had expected banishment. Danée wrote,

> I'm not going to live this way. Drinking, having sex to numb the pain—that's the easy way out and I'm not doing that any longer. I'm not proud of myself. I feel physically sick after last night. Those behaviors are not me. They are not at my core. They are horrible habits that I have developed to cope. I'm finished with the lies. No matter what the consequences may be, I'm not going to live this way. Pain will not be my gift to the world!

When Victoria processed her story, which was one of the most violent accounts of rape I had ever helped a survivor work through in therapy, she became physically nauseated and began to dissociate. Her therapy session to present her story took two hours alone, plus the ongoing work to process it afterward. Her story began with an excruciating and vicious gang rape at a fraternity party, which was quite clearly a planned assault. At one point I asked Victoria a question that she found grotesquely offensive, but which I asked for a specific reason: "how do you know that this was rape, and not just group sex?"

She and others in the room gasped at the apparent insensitivity of the question. Victoria answered angrily, "how about the fact that I was screaming, 'Stop it, stop it!' at the top of my lungs?"

I deliberately maintained an unfazed facial expression and asked, "and what else?"

"Isn't that f---ing enough?!"

"What else, Victoria? What else tells you this was rape and not just group sex?"

Victoria was repulsed by my questions, and answered even more angrily, "I was kicking at them, hitting them, clawing at them, and shrieking. What more do you f---ing *need*?"

Here is the reason I deliberately asked these questions. I have observed, through countless therapy sessions with rape survivors, that one of the after-effects of processing their stories is that they often hit a "wall" of self-doubt afterward. In particular, women who tend to intellectualize and become philosophical in therapy, who challenge me for proofs at each step of the process, or have to push themselves extra-hard to accept each step of progress, will also tend to go through a period when they will discount their own story's truth. "But what if it's all bulls—t?" asked Victoria, in tears after reading her story. "What if I have it wrong? What if I said 'yes' and don't remember? What if they didn't know they were raping me, and I led them on? How can I trust any of this?" She physically threw her notebook into a nearby chair.

Passing under a wave of self-doubt is very common after telling your story. As soon as Victoria threw her book aside I could answer her, "you know your story is true." Through tears she asked how I could say that. I was able to answer her with the same answers she had given me before: "Because you screamed 'stop it!' You kicked, you hit, you clawed. What more do you f---ing need?"

If I had not asked these questions earlier, it would have been too late to ask them now and get the same answers to reaffirm her story. In her moment of doubt she would have answered instead, "That's my whole point—how can I know it was rape and not just sex? What if I have it all wrong?" This wave of "what if my story isn't true and I have it all wrong?" self-doubt is a common impediment in many women's recovery.

There are some things you can do to keep yourself safe from these risks. First, simply being aware of them can help inoculate you from them; if you have this flood of "I'm bad and now everybody knows it" or "I've told my story, and now I'm starting to wonder if I even remember it right" thoughts, you can recall reading this section and remind yourself, "I'm *not* bad. This is a normal feeling. Lots of women go through this. I'm just frightened because I faced my demons head-on today, and it shook me." Or use the wording that suits you. But knowing that this is common and normal may help you not feel so dizzy with doubt if you encounter these emotions afterward.

Second, always have a support/ally throughout the process of rape recovery treatment. I do not advise that a boyfriend be that person, even if he *is* the love of your life (and nice and cute and smart), because the rape details will inevitably surface again your relationship, especially in sexual aspects. The best option is a face-to-face friend, one that you can actually be present with who can support you.

Third, remember your contract with your therapist and peers. Re-read it if necessary.

Fourth, journal about why your story causes you to feel these emotions. What thoughts and beliefs are surfacing which convince you your feelings are (or aren't) accurate? Begin to challenge yourself that just because you feel shame or guilt does not in any way mean that you *are* shameful or guilty; feeling an emotion is not the same as having proof that the emotion is accurate. Shame and guilt are built right into rape. The self-hating and defeated emotions among abuse survivors are the inaccurate ones, which come directly from the abuse (and from your abuser).

Fifth, if you are a woman who struggles with self-blaming thoughts or self-harming behaviors, do not choose a Friday to share your story. Weekends can be powerful triggers because there are fewer opportunities for support and more opportunities for substance abuse, isolation, or self-harm.

Not knowing when the dawn will come,
I open every door.
-Emily Dickinson

Part V: Identifying stuck points

Sharing your story can have a powerful effect in transforming you from a victim into a survivor. On the day you finally share your story—out loud—with others, your courage begins to outweigh your fears. You have taken control of the story, rather than your story keeping control of you.

The worst mistake you could make right now is to stall your forward progress and undo the success you have. Your breakthrough is remarkable, but it's fragile if you don't nourish it like a seedling. If you cancel your ongoing progress by dropping out of therapy, resuming substance abuse, withdrawing from groups, or hurting yourself, you run the risk of worsening your previous depression, which is self-betrayal. At this point, your mental health is at a crossroads: you could begin to find success you never thought possible, or you could reinforce harmful beliefs and habits.

As quickly as possible, begin this next phase of your recovery work. You will begin to analyze your story for stuck points. "Stuck Points" are parts of your story that are the most difficult to re-visit. You can find them in your story by looking for these things:

- Jumps in the story from one event to another, without any transition. The missing transition is probably a stuck point.
- Parts of the story where you find yourself avoiding the full details.
- Parts of the story that you can't write about.
- Parts of the story you can read, but sound numb and emotionless.
- Parts of the story where you are suddenly *flooded* with emotions.

A stuck point happens wherever there is a conflict between your old beliefs (or what you *want* to believe), and the reality of the rape.[1] This can also happen wherever the rape story seems to *confirm* a prior negative belief you have had about yourself. If you have trouble figuring out what your stuck points are, there's another handy way to detect them: your stuck points (at least some of them) will be the specific parts of the rape you flash back to or have nightmares about, and they will also be the particular questions you have about your rape that you avoid considering because you fear the answers would be too awful to bear.

Our tendency is to avoid these parts of the story. We skip over them, write very little about them, and feel deeply ashamed when they come to mind. But stuck points are precisely the ingredient in the "trauma stew" that will continue to generate flashbacks, nightmares, and the urges to cut or drink. The parts of the story we most want to avoid are the parts we must pay the most attention to.

If we complete therapy without really facing, writing, and exploring these points, we have permitted toxins from the rape to remain inside us. It's like taking out the trash but allowing spoiled garbage to stay hidden around the house—eventually, it will become poisonous again. It may be foul and awful to find the "rotting meat" of our stuck points and pull them out, but that's how we finally throw them away so we can heal.

Victoria had two major stuck points in her story. The first stuck point was that she felt ashamed of her inability to physically fight off multiple attackers during a fraternity party rape. She had always considered herself a "badass tough girl" and wore Doc Marten boots as a symbol of her fierce strength. But as she kicked in resistance, the weight of her boots exhausted her and the once-symbols of her empowerment had betrayed her. Victoria found a stuck point between her desire to be tough, and the weakness she felt about her story.

Her entire second rape was a stuck point in itself. Victoria not only wanted to be physically tough, but street-smart too, and she carried enormous self-blame that after one brutal fraternity rape, "I should have learned my lesson and never put myself in that position again." By being raped a second time, she believed, she had proven herself to be easily victimized—a woman who could never trust anyone because of her own judgment's betrayal. She would argue against me for the right to self-blame with all of her attorney intellect, boxing me into logical corners and semantic syllogisms. I certainly wasn't a better debater, or even smarter than Victoria, but I also knew that she had to throw her full artillery of self-blaming arguments at me so that every speck of her shame would be tested. If she were ever going to relinquish that shame, it would only be when she had thoroughly auditioned her self-shaming beliefs and convinced herself that they were untrue. I learned that even if her beliefs caused her pain, she would not give them up until she was convinced she had drained them of their last molecule of venom; only when they lost their power to inflict nagging doubts would she accept that she was truly innocent.

Your homework is to identify at least two stuck points and examine them. Choose the most potent, difficult stuck points you can think of—the very things that seem the

---

[1] Resick and Schnicke, p68.

most shameful. Then use your journal to go through the following activity.[2] Your therapist may be able to help identify stuck point you haven't even noticed yourself.

Below is a list of questions to be used in helping you challenge your toxic and shame-causing beliefs. Not all questions will apply to the belief/stuck point you have decided to work on. Answer as many of the questions as you can, and answer them *fully*—no shortcuts or quick answers.

Stuck Point #1. the part of my story where I feel the most shame, and the greatest urge to avoid the details is:

The belief this point causes me to think about myself is:

1. What is the evidence for and against this belief?
2. Are you confusing a habit with a fact? (example: "I tend to take blame from others; I've done it all my life, so maybe I'm feeling ashamed out of habit, not out of fact")
3. Are your interpretations of the situation too far removed from reality to be reliable? (example: "I dissociated and/or blacked out, so my assumptions about what happened aren't necessarily accurate")
4. Are you thinking in all-or-none terms? (example: things are either all good or all bad; I do everything right or everything wrong; if I make *one* mistake in a situation, the *whole* situation is my fault)
5. Are you using words or phrases that are extreme or exaggerated or minimized? (Exaggerated examples: always, never, forever, should, everyone, no one; "I am nothing; I am worthless; I will never be lovable; Everyone will reject me; Nobody can understand me; I can never forgive myself". Minimized examples: "This part is just so gross; nobody wants to hear it. I'll skip it." or "He gave me a push and it hurt" or "He made me do bad things.")
6. Are you taking selected examples out of context? (example: making a judgment without considering the entire situation; "I'm just exaggerating things, because seemed like a nice guy before that" or "He got me drunk because he wanted us to have fun, so it's my fault he raped me")
7. Are you making excuses? (example: excuses *for him* such as "he probably didn't know what he was doing because I didn't say or do more"; excuses to avoid things such as "This part of what happened was worse than what I actually wrote, but they get the gist.")
8. Is the source of information reliable? (example: is it appropriate to use things the rapist said to set your beliefs about what happened? Can misinformed friends be reliable advice-givers? Can the rapist's friends give accurate opinions of you?)

---

[2] Based on the clinical recommendations of Resick and Schnicke, Chapter 8.

9. Are your judgments based on feelings rather than facts? (example: "I feel I should have known what would happen" or "I feel embarrassed by the rape, which means I am a shameful person.")

Case Example

In working my way through this latest assignment on stuck points, it has struck me that it is absolutely about the details. The tiniest things that I skimmed over, ran past, hoped to avoid altogether - *those* are the things that cause me such distress. And, who in their right mind would WANT to deal with the stress if one can avoid it…right?

-Leitha Brogan

Leitha began her journaling with this entry:

> I read this again today. It is quite helpful in regard to two things. One, you mention 'stuck points'. I have tried to go back and make a list of my 'stuck points' and I believe the greatest hindrances to my recovery.
> 1) My abusive childhood
> 2) My age, I was 12
> 3) My invitation, I met him on the road, I thought he was cute and he talked to me. When I saw him again, I invited him over.
> 4) Things that they said to me during the attack.
> 5) Things I was made to say to them and how they used it after I said it.
> 6) My body and how it turned on my soul.
> 7) My injuries and the long-term pain they caused.
> 8) The humiliation they inflicted and the early introduction of sexually deviant practices.
> 9) Their threats to return.
> 10) My silence and how the events of that day lead me to very young promiscuity, and how confusing the search for sexual pleasure in a pre-teen girl hindered the same throughout my womanhood.
>
> I am a moral woman. I am a professional and have accomplished much in the life I have led since my rape. Much I am proud of, much I am ashamed of. I can look back and see. But it was difficult to live through those days immediately after my rape. I wanted to be dead, but lacked the courage to cause my death. I wanted to make them pay, but I made no accusation. I became my own worst enemy and allowed too many boys to use my body, because I wanted to feel something that I could not understand. I began to feel that the only way I would feel that again was with the violence attached to the initial sex act, so I sought pain during sex. I thought the pain would bring the pleasure. When it didn't I began to believe the things they had said to me…
>
> Self-blame is sometimes easier than letting one's self off the hook. Someone has to be responsible. There is a greater Me and a lesser Me. Sometimes I am able to listen to the sense the greater Me makes. Sometimes, I find it more comfortable to live as the lesser Me. I really want to give you any information I

can to help you help other women who have suffered the horrors of rape. If any of the pain I have suffered, by their hands or my own, will help one person, I will gladly share my story with you.

Leitha's journaling demonstrates one approach to this assignment. She originally wrote only those few one-line responses to the essay questions, because she wanted to avoid her worst stuck points while appearing to have complied with the assignment. When it didn't work—she was stalled in her progress—she realized that she had cheated herself out of healing by ducking the true details of these points. She knew she would have to re-visit her stuck points, taking them seriously an giving them more elaborate examination.

Her first stuck point was the contrast between being a trusting child and the unabashed, all-out cruelty inflicted on her by the abusers she had trusted. The stuck point was the schism between two apparent alternative explanations: "I was a foolish child" or "there are no trustworthy people." Within that schism, Leitha's desperate hope to believe that she could be innocent and there really are good people in this world had seemed to languish for decades. Note that the important word is "seemed." Here is Leitha's subsequent work on her stuck points, where she truly begins to explore and overcome them:

The belief this causes me to think about myself: I am not sure if this is so much a belief about the person, but, I can try to state what I "felt"... (felt/believed...?) Initially, there was shock. I simply couldn't believe this was the person I had met on the roadway. That person had been sweet, charming even. He had been so wrapped up in me, and I had been so thrilled by that single thing, that I had never even asked him his name (new admission about the name). [Later, years later it would cause me to wonder why I never asked him who he was, but when my son was little he'd tell me about a new friend at school and I'd ask the question of him...his response was always..."I dunno". So, maybe that is a normal thing.]

The evidence I was SHOCKED. I also felt an overwhelming sense of BETRAYAL. That emotion was such a force on me that day. It brought about a SADNESS that I can't forget. I also felt completely STUPID. How could I have ever thought there was any way he could be interested in me? I felt LONELY. The feeling of ALONENESS was stifling. That knowledge that there is no one coming to save you. That feeling of knowing your death is here...will it hurt worse than this? ...is this what death feels like? all of that entered my head that day, in that moment.

Are you confusing a habit with a fact? I suppose the idea that this was their fault never came in to play until I arrived here just now. WOW. I just realized that I had never entertained the idea this was their fault until this year. I have spent years upon years believing a lie, and basing my life choices upon that lie.

Are your interpretations of the situation too far removed from reality to be reliable? DISSOCIATION IS A GIFT, AND A SENTENCE. It is meant to be a way to aid us in times of severe trauma, and it works...your mind just 'breaks'...but, that break being the first sense that you don't have to 'be there' for the pain and degradation, feels good. So, you 'learn' it. You learn dissociation, and you use it...many times just because your life sucks and you want to step out of the role. That is when the 'sentence' begins. THAT IS WHEN THE FREEDOM OF ESCAPE BECOMES THE PRISON.

Are you thinking in all-or-none terms? I think that my belief drawn from these feelings cemented the fact that I already felt UNWORTHY. I already felt ALONE. I already felt SHAME. I already felt HUMILIATION. I already felt SET APART. So, when an act comes upon you, and the people performing that act tell you all of these feeling apply to you...that you are actually right to have felt these things, then...it sets in your mind, just like concrete.

Are you using words or phrases that are extreme or exaggerated?
Are you taking selected examples out of context? Yes, this detail thing has opened my eyes, and opened my rape account up to encompass my feelings, thoughts, and words. I said a lot that day, but I was told to say those things, many I didn't know what they meant, but they FELT dirty. So, those details are painful. Then there is what they said to me, that is also painful.

But the most painful and humiliating things they did and said, those are the things of detail I have had such trouble with. I had hope that I could heal without "going there", but in this assignment, we are instructed to look closely and not write scarcely...and when I do that I find the pain, the humiliation, and the despair I had hoped to bury. I feel like I am stirring it up, but, Kaye's idea for an assignment on words - my words, well, I think that will help me close my self again, in a healthy way.

Are you making excuses? ~~~~I am rambling here...avoiding answering the real question.

Is the source of information reliable? I have felt like a FRAUD. Many years in hiding from the truth can do that to you. I left that day with the knowledge I would keep the truth a secret from everyone, then, I'd never have to find words for this thing they did to me. I learned the hard way that won't work, that your mind and body find ways to expunge the ugliness on their own, when you don't actively participate to aid them.

Are your judgments based on feelings rather than facts? What they did, and what they said was just like them saying, "You really are worthless, and no one cares if we do this to you, because you deserve it, you asked for it, you earned it. This is just what happens when you are who you are. This is what happens when you invite men into your home and you are a girl, not a woman. This is what happens when you stand on the side of the road talking into car windows dressed in a half shirt and short shorts.

This is what happens when you let a man kiss you out the car window and no one is watching.... {OMG, I did that! I did let him kiss me from his car. I did that! I actually did that} I just now remembered that in writing this right now. These are words I have never written anywhere, but I just now remember the kiss. I feel like throwing up.

For many rape victims, the constant self-talk that "I should have been able to prevent it!" has become a habit rather than a fact. It can be very difficult to separate the reality that the rape was not preventable, from the feeling that you must have somehow failed to select the precisely-correct sequences of actions that would have stopped it. Be very watchful for evidence of this kind of belief in your writings; it is extremely common for rape victims to exalt the *habitual* guilty self-talk into a *fact* that is held as undeniably true.

Leitha demonstrates what I consider to be excellent stuck point work. Notice that she does not mask or minimize anything; in fact, she bravely documents and examines the *most* dreadful parts of her trauma. And at the end, she even states "I feel like throwing up." But here is her subsequent journaling after processing her writings:

> Right now, I am speechless. Right now, I have no words. But I will accept this assignment, for it makes perfect sense. Just like where we did the "rape stole/didn't steal" assignment, this makes perfect sense to me, and I thank you for it. The ugly and vile things are reverberating in my mind. I need new words that I can shout, and replace theirs. Yes, there are words I would have said, had I been given a choice, and I will think on them, and I'll be back to this. Thank you, thank you.

And the next day:

> I can't really express in words how helpful you have been with this. I have come back to this probably 10 times. I have re-read it, and even my dogs are getting depressed ...LOL. But, in re-reading it so much, it really isn't as hurtful as it was when I first wrote it. I suppose that is what is supposed to happen, so this must be working. This was quite draining, but I am already feeling better.

Danée's major stuck point was her reluctance to accept the truth that her family caretakers had purposefully abandoned her in the lone company of a known pedophile, not out of mere neglect, but with an intention of her being raped as a child. For Danée, accepting this truth meant relinquishing the last scrap of her fantasy that perhaps on some level she was mistaken about her entire childhood: her family loved her, protected her, and never meant for her to be harmed.

As often happens, the breakthrough came not from therapy, but from life. Danée and her mother were driving in the car together that afternoon. Her mother, continually drunk, was in the midst of another typical tirade against Danée, telling Danée how worthless and stupid she was. And then her mother let the truth slip: "When you were a kid, I should have let [him] hurt you even more!" Danée stopped the car and expelled her mother on the roadside, and drove away! Although her mother's words had been callous, they had also granted Danée something she needed: proof that Danée's memories were not warped by bizarre conspiracy theories. No, her mother actually *had* left Danée in the den of a pedophile for the purpose of causing her harm. When Danée did accept the true history instead, it was not accompanied with a serene break-through, light-bulb moment; it was with a burst of rage, in which Danée actually became physically violent, throwing objects while shrieking at her childhood guardians.

Until that epiphany, though, Danée had regarded herself as worthless. The by-product of relinquishing her enduring fantasy—her illusion that perhaps she could still be loved by her family—was the destructive alternative: if her family actually had been capable of loving children, then why was Danée never treated with warmth? The stuck point was hidden inside the answer Danée had feared for years: "perhaps my family could love, but just not love *me*." But by exposing and processing the stuck point, Danée was able to correctly relocate the blame back to her abusers, beginning with her mother: "She's still living in the sick family legend!"

As a result, when I asked Danée to write a description of her core self, her true inner personality, she instead gave me a list of disparaging terms: "I lie…I hate the way my body looks…I say what I think people want to hear. I'm a manipulator…I find my worth in what others think of me…I'm abusive…I feel no connection to my kids…" I pointed out that Danée was not describing herself, she was describing her *abusers*. Danée had so deeply internalized feelings of shame and worthlessness from her rapes that she believed her abusers had infected her with their personalities as well; it was as if she bore a parasite of sleaze deposited into her by them. I watched as Danée wrote in her journal, "Don't confuse habits with my core being. I'm not an abuser…They hand you feelings for you to carry for them, so that they don't have to…Me at my core: funny, witty, smart, thoughtful, energetic, outgoing, articulate, compassionate, likeable."

Freezing and paralysis during rape – "I just laid there and took it!"

At first, few rape victims can tolerate alternate explanations for their rapes. For example, you may habitually tell yourself "I should have fought more," without considering the possibility that you might have been harmed even worse if you had. Because rape is about power and control, a rapist will use a level of aggression that exceeds any resistance in order to maintain that control. Furthermore, during a traumatic assault the body's sympathetic nervous system takes over, instinctively regulating your behaviors for the sake of survival. That means your conscious mind stops choosing what to do, and your physical systems grab control, producing one of three basic responses: fight, flee, or freeze.

All three instincts have helpful and harmful aspects about them; they may either increase or decrease your safety. But contrary to what we see in movies and what we read in booklets promoted by the self-defense industry, the "fight instinct" is actually rather rare in both men and women. By far the most common instinct is the "freeze instinct," in which the body becomes very still, rigid, and silent. This is called "tonic immobility," and is a simple survival behavior. During rape, temporary paralysis is very common (it occurs in up to 88% of rape victims during the assault, according to studies) and entirely normal,[3] and probably even quite healthy.

---

[3] Finn, Robert. "Involuntary paralysis common during rape - Legal and TX Implications." OB/GYN News, Jan. 15, 2003. http://findarticles.com/p/articles/mi_m0CYD/is_2_38/ai_97767906

However, until someone explains to a survivor that this instinct is normal and appropriate, she will often spend years criticizing herself ("What's the matter with me? I just laid there! I'm such a fool! Why didn't I fight, or at least scream?"), and even lawyers and juries can be misled into lenience toward rapists whose victims are inaccurately described as "passive." This behavior is *not* "passive;" it is a biologically-driven form of *resistance*! But this fact is so rarely understood that rape victims often multiply their own sense of guilt and shame because of the freeze instinct. One study even found that the link between this "temporary paralysis" during rape and later feelings of guilt and self-blame are *directly* related to increased depression, anxiety, and PTSD later.[4]

This is why it is so crucial that rape survivors receive basic education about the body's adaptations to trauma, so that you can understand and accept these behaviors as *normal*, rather than as failure. "This is a biologically hard-wired response that just kicks in, typically when there's extreme fear coupled with physical restraint," states one study of victims' temporary paralysis during rape.[5] Jennifer Heidt, commenting on a study she helped organize, wrote, "if we can help to show them [in therapy] that they weren't letting this happen to themselves, that this is an unlearned response, that they were incapable of changing it, that they were incapable of fighting back, then we can help deal with that guilt."[6]

"Many people probably believe that they would exhibit strong physical resistance in response to sexual assault," states one research paper on the topic, "but the data do not support this…'freezing' was a very common victim response to sexual assault… engendered by an overwhelming sense of disbelief. While [tonic immobility] is often a source of shame to survivors, it has been argued to be a common self-preservation aid and a basic response to threatening situations."[7] Research found that this instinct to freeze was just as common among male victims of sexual assault as among females; gender made no difference in the likelihood of a person to freeze: "the woman who blames herself (or is blamed by others) for not 'fighting back' can be reassured that 'freezing' or partial freezing is a very common human response in fear situation and may be equally common in men."[8]

It can also be difficult to separate the issues of "compliance" with "consent." In most rapes where the victim is conscious, there is some degree of compliance with the rapist, simply as a reasonable way to protect herself from further harm. Although this is a very normal form of self-preservation, it can also produce one hell of a stuck point afterward:

- "The fact that I stopped struggling when he ordered me to means I am guilty of permitting the rape."
- "I removed my underpants when he told me to. That means I participated or led him on about sex."

---

[4] Heidt, J. M., Marx, B. P., & Forsyth, J. P. (2005). Tonic immobility and childhood sexual abuse: Evaluating the sequela of rape-induced paralysis. *Behaviour Research and Therapy*,*43*,1157–1171.
[5] Finn, op. cit.
[6] Ibid.
[7] Coxell, Adrian W. and King, Michael B. "Gender, sexual orientation, and sexual assault." *The Trauma of Sexual Assault*, 2002, p53.
[8] Ibid., p62.

- "I kept quiet and never screamed. Does that mean I wasn't really raped?"
- "My whole body froze and I couldn't move."
- "They always say 'no means no.' But I never said the word 'no' because I was paralyzed with fear."
- "I can't remember how I got into the closet [where the rape happened]…If I put myself there, it must mean I helped him rape me."

When a person is mugged, they instinctively freeze and will typically say to the attacker, "Take whatever you want." They will cooperatively hand over wallets, purses, watches, *anything* demanded of them, in a desperate, terrified hope that the assault will end without further injury or death. And nobody questions this cooperation; police even *advise* it as the correct course of action. People will support you and assure you that you did the right thing. Nobody blames you for carrying money by saying, well, didn't you realize that would only lead a robber on?" Nobody would blame you for all the times you willingly spent money by implying that this means you "have a history of giving it away, so aren't you just 'crying robbery' now?" Nobody would claim that the incident was probably just a cash transaction that "got out of hand" or you regretted later.

Yet when the violent assault becomes sexual, people implausibly lose all these same insights about the importance of compliance to reduce harm. Suddenly the guilty questions begin: "Why didn't I fight back? What if I had resisted more? Why did I stay quiet? Why did I freeze? Why did I take off something I wore when he ordered me to?"

These stuck points exist because of the gap between what we want to believe ("I would never 'let' anyone rape me") and what the rape itself seems to prove ("I must have failed to prevent rape. Or worse yet, I must have permitted it!"). It may seem like an unusual statement, but analyzing your stuck points is really a form of *forgiving yourself* for whatever actions you had to do to survive, and for whatever it's taken to cope since, and for whatever misguided self-blame you have felt in spite of the facts. Danée had to confront and thoroughly accept the apparent truth that her childhood "caretakers" had purposefully driven her to the home of a known pedophile, deposited her there with him, and unflinchingly driven away to actually *accommodate* sexual abuse; the agenda was to convince her of her worthlessness (as a four-year-old child!) so that she would become compliant with the family system of domination, control, and secrecy. Danée discovered during her "stuck point" work that she was neither weak nor willing, and that her younger self had never deserved the heaps of blame and guilt she had carried.

Challenging your stuck points

You have to crawl into your wounds to discover what your fears are. Once the bleeding starts, the cleansing can begin.

-Tori Amos

Do you see the truth here in your words? The rapist took away your control of the situation. You did not want it to happen. You tried to stop it. It happened anyway. There is no room for acceptance of blame in these words. None. You did all you could do to stop it. It takes time to get the message into your mind and heart that it isn't your fault. We have all reasoned our rapes as our own fault in some way, but we were wrong. Until I was able to admit I didn't cause my own rape, I had nightmares and flashbacks too. They have all but gone away as I have learned how to place blame where it belongs. I hope you will soon see, no matter who told you otherwise, you did not cause the rape. You simply do not have that kind of power over another human soul.

-Leitha Brogan

Stuck points are not easily demolished. They tend to be propped up by a network of faulty beliefs and values that seem so true that we seldom question them at all. For example, many women's statements to me, "I just think you should know, I have real trust issues with men," are based on the belief that "of *course* men are untrustworthy." And why would she ever question that belief? She had dozens of "proof examples" to support it. Another patient's stuck points included that her attacker was a boyfriend, that the rape was oral, and that the boyfriend continued to call her for dates and they even hugged afterward; this caused her to doubt that the assault was rape at all and to wonder if she had overreacted to the whole thing.

When you reread your writings, try to find examples of these and other forms of "thinking errors" that may be contributing to undeserved guilt and shame.

- ☐ **All-or-none thinking**: You see yourself or issues in extremes: all good or all bad. These thoughts usually use words like *everything, everyone, nothing, nobody, always, never*. Example: "Nothing ever changes" or "Everyone thinks I'm nothing but a _____" or "bad things *always* happen to me" or "You can't trust *anyone*." I see a lot of this language in the poetry of rape survivors, where poets will describe themselves as completely valueless, permanently injured, or totally hopeless. Another example: a caretaker displays a flaw of theirs, and you conclude, "I guess I should never have trusted you! You were tricking me like all the others!"

- ☐ **Mind-Reading:** You believe you know what other people are thinking, and assume they're having negative thoughts about you. You do this even though you have little evidence, and you don't consider other possibilities. Example: "I know that you think I'm disgusting!" or "My mom says she loves me, but I know she doesn't" or "I've told my story, and now everyone is thinking badly about me" or "I know you're not going to like this answer" or "he's only helping me so he can exploit me."

- ☐ **Emotional Reasoning:** Thinking with your feelings. You think something must *be* true because it *feels* true. Example: "I *feel* ugly, so I must really *be* ugly" or "I *feel* dirty, which means I *am* dirty and nobody will love me now" or "I *feel* like it was my fault, so it's absolutely true, and don't try to disagree!"

- ☐ **Discounting the Positive:** Believing that positive things you do or good things about you don't matter. You interpret good experiences into negative ones. Example: "So what if I'm smart? Nobody cares!" Or when someone compliments you, you think they're lying to be nice. Rape survivors often struggle with accepting compliments because they feel unworthy: "You may think that now, but if you *really* knew me, you'd know how awful I truly am!"

(Also: "My mom/dad/husband said s/he loves me, but it was only because we were in the therapist's office.")

☐ **Negative Filtering:** This is similar to "discounting the positive." You focus on negatives and ignore positives. "They're only being nice because they want something from me" or "people don't talk about the rape with me, so they must blame me or be ashamed of me."

☐ **Shoulds:** You criticize yourself by imagining all the ways you *should* have acted differently, even though there may be no evidence that different actions would have changed outcomes at all. "Shoulds" are a very common form of self-blame and shame: "I should have done this/not done that, and then I wouldn't have been raped." Shoulds usually apply to hindsight and what a survivor believes she ought to have done to have prevented her rape. This can also lead some women to harshly judge other women who have been raped and make critical comments toward or about them; this is done in an effort to create distance between the critic and the victim so that the critic can convince herself that *she* would never be hurt the way the victim was. For example: "you should have never gotten in that car! I *wish* some man would try that on me, 'cause I would beat him down!" Translation: "I don't want to be hurt like she was, so I will identify and attack any differences between her and me until I convince myself I would never be assaulted like she was." One woman wrote in her journal to me, "Oh no. Was he going to be mad at me? I shouldn't have started crying. I'm such an idiot."

☐ **Oversimplifying events, people, or feelings as good/bad or right/wrong:** You may tend to identify any mistakes or regrettable behaviors of your own, and then generalize them as an overall belief about rape itself. For example, "I had a beer to drink, which makes the rape my fault." Or: "He didn't mean to do that to me; he's always been a pretty direct kind of guy." Or: "I was raped by a man of a certain race or appearance, so now I fear all men, or men also of that race or appearance." Or: "Rape only happens when men force sexual intercourse on women. If my rapist used some other method besides penis-and-vagina intercourse, or if my attacker was a female, then it wasn't rape."

I often give my clients writing assignments specifically designed to nudge them toward news ways of wording their beliefs and feelings. For example, I have a collection of many, many journals and poems by rape victims who describe themselves in wholly negative terms. Common themes and images are of hearts being ripped out, souls being shattered, holes opening up inside, and emptiness; women may describe feeling they have "nothing left." These beliefs suggest all-or-none thinking ("I am completely bad/worthless now"), emotional reasoning ("I feel lost, therefore I am completely empty"), discounting the positive ("I am weak") and negative filtering ("I haven't told my family yet, which means I am awful").

Just casually browsing online rape recovery forums shows that stuck points can be so incredibly powerful that many women seem to *live* inside them. "I am so ugly and worthless" and "My life is just gross" and "I am dishonored and spoiled now" and "It happened again—I put myself in that position. How stupid I am!", *ad infinitum*, all show examples of stuck points that have been accepted and believed until some women have fused them to their very identities. Stuck points can be like parasites: they put up a fight when you try to cleanse them from your system. This is exactly what is happening when I challenge a victim's stuck point and she reacts with shock and outrage at me: "Can't you see how hard this is for me? Are you deliberately trying to be cruel? You claim to understand, but clearly you don't! If you knew how hard your words cut me, you would never have aimed them at me!" Notice the use of "challenge language," in which she sees the dialogue as a form of combat and oppression, rather than examination and change.

Writing about your stuck points can help identify which thinking errors your rape causes you to adopt, and how to challenge them. Journaling about stuck points forces you to ask questions like, "I may feel awful, but does that really *prove* I have no value?" and "I keep trying to convince myself it wasn't rape, but does that actually protect me, or *him*?" and so on. The assignment I described previously, in which a client had to write what parts of herself had *not* been taken or lost, challenges the "I am empty" imagery. This is not the usual "cheer up, smile, and focus on the positive" sugary advice that too many people offer to rape victims; this is a method of giving hard, sober attention to your beliefs and examining them for accuracy.

Rape teaches a woman many, many things—most of which are lies about herself. It is a powerful teacher, but a deceptive one. By generating potent emotions, it disguises itself as a source of truth about the woman, like a serpent constantly whispering to her, "See? You feel sad because you are a bad person. You feel empty because you are a living, breathing mistake. You feel dirty because you are an abomination. You don't talk to your family about the rape because you are a shameful secret-keeper." Because those emotions feel strong, we assume the beliefs they whisper to us must be true. But just like the artificial euphoria of being high or drunk doesn't actually mean we *are* happy, the overwhelming despair we feel during recovery from trauma doesn't mean we *are* bad and worthless, either. When a high wears off, we see our imperfections again. When we face and peel back the layers of our depression after rape, we see our *worth* again. This is why it pains me to see so many women trade the work of recovery for the easier cycle of drugs and alcohol; they sell off the opportunity to find real worth in themselves for a sequence of quick, superficial sensations. And that allows the false teachings of rape to continue to whisper to them, on and on: "you're bad…you're bad…you're bad…"

When you tell your story and explore your stuck points, it's your way of fighting back against rape.[9] You are really saying back to rape itself, "hell *no!* I'm not going to sit here and keep taking this from you! You keep telling me every day how bad and worthless I am, and how all these traumas in my life prove it. So let's take off the masks and see for real: I'm *not* bad, and you're lying to me! The reason I'm sad is because I'm *valuable* and I was hurt, not because I'm *worthless!*"

This becomes a new way of fighting back. Your journal is not an object of sadness; it is a weapon, a spell book, a *scripture,* that chases out the lies of rape the way a light makes cockroaches scurry off. Approach your journaling with a sense of angry, courageous, determined strength; you are picking a fight against rape itself every time you pick up your pen. If you choose to write endlessly about how empty, dark, broken, and ugly you are, you'll lose every battle. But when you call out the worst things rape

---

[9] Regehr, C., Cadell, S., and Jansen, K. "Perceptions of control and long-term recovery from rape." 1999 Am J Orthopsychiatry 69;1:110-5. Rape victims who had stronger beliefs in personal competence and control had less associated rates of depression and PTSD.

makes you think and feel, then challenge them, then shred and dispose of them with intelligence and insight and self-care, you will begin to kick rape's ass. (It feels good to read that, doesn't it?)

Andrea gave these words to each person who wrestles with the difficult work of battling her stuck points:

These journals are the toughest to get out and the most excruciating to share. But, getting these stuck points out of your spirit are the only way to healing! I am so very proud of you. When one of the group would have one of these days, the other group members would make sure at the end of group that she knew we were there for them. We would sit and offer even more support. We also knew/found out how hard the night was going to be for our group member.

If you can, picture us all around you; lifting you up for being so strong, crying for you, being so angry at your abusers that we are about to explode. We wish that we could give them what they deserve. Picture us sitting there with loving support in our eyes and amazed at your strength to survive these horrific things and people. Realize that in our group there is not one person who holds these as your actions and that we see no shame in what you did to survive. Picture us and see there is only love, only empathy, only understanding, and only amazement in our eyes for the girl that did what she had to do to have survived to become you. See what other survivors can see: what a beautiful, strong, and wonderful woman that you are here with us! And then know that you are TRULY AMAZING!

This is what I picture, us all there around you. My heart and my prayers are with you. I am so proud of you, you have worked so hard! Wrap your arms around yourself and give yourself a hug for me.

Your pain is the breaking of the shell that encloses your understanding
-Kahlil Gibran

Dealing with stuck points, questions, hardships, and setbacks during recovery

Many of us spend our whole lives running from feeling
with the mistaken belief that you cannot bear the pain.
But you have already borne the pain.
What you have not done is feel all you are beyond that pain.
-Kahlil Gibran

Changing self-talk

It's so easy to talk myself into depression, and so hard to talk myself out of it.
- 19-year-old patient

We resist peace because we don't know who we will be without the pain, without the struggle, without the nightmares, without the panic. Peace is unfamiliar to most of us.
- Danée

Relaxation and meditation are not the only ways to cope with stress, they are just the ones most frequently talked about. But there are some other techniques you can use to change the automatic thoughts you have about the stress and emotions you feel.

First, you must realize that thoughts precede emotions. If your therapist told you to try to become sad, you would have to think of something sad first, and then your emotions would change. If we can isolate and identify the thoughts we have that drive our emotions, we can begin to master the emotional responses we have to situations.

I want to introduce you to three parts of your personality, which you have met but may not recognize. Every person, man and woman, has these three voices, but we often train one or two of them to shut up because we don't think they have anything important to say. Here are your three inner guides:

The Warrior. This is the aggressive person within you. She can be helpful, but she can also get you into trouble. The Warrior responds to stress with power, which can be life-saving. But the Warrior can be a difficult person to be around for long, because she tends to take things out on others, project her own anger and skepticism onto others, doubt other peoples' honesty, and react with snippy comebacks. Because the Warrior believes that power is the best way to manage a problem, she may try to convince you to act invulnerable through drinking, drugs, sexual carelessness, and fighting. When you choose any response to conflict other than power, your inner Warrior will try to criticize you for it, telling you you're stupid, weak, worthless, and childish. A Warrior might lash out at others, and then become angry when the people we've hurt act like, well, hurt people. But a Warrior can also stick up for us, and the Warrior is the "hate it but do it anyway" strength that helps us persist through tough work. Beware, though, that the Warrior can keep some women in abusive relationships by saying to them, "you should be able to manage this! Just try harder!" The Warrior also causes some women to be attracted to abusers, because they seem powerful and they might remind us of someone we depended on as a child.

The Victim. This person inside of you is fragile. She feels helpless, hopeless, and incapable of changing a problem. The victim can be an energy drain on others, seeking reassurance and attention. The victim may cause you to put yourself down verbally, to prompt other people to counteract by sprinkling you with compliments to rescue you. Victims often depend on the input of others for assurance and permission. The victim does not resist negative thoughts; during a panic attack, for example, the victim accepts the panic as an inevitable weakness. The victim is the one who cries, "Who will love me now? I'm damaged!" or "I have nothing left to give, so people might as well take whatever they want from me from now on!" When someone is angry with you, the victim will tell you, "See? Everyone just picks on you! Pack up and leave the friendship." The victim is the person inside of you who wants you to constantly repeat unhealthy patterns because she believes nothing else would work, either. She is the one who says "yes, but…" to suggestions your therapist makes.

 The Elder. This is the wisdomkeeper, the healer, the mystic who keeps ancient knowledge and spirituality. The Elder learns from experiences, rather than regarding them as failures or accidents. She teaches you to use imagination as a tool, and points you toward new paths where goals seem impossibly unattainable at first. The Elder helps you replace former harmful ceremonies—cutting, drinking, sex, drugs—with new ceremonies that are valuable: journaling, art, talking, public activism. The Elder also urges you away from forms of entertainment that are superficial or toxic, and toward forms that are nourishing: intelligent music, insightful books, new friendships with other survivors and Elders, spirituality, and social action. The Elder is the person who reminds you that the way things have been is not the way they must always be: your family traditions, behavior patterns, and the misunderstandings do not limit and define you.

How these three voices debate while you are still traumatized

Imagine, hypothetically, that a woman who has been raped is now afraid that she will be unlovable and unattractive to a future mate. How would these voices speak?

The Warrior says, "Screw them! Who needs them anyway? I can do it alone. Men are a bunch of evildoers anyway, and can't be trusted. I don't need anyone but myself!"

The Victim says, "I'll be all alone. I'm unlovable, and people are only kind to me because they want something, and once they learn about my true self they will reject me. I have no other connection, besides sex and parties perhaps, with others."

The Elder says, "For all of human history, people have been hurt. Who are you to be any different? Your pain is small and you will outgrow it. Just wait it out."

Or you may be afraid of panic attacks

The Warrior says, "Victim, you are weak and annoying! People don't want to deal with you! Let ME take over, and we'll whip this thing. I can handle it with alcohol or marijuana. You should be ashamed of yourself for messing up!" The Warrior in a traumatized woman does not actually win battles, yet she promotes battle in nearly any situation. The Warrior distrusts all men, and rolls her eyes when empathetic men actually share of themselves—after all, says the Warrior, this *has* to be a phony put-on, right? The Warrior is embarrassed to be in therapy because she sees depression as a weakness and feels she should be able to "tough it out." Warriors hate to be seen crying.

The Victim says, "I'm going to panic, and everyone will see, and I'll be embarrassed." The Victim in a traumatized woman agrees with the Warrior that every situation is fraught with danger, but she does not agree with the Warrior that there is any way to fight back. The Victim, then, accepts danger as part of any relationship. She is the reason that many rape victims become vulnerable to domestic abuse and dating violence later, and why she seems to always pick the abusers in any group. Victims constantly chant words of self-doubt, and respond with "yes, but…" to any suggestion in therapy (followed by, "I've tried that already and it failed").

The Elder says, "I honestly have no idea why this panic attack is happening. It's strange and you are probably unique in this problem. You should probably start getting used to it as a fact of life." In a traumatized person, the Elder seldom presents useful wisdom. Rather, the Elder tries to help you appear like you have it all together when you're really falling apart inside: "I hardly ever think about the rape anymore; I'm over it; that's in the past; I've dealt with that issue already; what doesn't kill you makes you stronger, right?" The Elder in a traumatized person pretends that you have transcended or forgotten pain, usually by hiding behind your intellect or clever words.

How these guides converse when you are well-adjusted

Rather than having a debate so that one voice can emerge supreme, these three voices converse together inside a well-adjusted woman to develop a consensus in which each voice's strength becomes a part of the whole. For example, in the case of the woman who fears she will now be unlovable to future romantic partners, her Warrior and Elder both realize that it is her Victim who is doing the speaking. What would they say to the Victim to encourage her?

The Warrior would say, "I'm glad you are recognizing that you are hurt, because you can't ignore your injuries and still fight a battle. But you also can't go on being so scared! You've got me to help you, and you can try to initiate some quality relationships. If they don't work out, you can still do well. Let me protect you while you heal; I'll keep us from jumping into as new relationship too quickly so that we have time to take care of you first."

The Elder could say to the Victim, "These are ancient fears. Our people have been facing them for thousands of years, and it's scary to face rejection. But you're not weaker than anyone else who succeeds. Take some time to rebuild yourself, learn how to recognize dangerous relationships so that in your zeal and temptation you don't become entrapped by an abuser, and prepare yourself to be a bold, strong woman in a future relationship. There is no need to hasten into a relationship, but it is absolutely true that there are those people who will see your real worth, and not just your trauma."

The woman who is using these guides is allowing her Victim side to be expressed rather than masking it with false toughness (through the Warrior), or pretending to have it all together when she really still hurts (through the Elder). Instead, she refuses to accept the first conclusion she comes to ("nobody will love me now"), and patiently considers the input of these other messengers. She rebuilds her self-talk to allow for multiple insights, rather than just the first awful, catastrophic belief that comes to her.

In the well-adjusted woman, each guide has a time to be heard, and a time to be silent. For example, the Warrior may be necessary to sustain your commitment and perseverance during the legal process, if you prosecute. She may also need to stiffen your backbone and remain in control if you see your rapist in public again. If you are dating someone who begins to abuse, your Warrior must be able to speak up—not to start a fight back, but to say, "This is unacceptable. The cost for you doing that to me is that our relationship has just ended—permanently. I will not reconsider." The Warrior may begin to see alcohol as an enemy rather than friend, and become fiercely resistant to it. In families where girls are taught to be weak, cute, and to serve, the Warrior tends to be afraid to surface—"It'll get me in trouble! It's not allowed!" The Warrior especially needs resurrecting in women with eating disorders.

Yet the Warrior cannot be in constant control. For example, sometimes people will utter insensitive or misinformed comments about your trauma. If your Warrior takes over, you could make a fool of yourself by "going off" on them, ranting hysterically, and attacking, rather than allowing the Elder to step in and calmly say, "you know, a lot of people believe that, but I have learned that it is a myth. The truth is…" Warriors are fighters, not educators, and sometimes you'll need to shift into "educator" mode rather than "fighter" mode.

Furthermore, the Warrior tries to get you to reject entire relationships at any early sign of trouble. If a sister or father or friend doesn't return a call, the Warrior and Victim talk to each other and agree that you are being abandoned, that this person must not love you, and you should either spite them back or create some major chaotic crisis to force them to pay attention again. These two voices draw up a border that excludes the Elder's wisdom and challenges other people to either fully accept you, or face your wrath. (A person with "Borderline Personality Disorder" tends to have extra-loud Warrior and victim voices—and they are best friends—while the Elder is shunned. The result is "Take care of me without failing, or I will strike out—at either you or myself!")

Warrior and Victim voices often work together, to tragic ends. I once had a patient from a painful family life who explained to me, "The way to survive in our house is to never be the target. You are never safe. The strategy is to 'throw someone else under the bus' during hostile times so that they, not you, are the target instead. Always look for who else can be identified as a wrongdoer so that the family anger goes to them and not you." As a result, I observed—and even experienced—this patient's tendency to respond to inner emotional pain or family upheaval by looking outward for wrongdoers to blame and attack. The effect was to focus the family as a unified force against an external distraction, rather than having to confront the internal stuck points of troubled family life. Consequently, close and dear friendships were exterminated, role models were turned against, and her dwindling circle of allies eroded. The Victim voice could not bear to consider that it was *she*, and not *they,* who was in dysfunction, so she would accuse each new target of being the one who had changed and betrayed *her*: "You're not even the same person I once knew! I used to look up to you, and now you've changed!"

The Victim needs to be heard at times, too. I have worked with women who cannot grieve their rapes because they keep their Victim voice bound and gagged in the subconscious. They never cry, they never express deeper pain for their trauma; they "tough it out" instead. And usually, they fail at this. Self-injurers put their Victim voice in a tough position: they acknowledge that the Victim is real, but they will not let her speak. Instead, she shows up in the skin, but not in their words. Self-injurers need to allow their Victim to speak up, to put into words the pain that is being expressed in self-harming ways. I worked with a woman who was incredibly intellectual and could explain the origins, why's, and effects of her emotional pain. She could recite a narrative of her life like a case study, but she never showed emotion about it. With masterful vocabulary and academic skill she could dissect her life experiences, drawing insight and connections. She was gifted at explaining her pain, but not feeling it: "I hurt *because...*" If I asked her what she felt, and she would answer with what she *thought*. The trick was to get her to drop the "*...because*" and simply be able to declare, "*I hurt.*"

But there are times when the Victim monopolizes your life, too. I have had women in therapy who apologize for every incident when they merely express themselves. They act as if they have no right to stick up for themselves or have demands on anyone, and they follow-up with, "I'm so sorry! I didn't mean to raise my voice. I hope I didn't piss you off!" These are the women who guess at answers to my questions, trying to say what might make *me* happy rather than what she actually needs to say. They often answer questions with questions, or they make statements asked in a question-voice. They also often rely on "I don't know" answers during therapy. The Victim may try to fill your journal with dark poetry about how torn, broken, empty, alone, ugly, and abandoned she says you are. The Victim thinks that these poems are brave because they "express how I feel," when actually they simply chant "I'm bad, I'm bad" repeatedly.

One clear sign of a Victim who has monopolized a woman's voice is when a patient asks me to comment on her journal. But if I challenge or even dislike something she has written or drawn, she becomes irate and accuses, "you obviously just don't understand!" and withdraws. She has sought approval, not input. She wants flattery, not honesty. She feels personally invalidated when a detail of something she has said is challenged. Whether she feels so victimized that she expects *everything* she does to be wrong, or whether she feels so victimized that she feels entitled to total exemption from challenge, both viewpoints come from the Victim. I have had many clients whose feelings are hurt during group therapy, but instead of speaking up and addressing it with me they will simply start skipping groups without explanation, forcing the rest of us to guess at what has upset her. This emotional "hide and seek" is meant to manipulate our support, rather than overcome the problem itself.

The Elder has important things to say because she is able to step back from strong emotions and consider the "bigger picture," drawing on strength and wisdom from past lessons. The Elder learns from mistakes, and can interrupt the Warrior and Victim by saying, "Now, just wait and think about this for a sec…" The Elder plans responses to a crisis, rather than just reacting. When you lie in bed and think about what you "should have said" during a conflict that day, this might be your Elder speaking up (unless you're trying to find new-and-improved ways you could have slammed the other person, or ingenious ways to guilt them into backing down—the Warrior and Victim, respectively). You might notice that what the Elder has to say is usually more insightful and effective than what the Victim or Warrior actually *did* say at the time. When your instincts feel like responding to a crisis in the "old" ways, but instead you stop and think about what you have learned in therapy and how you want to change your reactions, this is your Elder stepping forward. When you ignore your therapeutic learning and go right for the habitual emotional reaction, you are silencing the Elder. An Elder can consider whether a person who is upset with you has a valid point; a Warrior would merely fight back and a Victim would slink off.

There are also times when the Elder should back off. There are times when calm, reasoned intellect just isn't the right reaction. For example, some women mask their pain by speaking and writing in eloquent or intellectual ways, but their communication skills become a clever form of avoidance of deeper feelings and plain statements. Journal writings about serious trauma become compositions full of similes, metaphors, descriptive phrases, and clever analogies—rather than direct, honest emotion. The Elder is the voice who writes her rape story like a poet or novelist. Questions about how a woman feels are answered by the Elder with, "I think that…" Therapy sessions tend to follow the pattern of dialogue about philosophical issues, rather than resolution of trauma. Or if a woman confronts an abuser or perpetrator, she does so in a very contrived, rehearsed manner in which she actually contemplates his side, responds back to them, and treats the encounter as a treaty negotiation; it's more of a conversation than a confrontation! When the Elder speaks up at the wrong time, she tries to be so transcendent, so rational, and so enlightened that she is in danger of minimizing rape or minimizing her response to a rapist ("we all make mistakes; we should judge the actions, not the person; in a way I'm glad this happened because I can learn about myself from it," etc.). The Elder can sit in group therapy and relate to topics on a rational, intellectual level, yet have difficulty connecting personal emotions to those same topics.

Other examples:

Fear of being alone
Warrior: "This is the Victim telling us how dangerous this is. But I can protect us all from things now. I can be bold and outspoken if I have to be, so I want to reassure the Victim that things will be okay. I'm 25 years old, and that means that for 9,124 days I've been safe, and on one day I wasn't."
Elder: "The Victim is partly right. We do need to be wise and careful, but what kind of life am I protecting if my caretaking prevents me from *living* any of it? The Warrior is making a good point, too: I am likely to be okay, and I have learned new skills to protect myself. It's time to go for a walk again!"

Nobody will love me

Victim: "I need to be honest that I have some doubts about being loveable now. That makes me vulnerable to manipulation by people who flatter me, and I should keep in mind that my hunger to be loved can draw me into relationships that may not be healthy. Whether I am loveable or not, I'm not really sure—but my Victim's voice might actually have some beneficial wisdom about keeping from harm in future relationships."

Warrior: "I should be the emotional bodyguard for a while. Since the Victim is vulnerable to lovers who may not be healthy, I should probably reinforce my walls just a bit. I need to make a contract with myself about what kind of partner I will accept, and what warning signs I will look for. If I am to be loved, it must be by someone of *my* choosing, not just by someone who chooses me."

Elder: "I agree with the reinforced walls—we call them 'boundaries'—but make sure they have windows and doors in them. Closing yourself off from others completely is unhealthy, and will guarantee that you will not be loved. There are many survivors who are happily married, loved, and cherished. Yes, there will be some jerks out there, and it's better to give trust too slowly than too quickly, but there are some amazing people who will love me. I don't need to become flirty, dumb myself down, or settle for losers just to have a relationship. What I *can* do is starting some of the many awesome books there are about how to recognize signs of manipulative and abusive partners!"

A simple formula can help you pull these voices together and produce the best choice of response during a decision. You and your therapist should work together on these worksheets, actually writing your answers out until they become second-nature to you.

The event that is affecting me right now is:

My immediate, instinctive thoughts about the event are:

My immediate, instinctive feelings about the event are:

Which guide is giving me those thoughts and feelings?
_____ Warrior   _____ Victim   _____ Elder

What are the risks of that guide being the only decision-maker in this situation?

What reactions docs that guide often lead me into, that I would like to change?

What "thinking errors" could this guide be committing?

All or None:

Mind-Reading:

Emotional Reasoning:

Discounting the Positive:

Negative Filtering:

Shoulds:

Oversimplifying:

What would the other two guides say to help you come up with the best reaction?

Using Your Story as a Weapon

You will occasionally feel the temptation to use your rape story as a weapon. It is possible to shock, stun, or repel people with your story, and even to use your rape to motivate sympathy and attention from others. But this would be your Victim speaking, hurling the word "rape" to convince others of your authentic trauma and the grim rationale for your own subsequent behaviors. But this also becomes a shameful ploy to seek attention and special treatment (or special exemption from responsibility), as in "I was raped, and so that's why I did drugs." This "I was hurt, so I'm entitled" mindset has its advantages, and is very tempting.

I once worked with a woman who would deflect any challenging statements or confrontations from group members by wailing loudly and becoming tearful, before tersely spitting out the rebuke, "I was *raped!* Can't you see that I am in *pain*? Can't you see what your words are doing to me?" This was a ruse to make her bulletproof by pretending to be exquisitely vulnerable, using her rape as kryptonite to paralyze therapists, group members, and family so that nobody could ever nudge her into alternate paths of behavior or beliefs. I refused to take the bait, and held up my hand and interrupted: "Oh, no! That isn't going to fly here. You are not so uniquely impaired that you deserve special exemption from hard work. This is not about remaining passive and fragile, and everyone else here has had to do this work too. You are not going to invoke victim status as a spell to keep hard insights and expectations away! There are no victims in here. There are women who work hard. If you are one of those women, we can continue."

Clearly, she did not greet my intervention with appreciation; she regarded it as callous and disrespectful for me to disallow her use of "rape status" for personal privilege. This crumbled her myth that rape therapists are ginger, doe-eyed Aunt Bea's who cradle and coo over victims, and awoke her to the stark reality that this work is hardcore, rugged, and bold. We, the therapists, are loving, but not marshmallows. She wanted her Victim to be exalted, and was keeping her Warrior and Elder mute.

But by remaining poised and calm, and by *not* using your story as a debate weapon, you allow your Elder to manage your reactions.

Using your story as a weapon is very dangerous to your own emotional health. Trying to convince people to be shocked, upset, or sympathetic by using your rape story works for a short time, but two things will happen. First, people will eventually stop being supportive and begin avoiding you because your continual and sudden revelations of disturbing trauma will drain them of energy. Your story should be shared in a way that promotes your own healing, not in a way that controls others. Second, your own sense of shame and depression will worsen. Using your story as a weapon works *because* it plays on the aspects of your story that are uncomfortable. It takes a story that you have been working to cleanse of its shame and guilt, and slaps shame and guilt labels all over it specifically *because* you can stun and manipulate others with those feelings. How can you finally heal away the shame and humiliation of your rape, if you use on the story to shame and humiliate?

If you use your rape as a go-to topic to shut down criticism, confrontation, or accountability from others, it might have worked only because it hurls something intended to repulse and disturb. It would give you a short-term "win" over temporary conversations, but it also leave you with newly-magnified labels of "gross and disturbing" to handle all over again. The whole point of rape recovery is to rid yourself of those very labels, not to make banners out of them!

In short, an authentic survivor does not claim the label of "rape" to alter other's treatment of her. Instead, she claims the label of "survivor" to alter her treatment of herself.

*You, created only a little lower than the angels,
Have crouched too long in the bruising darkness.*
-Maya Angelou

Why do some men rape? And why did it happen to me?

The more research that accumulates on the issue of why some men rape (and why rape is perpetrated almost *only* by males), the further we move away from the traditional perception of rapists as sick, psychotic, sociopathic monsters who lurk in the shadows. What we are finding is much more disturbing than that.

We are discovering, with more and more backing research, that rape is a behavioral outcome of the *normal* training of *normal* boys. As our culture continues to sexualize power and control as masculine, and submission and objectification as feminine, the problem of rape continue to be an outgrowth of what has become a "rape culture."

This is not an anti-male "guy-bashing" conclusion. On the contrary, it has become a concern of many men: fathers, male coaches, male sociologists, male psychologists, and male religious ministers who are increasingly vocal about the problem of toxic messages linking sex, power, and masculinity that pervades boys' lives. There are, of course, men who are deeply offended by this conclusion as well, and resist any implication that men share, let alone *own*, the burden of responsibility for the problem of rape. But I'm not particularly interested in protecting their anxieties or egos from an honest analysis of the problem of men's violence.

The brutal fact is that rape is an effective and almost-airtight method of gaining control over another person. As you are reading this, the statistical probability is that you not only know this to be true, but you are deeply enraged about it: fewer than 5% of all accused rapists ever spend *any* time in prison, and rape continues to be the most underreported crime in America. Men who rape are virtually assured of getting away with it. And even when their victim does report the crime and press charges, it is almost always *she* who then suffers the brunt of social scorn, doubt, and rejection.[1] There are few forms of power and control that are so complete in their ability to transfer power from victim to perpetrator, and so safe from consequences to the perpetrator.

Ours is a society that gives lip-service to the wider problem of rape, but does not engage the problem in meaningful ways. Political campaigns are full of rhetoric about "ending crime," yet the second most severe violent crime (beneath homicide) will seldom be named by a single candidate. Budgets that are increasingly conservative on social programs whittle funding away from rape crisis programs, leaving the bulk of grants for these programs to come from United Way or private contributions, with the result that rape crisis programs are shutting doors by the hundreds. The highest-risk age group for rape victimization is 13-24, but rape prevention educators have difficulty finding schools who will agree to host prevention programs.

Robert Jensen is in a good position to observe the effects of media on the public consciousness in his role as Professor of Journalism at the University of Texas at Austin. Jenson writes,

> In the contemporary United States, men generally are trained in a variety of ways to view sex as the acquisition of pleasure by the taking of women. Sex is a sphere in which men are trained to see themselves as naturally dominant and women as naturally passive. Women are objectified and women's sexuality is turned into a commodity that can be bought and sold. Sex becomes sexy because men are dominant and women are subordinate.
>
> …Again, the argument is not that all men believe this or act this way, but that such ideas are prevalent in the culture, transmitted from adult men to boys through direct instruction and modeling, by peer pressure among boys, and in mass media.
>
> The predictable result of this state of affairs is a culture in which sexualized violence, sexual violence and violence-by-sex is so common that it should be considered normal. Not normal in the sense of healthy or preferred, but an expression of the sexual norms of the culture, not violations of those norms. Rape is illegal, but the sexual ethic that underlies rape is woven into the fabric of the culture.[2]

Jensen is suggesting that rape does not happen because of some characteristic about the *woman* who is raped, but because of countless characteristics of *men who rape*, and the culture that produces those rapists. So while we may make rape illegal, our society also makes rape an integrated part of its culture. To state it boldly, we have a

---

[1] Campbell, R., et al. (2001). "Social reactions to rape victims: healing and hurtful effects on psychological and physical health outcomes." *Violence And Victims* 16;3:287-302. Rape victims who had someone believe their account or were allowed to talk about their experience in a manner they considered to be healing, had fewer subsequent emotional and physical problems.

[2] Jensen, Robert. "Rape is Normal." *Counterpunch*, Sept. 4, 2002. http://www.counterpunch.org/jensen0904.html

culture that raises rapists; rape is "culturally dictated, not culturally deviant."[3] Sociologist Patricia Yancey Martin reaches the same conclusion: "Rape is not a rare, mysterious aberration perpetrated by a few 'bad apples' but a practice available to all men (and boys) who believe they have *a right* to sex from women."[4] Note that she is not saying that all men have the propensity to rape; rather it is men who have a certain culturally-supplied belief system who will use rape. Her argument is not anti-male, and it is disturbingly true.

By treating rape as a "women's issue," we have isolated the male half of the population from participating in problem-solving, and probably made the problem worse by shifting attention (and blame) onto *women* as the ones responsible for preventing rape. As a result, many men's involvement in the issue of rape is limited to uttering the standard speech: "I would never rape anyone! I think that's so wrong!" The assumption of such men is that "I've taken a personal stand against rape, so I've done my part to fix the problem." Women in my therapy groups are almost always angered and offended by the simplistic platitudes they get from men who recite the same lines: "I respect women! I would never do that to a woman! I think the woman is a gift from God", and blah blah blah. But when men in my groups are pressed by their female peers for a deeper, more thoughtful reaction to the problem of rape trauma, many are typically stumped and unable to verbalize much beyond these platitudes. This is a shame, and it undervalues men as well as women. Men seldom order our lives, travel plans, and schedules to consider the possibility of violence, while women do so in dozens of ways every day.

Meanwhile, nearly 100% of rape victims blame *themselves* in some way for their own rapes. This also lends a lot of power to rapists, unintentionally, and as long as victims and survivors continue to swim in circles of self-blame the REAL culprits continue to get more and more powerful and suffer less and less confrontation of their behaviors.

In ancient history, rape was not seen as a crime against an individual, but a *property crime* in which the father or partner of an assaulted woman was the actual victim. The first rape laws protected women only in the same way that we pass laws making it illegal to vandalize someone's car; the intent was not to protect women, but to compensate *men* for the loss of value if a woman was "damaged." The Code of Hammurabi, humankind's first written set of laws, defined rape as a crime of adultery by the woman and prescribed her death by drowning. In Biblical law, the punishment for committing rape was that the raped woman would be stoned to death unless the rapist would agree to marry his victim and pay her father 50 shekels; the idea was that a woman was so devalued by rape that it punishes *the rapist* to have to carry her as a spousal "burden." The first rape mentioned in the Bible is described as a form of "humbling" a woman (Genesis 34). Right from the start, the power and control aspects of rape are remarkably clear!

In the 12th and 13th centuries, English Common Law stated that rape was indeed a crime and that the rapist, not the victim, would be punished by death. This may appear to be a progressive step in human law, except that husbands were exempt from any penalties for raping wives and the standards for proving rape were nearly impossible to meet.

---

[3] Baker, Katherine K. "Once a rapist? Motivational Evidence and Relevancy in Rape Law." *Harvard Law Review*, 110: 563, January 1997.
[4] Martin, 2005, p7.

In the last few years, biologists have put forth theories that rape is not a socialized or cultural behavior at all, but rather the natural result of evolutionary biology.[5] Drs. Thornhill and Palmer suggest that sociological and feminist explanation of rape as an act of power and control have not been tested for accuracy, and that these theories ignore the possibility that sex really might be a—or *the*—motivation to commit rape. They point to the importance of reproduction in evolutionary survival, primitive methods of accessing sexual stimulation, and brain differences between males and females that promote male aggression. Thornhill and Palmer received extraordinary criticism despite their defense that they are not excusing rape, merely trying to provide more accurate analysis of it for the purpose of improving prevention efforts.[6]

In this "biological theory," the role of social learning and culture are not dismissed, only augmented: "Social learning appears to be an immediate cause of rape, but it is just one of a multitude of equally important immediate causes. Also, rape is the result of ultimate or evolutionary causation."[7] Biological theory does *not* suggest that rape is morally neutral, inevitable, or unavoidable because of genes; on the contrary, the biologists who proposed it state very clearly that any evolutionary biology that may influence rape behavior is not supreme, and that another component of evolution is the ability and obligation of individuals to make conscious choices about their own conduct.

I am personally disappointed in biological theory because I do believe that rape is a socially-transmitted, learned behavior. I come to this conclusion not through indoctrination by feminist theory, liberal professors, or sociology coursework in universities, but in my personal observation of the lives of young men who accept and adopt the attitudes about power, masculinity, and sex offered to them by culture. My awareness of our culture's "rape training" leads me toward the conclusions of feminists, the professors, and the sociologists, rather than vice-versa.

I can even concede that there is more of a sexual aspect to rape than most other feminist theorists would allow, but only with a careful explanation: I see a sexual component to rape *not* in the sense that rape is an expression of sexuality. Rather, I acknowledge that culture has behaviorally trained many people to associate power and brutality with sexuality; the result is sexualized misuse of aggression for personal gratification. My belief orbits around the feminist "power and control" explanation for rape, but with the chilling caveat that power and control *are* treated as sexual dynamics in cultural messages.

The fact that rape victims can range in age from 6 months to 100+ years old, or that men rape other men,[8] would also seem to question the biological basis of rape as a form of reproduction, sexual action, or evolutionary trait. Since there is abundant research showing that the majority of rapists pre-plan their sexual assaults using intoxication, intimidation, and isolation as tools of control, it is also reasonable to conclude that rape is a conscious choice that reflects the values and beliefs of the rapist. A startling and horrifying case in point to support this conclusion comes in the remarks

---

[5] Thornhill, Randy; Palmer, Craig T. "A Natural History of Rape: Biological Bases of Sexual Coercion." MIT Press, Cambridge, MA. 2000.

[6] http://www.aec.at/festival2000/texte/randy_thornhill_e.htm

[7] Ibid.

[8] In the *majority* of male-on-male rapes, both the perpetrator and victim are heterosexual. I can't imagine a stronger demonstration that rape is about power and control rather than about sexual desire.

by Florida veteran circuit judge Gene Stephenson in 2004. Presiding over a rape case, Judge Stevenson commented on the record, "Why would he want to rape her? She doesn't look like a day at the beach." His statement was uttered as he viewed photos of a 57-year-old woman, beaten and bruised during the assault, during a hearing in which her attacker was being charged with raping, beating, kidnapping, and robbing the woman. What the judge was essentially saying is that something about the *victim* makes a man rape her; if she isn't pretty, then what other fact about *her* would make someone rape her?

Meanwhile, violence is the number one cause of injury against women in the United States, and those who advocate for societal changes to address this problem are mocked as "feminazis," with Rush Limbaugh propagating his own "undeniable truth of life" that "feminism was established so as to allow unattractive women easier access to the mainstream of society." The use of sexism and misogyny to maintain dominance is plain.

We also find that certain cultures are more "rape prone" than others. This alone suggests that cultural sociology tells us an important story about why rape happens. In cultures that are not prone to rape, males and females share more traits of equality. Religion is not seen as a purely "male" commodity, and women share authority with men in lawmaking, family, and transmission of culture. These cultures are neither patriarchal (males in power) nor matriarchal (females in power); they are *egalitarian* (power shared equally). Rather than a layered hierarchy of "who's above who," men and women constitute two symbolic halves of a circle. Such cultures do exist,[9] and in North America they would be found among many traditional indigenous peoples whose tribes managed a well-regulated balance between males and females for the purpose of sharing power, and among religious sects that extend leadership authority to both males and females in any capacity.

In the United States, rape crisis centers did not open until 1972, and in 1994 the Violence Against Women Act (VAWA, drafted by then-U.S. Senator Joseph Biden) finally secured federal funding for women's shelters and rape crisis programs (which increased in number from 15 to 2000 nationwide!). Before VAWA, women had to pay for their own forensic medical exams, which discouraged most women from seeking help. Even though VAWA has expanded the services available to women who had been battered or raped, it is continually at risk for severe budget cuts in Congress (one way to track your Senators' and Representatives' commitment to ending violence against women is to follow their positions on VAWA). Of course, the key question is: has it worked?

The first-ever Presidential initiative to combat violence against women was in 2010, and it increased funding for crisis centers, DNA testing, funding to clear the backlog of rape kits, and prosecution, as well as a proposed *doubling* of funds for VAWA. Health Care Reform also made it illegal for insurance companies to regard domestic violence as a "pre-existing condition" to deny medical coverage to abused women. As of this writing, the rape rate in the United States is less than *half* what it was a decade ago, and reporting rates are rising, not falling—we're actually winning![10]

---

[9] Noted examples include the Minangkabau, a rape free Indonesian society, and several traditional indigenous nations and societies.

[10] Bureau of Justice Statistics, *Criminal Victimization in the United States*, Sept. 15, 2011.

How feminist theory counteracts mainstream rape myths

Is rape a gender issue?

Mainstream rape myths: No. Rape is a "sex crime" caused by sexual urges that are out of control or "go too far."

Feminist theory: Yes. Rape is a logical consequence of a cultural system that disempowers women. Rape is one example of a continuum of mechanisms that maintain that imbalance of power.

Why does rape happen?

Mainstream rape myths: Rape is a result of men's "horniness," or of women's careless seductiveness. Men rape because a sexual opportunity is presented but requires force to be completed.

Feminist theory: Rape is the product and consequence of a toxic culture in which women are not valued and even seen as threats. Culture socializes rape behaviors by normalizing sex as a form of power, using sexualized violence as a form of entertainment, approving of violence as a legitimate tool of problem-solving, and directing scorn and suspicion toward women who come forward with rape allegations.

Are allegations of rape usually true or false?

Mainstream rape myths: Rape allegations are often careless and false accusations made by women who want financial rewards, celebrity status, sympathy and attention, or who seek to harm men with false claims. "Real rape" is different from "date rape."

Feminist theory: Rape allegations have been shown in years' worth of reputable research to be true in 92-98% of cases. The hostility shown toward women who report allegations of rape is a result of social legends about women as manipulative, vindictive game-players, or "sluts" who "cry rape" to protect their reputations and/or socially persecute men. The scorn directed at women who report rape is a reflection of a cultural system that uses prejudice as a tool to continue women's silence and self-blame.

What kind of person rapes?

Mainstream rape myths: Rapists are demented sickos and psychos who hide in shadows and attack prey. They are deviant from social norms, totally unlike "normal" boys and men. If a "normal" man is accused of rape, it is probably that he was stimulated into the act by a woman.

Feminist Theory: Statistically, 99.8% of rapes are perpetrated by males, and acquaintances are the most common attackers. Men who rape are, disturbingly, otherwise regarded as "normal" by conventional social standards.

Who is raped?

Mainstream rape myths: Rape happens to women who fail to use common sense and safety planning, or who "put themselves in the position" to be raped by engaging in substance use or alluring behaviors in the presence of men. "Real rape" happens when strangers break into houses at night and rape lone women or abduct women into alleys.

Feminist theory: 95% of rape reports are made by women, although both men and women can be raped. The age range of rape victims in the United States is from a few months old to over 100 years old, demonstrating that rape is not about sexual desire or biological drives, but about power and control. Statistically, one in five women will experience rape or attempted rape in her lifetime, although some studies place the number at one in four, and others at one in six.

Can rape be prevented or eliminated as a social problem?

Mainstream rape myths: No, because rape is caused by mental illness or by women's power to entice men into sexual urges beyond men's control. Both of these will always occur. The most likely way to reduce the problem of rape is for women to change their own behaviors, such as how they dress, where they go, and how they behave, so that men will not be influenced to rape.

Feminist theory: Yes, if two things happen. First, men must address other men and reclaim rape as a men's issue as much as a women's issue, setting standards for male conduct that do not approve of any form of violence toward women. And second, the status of women in society must be fundamentally improved so that women are equally valued, and not regarded as a weaker, hysterical, unreasonable, or subordinate population. This involves political action as well as change in families, theology, media, and economics.

What degree of blame does a victim have for rape?

Mainstream rape myths: Victims of rape deserve a share of the blame for their own contributions to the rape. If women did not drink, dance, dress attractively, or attract male attention, men would not rape. Therefore, if women have the power to instigate men to rape, women also deserve part of the blame. The problem of rape will not be changed through social action and education, but by advice to women about how to monitor their own actions so they do not cause themselves to be raped.

Feminist theory: None. The responsibility for rape is solely and completely on the shoulders of the perpetrator, who makes his own decision to commit an assault. But women are taught to engage in self-blame because of a social system that consistently regards rape victims as being at fault.

Cultures that are less "rape prone" tend to avoid rigid structures of gender roles ("this is men's work, that is women's work; A woman's place is such-and-such; a woman who has been abused put herself in that position," etc.) and authoritarian morality. Morals are seen as expressions of "the common good" rather than prescriptions for traditional roles which are enforced by shame or alienation. Religion in "rape free" societies is seen as a means of liberating both the individual and entire societies from oppression, injustice, or disempowerment, rather than a form of deity-sanctioned power and control where men are in charge.

When romance novels feature rape as the typical first contact between two characters who later become lovers; when musicians like Insane Clown Posse and Eminem can openly ridicule rape victims and not only retain their fans but get Grammy Awards for the music, when more and more pornography intentionally recreates rape as a form of erotica (the trend in porn is toward more explicit violence), when troubled "bad boys" are glamorized as the ultimate lovers, when "Pimp and Ho" costume parties have become normal themes, when children's Halloween costume catalogs feature "Pimp and

Ho" costumes for kids, when the word "pimp" has itself become a *positive* term, when video games like *Grand Theft Auto* award points for raping and beating bystander women (and when parents buy these games as gifts for kids), and when the woman accusing a sports hero of rape is targeted with scorn and hate while the accused rapist himself receives standing ovations by fans, we begin to see how rape has become "normalized" in culture. When social critics who share concerns for trends like these are mocked as "politically correct" and told to "get over it," we see that rape has not only become normalized, but *socially approved* as a pastime. In fact, active opposition to rape-culture is seen as the "strange" position to take, which may explain why so few males (by proportion) are part of the anti-rape movement.

For example, retail stores are now selling "Bratz"-brand padded bras to girls aged 7-10; I am not kidding. Reprints of the *Sweet Valley High* novels for preteen girls were edited to specifically alter the "perfect clothing size" from a 6 down to a 4; I am not kidding.[11] The "Talking Teen Barbie" doll included among its scripts, "Math class is tough!" Wal-Mart was protested for selling panties in child sizes printed with "Who Needs Credits Cards When You Have This?" over the crotch. Online toy companies sell pencil sharpeners molded to seem like women with spread legs, and a battery-powered voice squeals, "Ouch! That hurts! Help! Stop!"[12] Airports installed urinals sculpted in the form of women's open mouths; I am *still* not kidding.

There is more than one type of rapist, too. Just as there is no such thing as a "typical rape," there is no such thing as a "typical rapist." They include members of every race, religion, social class, and personality type. Men who rape are not insane, and they are not just "sowing wild oats" when it comes to sex; most rapists are men who have relationships in which sex is otherwise available to them. They are not perpetrating rape because there have no other way to get sex. Whenever a celebrity is accused of rape, I brace myself for the dozen-or-so times I will hear the ignorant comment, "*He* would never rape because he can get sex whenever he wants to anyway!" My reply is usually, "yeah, I'm sure he believed that, too."

Men who rape usually believe that what they have done is normal and acceptable. In their minds, they aren't doing anything that most other men would do in the same situation, too. So to be clear, it is not feminists who believe that all men are rapists; it is *rapists* who believe that all men are rapists.

Forensic psychologists have used the methods of profiling types of criminals to identify four primary types of men who rape. They are:

- **The Power-Assertive Type.** This is the typical "macho" guy, a tough guy, often an athlete. The power-assertive rapist has exaggerated beliefs about masculinity, and regards sex as the obligation of a woman to him. He commonly meets his victim at a bar or party, and most often has some acquaintance with the victim before the rape (the "date rapist"). He is physically aggressive, and is prepared to use some type of violence (hitting, slapping, threatening) to control his victim, but typically has no intention of killing her. He has no hesitation to use drugs or alcohol as a form of control, and is typically the type of rapist women describe in stories of waking up after drinking and finding she has been (or is being) sexually

---

[11] http://gawker.com/5004617/random-house-proudly-promoting-eating-disorders
[12] http://feministing.com/sexual_assault/

assaulted. He will often directly command his victim, "stop fighting back and it won't hurt so much" or similar statements. Begging and crying will not work with this guy; in fact, he sees it as confirmation of his male superiority over women. To him, this is not an act of rape, but an act of fierce sex, and he often steals a souvenir of the assault such as underpants, makeup, shoes, or jewelry. If he later teases her with the souvenir or about the rape itself, he regards it as a form of sarcastic after-play. He accounts for about 75% or more of rapes. Because he is often popular and does not consider himself a rapist, his tendency will be to assault several women during his life.

- **The Anger-Retaliatory Type.** This guy is hostile toward women and wants to punish and humiliate them. He is often an addict or mentally ill. The anger-retaliatory does not have a "type" of victim in mind, and doesn't target a specific woman. Rather, he creates an *opportunity* to rape. His assaults appear spontaneous and vicious but in fact they are deliberate. He is typically quite violent, and his violence escalates as his victim resists. This guy often feels that *he's* the victim of women's nature, and that women in general deserve punishment for whatever distress *he* feels.

- **The Power-Reassurance type.** This guy lacks confidence with women. He's often awkward and has difficulty establishing intimate relationships, and isn't a "tough" guy. He may be using rape to reassure himself that he is indeed "manly," yet he is the type least likely to be violent. He may use alcohol specifically to enhance his confidence and aggression in social situations. I have encountered this type of male in therapy and noticed that they often claim, quite convincingly, "I don't mean to hurt anyone! I'm just so awkward and unsure of the right way to do things with women!" Fortunately, this is also the rapist type with the best prognosis for prevention or rehabilitation. If he can be confronted by women and men *who do not make excuses for him* about his attitudes, and if he is offered alternative relationship skills, his chances of sexual aggression drop dramatically.

- **The Anger-Excitation Type.** This is the rarest, and most dangerous, type of rapist. This type accounts for about 2% of all rapes, yet he is the type portrayed in movies and TV shows because of the dramatic sadism he displays. This man is usually highly intelligent and very charming, and his crime is methodically planned. He is a repeat offender and his victims may or may not be strangers. He derives part of his sense of power from his ability to gain trust from women first before assaulting and injuring them. His entire goal is to inflict as much harm to his victim as he can, which makes him the most dangerous type.

What you will notice about all four types is that each of them operates from a principle of power and control. Rape is a product of their underlying beliefs and value systems, not a spontaneous urge for sexual contact. The act of rape describes the type of person the perpetrator is, not the type of person the victim is. This is crucially important to understand because so many victims begin to internalize their feelings about the rape and misconstrue it as something that happened to her because of some flaw, trait, or action of *hers*. Understanding the types of rapist can help you redirect your blame and anger where it should be, rather than toward yourself. There's nothing wrong with *you*; there's a lot wrong with the world you live in.

Let's also consider what *doesn't* cause a man to commit rape. I have read countless emails, websites, and flyers claiming to present information to help women "avoid being raped." I have noticed that there are two serious flaws that appear over and over in nearly all of them: First, they give lip-service to the fact that preventing rape is *men's* responsibility, but then the writers immediately revert back to the same clichés about ways *women* ought to change their behaviors, appearances, and freedoms to prevent rape. And second, they claim—with <u>no</u> basis in any published research whatsoever—that rapists have a "type" of victim they seek. The implication is that if you have any traits on their "victim type" list, you should alter yourself so you are a less likely victim. Both flaws actually blame *women* for rape, and hold women responsible for preventing—or by extension, failing to prevent—rape, while this blame is camouflaged as scholarly common-sense meant to empower and assist women.

Typically, these messages follow a similar course. They are often written by men, especially men who run self-defense programs for women.[13] Law enforcement officers are sometimes the credited source (which may not be true). They claim to be representing "FBI profiles" or "psychological studies." For the record, *no such studies exist.* If anything, published research overwhelmingly indicates that there are *not* "victim types" when it comes to rape, and that rapists cannot be identified by simple mannerisms, habits, looks, or secret handshakes.

The essays then list all sorts of bizarre claims about the types of women most likely to be raped. Some say it happens more to blondes, others say brunettes. If you have a ponytail, your risks increase because he'll see it as something to grab and hold. If you walk a certain way, make eye contact, fail to make eye contact, say something to him, don't say something to him, fight back, don't fight back, wear certain clothes (or even certain colors of clothing), you're told that your risk of being raped increases. By the end of the list, any woman reading or hearing these "helpful suggestions" is bewildered by all the countless trivia that "research" and "experts" claim will make her a victim!

So for the record: Rapists do *not* have a "type" of victim. This is absolutely essential to emphasize, because myths about "victim types" can keep women in cycles of self-blame for decades: "if I hadn't worn that; if I hadn't said that; if I hadn't done that; if I had done my hair differently; if I hadn't been pretty; if I had been with more guys at the time; if I had been away from *any* guys at the time…this wouldn't have happened to me!"

The question "why did it happen to me" isn't unimportant because it's your attempt to make sense of something that changed your life in a matter of minutes. The terrifying discovery that *anyone* can have that degree of power causes you to search for deeper insight. "Probably the most common reason for guilt is that survivors are forced to participate in their own dehumanization," writes Linda Braswell.[14]

[Potentially triggering media images on the next two pages]

---

[13] I fully support self-defense programs for women; research suggests that they are helpful for recovery. I am simply issuing a caution about certain claims that are often made about sexual assault in materials that market some of those programs.

[14] Braswell, Linda. *Quest For Respect: A Healing Guide For Survivors Of Rape.* 1992, p7.

Alcohol is deliberately used to facilitate the commission of rape. It is also treated as a joke by many, such as this "humor" poster from a college gift shop.

("...Well maybe if I'm drunk")

Many peoples' beliefs about rape come from "garbage" sources of information.

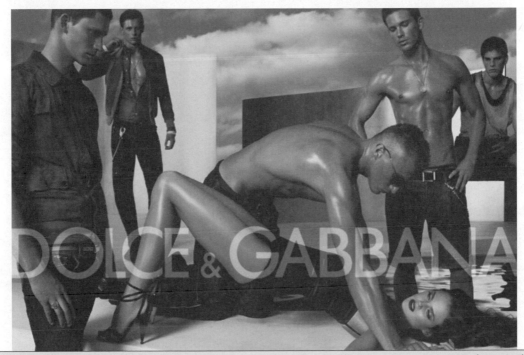

Fashion advertisements by Dolce & Gabbana and Calvin Klein portray power and control, in the presence of passively-interested onlookers, as sexy. Critics of the ad were mocked as "Politically correct" and "hysterical feminists."

How do you like your drunk girls?

⚪ Mobile

⚪ Immobile

[Vote]

These Free Drinks Aren't Going to Date Rape Themselves!

FILED UNDER: FOOD AND DRINK NIGHTLIFE

Source: *The L Magazine* online "Ladies Night" nightclub review

Ill take off my disguise,
The mask you met me in,
'Cuz I've got something for you to see
-Ani Difranco

The phrase "…put herself in that position" and blame

I am convinced that the single most damaging myth about rape comes from the "put myself [or 'herself'] in that position." I hear this phrase several times a week, and as often as not I hear it from women who have been raped. The phrase has been used in several ways:

- To blame victims. "She shouldn't have put herself in that position," says a critic. I hear men use this line in order to hand off responsibility for rape to women, implying that women are the ones who bear the duty to prevent rape. And I hear it from women criticizing one another, so that the critic can convince herself that she would never be harmed the way a rape victim has been because *she* would never put herself in such a position.

- To give the appearance of having "coping skills." I have heard rape victims use this phrase in an effort to demonstrate to others that she has "learned from her mistakes" and is "accepting personal responsibility" and will "take better care of herself." She does this by explaining that she will never "put herself in that position again."

- To allow ignorant or misguided therapists to inappropriately confront victims and survivors. I have heard colleagues in the mental health field harmfully confront their clients with this phrase as a way of "giving her a reality check" or "teaching her boundaries." Nonsense. I have also heard therapists construct an argument, based solely on flimsy pop psychology, that the woman who was raped must take responsibility for the rape. It sounds something like this:

"Can you control the actions of others?"

"No," comes the compliant reply.

"Then whose actions *can* you control?"

"Um, mine?"

The therapist smiles with the successful confrontation, while the rape victim wilts under the apparent logic of her blame. And with the stamp of authority, the therapist has just vandalized their client with the label of guilt.

"Then what could you do differently next time, to prevent yourself from being raped?"

I put this kind of therapy into the same garbage can as the line, "nobody can abuse you without your permission."[1] Any therapist who utters such trash ought never to counsel anyone who has survived abuse or trauma! Abuse and rape are two gigantic examples of why these phrases are pure nonsense. People *can*, and frequently *do*, abuse others "without their permission," and people *can*, and frequently *do*, control others against their will. Rapists *can* and *do* "put others in the position" of being raped—that is how 100% of rapes happen!

So the phrase "put myself/herself in that position" is used to appear insightful while it is victim-blaming in disguise. I Google-searched the phrase "put herself position rape" and found countless victim-blaming statements including:

- "While a rape is a tragic and undeserved by any standard, she willingly put herself in a compromising and dangerous position. Every person has to be responsible for the consequences of their own actions."
- "We can hold a woman responsible for conscious, careless actions that put her in a position of vulnerability."
- "How many cases have we read of a horrible attack and then thought 'but why oh why did she put herself in that position?' This is the real feeling behind the survey. The attacker is blamed 100% for the crime - No quibbles. But the victim can sometimes be at fault for putting themselves into a situation where this can happen."

I noticed a pattern in the results I browsed. Typically, the authors of each of the victim-blaming statements would give lip-service to the idea that rape is the rapist's fault ("The attacker is blamed 100% for the crime - No quibbles"), and then with the single word "but," set about dismantling the only true point they made. The gist seems to be "Sure, we're supposed to blame the rapist, and that's fine, but we all *really* know that rape happens because *women* do something wrong."

An example of this victim-blaming was apparent when the rapper Akon was filmed simulating a rape during a performance. Akon brought a 15-year-old girl (and local minister's daughter) onstage during a performance, and then held her down while he imitated sex in several positions. This was not simulated sex, it was simulated rape: throughout the footage, Akon grabs her, holds her down, pulls her back as she crawls

---

[1] A similar example is "We teach people how to treat us." While this is a handy maxim for setting expectations in healthy relationships, it is *not* useful in explaining the relationship between a rape victim and her perpetrator, or a victim and abuser.

away to escape the stage, and physically slings her around (and body slams her back down) to a cheering crowd, until concert security pull her to the side and take her away. The online reactions to the incident were bizarre; most people blamed the *girl* for being there and dressing in concert/nightclub clothing.

When we analyze the phrase "put herself in that position" more intelligently, we see that it is a very flawed, destructive way to explain rape. First, it suggests that rape is an inevitable act due to a combination of circumstances about *the woman*. The word "position" is a passive way to describe how rape happens. It suggests that there is a particular stew-pot of factors that leads to rape, and that these factors are a combination of happenstance plus the woman's own lapses of judgment. It's as if rape is an inevitable wrecking ball, just doing what wrecking balls do in wrecking ball situations, but women wander into their paths and suddenly become demolished because they ignore the signs and fences of a construction site ("I shouldn't have gone to that party; I shouldn't have been drinking; I shouldn't have walked alone…"). The outcome, while tragic, is ultimately the result of *her* negligence or willingness to be harmed.

Second, the phrase suggests that the cause of the rape is the woman, not the rapist. *She* put *herself* in that position: rape happens to a woman because of her choices and options. When women behave as if they are actually free people, they are raped as a result. There is no mention of any other person in the phrase, and no other person receives accusation or responsibility. But the victim is twice named: *she* put *herself* in that position. Phrases like this are partly why we think of rape as a "women's issue," with so few men positively involved in it. One weird and sad result of this common phrase is that it trains us, culturally, to think of rape as "that inevitable thing that happens," and distracts our focus from the real question *why* it happens to preoccupation with judging the victim's flaws. Rape is not "that inevitable thing that happens," it is a specific crime done by specific people with specific belief systems and methods.

Third, victim-blaming statements suggest that the way to prevent rape is for women to change or give up any rights, choices, or actions that supposedly trigger the rape "wrecking ball." The phrase lets men off the hook completely: we, as men, have no responsibility to address the use of power and control in our own lives, or to challenge media messages that glamorize sexual violence and demand/reward female submission, or to be a vocal alternative to the "men-only-have-one-thing-on-their-minds" legend. No, it's *women* who should change so men will stop raping them. It's *women* who should dress differently, act differently, and talk differently. Men can retain every basic right we want, because we're not in danger. So rather than changing the danger, let's change *women* by making them less free and more responsible for managing men's violence. This puts women is an impossibly schizoid trap: they are told they will be rejected if they fall short of men's concepts of beauty and submissiveness, yet they will also faulted for the violence that befalls them if they are attractive. The confusing answer, women are told, is to give up *more* of their rights and freedoms. The conclusion that violence is the natural "position" women will inhabit if women fail to surrender rights and liberties is chilling, yet it passes for common sense.

There is only one thing that causes a woman to be raped: a *rapist* puts her in that position. Yet there is no corresponding catchphrase that "*he* shouldn't have put her in that position." Why not? Who benefits and gains power by only using words that blame women as victims? In college there was hand-painted poster in a dorm that said, "Be careful, ladies! There have been 6 assaults on campus this week!" There was *no* corresponding poster that said, "Hey men, be respectful! There have been 6 assaults on campus this week!"

We tend to get confused by the "what if?" questions like, "What if she was drinking?" or "What if she was flirting?" or "What if she looked a certain way?" A better way to address these questions is to ask in return, "If she were doing any of those things, does it open permission for someone else to commit a felony assault against her?" or, "Do rapists rape because women drink?" or "Are men the powerless victims of women's prompts to commit rape?" I'm not denying that there is a need for reasoned, self-aware social safety by both women and men—indeed there is, and men and women both are capable of making poor choices—but we ought to ask whether *rape* is the reasonable, permissible consequence for *any* choice, let alone whether men can't stop ourselves from committing rape.

I have had clients who fault themselves for their rapes by stating "I should not have put myself in that position." When I ask them to describe the "position" they were in that somehow caused their rape, they will often list very mundane, everyday activities: "I shouldn't have been there, I shouldn't have worn that, I should have had a friend with me, I should have...shouldn't have..." I point out to them that these are activities women do every day, and rightfully so, and that none of these events caused a rape to happen. They will agree with me intellectually, but their gut *feelings* still tell them, "yeah, but if I hadn't done that, the rape wouldn't have happened. If I hadn't been there, the rape wouldn't have happened." Whether at a fraternity party or a car ride home, the conclusion is the same: "I shouldn't have been there. Somehow, this has to be my fault!"

One particular question can help to dispel that self-blame. I ask, "if *he*, the rapist, hadn't been there, would you have been raped while doing all the same things you did?" They will think for a moment, and then nearly always answer, "well no, of course not!" This nudges a shift in her thinking in which she begins to realize that no sequence of behaviors on her part would have caused a rape to happen if a *rapist* hadn't been present. Every rape that happens is determined 100% by a choice made by the rapist to commit rape, and nothing a woman does would cause rape to occur without *his* decision that it will occur.

Women may also come to the conclusion, "I don't think I caused the rape, but I think I created the opportunity through my poor choices. My rape was opportunistic; he (or they) saw me in the vulnerable position I had put myself, and raped me." But opportunities don't create rapists; rapists create opportunities.

Gradually, the layers of self-blame begin to evaporate as the truth of this starts to sink in. Even in the stereotypically "blame-able" scenarios such as a woman who is intoxicated, the bottom line is the truth of her innocence: no matter what she had done, no rape would have occurred without a rapist there to commit the crime, which brings us back to the statement that opportunities don't create rapists; rapists create opportunities.

Self-blame accounts for the bulk of all rape trauma symptoms. One of my mentors in rape work taught me, "Ninety percent of rape trauma recovery is undoing our tendency to self-blame. Ten percent is everything else. But the ten percent has to come *after* the end of self-blame; it can't happen while we're still ashamed and guilty."

*I was always looking outside myself for strength and confidence,
But it comes from within. It is there all the time.*
-Anna Freud

Comparing yourself to others in recovery

Nearly every client I've had in therapy goes through a period of feeling inferior about using time for herself. They make statements like, "I just feel guilty about taking up so much time!" or "I don't want to take away from someone else who really needs the help." Women who want to ask me a question even email me to ask my permission to email me! Much of this self-deprecation comes from the feeling that *I am too insignificant to deserve the loyalty and support of others. My life and my pain are trivial in comparison.* Rape survivors often engage in this kind of pain-comparison with one another, and may tend to devalue their own pain by imagining that everyone else is so much more advanced and deserving than she. I run a Healing Retreat for Survivors each year, and by far the most common fear that newcomers have is "I won't be as good as the others. They'll be so much further along in healing than I am!"

Suzanne S. put it this way: "I just feel stupid for being [in therapy] now. After hearing everyone else's stories, I feel like mine is so small. I should just be able to grow up and handle it instead of sitting here."

If you believe that you are diminished in worth because of your rape, you will have difficulty accepting the gift of concern when you receive it; Suzanne explained it this way: "It was like people [in the therapy group] cared so much about me, and I couldn't feel like I deserved it. It felt like I was accepting an award I knew I hadn't won. I was so afraid of being discovered, like they would eventually catch on to my scam and realize I really *am* pathetic and worthless, and then they'd be mad that I led them on by letting them care about me."

In her (remarkable) book, *The Rape Recovery Handbook*, Aphrodite Matsakis discussed the tendency of victims to discount their own right to recovery by comparing their own pain to the pain of other survivors. Matsakis writes,

> …There will always be women who are worse off than you. Even if another woman suffered more injuries than you did, you are entitled to grieve for your own pain, every bit of it. You are important too, and you owe it to yourself to recover as much as possible. If at some point you want to help others, the more recovery you have, the more insight and courage you will have to share.[1]

There is also the opposite form of comparison that can happen too, and it is very tragic and destructive, and fortunately much rarer. On occasion, I have observed victims of rape begin to almost *compete* for the recognition of worst trauma: one woman describes her rape experience in very basic ways, and another will respond with "I was raped too!" and begin to relate her own narrative. The effect is that the pain and worth of the first woman is diminished while someone else distracts the entire process with their own additional story. (This is especially likely in early stages of group therapy before trust and unity have developed; needy members can jostle for "place" in the group by auditioning their trauma stories to the others to prove they are worth attention)

Sometimes this competitive comparing can even be more aggressive, such as "Oh that's nothing—listen to *my* story!" I have found this among adolescent groups in particular, and to some extent among adults, where there can be a "queen bee" game to see whose lives have been the roughest, and whose pain deserves the most validation. This is a particularly gruesome and destructive behavior, and demonstrates a lack of empathy or support between group members.

In either case, the effect is to rank traumas so that some are considered "worse" than others—and hence more deserving of attention and care.

Pain is pain. There is no such thing as a rape that is "more deserving" of care than another rape. The only thing that varies is the readiness of the victim to work hard; if you are ready to take on this issue and see it through to the end—even when it upsets you and tests your strength—you are just as deserving of support as anyone else. Furthermore, don't give away the glory and honor for your achievements. Your success is yours, and does not belong to anyone else, including a therapist or the author of a book. When women offer me feedback that *Resurrection After Rape* worked, or even saved their lives, I humbly thank them but immediately return the honor for their success back to them. *You* have to do this work. Therefore, you deserve the praise for succeeding.

One final thought: don't allow yourself to glamorize someone else's recovery in a way that causes you to feel inferior. If you are dazzled by the apparent strength of another woman and you wish that you could be as strong as she, just remember that everyone's recovery is very different. The survivor you admire may have problems and hurts she has not yet revealed. She may be displaying a false strength because she feels insecure too. Or her response to rape trauma may simply be different. But no other survivor's life can be your measuring tool for how well or fast you should be progressing.

---

[1] Matsakis, Aphrodite. (2003) *the Rape Recovery Handbook*, Raincoast Books, p. 42.

The thing that is really hard, and really amazing,
is giving up on being perfect
And beginning the work of becoming yourself.
-Anna Quindlen

Personal history, "being perfect," and rape

Marie was certain she had considered the "larger context" of her rape in therapy because she had begun to realize that rape is a behavioral product of many cultural teachings about men, women, power, and sex. And she is right. But there was a more *personal* context that had not occurred to her until Week 5 of her treatment.

During her childhood, her older brother had been continually aggressive to her, taunting and insulting her and physically bullying her. She recalled him dragging her across the carpet while she resisted, and the memories of rug burns on her arms, legs, and shoulders returned to her. Astoundingly, while processing these events her skin re-experienced the actual *feeling* of burning, and several times while talking about these memories she would stop, pet her shoulder silently, and then shudder in disgust.

Marie recalled that as her brother's bullying worsened she had begun to resist less and less. This was because of natural conditioning: she had learned that resisting was never successful in halting his violence. She had also received family disapproval when she had objected to his bullying as a child: "You two knock it off!" and "You two go to your rooms!" (where his bullying escalated, now that they were secluded). The bullying was not sexually abusive, but it still taught her the futility of her efforts to resist him; his strength always won the battle. Marie's family pattern was to pretend that the real cause of family upheaval was due to some manufactured "enemy" on the outside, which united the family in distraction so they could ignore the ongoing dysfunction in the family itself.

Years later, she would be facing feelings of guilt and shame over her perception that she had not also sufficiently battled her rapist. Marie would alternate between self-criticism and depressed embarrassment that she had not been able to fight, kick, and hit powerfully enough to overwhelm him. "Why couldn't I do more?" she would ask.

But the larger context is that her abusive treatment since childhood, and the subsequent verbal scolding to mind her place and resume her "silent compliance," all collided on the day of her rape. The only lesson she had been given about her right to resist was that she had no such right. Resistance had never worked (and had even worsened the bullying and torment she faced as a child), and there was no permission for her to use her voice to assert herself. In short, she was well-trained to expect the failure of her own strength.

Even though she actually had resisted during her rape, she was conditioned by years of family experience to doubt her own strength, to expect to be diminished, to regard all encounters with men as inherently exploitative, and to see herself as a continual victim. Marie tended to talk tough about "Suvivorhood," but quickly reverted back to "victim mode" when she needed to rally the support of others to her side.

If you find yourself condemning or criticizing yourself constantly because you feel you did not "do enough" to resist, you may want to consider whether you had a similar life context. What messages were you given about your rights to resist? When you spoke up for yourself, was it honored or were you scolded for being impolite? Did you experience physical abuse or violence until you began to feel helpless to prevent it? Kaye wrote in her journal,

> I was raised to be polite. I was taught to respect my elders. I was to be lady-like, quiet, submissive and kind. I was taught to care about others, to serve others and look for the good in people. I saw the roles of men and women and I was always glad to be a female.
>
> I was taught that men are protectors, providers and problem solvers. They were there to love and take care of things... to take care of us, the women and children in their lives.
>
> I didn't really know that others were taught differently. I had exposure to womanizing, macho men in the movies, but the first encounter I had with it in real life was when the next-door neighbor showed up at our house in her underwear, beaten by her husband. I was quickly sent to my room as my parents dealt with it. It was never discussed.
>
> Being the trusting, polite and helpful girl... I wonder if that played into making me a good "victim."

If these apply to you, none of them means that you are weak or powerless. It simply means that you were conditioned—brainwashed—to doubt your strength. Chances are, you probably still doubt your strength and you may even believe that your rape is proof of your powerlessness. It sounds like this: "I'm so weak, and the rape proves it. I've always been hurt, and if I were stronger I could prevent things like this from happening to me. So obviously, they happen because I'm weak." This kind of triangular thinking becomes a form of "self-proof" in which we believe we're weak, and point to our trauma as verification.

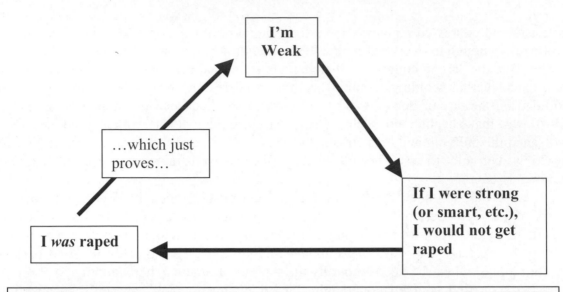

The cycle of self-blame in rape survivors: "I believe I'm weak, which means bad things will happen to me. And since bad things *have* happened to me, that proves I'm weak."

One victim had blamed herself for "weakness" until she began to examine her life lessons. She had grown up in a family where her father was very controlling and emotionally unpredictable. Her mother walked a delicate line between showing affection for her children and appeasing her husband to prevent his outbursts. This trapped her mother in a role of having to constantly assure her children, "you know your father really loves us," while having to abstain from any direct confrontation of his power in the family.

The result of this is that my client had an amazing inner life of imagination, poetry, journals, and insights, but it was all cocooned inside a very small, passive outer life. There were no role models to demonstrate boundaries, assertiveness, or self-defense. When she was raped, she had nobody to turn to because her father was enjoying all the privileges that male intimidation could offer, her mother was cycling through a "don't rock the boat" life, and the victim herself could only function in a "do-as-you're-told-and-keep-silent" system.

None of this means that the victim is at fault. I am not implying that anyone's family, childhood, or background "made" them a vulnerable person. What I *am* saying is that many of us grow up in systems where there is little support, or the so-called support is of the "pull yourself together and move on" –type. We never know a rape is about to happen, but when it does we come out of it with these emotional cavities already in place, and they impair how well we respond to the trauma at first. Rape is not a consequence of these things; but silence and self-blame afterward *are*.

More and more research is showing that your perception of the bond you have with your parents is also significant in determining the severity of your trauma after a rape. In one study, women rape victims who reported weaker bonds with their parents also reported greater indicators of stress, anxiety, and depression after being raped. In particular, the study noted that less affectionate and more controlling *fathers* correlated with deeper trauma impairment after rape.[1]

One of the most common family patterns I found among my patients is that as young girls they were raised to be people-pleasers. The purposes of their lives, all too often, were to "be perfect," to stay in their place, not rock the boat, and set the needs of others ahead of their own. I can spot this dynamic in group almost instantly when one patient becomes tearful or upset; the "people pleasers" will physically move from their seats, crowd around her, pet her, hold her, and make it their entire project that day to save their peer from feeling hard emotions. When I intervene and confront this interaction as inappropriate, they see me as incredibly cruel, unfeeling, and rejecting; their entire life's script is telling them, "nobody can be unhappy around me, because it is *my* role to fix them! I have to nurture others in their time of need, even if it means never focusing on myself and *my* needs!" In fact, they often perceive memories of their fathers "storming around" in even my gentlest effort to block their people-pleasing demonstrations.

Another way I can recognize this script in my patients is that nearly all women who were raised to be "servants and people pleasers" operate with a belief that they are meant to make things "perfect" and "right." But these are impossible goals, and there is a remarkable connection between these beliefs about having to be perfect, and women's dislike for their own bodies. The concepts of perfection, failure, usefulness, and happiness are internalized as *physical* experiences, which means there are nearly always two simultaneous beliefs at play: first, "I have to take care of other peoples' needs rather than my own, which would be selfish," and second, "I hate my body."

Anna Quindlen, a Pulitzer-prize winning journalist, described this in her book, *Being Perfect*. In it, she talks about the emptiness a woman feels when she has been raised to set the needs of others ahead of her own:

> Someday, sometime, you will be sitting somewhere. A berm overlooking a
> pond in Vermont. A seat on the subway. And something bad will have
> happened: you will have lost someone you loved, or failed at something at
> which you badly wanted to succeed. And sitting there, you will fall into the
> center of yourself. You will look for some core to sustain you. And if you have
> been perfect all your life and have managed to meet all the expectations of
> your family, your friends, your community, your society, chances are excellent
> that there will be a black hole where that core ought to be.

Many women lack the words or permission to even express the depths of this despair. By "permission," I mean that they, and maybe even you, have been trained since childhood to believe that the most important accomplishment for a woman is that she is helpful and nice to others, which means that any defiance or rebellion against this narrow role is met with suspicion and hostility, as if she is becoming "uppity" or "self-centered." You can verify this by listening to the compliments that adults give to young girls and noticing how limited and shallow those compliments are: "You're cute, you're sweet,

---

[1] Hauck, Simon, et al. (January 2007). "Parental bonding and emotional response to rape: A study of rape victims." Psychotherapy research, 17:1, pp83-90.

you're nice, you're pretty, you're sweet, you're cute, you're adorable, you're just a doll…" Songwriter Ani Difranco addresses these themes in her lyrics:

> Don't ask me why I'm crying
> I'm not going to tell you what's wrong…
> I want you to pay me for my beauty
> I think it's only right
> 'cause I have been paying for it
> all of my life

Difranco isn't merely addressing the problem of girls (and women) being trained into dutiful roles of beauty and submission; she specifically links this training to the victimization that women often endure as a direct result. In the same song:

> I was eleven years old
> He was as old as my dad
> And he took something from me
> I didn't even know that I had
> So don't tell me about decency
> Don't tell me about pride…

Ani Difranco's music explores these themes very often, and very intelligently. In another song, *Not a Pretty Girl*, she proposes that being "pretty" can even be a limitation because it brings with it an entire set of scripts and roles for the girl who strives to be perfect:

> I am not a pretty girl
> That is not what I do
> I ain't no damsel in distress
> and I don't need to be rescued
> so put me down, punk,
> maybe you'd prefer a maiden fair;
> isn't there a kitten stuck up a tree somewhere?
>
> I am not an angry girl
> but it seems like I've got everyone fooled
> every time I say something they find hard to hear
> they chalk it up to my anger
> and never to their own fear
> And imagine you're a girl
> just trying to finally come clean
> knowing full well they'd prefer you were dirty
> and smiling
>
> and I am sorry, but I am not a maiden fair
> and I am not a kitten stuck up a tree somewhere

I am not a pretty girl
I don't want to be a pretty girl
I want to be more than just a pretty girl

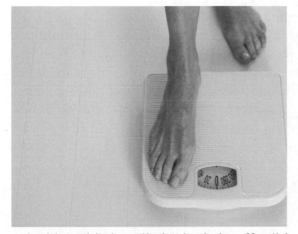 Insightful readers recognize by this point that I am not talking about merely the trait of "prettiness," nor am I saying that being attractive is bad. You recognize by this point that this is an issue that transcends image; the entire blueprint handed to nearly all young girls is one in which her qualities are superficially divided into outer (prettiness) and inner (keep your place and make yourself useful by taking care of others), and her life becomes limited by the very traits she has been told make her valuable! This is called "the halo effect" by psychologists: we tend to see one attribute about a person and attach all sorts of other labels to her as a result. So if a girl looks a certain way, she is assumed to have all sorts of other qualities as well.

The message is constant that some additional improvement must be made so she can finally feel acceptable. The accumulated burdens of submission, perfection, self-sacrifice, and "niceness" all combine to pressure women into self-deprivation in a futile quest to find a satisfaction that never comes. All of this is guided by the messages, "you must…you should…you must not…you cannot…" ("If I could just lose 5 more pounds, *then* I could…" or "If I just tried harder to help him, *then* he wouldn't…" and in the case of rape, "if I hadn't put myself in that position, and had done this instead, *then* I wouldn't have been raped.") From this message comes the selfless peacemakers, the rescuers, the I-can-save-hims, the givers, the sacrificers, the "stay in your place" girls. Even my bold, nonconformist feminist patients are saddled with the belief, "I have to achieve, and then achieve some more, to make myself okay."

When I say that these are the "starving girls," I am not (just) talking about food. When one young woman went to lunch with her father to finally talk with him about her rape, he spent the entire hour on his cell phone, doing office work. Perfectionism is a barrier that blinds parents to their own children.

When this already-dysfunctional system is further shattered by rape, several things happen. First, women are already culturally predisposed to internalize rape because lessons from family to friends to media, and even religion, all echo the same myths: if *you* would only do things properly, you wouldn't have to suffer. Second, these messages have already placed women at a self-esteem disadvantage, so a rape compounds this damage by convincing her, "if you thought your value was limited before, now it's *really* gone!" If our value comes from being attractive and perfect, then what happens when we feel ugly and useless after trauma? Or what happens if we feel attractive, but we suspect that attractiveness is what brought predators to us? One of my patients confessed at the end of therapy yesterday, "deep down I still struggle with the belief that I was raped *because* I am pretty." Imagine being caught in this trap, where service and prettiness are offered to a young woman as the means through which she becomes valued, and yet she also wrestles with the thought that perhaps these very "qualities" contributed to her rape!

I see countless women of all ages pulled to bits by this trap. On one hand, they strive for independence and maturity by becoming more "perfect," so that they can finally shut up that inner voice that accuses them of failing. But by striving for something that can never be reached, the voice actually becomes louder. If you are this woman, you find yourself running both toward and away from the same thing: an impossible standard of perfection. I believe that the pressure on girls and women to be care-takers for others before yourself, to be "useful" through constant selflessness, to be approved of by critics, and to strive for "right behaviors" to avoid being harmed or abused, are all part of why rape is a particularly devastating trauma. It attacks women right at the level where women are judged the most (their bodies), and then it also sledgehammers the guilty lesson, "this happened to you because *you* failed," which attacks women at their psychological, emotional, and spiritual core.

This, I propose, is partly why rape victims internalize their anger and shame after trauma. The "I have to do things right so I won't be hurt" philosophy may have been learned in families, but it is also a basic theme in daily cultural messages aimed at women. During therapy, two issues that seem to emerge over and over in rape victims are "am I doing this right?" and "I can't do anything right." In her book *Perfect Girls, Starving Daughters*, Courtney Martin pierces through the nonsense women are handed as a map of life and gets to the point:

> I want you to see it [body image and perfectionism pressures] for what it is—
> not a normal part of being a girl, not an acceptable way of moving through the
> world, but a destructive pathology that is stripping us of our potential.[2]

If you recognize your life in any of this description, begin working with your therapist to explore how they pertain to your lack of support or resources after your rape. You may have spent a long time after the rape in a cycle of lonely, self-destructive habits with the goal of soothing inner pain, seeking interconnection with others at any disastrous sexual price, or pushing yourself to physical limits just to test whether you still have an inner self at all. I hope that you can begin to see these behaviors as the results of external messages, rather than your own inner badness.

My goal in writing this section is to help many survivors reconsider their self-judgments about the ways they have responded to their rapes. Perhaps some readers will begin to recognize that even your self-destructive behaviors after the rape were not the result of being defective or warped as a person, but the result of years of life lessons that have *told* you to feel powerless (when you're not), *told* you to accept pain (when you shouldn't have to), and *told* you that these are the limits of your life (when they aren't).

---

[2] Martin, Courtney. *Perfect Girls, Starving Daughters*, p30.

*Courage is not the absence of fear,
but rather the judgment that something else
is more important than fear.*

Should I confront my rapist?

Most rape victims never want to see their perpetrator again, and feel deeply upset if they do encounter him. But occasionally, a woman will feel compelled to seek out her perpetrator and confront him. Almost always, her reason for doing this is to question him about his reasons for the rape. She is hoping that he will acknowledge the rape as real and provide some type of information to her that will fill in the gaps of her understanding. Very rarely will a woman want to confront a rapist purely to unleash anger on him; although it is common and normal to fantasize about doing so, it is uncommon that women actually undertake that project.

Research into this issue is clouded because there are so many variables to consider before knowing whether confrontation is the right thing to do: the circumstance and time of the rape, the type of rapist he is, his propensity to use violence, and your own emotional mindset. On this issue, forensic psychiatrist Dr. Robert Simon wrote,

> In some cases, confronting a rapist may burst his fantasy and bring his rape attempts to an end. In other instances, confrontation and resistance may trigger lethal violence from the rapist. As we have seen, some rapists are stimulated by resistance, others to expressions of fear.[1]

Aside from the safety concerns of confronting a man with a history of violence, there is the psychological damage that may come as a result of doing so. I'm worried

---

[1] Simon, Robert, MD. "Why Do They Rape? Examining The Inner Lives Of Rapists." In *Bad Men Do What Good Men Dream*, 1996, P88.

about this. If you confront a past abuser, they seldom (almost never) acknowledge their actions or respond to your needs. It is extremely rare that an abuser of any type, and in particular a rapist, will offer anything but denial and counter-criticism back at you. This means you don't actually get the answers you need from them, which can even cause you to regress into wondering all over again, "am I crazy?" When I interviewed men in prison convicted of rape, nearly every one of them still protested to me that they are innocent. These men, sitting in cells, convicted by *proof* from DNA, would still insist that they had never committed a crime, that it was consensual, that the woman was lying, and so on. Be prepared that if you confront a rapist, he is likely to reflect these same beliefs back at you as a counterattack, and it will hammer at the very same self-doubts you may already have. *You will not find answers or closure from your rapist.*

This is especially true if your rapist has never faced any consequence for the assault. If men in prison can continue to deny their guilt in the face of proof, then men who have had no consequences at all will deny guilt with even more ease. Sadly, rape is one of the least-successfully prosecuted violent crimes in America for several reasons. Investigators lack funding to test all DNA, and many "rape kits" of evidence sit in storage in police departments, untouched for years. District Attorneys are salaried, so they are inclined to prioritize cases that they can likely win which protect their "success rate" for elections.[2] Still, if an arrest is made there is an 80% chance of prosecution, although fewer than 17% of prosecuted men will serve time in prison for the rape.[3] Altogether, only about 5% of *all* rapists ever spend time in prison.

So the deck is stacked against the victim of the crime. Many rapists will actually convince themselves that the lack of legal consequences is proof they had committed no crime ("I didn't get caught, so you can't say I did anything wrong!"). Be aware that if you confront a rapist, he is very likely to deny any guilt or wrongdoing, robbing you of your goal of finding answers. His clever denials may also spur you into a flood of sudden self-doubt, questioning your own strength and even reconsidering whether you were raped at all; his denial can often trigger a rush of "maybe it's just me/I interpreted it wrong/I made a mistake/I shouldn't have caused trouble"-types of thoughts.

But here's the other thing: if you need something from *him* to get past this stuck point, it returns control *to* him over how your life continues. It's as if you are still missing part of a puzzle, and you need to get that piece from him before you can be complete, or unlock some door of understanding. If he chooses to grant you the missing piece of knowledge you seek, you believe you can proceed. But if he denies you that closure, you're stuck in front an incomplete puzzle or a locked door you can never pass through.

You've taken your power back from him by beginning to recover, so don't hand it back over by endowing him with the key to your emotional future. It gives him, and his choice to respond or not, all the power in what happens next.

Even if your best fantasy could come true about your rapist and he answered every question, acknowledged every fact, would it really help you heal? Even if he apologized and begged forgiveness, and stood before you as a new man who is somehow

---

[2] For more information about police reports and prosecution, see
http://www.justicewomen.com/handbook/part2_d.html or read Amanda Konradi's 2007 book, *Taking the Stand: Rape Survivors and the Prosecution of Rapists.*
[3] http://www.rainn.org/statistics/punishing-rapists.html

repentant for all the guilt of his crime, how would that help *you*? The apology would mean a lot, but you would still have all of your nightmares. You would still have your flashbacks. If you were a self-injurer, you would still have to contend with those urges. If you began a series of hurtful sexual relationships after your rape, you would still have all of that to address. You would still have your hurt. Trauma cannot be healed by anything your perpetrator might do.

If you are hoping to find some breakthrough in recovery through the act of seeking answers or insights or apologies from a rapist, then I must challenge your concept of what recovery is. This is a view of recovery that needs to wither away and die, because rapists do not hold keys to a survivor's recovery. Rapists do not hold answers to the question "why?" Rapists do not have insights into the ways you are hurt, or how to heal. Rapists tend to defend what they've done as normal, even deserved. And a rapist's words, even a miraculous "I'm sorry," cannot cleanse the hurt and anguish from the rape itself. Your recovery comes from sources other than him; it comes from within you. It comes from a network of relationships with other survivors. It comes from spirituality. It comes from self-education and public activism for other survivors. But the answers to your questions will not come from your abuser.

If you decide to confront your rapist, there are some considerations for personal safety—physically and emotionally—you should arrange. I have described my concerns, but I cannot claim that confronting a rapist is always wrong, or always right. It may be a disastrous choice, but for some survivors it may be the perfect thing to do. It depends on the reasons and methods of the confrontation.[4]

First, tell your therapist in advance that you are considering this! So many women embark on this confrontation all by themselves and conceal their intention from their therapist. One young woman explained to me, "I thought my therapist [a colleague of mine] would be mad at me!" No decent therapist would be angry about your choice, just concerned. (And if you are in a setting where you fear your therapist's anger, this alone is a problem to address! If fear of a therapist's anger impedes you, it's certainly not time to confront someone whose anger has *really* manifested violently in the past.)

Telling your therapist in advance can help them prepare you for the emotional upheaval of the event. They may also want to arrange a special session with you afterward to help you manage emotional fallout from the confrontation.

Second, never confront your abuser or rapist alone. Always be in a public, safe place, with a trusted peer near you. Have a phone with you.

Never engage in negotiation with your abuser. Abusers and rapists will regard this as a sign of weakness, not a sign of assertiveness or equality.

Never let your perpetrator refer to the rape using the words "we," as in "what we did." Abusers like to impose a "shared psychosis" upon their victims, which means they try to persuade their victims to buy into the perpetrator's own view of the abuse as a

---

[4] Cameron, C. (1994). Women survivors confronting their abusers: Issues, Decisions, and Outcomes. *Journal of Child Sexual Abuse*, 3. 7-35. See also: Roush, Dona June. "A Qualitative Study Of Sex Abuse Survivors' Experience Of Confronting The Perpetrator." Doctoral Dissertation, 1998. http://etd.lib.ttu.edu/theses/available/etd-09262008-31295013250815/

relationship rather than as a crime. The rape is about what *he* did, not what "we" did. Confront such language every time it is uttered.

Do not try to develop an understanding of him or why he did what he did. Attempts to learn whether he was abused or whether he had some personal difficulty that may have contributed to his actions is a form of excuse-making for him. Nor should you allow *him* to use these excuses either. After all, being abused or misunderstood does not create a rapist; women are abused and misunderstood too, yet women constitute only about 2 out of every 1000 rapists. Rapists can be people who were either abused or not, so don't allow some vague, fuzzy notion of "understanding his past" to distract from his pure guilt.

Never offer your rapist any form of intimacy. This sounds obvious, but I have known quite a few women who actually maintain some form of connection to their rapist, either by "hanging out" together, not leaving a party where he is, or replying to his text messages. One woman I worked with had even "friended" her rapist on Facebook.

Never try to guilt him into remorse by describing your life since the rape, including the pain and heartache you have endured, or the coping and success you have found in spite of him. Your life is none of his business. Describing your pain in the time since the rape can backfire by impressing him with just how powerful he really was over you. (Research suggests that the only confrontation that actually had a chance of producing new insight into the hurtfulness of their actions is confrontation that comes from *other men,* since rapists tend to discount the feelings of women and are often deluded into thinking that their sexual aggression is "normal guy stuff.")

Finally, and this is the most important thing of all, confront your rapist *only* because there is something you need to *say,* not something you need to *hear from him.* Decide in advance that his response, no matter what it is, will be irrelevant to you. You are not going to seek comfort, answers, or insights from him. You are going to personally express something *you* need to express. When he argues back, do not respond to any of what he says. Instead, use "bulletproof words" such as *however* and *nevertheless.* For example, if he tries to claim you consented or wanted the rape, reply, "However you see it, you have no right to treat anyone with such viciousness as you did me. However you excuse it in your own mind, what you did was abominable and it is you, not me, who deserves the guilt for it." Imagine his words rushing past you in the breeze so they don't get caught in your head.

An alternative to direct confrontation is to write a letter to your perpetrator, laying out what you would like to say to him or them if you could. This is not a letter that you will actually deliver; its purpose is to expel the emotions that you keep within yourself. Victoria wrote this letter to her multiple attackers:

> To Greg, Mike, and those of you whose names I can't recall or never knew—
>
> You are strangers to each other, but you all share something in common. Me. More specifically, my innocence. I'm not talking about my virginity; I gave that to someone I love and I gave it of my own free will. I'm talking about innocence.
>
> What do I mean, "Innocence?" I mean having faith in others, trusting them, trusting myself, having a sense of awe and wonder at life's mysteries, and a

belief and faith that the world is fair and just. Some of you stole pieces of my innocence from me and some of you were unwitting recipients of my own self-theft. Regardless of how you came to possess it, you all hold pieces of my innocence—my soul.

I want it back. All of it. Make no mistake: I'm not *asking* for it to be returned. I'm expressing my *intent* to reclaim that which is rightfully mine. I haven't yet figured out how I will reclaim my innocence, my birthright. I will love again, trust again, hope again, and be inspired again. I will be worthy again. I will love myself again.

None of you can stop me, and I will no longer stop myself.

A letter such as this can help you reconnect your emotions, direct the anger and blame where it ought to go, set a mandate for your own recovery, and prepare yourself with the words to say if you ever do encounter your rapist again and confront him.

If you have sufficient evidence to succeed, you can also file a lawsuit against a rapist. Lawsuits can demand compensation for pain and suffering, medical care, costs of therapy, time missed from work, and any other damage. Check http://www.rainn.org/public-policy/sexual-assault-issues/state-statutes-of-limitations for a chart of current state-by-state statutes of limitations for sexual assault. More and more states are eliminating the statute of limitations on rape altogether, as long as forensic evidence was collected *during* the initial time limitation.[5]

What if I see my rapist again unintentionally?

Some of my clients have done exceptionally well after therapy, only to hit a brick wall and fall back when they have inadvertently seen their rapist again in public. This can happen in several ways: what if you are a student, and he attends the same school? What if your perpetrator is a family member? What if you see each other at the mall or a gas station? What if you go to a party and he's there?

Even though you may have pictured his face in memory after memory for a long time, there's nothing as dreadful as actually seeing the person himself. There may be sudden feelings of panic and shakiness, and all the strength and confidence you've built up may wobble as if you were made of gelatin.

It is important to understand why these physical symptoms occur if you ever happen to see him again. Remember that the part of the brain responsible for fight-or-flight reactions is the amygdala. The amygdala scans all incoming senses—sight, sound, smell, touch—for any patterns that it recognizes as danger signals. When its scanner hits a "match," it sounds the alarm that temporarily reprograms your entire brain to enter "survival mode" rather than "stop and think about it" mode. Seeing your rapist is one of the strongest triggers there is!

---

[5] http://www.rainn.org/what-should-i-do/criminal-statutes-of-limitation/index.html

Despite all your best self-talk, empowering music in your car, journaling, and therapy, your brain reverts back into "trauma survival" mode: hyperventilating, tunnel vision, adrenaline, and fear, all of which are evolutionary adaptations to danger that work really well in the wild, but not so well in the aisle of the Buy-And-Bag Grocery.

Your reactions to seeing your rapist are probably perfectly normal. The problem is that many of my clients want so desperately to be able to stand up to him with warrior-like stamina and face him down, and when they find themselves quivering in the corner of a bathroom instead they tell themselves, "Damn, I'm just a wimp after all!" This self-talk ignites a sequence of more self-criticism, blame, and feeling powerless, none of which you deserve.

Fortunately, there is a way to prevent the amygdala from involuntarily taking over your brain with "trauma survival" instructions, and that's to consciously pre-plan for what you will do if your amygdala sounds the "warning" alarm upon seeing him. You may not be able to permanently stop your amygdala from sounding the alarm (and you wouldn't want to shut it off if you could; it keeps you from aimlessly wandering into dangerous places), but you *can* create a new set of instructions for it to send to your brain. If you can pre-determine what your amygdala will tell your brain to do upon seeing him, it will replace the amygdala's automatic message: "Panic! Hyperventilate! Faint! Hide! Shiver!"

If you want to prepare yourself to respond differently if you see your rapist, you will have to devote careful time to deliberately creating a new plan. It is important that you write your plan, don't merely think about it, because writing it down engages more parts of the brain and implants these plans into them more securely.

The first consideration in creating your plan is safety. If you see your rapist at a party, for example, that might be a strong indication it's time for you to leave! You probably should not confront him, attack him, or verbally accuse him in public, especially if you are intoxicated. Just leave. You don't have to explain to anyone why you need to leave, but make a contract with yourself *right now*, while reading this, that if you see him in a social setting, you will make your own safety a priority over anything else.

Journal: What are some examples of settings where it would be safer to leave than stay if you saw your rapist?

What statements will you begin to immediately tell yourself silently if you see him in public?
Examples:
- I'm okay; he can't hurt me now.
- I'm in control of what happens now, not him.
- I'm not going to panic. I'm going to stay in control of myself so I will be safe.
- If he makes rude expressions or comments toward me, I won't let them inside. They'll just bounce off and I'll deal with them later.
- I don't have to prove anything to him or myself. I just have to be calm.
- The only reason he had power last time was because I was terrified or confused. I'm not anymore, and now I know what he's like. That takes away his power!
- He's just a person. He has no abilities to control or hurt me.

- This is a tough moment for me, but I'm not going to harm myself after this is over. This is my moment to win power back by not collapsing.
- I'm not going to give him the satisfaction of seeing me whither.
- It angers me to see that his life is going on while I feel stuck, but the truth is that I'm the one who's really changing for the better. He's still the same a--hole.
- He may think he's cool and powerful, but in the end more people's lives will be improved by what I'm doing than anything he can ever do.
- There are things I would like to say to him, but it only gives him my attention and makes him think he matters in some way. If I lose it on him, it makes me look psycho. Dignity is my new weapon instead.
- I'll just blast Ani DiFranco's songs "Willing to Fight" and "Shameless" and "Superhero" from my car on my way home.

What actions will you *not* do if you see him again? It's important to rule certain responses out as "off limits" so that you don't perform them instinctively. Throwing a drink at him or vandalizing his car, for example.

If he sees you and speaks to you, what do you plan to say? You might want to write two versions of this one: first, what you would *like* to actually say, and second, what you probably *should* say instead. The first draft may be full of venom, which is fine—he deserves it!—but it won't actually help with your anxiety. The old notion of "letting off steam" isn't really true; going off on this guy in public tends to make women feel more anxious, not less, in real life. The second version, what you actually ought to say, must be short and to the point. For example, "I don't think we have anything to discuss." Or "I have no desire or intention of interacting with you again. Your past behaviors have shown you to be a person with no value to my life." And then leave without waiting for a reply.

If he mocks you, smirks, or tries to humiliate you, what will you do? I have *never* heard a single account from a woman in which it was productive to participate in a combative encounter with an abuser. Not once have I heard a "success story" in which a woman found just the perfect thing to say or do to neutralize a perpetrator in his tracks. In every story in which a woman has attempted comebacks or retaliation, the ultimate result has been a resurgence of panic, depression, fear, and embarrassment. The only outcome I have heard women consistently describe as positive and satisfying is to confidently walk out with class and dignity. Just leave. This is not a form of "running away scared," or a form of him "winning" again; on the contrary, this is a superb way in which *you* reclaim power and control from him.

If he stalks or harasses you, what will you do? Stalking is usually done to try to force some type of relationship to happen between the stalker and victim, but it can also occur simply to provide a sense of power to the stalker by frightening and humiliating the other person. Stalking is a high-risk, abusive behavior; it is not just creepy, it is also a crime.

Some stalking behaviors:

- Hanging around at your workplace or neighborhood.
- Phone calls, with or without messages. Calling and hanging up repeatedly count as harassment!
- Watching and tracking you; contacting people who know you to gather information about you. This can also including going through trash, public records, or even using detective agencies to monitor you.
- Retaliatory behaviors against you, such as filing or threatening lawsuits or false arrest charges against you, threatening suicide to you to manipulate you.
- Sending or leaving written notes, including emails or text messages.
- Sending manipulative gifts. These could be falsely romantic "flowers, cards" or purely bizarre and disturbing (pornography, rape jokes, photos or souvenirs from the rape).
- Lying to others about you in order to undermine your support network, which isolates you and expands the stalker/rapist's power and control.
- Threats and intimidation. This can include vandalism, physical assault, stern eye contact and facial expressions, "slashing the throat" motions, etc.
- Cyberstalking: using the Internet to harass or embarrass you. They may post websites or message board test about you, or they may even access your computer using spyware, keyloggers, etc. (Note: replying to you or your messages online does *not* constitute stalking/harassment. There is a reasonable expectation that a person may respond to public commentary that pertains to him/her, so be aware that if you post online about an individual, they are entitled to respond!)

Document *every* incident! Rather than ignoring the behavior, begin to keep a journal that records the time, date, and details of the harassment. Stalking does not always stop by ignoring it, so eventually you might need documentation to verify that you are being harassed. You will be tempted to ignore the behavior, telling yourself it will stop eventually. When you document an incident in your journal, include these details:
- Name of person committing the harassment;
- Date and time of day of the incident;
- Location of the incident;
- Exact details of the incident (including any spoken quotes);
- Any eyewitnesses

Keep any evidence such as emails, messages, gifts, or take pictures of graffiti/vandalism. Police reports are superb sources of documentation, so you may choose to contact police at every incident, regardless of whether they seem helpful or not. Each call generates a saved report that can be used legally to verify your claims against the stalker/perpetrator.

Make it clear to him that you do not want his attention. Only do this in person if the stalker has confronted you in person; otherwise, do not personally initiate contact, even to deliver this message. It is best if you have *no* contact with him while he is harassing you, because one of his goals is to force you to have contact of some type. I am not suggesting you should ignore the behavior; I am advising that someone else contact the stalker in your behalf to deliver the clear message that you will have nothing to do with him. That messenger could be a friend, teacher, manager, police officer, or someone else you can trust. It is also important that this message be the *only* message conveyed to the stalker; your messenger should not then continue to discuss or debate the matter with the stalker. Simply make the clear statement, and leave.

If you are being stalked or harassed at school or work, you may have special legal rights! By law, *any* school employee is required to intervene in your behalf if you report harassment. That means teachers, the lunch lady, the bus driver, or the maintenance man. They will report the complaint to the school administration. If schools have received reports of sexual harassment or stalking and they do not respond to protect you, they can be held liable in lawsuits; cases as high up as the Supreme Court have held that you have a constitutional right to harassment-free, safe education. See Nan Stein's book *Classrooms and Courtrooms* for specific cases and more information.

Likewise, many companies now have strict policies about harassment at work. Check your employee handbook first to find out whether a report should be made to a supervisor or to Human Resources directly, and what mandatory actions they will take, so that you are guaranteed certain courses of action if you want them, but not caught up in those actions if you don't want them.

Remember that stalking laws cut both ways: don't stalk or harass *him* either.

How Do I File a Complaint Under My State's Stalking Statute?
[From The National Center for the Victims of Crime Protocol, used with permission]

To file a complaint that will trigger an arrest and prosecution, it must be accompanied with sufficient evidence to establish "probable cause" that the stalker engaged in conduct that is illegal under the state's stalking statute. If law enforcement officials do not witness such conduct first-hand, it is often up to the victim to provide them with the evidence necessary to establish probable cause.

Again, victims would be well-advised to obtain a copy of their state's stalking statute[6] in order to gain a clear understanding of what conduct constitutes an offense under the statute. While most state stalking statutes are written in laymen's terms, the exact meaning of those terms is not always clear. Victims may wish to consult with law enforcement officials, prosecutors, or a private attorney for an explanation and interpretation of the specific stalking statute in question.

In other words, stalking victims are often put in a position of having to first prove their case to a law enforcement official before being afforded the opportunity to prove their case before a court of law. It is for this reason that it is crucial for stalking victims to

---

[6] Online at http://www.ncvc.org

document every stalking incident as thoroughly as possible, including collecting and keeping any videotapes, audiotapes, phone answering machine messages, photos of the stalker or property damage, letters sent, objects left, affidavits from eye witnesses, notes, etc. Experts also recommend that victims keep a journal to document all contacts and incidents, along with the time, date and other relevant information.

Regardless of whether or not they have sufficient evidence to prove a stalking violation, victims wishing to file a stalking complaint with law enforcement officials should do so at the earliest possible point in time. In some cases, victims may also be able to file a complaint in the jurisdiction where the offender resides, if it is different from the victim's.

If law enforcement officials refuse to investigate, or if they are not responsive to a complaint filed, victims may always directly approach their local prosecutor (also known in various jurisdictions as, the district attorney, state's attorney, commonwealth's attorney or state solicitor).

It is also recommended that any person who suspects or believes that they are currently being stalked should immediately seek the advice and assistance of local victim specialists in developing a personalized safety plan or action plan. Victim specialists can be found at local domestic violence or rape crisis programs -- which should be listed under "Community Services Numbers" or "Emergency Assistance Numbers" in the front section of the local phone book -- or in victim assistance programs located in most local prosecutors' offices and in some law enforcement agencies -- which should be listed under "Local, City or County Government" in the Blue Pages of the local phone book.

Seeing him does not sabotage your power

To my knowledge, and according to accounts from the hundreds of clients I have served in rape recovery therapy, there is *no single trigger* more powerful than seeing your perpetrator. Of all the possible reminders and anxiety-producers you will encounter—sights, sounds, smells, anniversaries, etc.—actually *seeing* him is the whopper of all triggers.

I have seen client after client "stumble" in their recovery after the unexpected trigger of seeing their rapist in public. They may have done fantastically and gathered all sorts of strength and power back to themselves, and then this one incident seems to demolish it all. But the important word here is "seems." I want you to remember that if you happen to see your perpetrator in public (including in court, if you are prosecuting), you may experience setbacks and struggles that *seem* to strip you of all your earned strength and power.

More than one former client of mine has had this experience. A young woman I once worked with had seen her rapist at a party—he saw her, smirked at her, and went back to pouring drinks down the throat of his new girlfriend—and she lapsed into days of heavy drinking, dissociation, and suicidal thoughts, alienating from all close relationships. "I felt ruined, like he was making all the decisions for me again," she said after returning to counseling sessions with me. "I wanted to have all the strength I had worked for, and in the end it was like I had no strength at all. I said if I ever saw him again I would crumble, and that's exactly what I did."

She talked about this moment extensively in therapy, and was able to realize that she felt anger not only at him for being there, having a party life, and seeming unaffected and even smug about what he had done to her, but she was also angry at herself. She had worked so hard and had built up so much strength that she wanted to pass any test in her recovery. When she had a nervous breakdown after seeing him, her conclusion was, "I have failed, I am not strong, I accomplished nothing. I'm right back where I started, and he has all the power—all he had to do was smirk, and down I go."

In one session, I asked her to list all of the ways he still had any sort of power or strength that exceeded her own. Thinking for a moment, she said "physical strength." We talked about how physical strength is simply a matter of biology, not a virtue or character trait, yet for her entire life this young woman had been taught that physical strength gave men the ultimate power to be unquestioned, sovereign, and privileged. She had been socialized to see physical strength as superior to any of her own strengths, and although she did not intellectually believe such things, her lifelong emotions kicked in at the sight of her rapist. When I asked her to describe the ways she was stronger than her rapist, she stammered, bounced her leg nervously, and went blank. "I…I don't know."

What she and I had to work on, then, was not a complete rebuilding of her strength and power, but a self-reminding of the power that *still existed within her*. She had taken on the issue of rape, and beaten it. She hadn't merely squeaked by; she had *nailed* it with flying colors. It wasn't that her rapist actually had power over her, it was that her self-talk lapsed back into its former script: "I can't do this; if I struggle, then I'm failing; I have no survivors as allies with me in this process; I'm alone in this agony…"

A huge part of what triggered this pain for her was that her rapist had appeared at the party with a girlfriend. Her personal guilt, which she held inside for a long time before she was ready to share it with me, was that she was afraid that the new girlfriend may be his next target, and yet my client had been so paralyzed she was unable to "save" her. Her belief was that she had failed not only herself, but failed the other woman—and by extension, *all* women—by not heroically rescuing the new girlfriend from a monster. It was difficult for her to separate being a survivor with being a savior, and to overcome the belief that if she wasn't saving someone (everyone) else, she was somehow betraying them.

But because this is the biggest trigger of them all, the monster at the end of the maze, the final showdown between the hero and the villain, it is perfectly normal to struggle and stumble at first. For any woman—you—to expect yourself to sail through it and cope perfectly the first time is to hold yourself to an unreasonable standard that has failure and self-blame built right into it. What any rape survivor must be able to do in this experience is to simply *forgive* herself for how difficult it is to work through this trigger. It will not be easy, it *will* send you spiraling at first, and you may begin to doubt yourself because of it.

So if you do see your perpetrator, and if the sight of him triggers an avalanche of distress and horror and regression, this is what you must remember:

1. It's not a failure on your part that this is tough for you. There is no bigger trigger than this. Give yourself permission to have an imperfect response, without assuming it means you have totally failed.
2. Nobody—*nobody!*—copes flawlessly with this the first time. Every woman in this situation later wishes afterward that she had responded differently. Not reacting the way you hoped you would is perfectly normal. If you are waiting for a time when things happen perfectly in your recovery, it will never happen.
3. Hitting a wall because of this trigger does not mean you are defeated, your strength is an illusion, or that you cannot recover.
4. If your distress has led back to a lapse in alcohol use, self-injury, or other harmful behaviors, do not wait passively for them to subside; retake control over yourself again as quickly as possible. Panicking and feeling distressed when you see him does not drain your strength and power; these behaviors *will* however.
5. The victory will mean more to you the more you have to struggle to win it. That's not very consoling at this moment, but it's absolutely true. It's one of those struggles that will scare you to death, yet is ultimately worth it.
6. This is the final battle, the last stuck point, the biggest challenge, to overcome. Don't flee it, literally or symbolically. This is the last locked door before total freedom. Hate it, fear it, struggle through it—and do it anyway. Once you have overcome this, what is left?

For help with stalking/harassment issues:

http://www.ncvc.org/ - National Center for Victims of Crime

http://www.thehotline.org/ - National Domestic Violence Hotline

http://www.haltabuse.org/ - Working to Halt Online Abuse

God help you if you are a phoenix
And you dare to rise up from the ash
A thousand eyes will smolder with jealousy
While you are just flying past
-Ani Difranco

Why does it emotionally destroy me when people downplay or misunderstand my rape?

Even when recovery has begun and progress continues, you may still be very vulnerable to the criticisms, or perceived criticisms, of others. Some people may ask questions that are simply insensitive. Others may struggle to say "the right thing," but instead utter something that really offends and bothers you. And sometimes people are just jerks who have ignorant opinions about the issue of rape. I once had a young client whose father *used* her rape against her as a form of discipline: "If you don't mind me, I'll take you back [where the assault happened] and you can get yourself raped again! Then you can tell me if it's worth it to not follow my rules!"

Misguided comments usually come from people's common misunderstanding of rape as a sexual event. Without good information about rape, people still believe that rape is the end result of sexual libido (horniness) that gets out of control. As a result, many people don't even know why their own misinformation is wrong—they see rape as a form of aggressive sex, as rape has often been romanticized in media (which is why people in the media still refer to sexual abuse of students by teachers as "affairs," or regard boys who were molested by female abusers as "lucky"). The misguided view of rape believes that the goal of rape is sex. "Men lose their judgment about sex," the belief goes, "and can't think straight in those situations."

The real truth is that rapists use sex to get power. Sex is the method, not the goal, of rape. (This is also why heterosexual men rape other heterosexual men: it's not about sex or desire, it's about power and control). But until people see this as a hate crime rather than a sex crime, they still consider rape as a sexual issue. If it *were* just a sexual issue, it would be much easier to move past.

The idea of rape being "no big deal" (along with the comment "you should be over it by now" or similar ways of minimizing the trauma) is repulsive to you because it denies the core truth that you have struggled so hard to embrace: that it *was* a trauma which did not invite and tried to resist, and it has been life-changing. The question "was it really no big deal?" becomes a stuck point because it drives a wedge between what you've worked so hard to achieve, versus the belief that people will forever misunderstand you. At this point in your recovery it's usually not so much that people's comments have you wondering if they're actually right—you know by now that they're not right—it's that people having those beliefs at all causes to you see just how distant other peoples' beliefs are from yours. The more ignorant the comment, the larger the gap of blindness that separates people from really understanding you—their ignorance becomes *your* loneliness.

People's ignorant comments appear to prove your worst fear: that you really are impossible to understand, or that your feelings really are completely unique and alien. When someone makes a rude or dismissive comment to a survivor about rape, there can still be a tendency for the survivor to interpret the comment as proof of *her own* defective thinking, rather than proof of the *critic's* defective thinking.

I once had a teen make a rude joke during a presentation I was giving. He made the comment that "women like it, and if they can't stop it they might as well lay back and enjoy it." Right in front of the entire audience, I verbally *nuked* this kid, until he was little more than a greasy spot in his chair. I lit into him hard, and sternly told him how ashamed of himself he should be. And I didn't let up: I went off! "How *dare* you?! I can't believe something so unbelievably ignorant just came out of your mouth!" (and other choice statements).

Later, I felt guilty like I'd lost control, lost my cool, and acted horribly. But when I consulted with my peers who also work in rape prevention and treatment, they affirmed my response completely. They made a superb point: Not only did that kid need strong confrontation, but the rest of the *audience* needed to see it. They need to *see* an example of someone rebuking that kind of ignorance, refusing to coolly tolerate it, and opposing it with passion, not just a blasé "well, let's talk about that idea…" style. So few people ever see anyone oppose and correct rape myths with much passion, and we need to see incorrect beliefs being confronted--not just in the dull tone of pamphlets, articles, and books, but with energized and strong voices. Besides, they pointed out, there may have been girls in the group who were rape victims, who needed to see an advocate on their side. They—just like the boy—needed to see *anyone* stand up to those kinds of comments so they would know that they're not totally alone.

The tendency to "discount the positive" can also be part of the reason why you may be especially sensitive to negative comments about your rape. I had a group of men and women together in therapy for depression once, and a woman finally made the intellectual connection between her rape a year ago and her depression right now. She began to expound on how her rape had affected her and what she was doing to recover from it. When she was finished, the entire group applauded and cheered her. Well, almost; there was one younger guy in the group who sort of snickered and smirked just a little bit. But twelve other people had *applauded* for her! Literally, they clapped and cheered!

About a month after she discharged from the group, this young client returned to treatment again. As we were reviewing her past progress, I reminded her of that ground-breaking group experience. But as I described the group, she was completely baffled and didn't remember *anything* that matched my description. What she did remember, though, was that one guy in the group who smirked! When I asked her, "But what about the other dozen people, men and women, who clapped and cheered for your breakthrough?" her eyes widened in amazement.

"People clapped for me?" she asked.

She truly could not remember the dozen people who applauded her. She remembered the one jerk.

It can be very difficult to face people whose beliefs about rape are so distorted. There are a couple of things you can do, though. First, remember that at one time *you* probably had misunderstandings about rape. You've had to fight an entire war inside of you to replace them with better beliefs. Someone who hasn't done the same amount of work as you won't be as insightful as you about rape.

Second, remember that having incorrect information about rape isn't entirely that person's fault. Actually, I'd be amazed if most people *didn't* have some defective beliefs about rape because most of our education on the subject comes from garbage sources: movies, romance novels, TV dramas, gossip, advertising, and porn.[1] It's not fair, but it's true, that being a rape survivor gives you a new job to do: you become a source of information for other people, and hopefully that information is correct. Otherwise, people's knowledge about rape remains a blank bulletin board to be filled by whatever images are carelessly tossed out from media.

I have noticed one *positive* result of an encounter with an ignorant or negative person. In therapy groups, members are nearly always supportive and accepting of one another. I can go for months and not witness a single act of rejection or hostility. But once in a rare while, I will be surprised at someone's stark lack of sensitivity. There seems to be nothing positive at all about this, until we revisit the incident in hindsight.

During a session in which several women were processing their sexual assault experiences, one woman—who was not a participant in the topic—became extremely agitated. She hissed out, "Well here's an idea! If you don't want to be raped, quit being so stupid! You think the rest of us want to hear all this crap? Quit putting yourself in those situations, so the rest of us don't have to listen to it!" The entire group was shocked, and I confronted her directly, telling her firmly "that's enough!" and directing her to either stop, or leave.

What happened next was startling. Two young group members, who had been struggling with self-blame, challenged her. They angrily told her that they had a right to be heard, that their pain was as real as anyone else's, and nobody could order them to stop talking. Furthermore, they continued, her opinions about rape were terribly ignorant.

---

[1] Buddie, Amy M. and Miller, Arthur G. (August, 2001). "Beyond Rape Myths: A More Complex View of Perceptions of Rape Victims." *Sex Roles,* 45:3/4, 139-160

Mayerson, Suzin e., et al. (September, 1987). "The effects of rape myth pornography on women's attitudes and the mediating role of sex role stereotyping." Sex Roles (journal), 17:5-6, pp321-338.

Nagel, Barbara, et. al. (June, 2005). "Attitudes Toward Victims of Rape: Effects of Gender, Race, Religion and Class." *Journal of Interpersonal Violence,* 20:6, 725-737.

They angrily debated back at her why they had not "put ourselves in that position," how they had not been given a chance to withhold consent because of the force and terror used against them, and how it has affected them to be treated in this way. They also told their critic what it did to them to hear her feedback.

But that marked a turning point in their therapy. Until that point, these two patients had been very defensive and timid about their rapes. But when they were answering their insensitive critic, suddenly they were fighting back against her words, which had also formerly been their *own* critical self-talk. By debating back against those ideas, they were able to confront and defeat them. They found themselves saying things with conviction that they had been unable to say.

Where is the hand for me to reach?
Where is the moral I'll never teach myself?
In all the black, in all the grief,
I am redeemed.
-Charlotte Martin

What if my body had a sexual response during the rape?

To a degree far greater than in men, women express emotional sensations as physical ones. You may recall times when being depressed or upset resulted in the physical feeling of nausea, or a headache, or a tightened body. Food and appetite are often used as voices by women in distress, and a woman's body is regarded in our culture as the *primary* means of judging her worth as a person. While you and I may personally reject the use of physical standards as the measure of a person's value, we live in a society that generally does and we cannot help but absorb messages that suggest to us that what we feel about our bodies is a reflection of who we are as people.

One of the least-discussed but most significant aspects about sexual assault is the possibility that some women's bodies may experience a sexual response to the assault. While not common, it is quite natural that a woman would experience the physiological effects of arousal, and even orgasm, which can be extremely confusing and upsetting to her later. I have found that this single phenomenon can produce the strongest stuck points of all because of the guilt and shame it can cause the survivor, to the point that some have strongly resisted even discussing or reading about this experience.

Cassie had been in treatment four times with four previous therapists, but her substance abuse and self-injury persisted. She was in the throes of self-doubt because her earnest work hadn't seemed to produce lasting recovery from rape, and her conclusion was that she must simply be a weak, defeated woman. As we progressed through therapy, though, we came to the issue of "stuck points" in her story. Cassie had come to trust me, and began to talk one day with a very familiar phrase: "I've never told anyone this before, but..." She then disclosed what she thought was the most shameful thing in her whole life: she had experienced orgasm during her sexual assault three years earlier.

Cassie's stuck point was that she felt she had "led him on" by being sexually responsive during the assault, which stirred up a swarm of stinging thoughts she had kept to herself: Was it really rape? Was it something she subconsciously wanted or enjoyed? Was she guilty of causing what he had done to her? And if her body responded in such a way, did it prove she is profoundly mentally disturbed for such a thing? These thoughts made therapy with Cassie very challenging because they prevented her from accepting the truth that she shared no fault for her rape. Cassie was also extremely angry at her body, which she felt had betrayed her, and would angrily exclaim, "I f---ing HATE being a woman!" Cassie was trapped between two conflicted thoughts: "I hate what happened to me" and "what could it mean that I hated something that resulted in a sensation most people associate with pleasure?" Needless to say, this was a delicate matter requiring care and empathy.

Cassie's story is her own, but it also typifies the kinds of mental "blocks" and inward guilt that women can feel when they have experienced this kind of physical response. When I asked Cassie to summarize what she thought this buried secret really meant, she thought and answered, "The word 'no' doesn't seem to count. My own body didn't listen to it. So it's as if I never said it."

Part of the answer to Cassie's self-crucifying beliefs was a simple lesson in biology. She had believed that a physical sexual response to her rape meant that she had accepted, and even encouraged, her attacker's acts of violence. But as awkward as it was for her to help me discuss the biology of *her* body, she trusted me and it was important for her to understand some facts she had overlooked. For example, the production of moisture in her vagina was not a result of physical or psychological desire for what was happening to her. On the contrary, it was a form of *self-defense*. Her body had adapted to the sexual assault by responding in a way that would minimize injury and reduce the sensations of pain by secreting fluid so that the invasion by a penis would be less physically severe. By doing this, her body was not betraying her, but sparing her from whatever agony it could. Her body had allied with her, not with him, in doing this.

She also learned that the clitoris is a bundle of about 8000-30,000 nerve fibers, twice as many as are found in a penis and more than in any other part of a woman's body. During trauma, the sympathetic nervous system takes over physical functions of the body, and an evolutionary "fight-or-flight" response causes all of the body's nerves to become hypersensitive. While this adaptation is useful in prehistoric survival situations, it is an anachronism in situations like rape—but no less natural. Is orgasm "proof" that a rape victim "enjoyed it?" Absolutely not! In fact, in this context it is proof that her body was traumatized and responding as such; all of her body's physical systems become hyperactive for the sake of survival. The clitoris is part of the nervous system, and when it hyper-performs, it does so in a way that causes a specific physical feeling. This feeling is not necessarily an expression about pleasure, acceptance, consent, or desire; it is simply a physical reaction.

An analogy would be that when someone tickles you, even against your will, your body responds by laughing and smiling. These responses are programmed into the sensation of being tickled, but have *nothing* to do with enjoying or welcoming it; people will laugh during tickling even when they hate it.

Dr. Eliana Gil, a specialist in treating abuse and trauma, wrote about a brilliant technique to demonstrate this to an adolescent rape survivor she counseled. Dr. Gil's patient, Anna, felt the same shame and betrayal as Cassie did in my sessions, and this caused a similar obstacle to therapy. Dr. Gil brought a fresh onion to a therapy session with Anna, and began to slice it apart. As she did this, both she and Anna began to cry. "What's happening?" asked Dr. Gil. Anna described how the smell and fumes from the onion had caused her to become tearful. Dr. Gil pointed out that even though they were both crying, neither of them was sad.

This caused Anna to reconsider her beliefs about what a bodily reaction really says, or doesn't say, about a person's actual emotions. Anna was able to understand that sometimes the body has reactions that *seem* to represent certain emotions, but don't; they are purely biological behaviors. "It's like what happened to my body…when he touched me in certain places, I got wet, and I got off," Anna realized. Dr. Gil summarizes, "She now had a way of understanding that her orgasm was not compliance with sexual abuse, but a way in which her body reacted…Anna now had a new narrative about her early experiences."[1]

For many women, a sexual response during rape becomes a "trigger" for negative beliefs about themselves during later consensual sexual experiences. If you associate sexual response with assault or with "badness" in yourself, you may consciously or unconsciously suppress sexual sensations at all. Libido, sexuality, and even orgasm become misunderstood as immoral or dirty sensations that you does not want or deserve, and some women temporarily lose the ability to orgasm at all after a rape, which she previously may have been able to do. While some women become extremely sexually active in the aftermath of rape (which has nothing to do with pleasure, and more to do with feeling powerless and empty), many become actively disinterested in sex at all.

These self-judgments can cause a woman to be fearful of sex, to have to be intoxicated to have sex, to dissociate during sex, and even to have sexual thoughts and fantasies that are inconsistent with her own previous sexual identity. Others may even have sexual arousal responses while reading a book like this one, and may become horrified with themselves as "sick" or "perverted." But that is not at all what that means; it simply means that the body has associated certain physical responses with the memories of rape, and it has nothing to do with desire or pleasure. This is also not a permanent damage; sexuality can heal after rape and even become enjoyable again.

Lisa was anally raped at age 12, and had difficulty even talking about the assault because she was so embarrassed by the details. But as Lisa came to trust me, she opened up emotionally and shared some of her self-shaming beliefs about her rape. Lisa's rapist, an older boy, had groomed Lisa for rape by engaging in various forms of pleasurable touch at first. He had lavished positive attention on Lisa, and begun to affectionately caress her, and then kiss her. All of this felt good to Lisa, which made it hard for Lisa to cope with self-blame after her rape.

As a woman in her 30s, Lisa had become an addict of alcohol and methamphetamine, and had spent several weeks in a hospital after a suicide attempt. In therapy sessions with me, she was terrified to confess that at first she had liked the older boy's physical attention, which had been soft and gentle, not vicious. Lisa's stuck point was her

[1] Gil, Eliana. (1996) *Treating Abused Adolescents*, Guilford Press, New York, pp116-117.

belief that by responding pleasurably to these forms of touch, she had "sent the wrong signals" and "caused him to rape" her.

Furthermore, Lisa had subconsciously begun to link the pleasure of touch with the violence of rape. She shut off her body's receptiveness to pleasure because she feared that if she felt pleasurably stimulated again, it would lead to her being re-victimized. She also shamed herself as "bad" for feeling any sexual pleasure at all because she had believed that rape was a consequence of her pleasure feelings; in Lisa's mind, if she ever *did* want sexual stimulation as an adult, it would make her as sick as her rapist. Consequently, she tended to either dissociate during sex with her husband, or use drugs before sex.

In therapy, Lisa began to explore the differences between rape and sexuality. She had believed, for example, that being raped was her first sexual experience, and she was baffled when I responded that rape is *not* a sexual experience, and that she had not "lost" her virginity from rape. Lisa also believed that *all* sex was about power and control, which meant she expected rape-like feelings in any sexual encounter—even safe, consensual ones. Since she was either dissociated or drunk during sex, she had never really felt any sexual happiness that would challenge her beliefs. Because she blamed herself for "feeling good" during the victim-grooming stage before her rape, Lisa had carried intense shame for twenty years which deprived her of enjoying any pleasure from *authentic* lovemaking.

If any of this applies to you, do not avoid the issue in therapy! This can represent one of the most painful stuck points in your story, and until you can resolve your guilt and accept these issues as perfectly normal, blameless, physical functions they can continue to sabotage your recovery. Lisa had been in inpatient treatment for weeks without her story coming out. Cassie had attempted therapy four times before she was brave enough to address this stuck point, and the result was that four times she was unable to remain sober until this core of guilt and shame was exposed and extinguished.

I don't know what to do
Can the damage be undone?
I swore to God I'd never be
What I've become
　　　　　　-Beth Hart

Why did I become promiscuous after the rape?

Looking online for the topic of sexuality after rape, I came across a question posed by a young man asking for feedback about a girl he knew who had been raped, but who became very sexually active within months afterward. Sadly, many people's ignorance offered him such replies as, "I think she's lying to get attention. There's no comfort in other men's beds when a man has just violated you" and "I think she's totally fibbing! I can't see how she could have sex when she was just so recently humiliated and degraded (supposedly)."

While some women become very conflicted about sex and avoid any physical, visual, or psychological sexual stimulation, others may actually become hypersexual after trauma. I have had countless clients who embarked on a series of hurtful, loveless, and deeply humiliating sexual encounters after rape or sexual abuse, and very little literature gives any attention to this taboo topic. The stories I hear are very similar: "I didn't even like sex! I hated it! But I kept doing it."

"I had to be drunk off my ass to get through it."

"It got to the point where I'd tell a guy to bring a case of beer with him if he wanted to meet me, because I knew what would happen."

"It was just something that was *expected* of me, which I gave into because I didn't know any other way to be. I hated the expectations."

"I tried to play it off like I just had a wild party life, like I was 'Queen of the Girls Gone Wild,' but inside I was dying. And everyone thought I was so naughty!"

"Ugh! It wasn't even good! I just wanted the guys I was with to get it over with so they would leave me alone!"

"I've turned into such a slut."

"I'm nothing but a slut."

"I'm a slut."

I have never met a slut. The word isn't part of my daily vocabulary, but it's exactly the word I have heard countless women use to label themselves. I have met women who are commonly *called* a slut by others or by themselves, but whenever I look deeper than the label I always find someone else: I find an amazing girl who is hurting badly.

I am proposing a whole new way of describing this pattern. I suggest we end labels like "slut" or "promiscuous." And frankly, the word "hypersexuality" isn't much better; it's the same label perfumed with clinical terminology. I'm not even thrilled with the term "sexual self-injury," which is a term *I* coined to use with clients. If we want to understand the problem of sexual compulsivity after rape, we need to explore the concept of *sexualized grieving*.

Grief after rape can take many forms, and as a therapist I believe that *all* actions are efforts to meet a need. If we can understand behaviors as responses to unmet needs, what could we learn about the girl who labels herself "slut" and becomes passively sexually vulnerable to unloving partners? Instead of trying to label something, what if we tried to understand the hidden needs and hurts beneath it?

If I were to say that people express grief with alcohol, nearly everyone would understand and agree.

If I said that people express grief through drug use, nearly everyone would understand and agree.

If I said that people express grief through self-injury, nearly everyone would understand and agree.

But if I said that people can express their grief through sex, suddenly people stop and gasp, "say *what?!*"

If you became more sexually active and vulnerable after your rape, it is important to stop using negative self-labeling like "promiscuous" or "slut," and understand your process in a new way. Your sexual actions are *not* the result of your faulty morals, your badness, or your low worth as a woman. Chances are, you've been doing this and not even knowing why, perhaps not even enjoying it at all (even if you've pretended to). Your sexual actions are the result of your *pain*. It is your inner hurt, not your personal worth, that has driven this cycle.[1] Your actions are a sign of despair and grief that have no words yet, and can only be brought to life through certain behaviors. By routinely using sex to give voice to your emotions, you are reconnecting yourself to the meaninglessness and humiliation of your rape through meaningless and humiliating sex, in the effort to somehow give your grief an opportunity to finally emerge and become expressed. Instead, though, the cycle has probably added new layers to your grief by adding guilt, negative labeling, and perhaps even a social reputation that makes it even

---

[1] Hillis, S. D., et al. "Adverse childhood experiences and sexual risk behaviors in women: a retrospective cohort study." 2001 Fam Plann Perspect 33;5:206-11. "Women with a history of childhood physical or sexual abuse had a significant increase in risky sexual behaviors, including earlier sexual experiences and likelihood of greater than 30 partners."

harder for uninformed people to accept and support you as a victim of rape. Rachel journaled about the shame she had felt during her experiences of sexualized grieving:

> We have taught and allowed ourselves and everyone around us treat and even refer to us as "sluts" or "whores" because we self injure using sex. We don't allow anyone that can have a positive attitude on us near us and we don't believe anything positive they say to us or about us. So what the hell is wrong with us? This is what we want right? We want to heal, we want people to see and know us as a person, a strong woman, whole and healed, but we refuse to allow ourselves to become that.

Sexualized grieving is an attempt by a rape or sexual abuse victim to grieve her brokenness through the desperate effort to reconnect her body and emotions. There are several reasons why some women begin to use sexual activity as an expression of inner conflict.

For one, sex is continually represented as the ultimate path to happiness and pleasure. Right or wrong, this is the persistent legend about sex in *most* of its representations around us. Sex-as-pleasure messages rarely even hint at the possibility of consequences; from TV to movies to songs, females are shown as sexualized creatures. For the same reason that drugs and alcohol are appealing to trauma survivors, sex is promoted as a means of pleasure and fulfillment. When sex fails to provide that promised pleasure and delivers instead more layers of hurt, humiliation, and depression, a woman who has been raped is particularly likely to conclude, "this must prove there's something wrong with *me.*"

A brilliant woman who was in therapy with me shared her story with me about her sexual promiscuity after rape. She told me that she had begun seeking more and more male sex partners, and she had begun to notice that over time she had also sought men who were increasingly vicious. She even began telling them, "*make* it hurt!" She said to me, "and if they couldn't hurt me enough, I'd find someone else who would." My patient had eventually come to the heartbreaking conclusion, "I hated myself and was using men as a form of self-injury. I realized I was raping *myself,* again and again." Her response to this dawning insight was amazing: she realized that her approach to sex was addictive and lethal, and she had to stop. So she immediately pledged with herself to become celibate, and has kept that pledge now for three years (and counting). She explained, "I feel so free now! I am finally getting to know *me,* and I really like who I'm becoming."

Some women have described to me that being the initiator of sex—even meaningless or harmful sex—is a personal form of seeking control over the process of sex itself. One client, a 54-year-old woman, journaled to me,

> I know what it's like when I'm *not* in control of my body or my choices, and it's awful. I think I used sex afterward in an effort to *find* some sense of control, like, "let's see what happens when *I'm* the one who causes this to happen, instead of someone else." I used sex to feel like I could control others. Suddenly I could be the one to approach men, and they'd do exactly what I wanted them to. I hated the fact that it was sex, and only sex, that seemed to give me that power, but I felt so low as a woman that I thought it was all I had left.

This same client later returned to the topic of sex-as-power, and examined it more closely. She came to realize that promiscuous sex wasn't just her way of seeking control over her sexual self again, but also that she felt so damaged and empty inside that sex was the *only* means through which men would relate to her now. Her journaling reflected,

> I just knew I was a bad person. I had to be; I mean, I was raped, right? So that meant, in my mind, that if people really knew me on a personal level, they'd reject me. I'd lead with sex because it gave me a way to connect with people, but at the same time it shielded me from really being *known* by them. It was my way of trading: I'll let you know this part of me, but not the other parts of me, so that I can have connections without the risk of rejection. But what it really did was prevent anyone from connecting with me at all, and then gave me a dozen more reasons to believe I was bad.

Another young woman wrote in her journal,

> Since I was so young when it happened, my search for sexuality put me in the backseats and sleeping bags of lots of teenaged boys who must have thought they'd hit the mother-lode with a 13-14 year old girl who would allow so much to be done to her body by their hand. And, as horrible as it was, some of what had been done to me during the rape I 'taught' to the boys my brother brought home after school. So I have A LOT of guilt, and a lot of shame, and a lot to seek forgiveness for. But I am honest to a fault. I am honest with my accounts of my rape, I am honest with my therapist, and I am honest with myself.

Laura, one young client of mine, had another way to explain it; "I just thought [my rape] was sex. I said to myself, 'well, at least now I've had sex. I'll have something to talk to my friends about!' But I never did talk to them about it because I couldn't believe this (rape) is what sex really was…It's like, if this is what people are so happy about, and I hate it, what's wrong with *me*?" Laura did not initially recognize what happened to her as an assault, and thought it was the same kind of sexual experience that all her friends were having too.

Andrea, a 16-year-old, wrote,

> Every guy that I have been with has accused me of cheating on them. Sometimes I feel like I need to spend all my time with that person to prove that I didn't and wouldn't cheat on them.
>
> After that day [when I was raped], I think I became more sexually involved rather than less. I wasn't scared of guys doing things to me anymore and to an extent I liked it. I mean, if I *let* them do it, then it's okay right? Well at least that is what my mindset was. It just frustrates me now because I do like a lot of these things, and I feel like I'm supposed to hate them. I'm still not sexually active but I let guys do other things…Basically everything short of having sex or oral sex.

Some clients of mine have even returned to their perpetrators and sought relationships—even sexual ones—with them. When they realized later that they were raped, they felt deeply ashamed by their choices. This is particularly common in marriages or dating relationships where abuse happens; a survey by the National Victim Center in Arlington, Virginia, states that 10% of all sexual assault cases reported by women involve a husband or ex-husband. In such cases, the ongoing relationship may include continued sexual coercion. But in others, there may be a different explanation, as we will see.

A 16-year-old girl who had been raped explained her decision to return to the boyfriend who had raped her twice:

> One problem down. I told him I would start dating him, he just has to stop hurting people. He seems to be having a breakdown because he said he was sorry and that he just got mad, and hopefully having someone to care for him will help him stop, or so he says. I just hope he can find an answer to why he's doing these horrible things. I'm meeting him tomorrow to go out to some club. He also promised there is going to be no drinking or getting high. Well, maybe the only way to get over this rape is to help see why he did it in the first place, but he's won and the fight is over.

The danger in her mindset is clear. This is a VERY common path that leads women into relationships with abusers: "He seems sorry; he's going to change; he just needs someone to care for him." Nobody can love an abuser into wholeness, and that there is no such thing as an abuse victim who can rehabilitate their own abuser. The idea that he just needs someone to truly care for him is dangerous because it entitles his emotional needs and demands to a level of importance higher than yours. In this kind of relationship, you would find yourself trying harder and harder to "understand" and "help" him, and the worse her gets the harder you have to try to "fix" him. This is a deadly desire that many women have expressed: "I could heal if I just knew why he did it. And the way to find out why he did it is to give him another chance."

Linda, a 40-year-old client, had been raped at gunpoint by her first husband, which caused her to leave him immediately. But after she had left him, she returned to him twice for sexual intercourse. She was deeply ashamed to disclose this to me, and it represented a massive stuck point in her rape narrative. "Why would I have done that? How sick am I?" As we examined this history, several truths emerged. Linda had initially refused to believe that what he had done was rape, despite the unambiguous fact that it was. She had not wanted her last memory of him to be a traumatic one, and the only way she could undo the conflict between her reluctance to accept that she had been raped and the actuality of what happened was for her to conclude that *she* had simply misunderstood his sexual conduct.

In order to compile evidence that would support her "I-wasn't-really-raped" belief, Linda had to replace her last memory of her husband's assault with different memories. She had sought him, sexually, for the very purpose of constructing new memories that could overlay the traumatic one, and on which she could build her preferred beliefs about herself: "I wasn't really raped; it was just my misunderstanding of what he was doing. See? We had sex again, and it was fine. Doesn't that prove he's not a rapist and I'm not a victim?" For many women, sexual actions after rape are just that: an attempt to "prove" to one's self that she is not a "victim." But the actual outcome, unfortunately, is that her sexual actions cause her to have *more* self-blaming beliefs. In the mind of a rape or abuse victim, sex becomes evidence that you *are* bad and weak, rather than evidence that you're not.[2]

In some cases, sexuality isn't a woman's effort to escape from rape, but her effort to gather proofs and confirmation of her beliefs about men and rape. Victoria told me her stories of seeking sexual partners of the worst kind: incredibly abusive men. She would deliberately find men who were vicious, and then urge them to impose all manner of degrading, violent, and hateful actions upon her. With tears streaming down her face, Victoria told me that she had searched out more and more inhuman forms of sex, yet the slightest touch of someone she loved would make her nauseated. "Why am I this way?" she asked. "Am I just totally f----d up?"

As we processed this in therapy, several things emerged. Victoria had been using sex as a form of self-injury, in which she would inflict on her body what she thought it deserved. The reason she was becoming more ferocious is that she was also trying to find the limits of her humanness. "I knew that human instinct is to try to survive. I kept forcing more and more pain on myself, through sex, hoping that at some point my humanness would awaken and scream out in self-preservation. I wanted to shock myself into reviving, to see whether something human still remained," she said through tears. "When I never got into self-protection mode, I either had to push the limits further to see if *that* would finally do it, or I'd have to accept that I had no human survival instincts left."

But then why would she recoil from the sensitive touch of someone she loved? Victoria realized during therapy that another way to reconnect with her humanness is to respond to the positive touch of another person. But if she were to find a way to connect with someone in a way that clarified her value as a person, one consequence would be a sudden flood of shame; after all, how could a good human being also be committing such atrocities against herself? She wanted the will to resist and survive, yet she knew that this would also bring the realization that she had been self-abusive in her search for it. So Victoria began to seek *only* harmful touch, to avoid positive touch, and even to warn "decent guys" to stay away from her.

Morgan was convinced there were no such things as "decent guys" and perceived perpetrators all around her. Malekind was a fallen and disappointing form of life, in her view. She believed that men were fundamentally incapable of controlling themselves, and that even "nice" qualities were forms of camouflage designed to trick her into submission. So Morgan developed a test to prove her thesis: she would present herself as a sexual option in relationships with men, and then conclude her beliefs about men were correct as guy after guy flunked: as they enthusiastically accepted her sexual advances, she regarded them as just one more failure of men in her life. Her test became its own proof.

---

[2] Southern, S. "The Tie that Binds: Sadomasochism in Female Addicted Trauma Survivors." *Sexual Addiction and Compulsivity*, 9:4, January 2002, pp209-229. "Women who develop addictive disorders to survive life trauma present a wide array of variant behaviors...including self-injurious behavior, eating disorders, and sexual addiction...Survivors turn childhood tragedy into triumph through sadomasochistic re-enactments of life trauma."

This not only caused Morgan to pass through several years of unhappy and abusive relationships, it also caused her to develop two very strong beliefs: "I am a worthless slut," and "rape is inevitable." Since her sexual testing of men had "proven" to her with apparent accuracy that men cannot use sex respectfully, her natural conclusion was that every woman in every social situation was at risk for whatever form of rape would inevitably, unstoppably, happen.

Then something even more tragic happened: Morgan changed the reason for her use of sex. Instead of using it as a test of malekind's failures—which was heartbreaking enough for this young woman—she began to use sex as a form of self-sacrifice to *save* other women from the inevitability of rape. She believed that since rape was incvitable, and she was already ruined, why not allow men to dump their hate and abuse into her rather than into other women who were innocent? Morgan found an excruciatingly sad way to capture her thoughts: while lovers "make love" with one another, men "make hate" to her. She became the voluntary martyr, actively seeking out sexual abuse by guys so that other women would be spared their turns as the victims.

In her journal, Morgan wrote very explicitly that she saw herself as a "spoiled martyr," willing to be a target for men's sexual viciousness so that other, purer, women would be spared the shame. Morgan unabashedly described her plan to seek the attention of predatory men and spare other women from becoming the same empty, rotting, dishonored creature that she believed herself to be. Morgan fantasized that in some way she was owed countless debts of gratitude and thanks from women, who actually never knew Morgan had saved each of them by taking their place as the victim. This locked Morgan into an unending cycle of feeling worthless and ruined, sustained only by the false belief that she was redeeming herself by voluntarily absorbing more ruin night after night.

What is interesting in Morgan's perspective is her dual assumption that rape is inevitable, but that men who rape are yet able to make choices about their actions. She had reasoned (correctly) that rapists are making deliberate choices, as opposed to the myth that rapists simply lose control of their actions. Her conclusion, though, was that she could influence those choices by attracting the assault toward herself so that other women would be spared. She was living in a conflicted philosophy in which her own degradation was meaningless and meaningful at once; she thought of herself as having less and less value, except in her "merciful" role as the martyr/bait. This created a deadly combination of beliefs that could have literally killed Morgan if it had continued for much longer. By seeing hcr perpetual abuse as a way for her to still have worth, she had never questioned the ongoing cycle.

In therapy, she and I began to question these beliefs. "Have you ever considered," I asked, "that if rape is a socially-learned behavior, you are *contributing* lessons that support it?" Morgan was stunned and a bit annoyed, but I pressed on. "You see yourself as taking a 'hit' for other women so they never have to go through rape. But rapists don't usually rape once and then 'get it out of their systems.' They almost always continue to commit other rapes. So you haven't stopped the cycle of rape at all. And what you *are* doing is presenting a lesson about women that rapists will find appealing because it will support their beliefs."

Morgan's leg began to vibrate furiously as she considered these words. She stared intently downward at her journal, gazing at her handwriting.

I continued. "You're a brilliant young woman. But you're not showing these men what a brilliant woman really is, you're showing them that even brilliant, strong women are readily abusable. You're showing them that even the most amazing women are really there to be used, and willingly so. So your actions are teaching them lessons that support their rape beliefs. And when they're done with you, they move on in their lives to continue their behaviors, because in their minds, *you've* proven that their beliefs about women are right. That makes life *less* safe for the women around you, not more. You're not using yourself to change thoughts and attitudes about women, men and rape, you're *verifying* the myths some men have about women and rape."

"I never thought of it that way. Damn it, Matt!"

Risking that I could make one more point without Morgan shutting down, I uttered the most confrontational statement I had ever made to her. "You just might owe women an apology for how you've taught abusive men that their actions are justified, and that women really are available for their purposes. You may have saved some women from one loss, but you haven't given them any victories."

At this point, I am walking a fine line. I have to be able to point out the deadly truth about Morgan's beliefs and actions, without engaging in victim-blaming. I have to find the balance between bold accountability and shame. I am appealing to Morgan's feminism by framing this as an anti-woman ideology as opposed to a woman-saving practice, and I'm not sure if I've succeeded in breaking through or just pissing her off. But I know that if Morgan's thinking doesn't change, it will have fatal consequences because Morgan had developed a habitual use of binge drinking to help her proceed with each act of sexual self-sacrifice, plus self-injury to confirm and express her self-hatred, culminating in several serious suicide attempts as her way out of her shame.

Morgan's hand scurried across her journal, and I asked her what she's writing. She was writing down the things I had said.

She heard the point!

And I know it's all changed. Her thoughts about sex, her own worth, and her purpose as a woman in the world, will never be the same. Tearfully, Morgan cried "I can't believe what I've done! How could I have done that to *myself?* I deserve better!"

In one single session, Morgan had moved from "I am rotting at the core" to "*I deserve better!*"

After all this has passed, I still will remain
After I've cried my last, there'll be beauty from pain
Though it won't be today,
Someday I'll hope again
And there'll be beauty from pain.
-Superchick

Can sex be enjoyable again?
Why do I have to be numb to have sex?

While some women may recover their sense of sexual pleasure within a few months after rape, I have not encountered *any* rape survivors who did not experience some type of disruption of sexuality. In fact, "sexual dysfunction" (I dislike that term, by the way) is so common among survivors of rape that some studies have even discovered that the majority of women who report sexual avoidance or dysfunction have some type of sexual trauma in their background.[1] This suggests that sexual trauma is an extremely powerful disruptor of sexual pleasure later in life for most women who have experienced it.[2]

Sexual dysfunction can occur for many reasons, including diabetes, depression, some forms of birth control pills and antidepressants, illness, and eating disorders. So it's important not to assume that any disruption of your sexual life is automatically connected to rape, but it is also common sense that one of the profound effects of rape would be a

---

[1] Becker, JV; Skinner, LV; Abel, GG; and Treacy, EC. (1982) "Incidence and types of sexual dysfunctions in rape and incest victims." Journal of sex & marital therapy. Spring;8(1):65-74. "56% of these victims experienced sexual dysfunctions postassault; 71% of these subjects reported that the sexual assault precipitated the dysfunction. Fear of sex, arousal or desire dysfunctions were the most common sexual problems presented within this victim sample."
[2] Meston, C. M. and Heiman, J. R. "Sexual abuse and sexual function: an examination of sexually relevant cognitive processes." 2000 J Consult Clin Psychol 68;3:399-406

diminished sense of pleasure from sexual contact. For some clients of mine, there was a long-term loss of interest in sex, and/or aversion to sexual encounters. Often, these issues caused problems in marriages. I have also worked with clients whose eagerness to regain sexual mastery over themselves resulted in escalating use of pornography, masturbation, and sex obsession, but these also became dysfunctions in their lives and sometimes even compounded their shaming self-concepts.

Dr. Patrick Carnes suggests the term "sexual anorexia" to describe the denial or repulsion of appetite because of a person's negative or rejecting view of themselves. Dr. Carnes points on that the word *anorexia* is not specifically a food-related term, but a Greek word (*An-Orexis*) meaning "denial of appetite." He describes sexual anorexia as "...the agonizing struggle for control over the self...Both [sexual and food anorexia] share the same extreme self-hatred and sense of profound alienation."[3] Dr. Carnes identifies the following traits of sexual anorexia:

- A dread of sexual pleasure
- A morbid and persistent fear of sexual contact
- Obsession and hypervigilance around sexual matters
- Avoidance of anything connected with sex
- Preoccupation with others being sexual
- Distortions of body appearance, real or imagined
- Extreme loathing of bodily functions
- Obsessive self-doubt about sexual adequacy
- Obsessive worry or concern about the sexual intentions of others
- Shame and self-loathing over sexual experiences
- Depression about sexual adequacy and functioning
- Intimacy avoidance because of sexual fear[4]

But there is also an abundance of bad, even insulting, advice offered to women who are experiencing sexual dysfunction. Some books and websites advise persistently re-trying sex until you become more "successful" at recovering your pleasure. I would caution that this approach is likely to further entrench your trauma rather than diminish it, because it develops a routine habit of associating sexuality with personal disgust and a sense of "failure" on your part. It minimizes the real role of trauma in your sexual life, and wrongly persuades you to believe that your feelings toward sex come from personal weakness, fragility, or timidity. Notice, also, that this disruption in sexual pleasure (or even sexual happiness) is *not* a result of being "frigid," which is often a term used to disparage women who refuse to subordinate to the sexual intentions of others. The symptoms of sexual dysfunction in rape survivors are no less natural than the loss of hearing in the ears of a person who has survived a bomb explosion—of *course* the body will bear impact of trauma.

Yes, sexuality can and probably will become enjoyable again, especially with the passage of time. There are some forms of self-care that can promote this aspect of your recovery. Perhaps most important is that you not begin a new sexual relationship quickly

---

[3] Ph.D., PatrickCarnes; Joseph Moriarity. (1997). "Sexual Anorexia: Overcoming Sexual Self-Hatred." Hazelden. p2.
[4] Ibid, partial list from source material

after rape. It is impossible to sustain a healthy relationship while you feel damaged, unknowable, and undeserving of respect, and these are extremely common forms of self-judgment among victims. Remember that immediately after the rape you will be in the Crisis stage of recovery, in which assertiveness and decision-making are extremely difficult. Additionally, many women who have been raped initially find it very hard to say "no" to pressures in relationships if they have lost faith that their "no" counts for anything. Recovery from rape involves restoring the power of "no" and your trust in your own strength. But until then, there is a higher risk that rape victims may enter controlling relationships.[5]

Sexual trauma need not be limited to acts of rape, either. Trauma can take many forms: sleazy mockery of your body or sexual self as a child by bullies; physical trauma resulting in damage to the body that you fear is unattractive; sexual harassment; exposure to pornography in childhood; verbal put-downs in childhood that you are "ugly" or "fat", etc. Notice that something does not necessarily have to be illegal to still be traumatic. Research also finds that the younger you are when you experience trauma, the more you will struggle with efforts to cope with it. Why? Because when the trauma happens during the time of life when you are forming your beliefs and instinctive responses, which will guide you through your lifetime.

Sexual recovery simply cannot happen while any form of relationship abuse continues. Sexuality must be based on equality with your partner, mutual respect, and a consistent feeling of safety by both people. If you have a partner who uses sex for personal gratification at your expense, it compounds your trauma by reinforcing the "I'm only good to be used by others" self-talk. Likewise, a partner who verbally or physically mistreats you, humiliates you, shames you, or disregards your right to equality is communicating a clear message to you that you are unworthy of respect and choice. This adds another layer to the messages that rape itself sends. Consequently, sex will not be a form of mutuality and pleasure, but a chore, an obligation, an expectation, a duty, even a punishment. Since our ability to cope with trauma is also shaped by how other people react to our experiences, it becomes more difficult (or impossible) to recover from trauma while involved in any form of abusive relationship.

Have you ever given consent to sexual behavior, and yet felt traumatized afterward and not understood why? Have you ever sabotaged sexual encounters by picking fights, becoming disinterested, or distracted, moments before making love? Have you ever wondered whether *all* sex is traumatizing and awful? *Most* women report that they have had consensual sexual experiences that still left them feeling ashamed or degraded, including losing virginity in ways that were anything from distressing to downright traumatic. These events "program" your mind to define sex as an overpowering and shaming encounter; they not only change your beliefs, but even your very brain structures. Consequently, when you approach a similar situation in the future, your brain "fires" in similar ways as when you first experienced sex as a trauma.

This means that rushing into a new relationship after rape could be a disastrous choice. Saying no to a relationship option may be extremely difficult, though, for several reasons, not the least of which is that the rape may have obliterated your faith in the "no"

---

[5] When a person is harmed by a trusted caretaker, her ability to form new trusting relationships is more seriously injured. The risk of rape victims ending up in abusive relationships is *much* higher among victims whose perpetrators were family members, intimate partners, or other trusted persons.

option itself. But when you are at a low point because of rape, it can be comforting to receive affectionate attention which seems to soothe your painful self-talk about being worthless or unlovable. Some women seek dating partners very quickly after rape, both to reinforce her own confidence that she can still find acceptance, but also to recruit a protector of some type. (This is true whether the woman is straight or lesbian)

If you are already in a sexual relationship, it is inevitable that rape will disrupt your normal sexual routine for some time. It is essential that your partner understand this, and there must be no pressure or guilt directed at you to "perform" as before. Many survivors, let alone their partners, have not fully recognized the extent to which their trauma has impacted their sexuality, partly because what you sense about sex may not feel like an "effect" or "result" of anything; it simply seems to be that sex lacks meaning and pleasure for you. "It's no big deal, I don't see what everyone makes such a fuss about. I mean, I do have sex once in a while, but it's like I'm barely there at all, just waiting on it to be over," explained Maria in therapy. The same can be just as true for the survivor who continually seeks sex, even though this too fails to provide fulfillment and happiness to her.

Journal essay: Complete the following statement.
"Sex is…"

(I have been enlightened, but not surprised, by the number of rape survivors who answer with a list of words such as *dirty, violent, disgusting, a weapon, bad, scary,* and *torture.* None of these words describe sex; they describe *rape.* Your journal can reveal what messages rape has given you about sex, and thus about your sexuality. Recognizing this is a step toward beginning to challenge this and differentiate between sexuality and abuse)

It may be difficult to fully know the way your sexuality has been impacted because it hurts to recognize how extensively the ripple-effects of rape have really affected your life. It's not fair or reasonable that any one thing, no matter how traumatic, should have the power to bring such disruption. And sexuality is one of the forms in which your perpetrator affects not only you personally, but affects your intimate partners by extension.

Until you know and understand the effects of rape on your sexuality, the risk is that sex itself will continue to echo the negative self-talk you might have about your body, your worth to your sexual partners, and even your role in life. Sexual trauma in any form generates negative, shaming messages about sex, especially until we fully realize that rape and sexual abuse are not forms of sexual expression. We adopt the mindset that rape or abuse are representations of sex, and sex itself becomes as "dirty" as we feel *we* are. If we think of rape as a sex act, then of course we are more likely to shun sex! Sex has been defined to us as a weapon, rather than a form of meaningful, pleasurable, and healthy connection between equals! We are unable to dismantle the "dysfunctional sex mindset" and redefine sex as a healthy experience of love and mutuality.

One of the immediate dangers of this thinking is that we are left undefended against further abusive experiences with sex. If we regard sex as a form of manipulation, control, or punishment, then even when we attempt to engage in a sexual life we are misled by these beliefs into accepting inexcusable, abusive behaviors as "just what sex is."

Journal Exercise: Use your journal to write your thoughts about these questions. Go beyond "Yes/No" answers and spend some time examining these ideas.

How has sex become a chore or duty you *must* perform for another person?
Is sex becoming a form of behavior you do to "get" someone else in a relationship?
Has sex begun to feel dirty or bad?
Does sex hurt more physically or emotionally? How?
What memories, triggers, or flashbacks does sexual intimacy cause for you?
Do you regard sex as some*thing* you either give or get? Is sex something done *to* another person?
Consider the slang terms used to describe sex:
> **Hitting it**
> **Kicking it**
> **Nailing her**
> **Scoring**
> **Getting some**
> **Knocking her**
> **Screwing her**

What do these terms suggest about the attitudes toward sex that are common in society?
Do you believe that sex benefits men more than women? Why, or why not?
Do sexual partners have any responsibilities toward one another during sex? What are they?
Does sex become something demanded of you by others?
Do you ever provide sex too quickly in relationships out of fear of losing a partner?
Do you use sex as a way to avoid painful emotions? To express them?
Do you avoid sex, even with someone you truly love?
Do you feel guilty about saying "no" to someone's sexual advances?
Do you have to use alcohol or drugs to "get through" sex?
Do you hate your body (or certain parts of it), or hate being a woman, at times?
Are you sometimes confused whether you are gay or straight?
Do you find yourself wanting sex for reasons you believe are wrong?
Do you expect to be loved only if you give sex?
Do you worry that you are as "sick" as your rapist if you want sex?
Do you wish you lived in a sexless world?
Do you have difficulty forgiving yourself for your sexual history?
Do you fear that becoming sexually pleasurable will cause rape again?
Do you have sex with partners because you would feel guilty about denying them?
Are you afraid that sex will cause the same physical pain that rape may have caused?

As you complete your journaling about these items, you might begin to notice that the effects of trauma have been deeper than you first realized. You may also find that certain questions hit "bull's-eyes" for you, and bring up a lot of emotion or the desire to avoid that particular topic. Review your answers and consider which ones expressed the most intense emotions, and also whether any answers indicate possible dangers to you. Do you see any trends in your answers? For example, do you find yourself desperately seeking pleasure or connection, yet avoiding sex? Or perhaps it's the other way around: some survivors *only* engage in sexual connection with others because they believe that other forms of connection and intimacy are not possible anymore.

You can also consider your answers from a Before/After perspective. In your journal, you can divide a page in half and label the columns,

Before my rape, I…   **After my rape, I…**

Write under each heading how you thought about and experienced sex, and you may begin to see that your responses now are different than they might have been prior to the rape. For many women, it is difficult to recall pre-rape attitudes (especially if they have blocked or suppressed them because of a "stuck point" belief that "those beliefs of mine contributed to my being raped"). You can approach family members and friends for information, without having to reveal that you are processing your sexuality in therapy, by asking them the simple question, "I am having trouble remembering the kind of person I used to be before my rape. Can you describe what I was like and how I seem to have changed?"

By all means, continue to revisit your journaling at future points. Journaling is meant to capture your feelings at one point in your long life, not carve them into stone. This is precisely why I instruct clients to date and never discard all their journal entries. If your views of personal sexuality have changed from past to present, they will also change from present to future.

Improving your sexual life

To begin overcoming your trauma's effects on your sexuality, you should set goals for yourself. What would you *like* for your sexuality to become? How would you *like* for sex to fit into your life? Consider some of these changes and write about the ones that might apply to you:

- I would like to feel less guilt about my sexual feelings
- I would like to be less ashamed of my body or sexual performance
- I would like to have more control over my choice of sexual partners
- I would like to have relationships that are intimate in ways other than sexually
- I would like to engage in sex without dissociating
- I would like to engage in sex without being drunk or high
- I would like to trust my own sexual instincts better
- Other

Avoid goals that are fantastically unrealistic ("I want a perfect sex life" or "I want to only have great sex").

In order to reach these goals, you will need to understand what a healthy concept of sexuality really is. This is difficult, because we are flooded with billions of sick and dysfunctional messages about sexuality from every aspect of life, while healthy messages are rare. It's easy to find advertisements, movies, magazines, and songs that portray sex as a sleazy, secretive, exploitive, manipulative, and controlling form of behavior, but very difficult to find representations of sex as something sacred, delightful, mutual, or even clean. My simplest definition of "healthy sexuality" is that it is any expression of sexuality that uplifts the human worth of any person involved, and enhances self-worth rather than diminishing it. This definition automatically filters out sex approached through manipulation, coercion, shame, fear, or obligation. It also challenges the concept of sex as something one has to "get through" for the sake of another person's pleasure or power.

What is your definition of "healthy sexuality?" How do you know when you are ready to have sex? What criteria do you have for the type of partner whom you will accept for this level of intimacy? And finally, what fears do you have about sexuality itself?

Journal essay: What is the difference between sexuality and rape?

The next step is to look at the goals you have chosen, and decide how you will know when you have achieved them. For example, if you chose the goal, "I want to feel less guilty about my sexual feelings," the next question is, "What do you feel guilty about?" (example: "I feel guilty that I had a lot of drunken sex after my rape" or "I feel guilty that my rapist was a family member", etc.). Then, "What will you be able to do (or stop doing) when this guilt has vanished?" (example: "I will finally be able to understand that my sexual promiscuity was an expression of grief, not my badness, and I can forgive myself" or, "I will be able to tell others without shame that I am a rape survivor", etc.). Notice that these are based on concrete steps, not vague concepts, which can tell you when you have met your goals.

Journal Activity using one goal as an example:

My goal:

What beliefs and feelings block this goal:

What will I be able to do (or stop doing) when I succeed at this goal?

Repeat this activity for each goal you have chosen.

It is important that you are making these changes only for yourself, not for anyone else. Your sexual recovery must never, ever be done as a way to appease an impatient sexual partner, or because you feel guilty about not sexually performing as you feel you "should" for another person. Approaching recovery from those motivations will cause further impairment, not sexual liberation, because they are still based on you adopting the role of a sacrificial provider for another person's needs, and no woman can recover from rape while this role remains the limit of her sexual life. After all, sexual abuse is based on one person having to surrender to and accommodate another person's sexual demands and feelings, without reciprocal regard for her own. A rape victim already struggles with the message that sexuality is not her right, and that sexuality exists only for the benefit of other people.

Nor does becoming sexually recovered necessarily mean that you will begin to engage in sex. Perhaps sexual recovery for you means that you will finally have the confidence and option of abstinence, or that you will be less vulnerable to the manipulations of sexual con-artists. Sexual recovery has *nothing* to do with how great sex feels—sorry!—and *everything* to do with your own rights and choices over your sexual self. A sexually-recovered woman is free of the burden of "Should" messages: "I *should* give him/her sex so they will love me; I *should* take care of his/her needs; I *should* like having sex; I *should* give others what they want and expect…" Nobody can recover your sexuality for you; it is done by you for yourself.

The five conditions for healthy sexuality (CERTS)

Messages about sexual perversion surround us, and violence is increasingly eroticized as sensual. We only have to glance at fashion magazine ads or music videos to see this. But messages about healthy, intimate forms of sexuality are rare and it is no wonder we are left confused. "The five conditions for healthy sexuality—consent, equality, respect, trust, and safety (CERTS)—are seldom taught at home or in school, or reinforced in our culture," writes Wendy Maltz.[6]

Just as Maltz identifies five conditions for healthy sexuality, she also identifies five red-flags of abusive mindsets toward sex:

1. Sex is uncontrollable
2. Sex is hurtful
3. Sex is a commodity
4. Sex is secretive
5. Sex has no moral boundaries.[7]

Sex, Maltz points out, is a normal biological drive. It has healing properties when used responsibly, and can be an expression of love and mutual desire. It is not a service that is taken or demanded, and healthy sex does not cause either person to feel they have lost part of themselves to the other.

If sex is a part of our normal human lives, where did we get the idea that sex is bad? The most likely answer, if you are reading this book, is that you have begun to believe that sex is bad because you believe *you* are bad. In fact, many women I've counseled feel remorseful and ashamed when they engage in even the mildest of sexually-exciting behaviors, because they fear that *any* experimentation is deviant, and

---

[6] Maltz, Wendy. *The Sexual Healing Journey*, Quill publishing, 2001, p84.
[7] Ibid, 85.

thus makes them more like their perpetrators. Rape survivors often draw either of two conclusions from the trauma of rape:

- I was raped because I was bad
- I am bad now because I was raped

Many people grew up in families where sexuality was punished as a naughty, immoral drive. Questions about sex were responded to with shaming embarrassment (or even anger), and curiosity was regarded as perversion. Being mocked or humiliated because of normal childhood rituals such as masturbation or interest in naked bodies solidifies a child's belief that these curiosities are bad—and thus the *child* is bad for her secret that she is very much intrigued by them anyway. If sexual abuse or rape occurs, this lifelong mindset about sex teaches the victim to conclude, "I was raped because I was bad. My being a sexual person is what compelled someone else to misuse me!"

I have had countless women in therapy who say to me, "I've always had a sort of 'sexual energy' about me. Do you think it's why I was raped?" *Of course not!* The 'sexual energy' is an entirely normal part of being human. It is our childhood messages to be ashamed of that sexuality that cause our tendency to look *inward* for some flaw in ourselves to explain why the rape happened.

In some cases, the abuser or rapist themselves may be the person feeding you messages about your sexuality being bad. One of the reasons I ask clients to write their memories of what their rapist said during the assault is because of the frequency that an offender *teaches* her to hate her sexuality with verbal taunts: "you're a real slut, aren't you? You really like this! You're so sexy I can't control myself!" and so on. As these words reverberate down the corridors of time, the survivor imprints herself with the red-hot brand, "*dirty*." Not a person, not a spirit, but a *thing*, a sexual object, without other worth. Rita, a 51-year-old patient of mine, expressed it this way:

> I became nothing because that was the only choice. [My offender] told me that I was the one who seduced *him* and brought on the rape, and he said I was only getting what I deserved. So between the choice of being his deliberately-planned object of rape, or being nothing, I chose nothing. I had no identity in my own mind except for rape itself—I *became* a pure victim, rather than a woman who was victimized. For years, I was just an empty pod, filling up with alcohol and anything else, because the only other thing I was full of, was rape.

In order to develop the five conditions of healthy sexuality, it's not enough to simply rid ourselves of our negative beliefs about sex and self; we must replace them with healthier alternatives. For some reason, it's easier for many rape victims to get away from the "I'm bad and awful" part, but much more difficult to accept the "I'm good and deserving of love" part.

Journal entry: Why is it hard for a rape survivor to re-experience herself as good, whole, and lovable again?

Why do you want to stop any of your sexual behaviors or thoughts?

One way to replace our negative beliefs with positive ones is to rediscover your voice and courage about sexuality. Often, women in the early stages of rape trauma have difficulty setting boundaries, asserting choices, or speaking up about personal needs. It is impossible to develop all the CERTS qualities if you are unable to assert or negotiate your terms and rights, or to describe your emotions and thoughts to your partner. Some women in therapy with me have disclosed being terrified that if they do begin to speak up about their sexual needs—including the need to *not* engage in sex sometimes—that they will upset or lose their partner. I have observed, though, that in healthy relationships the opposite occurs: their intimate partners feel a new sense of *hope* for the relationship. If you are in a relationship where your concerns, rights, or feelings about sex are not discussed or respected, this is a red flag of a serious power imbalance between you and your partner.

Rita, who had chosen to become "nothing" and "empty" because of how her rapist had mocked her during his assault, struggled with her inability to speak to her husband about her sexual fears and wants. She was only able to engage in sex when she was extremely drunk, and felt desperate to escape her body until he was finished. Sex, for Rita, became a perfect symbol for how she saw herself as a woman: an "empty pod, waiting to be filled." During therapy, Rita began to use these steps to redefine sexuality. She was able to transform her understanding of sex away from something punitive, dirty, and degrading, and to see it as natural and interconnecting. The vital step in accomplishing this was when she was finally able to differentiate between real sexuality and rape.

When Rita began to tell her husband that sex made her feel vacant and hollow, her husband was initially defensive—"why are you only telling me this now?"—but softened when he realized that Rita was describing the effects of her rape, not criticizing his sexual performance. Her husband revealed that he had been aware of Rita's discomfort during sex but had inwardly criticized himself for it, believing that he was an incompetent lover. When he realized that he was not at fault and that Rita was now able to describe her feelings and lead him to a better understanding, he became very excited and hopeful. He explained that the improved communication from Rita reassured him that he would be less likely to hurt her feelings, sexually, and more likely to collaborate with her in the development of a better sex life. Rita's new ability to verbalize her thoughts to him meant that she no longer had to dissociate during sex (while faking pleasure at the same time), and could rediscover her husband as a true partner, rather than someone "doing something to me."

Women who dissociate during sex tend to also experience negative feelings and beliefs about themselves and their bodies. They become anxious and uncomfortable when they are brought into contact with strong feelings (and sex is certainly a strong feeling!), so rather than explore and understand those feelings they turn them off entirely. This is not only true during sex; it is also true during these women's more inward, thoughtful, and quiet times of life. If you are a woman who dissociates during sex, you are probably also a woman who resists deeper examination of her interior world, because you fear that such examination will uncover difficult emotions. Such women also tend to rush through sexual motions with a "let's get it over with" mindset. The body cannot remain connected to sensation when the mind has already switched itself off.

Teresa, a 25-year-old rape survivor, struggled to change her habit of allowing others to use her. "I have stopped letting others walk all over me. My ex-husband was the final straw," she journaled. "I demand what I want in relationships now, and if I don't get it then I am gone. It's not a selfish thing, it's an 'I have waited my entire life to be loved and cherished and be with someone who would make me feel precious instead of feeling dirty' thing."

The next step to developing CERTS is to treat your own body with respect. This involves two accomplishments: taking physical care of your body, and accepting your body as something valuable you deserve to inhabit.

When abuse and rape survivors internalize the message that their bodies are bad, they tend to punish their bodies. By engaging in drug abuse, nicotine addiction, alcoholism, self-injury, or eating disorders, the body becomes the recipient of the victim's self-directed anger, powerlessness, and self-rejection. By mistreating our own bodies out of grief, we are not *expressing* grief, but reinforcing it. If we already feel ashamed, we compound those shaming beliefs when we re-abuse ourselves.

Women who develop eating disorders and self-injury habits also disrupt their brain's nervous system, which is the system that regulates messages of pleasure. One effect is the development of a syndrome called *anhedonia*, which is the loss of the brain's ability to feel pleasure at all. As levels of the neurotransmitter dopamine drop, the brain's nerve connections fail to transmit messages of pleasure from the body. The sensation that remains, then, is very much like drug withdrawal: apathetic, bleak, numbness in which happiness itself feels distant. Online rape recovery forums are full of women who openly acknowledge self-injury and eating disorders, and whose writings are characterized by desolate misery. More and more evidence suggests that the abuse of our bodies causes the emotional deadness, rather than vice-versa!

Being willing to inhabit your own body can be very difficult for a survivor, too. Dissociation can become an easier habit than consciously feeling "in the moment," especially when sexual abuse or rape has caused a woman to reject her own body as "ugly" or "bad." I often hear women deny that they regard their bodies in these ways, but when I ask how it would feel to closely examine themselves in a mirror they wince with disgust and confess that they can't bear it.

Cassandra was a 17-year-old punk rocker with a genius IQ. She denied any history of trauma or abuse, and had bounced from therapist to therapist for "depression and anxiety," her standard self-description. She would look with innocent eyes and say she had "no idea" why she was so depressed. Cassandra also acknowledged self-injury, although her arms showed no signs of wounds. For some reason, not a single previous therapist had inquired about the nature of her self-injury or just how she was hurting herself, if not in the more common act of cutting and scratching her forearms. When I asked, she blushed and began to tell me. "I mostly do it under my shirt and underwear so nobody can see the marks." I told her that I obviously was not going to ask to see her injuries, but wondered if she would describe them to me.

"I carve criss-crosses on my breasts. And I carved the word UGLY on my stomach with an arrow pointing down."

Just having this information filled in all the missing answers. Nobody carves an arrow to their groin with the word *UGLY* without deeper meaning. I instinctively knew that these were signs of rape. When I cautiously approached the question she began to cry and said that she had never told anyone, but that she had indeed been raped by a boyfriend three years earlier. But none of her previous therapists had even asked.

What her actions revealed, though, was not just that she was engaged in self-injury but that she also rejected herself as deformed and hideous. Cassandra specifically rejected her vagina as ugly, and had journaled about being embarrassed to even be a girl or to have anyone see "that ugly part." What this suggested is that Cassandra faulted herself, her *femininity*, as the cause of her rape, rather than blaming her boyfriend who had raped her (she had dated a few boys before coming out as gay). Consequently, she dissociated so thoroughly during sex that she could not even recall sexual encounters afterward. Dissociation had become her way of passively punishing her body for "betraying" her, and cutting words and arrows into her flesh became her way of secretly expressing herself. She had imaginatively transformed her body into the perpetrator rather than the victim, and convinced herself she was "fighting back" by attacking herself.

One of the main reasons Cassandra blamed her body as the culprit of her trauma was that she was mystified by the automatic responses she had to triggers. She had begun to stiffen and reject hugs from family members after her rape, and certain scents (cologne and cigarettes) caused her to experience maddening panic attacks. When men stood above while speaking to her as she remained seated in front of them, she became extremely nervous and images of her rape would flicker through her mind. On some level she knew these emotional responses were irrational, but this only reinforced her belief that she was really crazy, or weak, or both. If the source of her triggers and panic were within her, she reasoned, then the cause of her rape must be within herself as well.

By learning to recognize her body's responses to trauma and accepting them as natural neurological processes rather than blunders or failures on her part, Cassandra was gradually able to "forgive" her body. Once she had redefined her body as innocent, she was able to remain conscious within it and gradually phase out her dissociation. And then, finally, she was able to rebuild her body-mind-spirit link, which allowed her to see herself as a whole woman, not a flawed soul trapped in a defective shell.

Other women have difficulty feeling pleasure because they see their bodies as "crime scenes," and cannot mentally transform their beliefs about themselves. Unfortunately, a lot of social conditioning teaches women (and men) to define "good sex" based on phony values, such as body attractiveness (weight, appearance). But relying on physical senses only, without intimacy, trust, and openness, cannot provide you with fulfillment.

Remember, too, that body cells constantly replicate. They die, are dismantled by a process called Phagocytosis, and are replaced by entirely new cells. This means that the age of the tissues of your body is much *younger* than your actual age. Your body is younger than you are, and the cells you were made of a few years ago are now entirely gone. In other words, the human body constantly regenerates.[8] Only your DNA remains unchanged. What does this mean? It means that the body you are living in, as you read this *right now,* is not the body you were raped in. It also means that since your DNA remains unchanged, you are – at a molecular level – the same person you were always

---

[8] Spalding KL, Bhardwaj RD, Buchholz BA, Druid H, Frisen J. (2005) "Retrospective birth dating of cells in humans." *Cell.* 122:133-43.

meant to be, and rape cannot change that. You are physically a different person than the rape victim you once were, and your body is not a raped body any longer. It has regenerated, and will continue to regenerate through your entire life. When you look into a mirror, you are no longer seeing a body that was raped; that body has died and been replaced by entirely new matter. You are *not* living inside the shell of a rape victim.

The third step to developing CERTS sexuality is to break sexual habits associated with trauma and progress toward a more healthy set of sexual behaviors. This can certainly include voluntary celibacy, especially if sex has become a compulsion or if you find yourself moving toward sex too quickly with new partners. Celibacy may be particularly advisable if you are prone to dissociation or intoxication during sex, which creates immense risks and vulnerabilities for abuse. However, changing habits and behaviors is the most difficult step in sexual recovery.

One reason this can be difficult is that often we may not even be aware of what healthy sex *is*. If your sexual trauma began early in life, or if you grew up in an environment with poor boundaries or persistent conflict and abuse, the model of sexuality you have been given will likely be greatly flawed; sexuality in these environments tends to be secretive and manipulative, and is seen as something given (or lost) for the advantage of another person. It can be hard to redefine sex as something okay to enjoy.

Many women have told me that they resist the idea that their own bodies can be sources of pleasure. To them, it feels perverted to even imagine physical pleasure, based on a fear that such enjoyment might parallel the mindset of their abusers. It does not. Sexual violence is not anywhere on the continuum of types of intimate physical pleasure, and it is not wicked or unhealthy to accept your body as a potential source of pleasure again. (In fact, a case could be made that healthy, playful sexual pleasure sets you further *apart* from your rapist!)

Your therapist will be particularly helpful in this area, so do not hesitate to ask questions about healthy sexuality. It can feel embarrassing to acknowledge that this entire area of life continues to mystify, but the benefits of exploring this will far outweigh the risks.

In addition to your therapist, there are books and videos developed specifically for survivors of sexual abuse and rape that address recovery of sexuality. Among my personal favorites is Wendy Maltz's *The Sexual Healing Journey*. Maltz also offers a website, healthysex.com, which provides extensive information and superb videos for trauma survivors about the topic of sexuality.

Last, there needs to be some type of a "relapse prevention plan" for your sexual recovery. The most important part of planning for successful recovery is denying yourself permission to fail, but granting yourself forgiveness when you do. Recovery is never perfect from the first attempt, and you can easily become frustrated if you expect your sex life to completely turn around simply because you have determined that it must. Relapse is a part of the normal process of recovery, and it is healthier to redefine them as opportunities for learning rather than failures.

Relapse prevention plan for sexuality

By "relapse," I am not treating anyone's sexuality as an addiction, necessarily, nor a pathology. In some cases the term "addiction" might accurately apply; in other cases the term "sexual anorexia" might fit. For others, sexuality may not be dysfunctional at all in its actual patterns of behavior, but it may be removed from its purpose as a source of pleasure, connection, and mutuality with a loving partner. The "relapse" I am describing could be the act of returning to prior sexual behaviors that are disempowering to you, or it could simply mean the return of sexual avoidance and anhedonia.

In preventing sexual relapse, the first step is to form a contract with yourself that guides your own sexual conduct, limits, and criteria. Some women realize they must commit to a period of sexual abstinence while they develop their plans and give their recovery momentum; clients of mine have set anywhere from ten-day to two-year goals of sexual "vacation." This is not a form of avoidance, but a form of relief in which you can sidestep sexual pressures in order to rebuild your sexuality. To begin this, complete the following preliminary exercise.

Journal Entry: What sexual practices of yours do you wish to change? What sexual *feelings* of yours do you wish to change?

Rachel completed this journaling for therapy and wrote, "I tend to have sex too early in new relationships, and then I disconnect from my partner afterward. I need to postpone sex until the relationship has become healthy and committed. I also tend to dissociate during sex. I need to make direct eye contact and verbally communicate with my partner throughout sex until I have a new habit of not dissociating."

Michelle wrote, "My biggest mistake is that I keep thinking sex is something that *has* to happen, not a choice I can make. So to deal with it, I will get very drunk so I don't have a lot of feelings about sex. It means I barely care about sex, and I barely care about the guy I'm with. I wasn't like that before my rape."

Other clients of mine have written journal entries like, "I would like to stop using physical pain as a part of sex," and "I would like to stop pretending to love sex when I don't" and for a teen-age girl, "I need to stop looking for older men as sex partners."

Once you have identified the areas of your sexuality you would like to change, begin to explore what needs those areas used to fill in your life. It may sound strange to think that *all* actions are needs trying to be met, but the realization can help us understand why we act as we do. For example, Rachel realized that she tended to have sex early in relationships to reassure herself that she was still desirable to men, but once she had sex with a new partner she felt ashamed rather than validated. Her choice to distance from men right afterward reflected her need to recover from shame. Michelle approached sex with a sense of being powerless; it was difficult for her to finally realize that she was doing this to prove her guilty feelings about her rape to herself. If she could continually verify that she is powerless over sex, then her self-blame for rape would feel truer and truer. Michelle's need to be right about self-blaming beliefs made her recovery extremely difficult because of the double issue of guilt and self-harming sex. My teen-age client who was sexually involved with much older men was looking for a suitor who would seduce her with flattery about how mature, sexy, and complex she was. She craved this feedback to fulfill her need for validation by older men (which her father had never given her), and exchanged sex for this flattery to keep the cycle going.

Women who misplace the blame for their rapes onto themselves have more difficulty recreating a positive sexual life. This may partly be because she fears having her guilt discovered by a partner who becomes too close, or it may be because she fears she will "trigger" a similar trauma again by behaving in ways that she believes had caused her previous rape. These feelings of shame, as well as unresolved anger, can lead to her either shunning sex altogether (sexual anorexia), or engaging in "repetition compulsion" – the subconscious attempt to continually re-create her traumatic experience(s) in an effort to understand and master it.

Use your therapy sessions to courageously examine: "what needs are being met by the current condition of my sexual life? Is my sexual conduct being used to prove something, or to disprove something, about myself?" These questions might simultaneously intrigue and annoy you. One client of mine even recognized that despite her physical enjoyment of sex with her husband, she tended to become irritable and frustrated soon afterward because she was approaching sex with the belief that she was obligated to perform for him, which triggered her feelings of guilt and worthlessness from her rape.

For some women, having a support group is very helpful in sexual recovery. If your therapist offers group therapy, you may already have such a support group in place. Other clients of mine have attended SLAA (Sex/Love Addicts Anonymous), and found these groups to be very positive and helpful, in contrast to the embarrassment and shame my clients first felt when they considered attending any group with "*that* name." Even a single role model/mentor can make a huge difference if a support group is unavailable. I do not regard online forums to be anything close to a substitute for face-to-face support.

Journal entry: What are your new ground rules for healthy sex? What rights and conditions will you require when it comes to sex?

Finally, your intimate partner will likely need a lot of education about the effects of sexual assault. This means having some uncomfortable discussions with him or her. If you have not disclosed your rape to your partner, I am not saying that you must do so immediately in a new relationship. Rape is a personal experience, and you own the rights to your memories and privacy. You have no reason to feel guilty about keeping your rape private until *you* decide that you are ready to reveal it to anyone. Nor should you feel that you are "keeping secrets," and nobody ought to pressure you to reveal more than you are ready to reveal. There will come a time in a committed relationship when you will need to open and discuss this issue with a life partner, though, and there are some ways to help that conversation go more smoothly. Occasionally a woman will write to me by email and ask me, "how do I address this with my husband?" but when I reply with suggestions, she responds, "but he doesn't even know I've been raped." I think that by this point (marriage) such a discussion is long-overdue, and there just aren't any good ways to address serious issues in a marriage when the root of those issues cannot even be divulged to one's life partner.

Not all partners are equipped with the insight and maturity to appropriately handle issues like rape. Your judgment is the best tool for predicting how your partner will react. I have observed partners who were supportive and nurturing, and I have observed partners who became frustrated ("why are you only telling me this now?") and even critical. Some of this is a result of their feeling hurt by the discovery that you have had a complex inner emotional world that they have not shared, or the realization that despite their best efforts you have simply not found sex enjoyable. While you may find that your partner needs you to educate him or her about rape recovery, it should not become your job to offer them "therapy" to soothe their own discomforts about this issue. If your partner seems to need help with their own emotions about your rape, it ought to take place in a counseling session, either as a couple or by your partner individually.

When you discuss this with your partner, you do *not* have any obligation to defend your innocence, convince anyone of the facts of the abuse, or justify your traumatized responses. Your partner may press you for more on these issues, but a short, concise summary is perfectly acceptable; the purpose of the disclosure is to build an alliance with your partner toward sexual recovery in the here-and-now. Any specific details given about your rape ought to be presented during a scheduled therapy session.

My website (www.resurrectionafterrape.org) includes a downloadable booklet called "A Man's Guide To Helping A Woman Who Has Been Raped," to offer husbands and boyfriend some advice. There are also resources that can expand on these ideas and assist women in same-sex relationships. I have observed that the majority of books on this topic are written for partners of women who have survived childhood sexual abuse specifically, which may or may not also apply, but they are highly applicable to survivors of rape as well. In particular, I recommend these books:

What About Me? A Guide for Men Helping Female Partners Deal with Childhood Sexual Abuse by Grant Cameron
• **ISBN-13:** 978-0921165385

The Sexual Healing Journey: A Guide for Survivors of Sexual Abuse by Wendy Maltz
• **ISBN-13:** 978-0060959647

Reclaiming Desire: 4 Keys to Finding your Lost Libido by Andrew Goldstein, M.D., and Marianne Brandon, M.D.
•   **ISBN-13:** 978-1579546830

How do I know if I'm ready for sex?
(Some items apply specifically to adolescents)

Research suggests that people who engage in sexual activity before the age of 16 *usually*—not just "often"—suffer negative emotional and physical consequences.

1. You must be able to handle the potential consequences, such as pregnancy. Are you in a position to comfortably care for a baby? (That means you have the time, the money, the knowledge, the sobriety, and the patience.)

2. Would the majority of trusted adults in your life agree that you have reached the level of maturity and emotional health necessary to have a sexual relationship?

3. Have you known your partner deeply for many months without having sex?

4. Are you aware of all of the possible sexual infections that can occur? Do you know which methods of protection are helpful in preventing them, and which methods are not? Do you know what number of people your age are carriers of an infection?

5. Do you know what HIV is, and are you aware that the HIV rate among adults is dropping, while the majority of new cases are among *teens*? Do you know how HIV is different from AIDS? Do you know what is involved in HIV treatment?

6. Even if your partner tests "clean" for diseases, do you know that that does not mean that he or she is guaranteed to be disease-free until a follow-up test is done three months later?

7. Do you know where to get help for a sexual infection, should one occur? Do you have the money to pay for these treatments?

8. Do you understand how to properly use birth control, and do you have access to effective forms of birth control? Have you and your partner talked at length about risk reduction? Do you understand your religion's teachings about birth control?

9. Do you understand what happens in the human body during sexual intercourse? For example, are you aware that females can get pregnant at *any* time during their monthly cycle? Are you aware that sperm can stay alive inside a body for several days?

10. Does having sex mean sneaking off somewhere? Is having sex something you have to hide from others? Sneaking and hiding are evidence of the "abuse mindset" of sex.

11. Do you or your partner have a habit of becoming sexual very quickly with new partners at the beginning of a romance? That would be a warning sign.

12. Do you have religious beliefs about sex that you have considered and talked over?

13. Would you feel guilty or ashamed if your family knew about your sexual activity?

14. If the idea of sex scares you, can you say you are ready for sex yet?

15. If you have not received *deep* therapy for any sexual abuse, then having sex may be emotionally damaging.

16. If you are considering sex to make your partner happy, your relationship is not ready for sexuality.

17. If your partner uses guilt or pressure about sex, your partner is not ready.

18. Are you are considering sex to hold on to your partner?

19. Do either of you are use sex to "make up" after fighting or abuse?

20. Do you have criteria for a partner other than just attraction, pleasure, and desire?

21. Do you know how the laws in your state define sexual consent?

22. Does your partner respect your wishes when you say "no"? Are you *able* to say no when you want to?

23. Would you become devastated or suicidal if someday you lost your relationship with this partner?

24. Has there been any abuse—physical, emotional, sexual—at any point in the relationship?

25. Are you considering sex because you are eager to have another person's attention or flattery?

26. Is there a wide age difference between you and your partner? That would be a warning sign. Over 60% of teen pregnancies are fathered by a male 5 or more years older than the female.

27. Can you argue with your partner without feeling afraid of them, and without either of you becoming abusive or overpowering toward the other?

28. Do you feel proud and dignified about your decisions after you make those decisions, or do you doubt yourself and feel uncomfortable?

And while I stood there
I saw more than I can tell,
and I understood more than I saw;
for I was seeing in a sacred manner.
-Black Elk

Do I have to have an "A-ha!" moment in therapy?

In this book, I have described some tremendous and impressive breakthroughs in therapy that other women have accomplished. It may give the impression that recovery from rape is a process that finally "clicks" into place, and suddenly all mysteries and pains are answered, like a light coming on: "Extra! Extra! I'm healed!"

Not only is this *not* the case, but on the contrary I have been wary and doubtful about recovery that seems to come "all at once" through a single breakthrough. Nothing about rape (or trauma) is resolved by a cathartic flood of insight, in which there is a sudden awareness of truth, hope, and complete insight. In fact, I might even suggest that a sudden "A-ha!" moment can be a form of *avoidance*, not of recovery, in which a woman appears to soar to health so that further difficult work becomes unnecessary. I have more confidence in the recovery that comes through the process of hard labor than from exuberant proclamations of success. Danée stumbled often or tried to fool me and avoid deeper feelings, and Victoria resisted, questioned, and fought me at every step through the work. Women on my web community work so hard for so long that they actually throw this book angrily, calling it "that damned book!" Healing comes through struggle, not a sudden singular lottery-win.

The real work of rape recovery is peppered with victories and "A-ha!" moments, but not in a way that brings complete resolution in a single stroke. It is a complex, lengthy process that will involve homework, confrontation, confusion, and possibly conflict between you and your therapist. Psychiatric medication plays an important role in stabilizing anxiety and depression, not to "cure" rape trauma, but to equip you with the steadiness to do the *inner* work of recovery. But recovery itself is work.

You might consider rape recovery to be like creating a new piece of jewelry. A jeweler cannot pick up one piece of stone and proclaim it finished; each component has to be individually treated. The strand of the necklace would be your faith in yourself, which holds all of your work together. Nothing can sustain your recovery if you lack belief in yourself, and the belief that you *will* get better.

Therapy is the grindstone you use to shape and polish every gem you will place in your jewelry. It takes friction, heat, and pressure to transform each gem from a rough stone into a sparkling, complete jewel.

Your "A-ha!" moments will be many, and each one of these moments is the act of stringing a new bead onto your necklace. Obviously, your masterpiece will not be complete as a result of a single "A-ha!" moment, but from a sequence of them that gradually draws all of the separate pieces together into a beautiful, new whole.

Spirituality is the clasp of the necklace, which holds the beauty of the whole work close to you so that others can see and marvel at it, and which prevents you from losing what you've constructed; if your spirituality is weak, like a broken clasp, you are at risk for losing the entire necklace without even realizing it.

Many women are in a rush to complete their recovery, and a very common mistake is to try to succeed too quickly (or to dash away at the first tough moment, conflict, or confrontation). But speeding through journal activities and readings is not the same as true recovery; even though you end up with a full journal and an impressive reading list, you may not have truly absorbed the insights you could have. Approach recovery like a fine meal: by savoring each part and proceeding slowly, you have a more complete experience than if you shred through it from drive-thru therapy.

Why do I sometimes get angry at my therapist during the work we do?

Seems like the best therapy is the therapy that sucks so badly while we're there.
-Leitha Brogan

My clients have coined a term that they use to tease me about the various ways I apparently have of provoking them in therapy. "Damn you, Matt! moments" are how they describe when issues brought up in therapy challenge their beliefs, or bring things to their attention that they would prefer to avoid.

If your worldview had been successful at sustaining you, you would not have been in trauma. Part of the purpose for therapy is to nudge you into new beliefs and improved ways of considering the world and your place in it. You can't truly transform yourself if you are still harboring the same thoughts and beliefs at the end that you had at the beginning, and "recovery" is not just a way of becoming more eloquent at describing your problems. In the course of healing, many beliefs that you feel in your gut are absolutely true, will be confronted and challenged by your therapist. While the purpose of this is to help you learn how to question your own assumptions about yourself, it *feels* like disrespect at the time because it seems someone is questioning a belief you are absolutely convinced is true. If a therapist questions a belief that you have accepted as truth, it feels like they either do not respect your perspective, or they truly "don't get it" because they can't accept the same obvious truths you accept.

Laura was angry at me when she asked me if her experience was rape and I said yes. She didn't disagree with the answer, but criticized me for giving it to her because she was certain that if I'd only lied and said "no" it would have spared her five weeks of painful therapy. But what if I had told her it wasn't rape? Could there have been consequences to a lie that spared her short-term distress? We could have wasted weeks of therapy pretending that her stress, self-injury, and alcoholism were caused by a flat tire, or by arguments with her sister, or by bad hair days, and *none* of her problems would have improved. And if I had said that her experience was not rape, I would have been guilty of sending her back into ongoing abusive relationships, and given her abusers the therapist's "seal of approval" that what they were doing to her was acceptable. She would have tolerated such forms of sexual abuse from men for years to come—after all, hadn't her therapist told her it was "not rape"?

In many studies looking at what factors affect a successful outcome of therapy, clinical methodology actually comes in at third place. The two most important factors are the therapist-client bond, and the client's hope and expectation of improvement. The close alliance between the therapist and the client isn't just a minor concern; it's the *foundation* of positive outcome. One journal reviewed over 100 previous outcome studies and found that specific techniques used by the therapist accounted for only 30% of the positive outcome. However, the quality of the bond between the therapist and client predicted the results more than 40% of the time![1] The days of the therapist as the stoic, detached observer are ending as we find that a warm and caring bond between client and therapist may be what promotes the greatest success.

What does this mean in plain language? It means that there is objective data that consistently finds that how the therapist and client *feel* about each other matters. In fact, it is the top predictor of the outcome. It isn't an indicator of "poor boundaries" or "inappropriate emotion" for the therapist to care deeply about his client (and vice-versa); it is probably the most crucial, necessary, vital aspect of treatment. In the book *How to Fail as a Therapist*, the authors (Ph.D.'s in psychology) include a specific warning against the error of "emphasizing technique over relationship-building." The authors state,

> The lesson here is one that is all too commonly missed: The therapeutic relationship trumps technique...interviews with clients repeatedly show that even though you may have all of your licenses, credentials, and degrees prominently and tastefully displayed on your office walls, it takes time and relationship building to gain the confidence of most clients.

Another mistake therapists make is failing to communicate sufficient empathy and signs of support for their client. It is *essential* that a therapist show a warm sense of support, care, and dedication to his or her client. I can have the best books, research, and techniques training in the world, but until I am able to show genuine affection and connection to my clients, it means nothing. Many clients terminate therapy because they feel that their therapists lack these qualities. One research study is so bold as to state, "It is imperative that clinicians remember that decades of research consistently demonstrates

---

[1] Lambert, M., J. & Barley, D., E. (2001). Research Summary on the therapeutic relationship and psychotherapy outcome. *Psychotherapy*, 38, 4, 357-361.

that relationship factors correlate more highly with client outcome than do specialized treatment techniques."[2] More and more research calls upon therapists to enter the client's world, specifically to strip the therapist of all desires to condemn or evaluate the client's life experiences.[3]

This can be difficult, too, because as a therapist I had to be able to say difficult and painful things to my clients--they have nicknamed them "Damn you, Matt! Moments" (or "DYM's" for short)--and some aren't ready. Some clients don't want corrections in their thinking, they want sympathy and acknowledgment of their pain. This can be tough, because as gentle and compassionate as I am I don't have a molecule in me that is willing to simply validate pain to allow a hurting person to remain otherwise stalled in recovery. I would regard such as "velvet-gloved abuse." Unfortunately, it is soothing to many clients who invest in years and years of therapy for the same issues, achieving nothing more than expensive sympathy.

As a result, when someone complains of flashbacks, panic attacks, distress, self-injury, and suicidal thoughts, I have to tell her directly and honestly that these things do not get better on their own with the passing of time; in fact, they get worse. I have to tell her that the only way out of this is *through* it—to stop fleeing and face it directly, and use clinically-guided techniques to overcome these pains. Some people are ready to hear this and it offers them hope for a way out; others are shocked at my "cruelty" because of my refusal to soothe, pet, and console them in their present state. But this blunt, difficult realism can be part of a healthy therapist-client relationship; my patients have all known that regardless of my love and care for them, they will never receive watered-down condescension. As a result, they trust feedback to be clear, honest, and given with genuine concern for them. They have also all known that they could dispute things with me, disagree, confront me, even lash out at me, and I would not, under any circumstance, retaliate. But the therapist-client bond is a close and deeply personal one. This gives the dynamic itself immense power to inspire feelings of anger, just as well as hope and trust. Andrea found that to be a valuable part of her recovery:

> Who would tell a technique-only therapist the personal things that we do?
> It is impossible for me to even conceive telling those to anyone that I have not built a bond with. I hadn't told anyone at all and had kept it to myself for 20-ish years. Time will definitely not heal you! I tried that for so many years and it hit me in the face over and over again.

> If you realize that you can make poor choices and your therapist isn't going to let that fly, you develop a respect that is relative to your closest friend looking at you and saying, "Yea right!" If you know you are going to get back the truth, the bare bones of it, and that it is not a textbook answer you become willing to work/fight through it. It is truly about you and your life experiences.

---

[2] Constaquay, L. G., Goldfried, M. R., Wiser, S., Raue, P.J., Hayes, A.M. (1996). Predicting the effect of Cognitive therapy for depression: A study of unique and common factors. *Journal of Consulting and Clinical Psychology,* 65, 497-504.
[3] Singer, Richard A. Jr. "The Therapeutic Relationship is the Most Important Ingredient in Successful Therapy." http://www.selfgrowth.com/articles/Singer7.html

Some clients want their therapists to tell them directly what things mean and how to fix them, but what a therapist *actually* does is to provide education about the issues you face, while helping you draw connections between the feelings you have, why you have them, and how to alter or cope with them. Andrea wrote this advice to all women looking for ways to invest in their own recovery:

> Find a therapist that will take those leaps with you, but not for you. A therapist not afraid to make you mad, or ask the tough questions, and that actually expects nothing less than your whole truth and hard work. A therapist that you bond with and who you do not want to let down. Because, truth be told we all too often let ourselves down and are used to doing that. Then, after a while you realize, "I am not going to let myself down, anymore! I deserve the best me and to Love myself!" It is the only thing that worked for me and I am very thankful! Life is more alive now, because I am living it!

A second reason clients may become angry with their therapist is that the therapist fails to offer the "perfect provider" persona that some clients crave. Dr. Otto Kernberg, regarded the most-cited living psychoanalyst, proposes that in "transference-focused psychotherapy" some clients will experience oscillations between idealizing their therapist, and then abruptly (and strenuously) despising that same therapist after perceiving some slight, flaw, or offense by the therapist. Kernberg suggests that this is because of a subconscious belief that a perfect caretaker ought to exist for the client, who initially clings to hope that the role will be filled by the therapist. When the therapist inevitably fails—they are human and fallible, of course—the client feels betrayed, swindled, exploited, "sold out." It is not uncommon for such clients to target the therapist with accusations like, "You've changed! I thought you understood, but you're just thinking about yourself!" or, "I looked up to you, and you let me down!"

But if we can accept flawed people with imperfect lives and still treasure one another, then perhaps we have hope. Your therapist will fail you at times—it is a fact. They will disappoint you, misunderstand you, and even offend you. If you see this as betrayal, then you are holding your therapist to too high a standard for any human. But if you can accept such flaws in the context of their humanness and also remember your own history of mistakes, regrets, and struggles, then you and your therapist will likely be able to succeed.

Another reason some clients become angry at their therapist is that the duration of therapy itself is coming to an end. "If you think it's hard to end a relationship with a lover or spouse, try breaking up with your psychotherapist," wrote Dr. Richard Friedman.[4] The bond formed between a client and therapist is powerful, especially when the therapy has succeeded in improving your life. If your therapist has been a good one, you have come through an experience of being listened to, accepted, respected, and inspired. Approaching the end of therapy can trigger fear of abandonment, and even anger at the therapist for choosing to abandon you. Dr. Friedman states,

---

[4] Friedman, Richard MD. "How to Figure Out When Therapy Is Over." *New York Times,* Oct. 30, 2007. http://www.nytimes.com/2007/10/30/health/views/30beha.html

The term "cure," I think, is illusory — even undesirable — because there will always be problems to repair. Having no problems is an unrealistic goal. It's more important for patients to be able to deal with their problems and to handle adversity when it inevitably arises. Still, even when patients feel that they have accomplished something important in therapy and feel "good enough," it is not always easy to say goodbye to a therapist.[5]

What I would like patients to realize is that therapists cannot help but develop bonds and feelings toward those they serve, as well. This is called counter-transference, and it describes the way *therapists* feel toward *you*. I found it very difficult to part with certain patients of mine, but at the same time I was gratified to know that he or she had become ready to go. I am always thrilled when a former patient returns to visit me or sends me a card or phone call to let me know how well she is doing. Moments before writing this, in fact, a very special former patient dropped by my office, smiling and laughing and telling me how well her life is going. Please make a point of re-contacting your own therapist down the road and letting them know how you are doing, and how much the process has meant to you.

If you feel angry at your therapist, by all means talk to him or her. Often, there are amazing lessons hidden inside the emotion of anger, and examining the causes and effects of your anger toward your therapist can reveal some startling buried beliefs.

There are some conflicts, though, that necessitate an ending of the relationship between you and your therapist. If any of these is happening, your anger is serving you well by telling you that separation and finding a new therapist are urgent:

- A therapist who blames victims of rape;
- A therapist who uses "rape jokes" to try to distract you from depression
- A therapist whose approach to rape trauma is superficial, such as "put it in the back of your mind" or "think happy thoughts, and only focus on the positive!";
- A therapist who is continually unprepared or late for sessions, or unreliable;
- A therapist who flirts, teases, or suggestively touches you, or promotes any other form of sensual contact or relationship;
- A therapist whose *own* trauma issues continually surface in the session, causing them to redirect the topic to their own experiences and feelings rather than yours;
- A therapist who focuses only on surface problems like substance abuse, without helping you examine the trauma that underlies them;
- A therapist who suggests that they, and they alone, are the only ones truly capable of understanding and helping you;
- A therapist who does not actually have clinical training, and is motivated more by religious or personal zeal for a cause than by knowledge and experience.

I have heard many horror stories of awful therapists harming patients by approaching rape therapy with no skill or experience. One young woman described her experiences with "Doctor Jerk" (her term, not mine), who committed several unforgivable offenses in the first session alone. Dr. Jerk was insensitive and would bark at her with "Why are you crying? Stop crying and talk!" and "you have serious

---

[5] Friedman, op. cit.

problems!" He asked her in the first session, "So, what did it feel like to get raped?" and then asked her to stand and physically pose to demonstrate how her attacker had held her during her rape so he could understand. She later shared, "All I could think was this guy is a real sicko who's getting his kicks off of hearing what happened to me."

Another college student approached me just a week ago as I write this, and told me that her perpetrator had been her abusive husband. Among his many other forms of abuse, he had also driven her down with his car, striking her and causing injuries requiring tendon surgery. But her therapist, a female, advised her to return home to him, plead with him to take her back, and make the marriage work. She knew this was ridiculous advice, but she wanted to ask if I thought the counselors at her local women's crisis center would take the same approach. I assured her that no therapist worth their salt would have ever spouted such nonsense, which I characterized as "psychological vandalism."

One woman emailed me to describe her experience with a counselor, who told the client that "other women had it worse than her" and that she "couldn't really see what impact the rape had" on her. The counselor said that the client's depression and low self-esteem were just ways she was "stuck," and that she needed to move on.

The point isn't to scare you with horror stories of what can go wrong. I do think you should be determined to only accept the quality of care you deserve, though, and be aware that there are fools out there who inflict damage on rape victims because of their own ignorance. Don't allow meekness or humility to keep you in an "abusive relationship" with an incompetent therapist, and don't assume that "licensed" means "capable."

Finally, be honest with your therapist. Some of the most painful outcomes I have experienced came at the end of weeks, even months, of constant positive feedback by the client. Over and over they assured me that they liked and benefited from the direction and style of our work. Only much later did they abruptly reverse this feedback, arguing that I "should have just known" that they had felt differently. Therapists are not mind-readers, and depend on feedback and honest direction from clients. A 16-year-old wrote this journal about her angriest moment in therapy:

I informed my therapist I was quitting today; he inquired why. I told him I couldn't take his pushing me...he said "If you aren't pushed you just shut down and that doesn't get you anywhere." He was right.

So I told him it was because therapy wasn't helping me at all!
We talked a bit and then he asked, "Why were you raped?"
I said "because my dad decided to take advantage of me" (which was my rehearsed response). He then asked a buncha stuff he never asked before:
"Why didn't you fight him off?"
"Because I was a kid! I was scared, he told me this was my punishment and I deserved it and I believed him because I trusted him."
"Then it's your fault for trusting him, isn't it?"
"No! He was my daddy and he made me believe I could trust him! That's not my fault!"
"But you did deserve it, didn't you?"
(At this point I was PISSED!) "NO I WAS $#@&ING 8 YEARS OLD! THERE'S NOTHING I COULD HAVE DONE TO DESERVE THAT!"

He then said, "On day one you told me it was your fault because you trusted him and didn't fight back and you deserved it."
I was like, "oh yeah...I did say that didn't I?"

The last thing he asked was, "Still think therapy doesn't help?"

Needless to say I didn't quit.

Perhaps my favorite *A-ha moment* of all time happened with Danée. It is well-known that women who have experienced childhood sexual abuse often feel a resurgence of trauma symptoms when they have a child who nears the same age. Danée's rapes began when she was four, and I learned that Danée's youngest daughter was about to have her fourth birthday during the weekend. This would be a powerful trigger, but also an opportunity for Danée to have an "a-ha moment." Danée was in the throes of intense self-blame while working through stuck points, and just could not seem to relinquish her stubborn belief that if she had not been so weak, she could have fought off her uncle during her rapes. Therefore, she must certainly have been a failed child.

I asked Danée to spend extra time with her daughter that weekend, away from all the usual birthday celebrations. I gave Danée two assignments: look at her own four-year-old girl and consider whether Danée really believes that such a child ought to be able to fend off an adult. And second, she had to read *The Velveteen Rabbit* to her daughter.

For those unfamiliar with the book, it is a children's story that examines what it means to be a real, living being, as opposed to a mere disposable toy. This would be the perfect symbol for Danée's own existential crisis: could she ever be more than a discarded *thing*? In the book, the toy rabbit learns that becoming *real* is a painful, uncomfortable process that only happens when a child loves you. At times, the process is painful. But once a person becomes *real* through acts of love, they can never again be seen as ugly.

I knew this book contained hidden treasure for Danée as she read it to her own four-year-old. Danée would not only identify with the toy rabbit, yearning to be loved, but she would also identify with the child who could love another. After her daughter had gone to sleep, Danée wrote:

> ALL THE STRUGGLES + CHALLENGES ONLY MAKE US MORE REAL + LOVEABLE
>
> BEING REAL TRANSFORMS US.
>
> YOU DON'T HAVE TO BE PERFECT TO BE WORTHY.

People are like stained glass windows. They sparkle and shine when the sun is out, but when the darkness sets in, their true beauty is revealed only if there is a light from within

-Elisabeth Kübler Ross

Is it normal to be angry at God now?

I grew up in a Christian family and always loved God, but then I was raped and abused for years by my cousin, and yet to everyone else they were the "perfect" Christians. So from about grade 9 to grade 11 I wanted nothing to do with God. If that was what a Christian was, I wanted nothing to do with it. I was so angry and thought if there was a God and He allowed those things to happen, I didn't want anything to do with God. I was going to end my life. I did make up with God because of the kindness of someone else, and being accepted for who I was. I still go through times I get mad at Him. God can handle you being mad at him....it's ok! But He also wants to love you and is hurting with you.

-Retta, 23.

I am not going to preach, scold, or advocate for any particular spiritual system over others. But the impact of rape on spirituality is such a common injury that it cannot be ignored, either. I have had clients who drew closer to their concept of God after rape, but many also draw away from God, or spirituality, or religion. For some readers, religion and spiritually may be a non-issue, and this section may not apply at all.

Freud suggested that humans need spirituality to soothe our anxiety about being mortal. Our fear of eventual death, he said, is what causes us to cling to beliefs, ceremonies, and religious systems that give meaning to our lives (and afterlives). If spirituality is where we find the meaning of life to soothe our fears about death and loss, then it makes sense that a rape survivor would either reject, or cling desperately to, spirituality.

If you believe that because of rape, spirituality has failed in its promise to offer protection, comfort, or meaning to our lives, it is possible that you will reject spirituality as a failure itself, or as a maker of false promises, or as a phony system of rules that don't actually work. "I didn't get angry with God. I just decided that He didn't exist," wrote Kaye. "You can't be angry with someone that doesn't exist."

If you, through your rape, have become desperate for a source of comfort, meaning, and reassurance about your life's worth, then it is likely you will seek those things through some form of spirituality. And if you have a stuck point that "I was raped because I broke a rule and acted wrong," you're more likely to seek fundamentalist religious systems that offer divine blessing in exchange for adherence to strict moral codes.

Some rape survivors become spiritually experimental, exploring alternate religious traditions other than what she has grown up with, or adopting a liberally-minded philosophy of the worth of all persons and interconnectedness of all life. Others, however, may tend to do the opposite and cling to a more conservative creed in which morals and conduct are precisely prescribed. This is attractive because it offers concise limits which regulate behaviors, and which may promise God's acceptance and protection in exchange for dutiful obedience. For someone struggling with the thought that "I must have done something bad if I've been hurt this way," a more strict religious system may provide the sought-for promise of redemption. My concern, however, is that it may also reinforce the negative "stuck point" of traumatized thinking by suggesting that you were indeed hurt because of your *own* improper conduct or immorality. The question "who betrayed who?" becomes crucial to that survivor: did God betray me, or did I betray God? For example, Leitha wrote in her journal,

> I BEGGED silently during my attack, that God would send me help. That He would make the physical pain I was feeling come to an end. And I believed that He could, and that He would, because I was told I was His child and that he loved me. But the attack continued, and horrible things were being done to my body, and I couldn't understand why God wasn't helping me. But, as the violence against my body continued, I came to believe--to resign myself--that God was not sending help because I deserved what was happening to me. I had disobeyed my parents and I had broken house rules, and this was my punishment. And I was not angry with God at that point, I was angry with myself for my participating in this awful thing happening to me.

But the same benefits promised by spirituality/religion are often the very reasons you may be *angry* at God: Where is the protection you thought was promised? If God gives meaning to life, what could your life *possibly* mean if God permitted someone to harm you? If God really cares, where was God when you were raped? If men can be so vicious, how can we reconcile with a God who is often described as a "He?" Hennah journaled,

> Initially I believe that it was my faith in God that brought me through my childhood. As I am now going through it all over again, I have developed a

> different perspective. I have always had an unwavering faith. I was the rock. I loved God. I had a close and personal relationship with him. I didn't just pray, but I talked to him. When I was attacked, I was shattered. I was *violently* attacked, and was seriously thinking "enough already!" I still believe in him, but I'm mad. I can't seem to reconcile the love He has for me with the idea that He let this happen. If He's omniscient, then He saw this, and still it happened.

Danée also experienced intense anger toward God, because Danée could not reconcile the typical church description of an all-loving Father with her years of sexual abuse and rape as a child by family members. "I feel abandoned by God. It's like He too has closed his eyes. I feel angry that I never experienced a childhood. I never knew what it feels like to sit on my mother's laps and be rocked to sleep."

I have my own opinions, but I cannot simply write what *I* think and expect it to be *your* answer. However, I can offer you what many women have described as their way of answering these deep, agonizing questions. Let me preface by acknowledging that it's just impossible to propose answers that would fulfill every religious and cultural tradition, so please don't regard it as "exclusion" that such gaps are inevitable. I'm hoping to share the *processes* through which other women found answers, not to give those answers as final conclusions.

Have you ever considered that being angry at God is *respectful*, rather than disrespectful, to God? By challenging and questioning God, you are acknowledging God's responsibility—God's "ability to respond"—to you. Although you are confused and disappointed by God's apparent lack of comfort or aid to you, you are still asking for reasonable answers about God's involvement in your recovery. It is absolutely normal to be angry at God; in fact, it is just as important for you to express *these* feelings in your recovery as it is to express your other feelings of sadness and anger.

From this point of view, anger at God is not blasphemy, sin, or arrogance; it is a powerful search for meaning in life beyond rape. If all actions are needs trying to be met, your anger at God is your process of struggling to find answers and personal worth as a rape survivor. Besides, if you are angry at God, God already knows it and knows why, and can take it.

Some women have told me that their answer to these questions is that God must be testing their faith through trauma. This is a common theory among trauma survivors in general, not just rape, but it brings up some disturbing questions about God perhaps more than it resolves them. For example, if God tolerates, even arranges, for suffering to happen as a way of "testing" our faith, do we really find that God is all-loving? Or does it make God more of a manipulative, abusive authority, using pain to regulate us? If God even *needs* to test us to determine the outcome of our faith, is such a God actually all-knowing? If so, is this really the kind of God who can comfort us or even love us? I do not believe that rape is God's will (but recovery is), nor can I accept trauma as God's way of "testing" our faith. Hennah considered this issue in her journal as well:

> When I think about this, I start to wonder if God is just toying with us, but then I get a little deeper. If there are trials to be had, then the Lord knows that his faithful are better equipped to handle them. Where one person may be shattered permanently, I have the strength to endure. He doesn't want me to

> suffer, but He knows that He has given to me the tools of faith, to better prepare me.

I also find myself rejecting the slogan, "what doesn't kill us makes us stronger." While this sounds like an attractive maxim that finds strength in the midst of upheaval, *it's just not true*. Abuse, rape, incest, and violence do *not* make us stronger. I cannot identify a single way in which any of these experiences is anything but damaging. *Recovery* from these traumas will make us stronger, but the traumas themselves do not. The effort to find some "silver lining" or "moral lesson" in rape is misguided, and even toxic, because it prevents us from radiating the full depth of outrage we ought to have for these tragedies.

I might be able to go along with a modified slogan: "Recovery from what doesn't kill us makes us stronger." That's been true every time, and it's not a minor difference.

Another reason you may be feeling angry at God is that God did not seem to uphold the lessons you were taught as a child. Unfortunately, a lot of rotten, useless theology is given to children, disguised as "religion." We are often taught, for example, that worshipping God in some particular religious tradition will grant us a supernatural immunity from life's struggles, as if God wraps a bubble of protection around us. We are enchanted with stories from long ago of prophets and holy men and soldiers who were implausibly spared from death in furnaces, battlefields, combat with giants, even persecution and execution.

What we are *not* told, as children, is that true spirituality is not a form of protective spell-casting that guarantees a safe life. Rather, spirituality is the complex set of responsibilities, values, and insights that urge us to go *into* storms, survive them, and then pass along healing comfort to others in their storms. Spirituality does not anesthetize pain, it asks us to stand in solidarity with the hurting. From Christianity to Buddhism to Hinduism to Islam to Paganism to Indigenous religions, the message is issued again and again:

> This path is a difficult, narrow, even painful path. Following it does not guarantee your blissful invulnerability; it may even guarantee you turmoil. But it offers you *hope* that your struggles do not diminish your worth as a created person, and it will lead you toward others who are also hurting, who need you.

Perhaps much of our anger at God is for God's apparent failure to live up to a role God was never supposed to be in. It is not so much the failure of God, but a failure of childhood fairy-tales *about* God, that disgusts us. If we can reconsider religion as a way of recognizing our interconnection within a community of living souls, rather than a simplistic fortress against the minions of trauma, perhaps we can reconsider its role in our recovery. It is *not* God's will, or fault, that any person has been raped. It *is* God's will, and God's work, that survivors find one another and support one another through the healing process. God's action, then is not found in the trauma but in our response to it.

Some women have difficulty with the traditionally-male gender of God, as God is described in scriptures and sermons. If your perpetrators have been men, this might be an obstacle for you. If your perpetrator was a father, it can be difficult to refer to God as

"Father." For some women, avoiding the male terms for God alleviates these stresses, but it may also cause new feelings of guilt for rejecting the lessons they have learned in church and Sunday School about what God is!

"Alternative" and indigenous (tribal) religions are not typically male-oriented; God can be seen as genderless (neither male nor female), or even gender-full (wholly male *and* female). The "Father God/Mother Earth" duality in tribal theology suggests a balance between male and female, like two halves of a circle, in which men and women both share in an egalitarian relationship.

Even Biblical scholarship shows that God has traits of both a father and a mother, despite the typical He/Him descriptions of God in church. Several Abrahamic scriptures specifically deny that God is a *man* at all, despite the cultural and literary preferences for "He/Him" pronouns in ancient writings:

> **Numbers 23:19** God is not a man, that he should lie, nor a son of man, that he should change his mind. Does he speak and then not act? Does he promise and not fulfill?

> **1 Samuel 15:29** He who is the Glory of Israel does not lie or change his mind; for he is not a man, that he should change his mind

> **Romans 1:23** [foolish people] exchanged the glory of the immortal God for images made to look like mortal man. . .

In fact, we find that God encompasses the best of both genders:

> **Genesis 1:27** So God created man in his own image, in the image of God he created him; male and female he created them.

This verse implies that in order for creation to fully reflect God's image, both male and female are needed. Again, the words "He" and "His" reflect convenience in writing, and are actually gender-neutral in a purely grammatical sense, which in context now seems self-evident. I do not believe that these interpretations are heterosexist; gay and lesbian people can accommodate these interpretations as well. These ways of seeing God as gender-full simply describe the complexity of God's personality as it is fully experienced to any person.

One conservative Christian writer even took this insight to its full conclusion as it applies to survivors of sexual assault and abuse:

> There are hearts for whom the words, 'Daddy is home' are the most chilling, terrifying words that could ever pierce the air. Tragically, these dear people cannot even imagine how those same words flood millions of hearts with delight, making them feel warm, secure and content. That children can beam from ear to ear at the sound of a father's entry staggers their imagination. So different is their father that they find it almost beyond belief that there are those for whom their father is not only their protector and hero; Daddy is fun.

There are children who know that in their Daddy's eyes they are as close to perfection as any child could get. These greatly loved children know it is not because they are special; they think all fathers are like that.

When seeking to portray something that nothing in the universe can match, it is a communicator's nightmare that what for some people conveys the most powerfully evocative and accurate picture, is for other equally important people so far off beam as to be considerably worse than nothing.

If the Christian God is even remotely like the person many people know as father, we would have good reason for rejecting and despising him.[1]

We also find many verses that describe the love of God as a *mother's* love:

Isaiah 66:13 As a mother comforts her child, so will I comfort you . . .

Isaiah 66:12 For thus says the Lord, ' . . . you shall be nursed, you shall be carried on her hip, and be trotted on her [God's maternal] knees . . .'

Matthew 23:37 O Jerusalem, Jerusalem, you who kill the prophets and stone those sent to you, how often I have longed to gather your children together, as a hen gathers her chicks under her wings, but you were not willing.

We find verses about God giving birth to us (Deuteronomy 32:18), giving birth to earth itself (Psalms 90:2), and caring for God's newborns by nursing us (Numbers 11:12). We even find verses that specifically address God's role in replacing a parent who has been abusive: "Though my father and mother forsake me, God will receive me." (Psalm 27:10)

Once where Jesus tells His followers to "be compassionate as God is compassionate," the word *compassion* is translated from the Jewish word for *womb*. Jesus is telling people to feel mother-like compassion for one another, just as God is womb-like in compassion for all of us.

Other clients of mine have reconsidered their beliefs about the forces of good and evil in the world, too. As they have studied the causes and effects of rape, some women have begun to doubt that "evil" is something mystical that comes from literal demons, but rather something that comes from a human-made system of power, control, and selfishness. As humans have organized our social systems around values that are contrary to God's will, *we* (humans, not "we" rape survivors) produce the evil actions that bring so much trauma upon one another.

For example, as sexualized violence, cruelty, abuse, and hatred are normalized every day in reality TV, song lyrics, romance novels, movies, advertisements, and jokes, the effect of this warped system is that it produces the "smog" of "evilness" that warps

---

[1] "Mother God? Surprising discoveries by a conservative Christian about the gender of God and motherly love of God" http://net-burst.net/god/mother.htm

human behaviors right along with it. These aren't the works of little demons creeping about, but the destructive ("evil") works of humankind making abusive choices rather than compassionate ones. Rape, then, isn't something God has permitted, tolerated, or been passive about. Rape isn't something God uses to test faith or punish disobedient daughters. It's something that emerges from a social system that devalues women and values power and control instead. We are misdirecting our anger at God, when perhaps it ought to be directed at a society right before our eyes that tolerates and even *rewards* cruelty as entertainment. Perhaps God is just as angry as we are, right beside us, right *within* us, about the same things, while we wonder "Where is God?"

If any of this theory is even partly true, then authentic spirituality means more than "good" inner beliefs and "warm" thoughts and vague slogans about love. It would mean that authentic spirituality requires action as God asks us to directly confront and challenge the sickness of social systems that exalt abuse while demeaning anyone, women or men. When a rapper who jokes about murdering and abusing "bitches" gets a Grammy award, is this just a petty matter for too-sensitive bleeding hearts with too much free time? Or has it become a *spiritual* issue, which we should confront? If evil is a byproduct of *voluntarily-perverted* culture, then it becomes very Godly when we stand up and protest.

Likewise, when a woman accuses a celebrity of rape and then becomes nationally scorned while the celebrity is cheered and treated as a victimized hero, what should we do? If we're not willing to speak in defense for other women who come forward to report rape, then we're contributing to our society's *tolerance* of rape. It would be unfair for us to fail to challenge these wrongs, and yet wonder why God is not stepping in to do what we won't. I do believe that activism for social justice is one of the more powerful ways we can find God and spirituality.[2] I also believe that failing to act for social justice is one of the most common reasons we *lose* God and spirituality. If we oppose rape, we need to get off of the rapist's side.

Fay's journaling wrestled with this: "I'm still trying to figure out my own sense of purpose in life, at the moment I just do what I can on a small scale, like trying to practice 'backyard ecology' in my garden; and I've drafted up a will to ensure my house goes to Women's Aid after I die. I'm just not yet sure I've found exactly where I need to be in life, but I'm working on it." Lucinda pondered, "God is truly very good. I didn't used to think so...I used to think that he was punishing me—for what, I could not understand—but I think very differently about the Creator at this point. He knows me well."

My tribespeople, the Ojibway, are the original inventors of the well-known dream catcher. Unfortunately, dream catchers have become popularized as trendy souvenirs sold everywhere from gift shops to truck stops, and they are usually trivialized with a paper

---

[2] Author Andrew Harvey calls this "Sacred Activism" and explains, "A spirituality that is only private and self-absorbed, one devoid of an authentic political and social consciousness, does little to halt the suicidal juggernaut of history. On the other hand, an activism that is not purified by profound spiritual and psychological self-awareness and rooted in divine truth, wisdom, and compassion will only perpetuate the problem it is trying to solve, however righteous its intentions. When, however, the deepest and most grounded spiritual vision is married to a practical and pragmatic drive to transform all existing political, economic, and social institutions, a holy force - the power of wisdom and love in action - is born. This force I define as Sacred Activism." www.andrewharvey.net

tag that explains "the legend of the dream catcher," which is nearly always some goofy statement about how dream catchers "catch bad dreams and let good ones through to us."

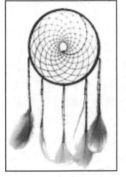

This is *not* the fundamental purpose of a dream catcher! A dream catcher, with its woven web of rhythmic spirals inside a hoop of willow wood, is actually an object that symbolizes the interconnected community around us. The web of strands represents the many points of connection and bonding between ourselves and others, each connected to others, who are connected to others, and so forth, within the enveloping hoop of God. The teaching has nothing to do with kids' dreams and magical webs; the teaching is that true strength is found in the complex interconnectedness we build between ourselves and others, in an ever-expanding circle. If we try to defend ourselves from things that will hurt us, we will fail if we try alone. But if we build bonds with others and nurture these relationships, our defense against adversity becomes stronger. In this model, God is not an overseer who passively watches as people hurt one another in some cruel drama that God never stops. God becomes the deeper spirit that exists in and through all things, binding us all together. Thus, "God" is present in the act of connection, and not present in the act of harm.

C.D. wrote, "For the past couple of weeks I have fallen asleep praying and it has actually been helping me with nightmares and flashbacks. I just pray whenever I can and it helps. No matter how mad I have been, it has helped. Because He doesn't care how mad you are... He is there."

I asked Danée what she felt about God now. Danée, who had journaled that she felt abandoned by God, told me, "I have a hard time being around church people, because so many church people failed to ever reach out while I was being hurt. And when they knew I was hurt, they turned away. But I do believe in God, and I find God in the loving connections I make with other people. God, for me, is not up in the sky. God is in the bonds we make with people who love us." I asked Danée whether she believed that God was present during her rapes. "Of course," she said. "They weren't things God willed or wanted to happen. God was there with me and grieved with me. And I think God has guided my recovery, sometimes by using things like lost memories to protect me…Amnesia can be a blessing."

Journal Activities:
Write about your spiritual beliefs. What experiences have you had that affected your spirituality, either positively or negatively?
What does your spiritual background tell you about the purpose of life?
What do you think God wants to say to innocent people who suffer?
What does it mean to be a human being having a spiritual experience? What does it mean to be a spiritual being having a human experience?
Where is God? Does God come and go? How can a human sense God's presence, and where do you go to sense it?
Did your rape change your spiritual beliefs, or confirm them?
Does spirituality allow you to remain silent and invisible? Does it require you to become openly active for other survivors?
Is spirituality something you keep privately within, or something that connects you

with others?
Does your spirituality require you to *act*, to follow certain ethics, or merely to think and believe good things?

One of the more difficult parts of spiritually recovering is to look back at your story through the question, "Where is God in this story?" Our emotions will reply, "God is nowhere in this story, of course!" and it can be tempting to leave it at that. But in individual and group therapy you may be able to discover some remarkable interventions you may have missed before.

As a Sister of Mercy, Marilyn Lacey has worked with oppressed people worldwide, such as refugees and war survivors. In her book, *This Flowing Toward Me*, she tells of a time when she became so overcome with the injustice, violence, and abuse she saw all around her that she became angry at God for God's apparent failure to intervene. But during a peaceful moment sitting in her garden, Marilyn felt God speaking back to her, and received tremendous words of counsel. Marilyn allowed me to use those words, and to alter them to apply to rape survivors. Here is her account of what God said back to her:

> You know that's not how it is, Marilyn, though I understand why you feel this way. I have many children. Some of them have locked your sisters out of my house. My heart is out there with them, but I've left people free. They do with me as they please. You see, love can't force anything. I'm as powerless, really, as a quadriplegic. They surround me with linen and candles, with solemn processions and profusions of flowers, and they deluge me with their prayers. But oddly enough, only a few of them really take notice of their brothers and sisters. It breaks my heart, too.
>
> I'm glad you've noticed them. Go ahead; be angry, but please don't hate me. I am with you in this, more than you could ever realize. And I am with your brothers and sisters, too, even as I am blamed for the burdens they now bear. Come now, let your tears flow. See, I am weeping with you.[3]

Laura had rejected God after her rape, believing that if God was a protective deity then God had failed her. After all, she reasoned, how can there be a God if Laura had been raped? It is very tempting for a therapist to promote their own personal views to answer such questions, but unless you have specifically sought a therapist who uses religious methods, this should not be done in your sessions. I was not able to give Laura my own views about whether God was or wasn't part of her recovery.

A month later as Laura prepared to graduate from therapy, she had gone apartment-hunting with her roommate. Laura had decided to move to a different county to avoid unhealthy relationships in her home town, and had settled on an apartment and was about to sign the lease. But as she left the apartment, she saw something astonishing:

---

[3] Lacey, Marilyn, R.S.M. *This Flowing Toward Me: A story of God arriving in strangers.* Ave Maria Press, 2009, p50. Used, and adapted, with permission of the author.

the car belonging to her rapist was parked a few doors down! She had been minutes away from moving within yards of him!

This was a county over from her home. If her rapist had been at work, driving around, or even lived on the other side of the building, Laura never would have seen the car. She would have been trapped in a very dangerous place for the next twelve months. As we talked about this, Laura remarked, "I'm still mad at God, but I think this was a God thing. I mean, how else would that have happened? Come on!"

Sometimes even symbolic experiences can translate to meaningful spiritual insights. I began to notice that in my group therapy studio, which was on the ninth floor, a large, lone hawk would hover just a few feet outside the window. Aside from being a beautiful animal, a hawk is meaningful to me: in my tribe, hawks represent steadiness and direction, healing, and insight. They also figure in to our creation story as a seeker of persons who make efforts to live spiritually, and hawks have become a symbol of "Protectors of Survivor's Spirits." Many survivors use a hawk as their representation of strength, and offer prayers for other survivors each time they see one circling over a field. I like that it transforms the hawk from its customary symbol as a predator into a new symbol as a watcher and hope-giver.

You can identify your own symbols, of course. Each person should identify something personally meaningful to them, so that reminders of success begin to outnumber triggers of struggle. Ashley, who works in the medical field, found insight from a patient during a conversation just before the patient's death:

> So last night I kinda came down hard on myself, but in the long run by the end of my shift I was feeling a little better. After talking to a dying patient last night I decided that I need to take some of my own advice. My patient was telling me how she's depressed that she's dying of pancreatic cancer and how she can't believe that she's going to be leaving her husband. I was changing a bag of saline when she said it. I stopped, sat down next to her, looked her in the eye and said "Just remember, God doesn't give us more then we can handle. Sometimes God challenges us and our faith, but it's never more then we can handle. It will take time but your husband will eventually heal from it and I'm sure he will have others helping him out." I stood back up and finished putting the bag back in the pressure infuser and it was like a light bulb came on. I need to start taking my own advice. Granted, my rapist ruined my life and changed me forever, granted I'll never be the person I was before. But I can work towards healing and I can work towards being a better person and can be happy again.

Kaye, who wrote earlier that she had simply stopped believing in God after her rape, added these words to her story afterward:

> The problem was that I knew that I decided not to believe in God without any real or valid reason. I simply went with my feelings on the matter. And so, I reached a point of really wanting to know, one way or the other. I started seeking God, figuring that if God was real, then God could be found.
>
> After months of this, I found God... I had a very real encounter with God that

changed my life drastically, completely and forever. It was after that, that I began my healing journey.

Hennah concluded her journaling by writing,

We are allowed to be angry with God. We are allowed to question. It is the trials that we go through that strengthen our faith. With each fracture, once repaired, it is stronger than before. We just have to be patient and persistent with it. I can't expect to regain my faith without trying to regain it. I am angry, but even through writing this, I have once again gained insight. This is how we grow.

I like the words that scholar Andrew Harvey used to describe the connection between God and the woman who seeks:

As the seeker deepens her experience…an astounding secret starts to derange her—she realizes that what she read in the great mystical books of every tradition is not poetry or enthusiastic exaggeration, but a literal and all-shattering truth: that she and the Beloved are not separate but one, and that the One she is looking for is also looking for her…That everything is held together by the force of love, that every atom is drunk on this love, and that the universe that before seemed so orderly is in fact always reeling in drunken, ecstatic dance.[4]

---

[4] Harvey, Andrew. *Perfume of the Desert*. Wheaton, IL: Quest Books, 1999, p33.

Feeling the pinch, feeling the hope
Feeling the void deep in my soul
Feeling my feelings so out of control
'Cause the years have not been kind to me, I know
                              -Concrete Blonde

What is the link between rape and self-injury?

People out there must be told about the self-loathing that follows rape and how it's the greatest breakage in divine law to mutilate themselves, as I have done.

-Tori Amos

Although I was a Self-Injurer before the rape, it only got worse afterwards. And when I didn't hurt myself physically, I think I kind of ran to guys to let them hurt me. I feel like I deserve more cuts, and more scars. More marks. Because I'm told I'm pretty so much and was told this by my ex-boyfriend until I was tired of hearing it. Tired of hearing I was "perfect" especially when I didn't think that I was. I cut because it physically made me feel better and because it meant that I was NOT perfect.

-Andrea, 16.

Self-injury (which I prefer over the inaccurate term, "self-mutilation") is the act of inflicting harm on one's own body to effect a change in inner emotions. This can include hitting, burning, hair-pulling, scratching, and cutting one's self. I am writing this section to those who self-injure, so the assumption I will make is that addressing the reader as "you" when discussing a self-injurer, applies.

To someone who is not a self-injurer, it may seem baffling that anyone would deliberately cause themselves pain or inflict such injury. Even to many self-injurers, this may also be a point of confusion: "What would make me do something like this? Am I sick? Am I a freak?" But to a self-injurer, the compulsion to cut or scratch (or otherwise harm) yourself can feel so overwhelming it becomes almost a *need*, not a desire or habit.

If you are a self-injurer, you may not even be aware of the inner motivations that drive these behaviors. Some women have recognized the connection between their self-injury and trauma, but others may have mistaken them as separate issues. I suggest that the link between the two is very strong.

Self-injury is far more common among females than males, although males are increasing these behaviors. The practice of self-injury (SI) tends to begin in adolescence, and may continue through adult years.[1] Many self-injuring behaviors gradually end in about 3 years (according to some studies), but I have worked with clients whose SI has persisted for a decade or more. The clinical research into self-injury identifies a common set of characteristics among women who self-injure:

> The typical subject is a 28-year-old Caucasian who first deliberately harmed herself at age 14. Skin cutting is her usual practice, but she has used other methods such as skin burning and self-hitting, and she has injured herself on at least 50 occasions. Her decision to self-mutilate is impulsive and results in temporary relief from symptoms such as racing thoughts, depersonalization, and marked anxiety. She now has or has had an eating disorder, and may be concerned about her drinking. She has been a heavy utilizer of medical and mental health services, although treatment generally has been unsatisfactory. In desperation over her inability to control her self-mutilative behavior this typical subject has attempted suicide by a drug overdose.[2]

Women who use SI say that they typically have one of two reasons for the behavior: to feel more, or to feel less. By inflicting an injury on the body, the person diverts emotional energy away from anxiety, depression, or frustration, and the replacement sensation—either pain or numb dissociation—becomes a sensation she feels she can control. For a woman whose inner pain is the result of abuse or trauma in which she had *no* control, this can become a clever, but addictive, way to find temporary relief.

In my work with self-injurers, I have observed several recurring themes in the thoughts and beliefs that precede the act of SI. These include:

- I can trick my brain into becoming numb so that I don't feel distress
- I am shameful and dirty, and I deserve punishment
- This is the only form of pain in my life I can control by myself
- These injuries are the only ones I can successfully nurture and heal
- This is the only way I can express inner feelings with an outward action
- This is how I prove to others that what I feel is genuine

Which of these are some of your reasons for self-injuring?

_____To convince others my pain is genuine

_____To attract sympathy and attention

---

[1] Kluger, Jeffrey. "The Cruelest Cut." *TIME*, May 16, 2005, p49-50.
[2] Favazza, A. R. and Conterio, K. "Female habitual self-mutilators." 1989 *Acta Psychiatr Scand.* 79:3. pp283-9.

____To cause physical pain which distracts from emotional pain

____To cause numbness that stops emotional pain

____To belong to a group of other self-injurers

____To prove to people that I can't be controlled

____To give myself a ritual of caring for the wounds

____It just seems cool for some reason

____It's become an addiction I can't stop

____I think I deserve punishment for bad things

The emotional side of self-injury

It has become very helpful for me when working with clients who self-injure to think of SI as a form of communication, in which the body has become a journal rather than a target. If I can become sensitive enough to comprehend what a set of injuries expresses about the woman who bears them, I can begin to absorb new ways of understanding *her*. I try to teach this to the frustrated and judgmental family members of self-injurers who struggle to understand these behaviors.

For example, I have found that some women use cutting to express their feelings about their lives. Women who cut in straight, parallel, even lines that aren't very deep are usually searching for stability and control. Their injuries themselves are a form of order: they are even, measured, and done with intentionality and care. These injuries speak to me of a woman who feels lost in a whirlwind of other peoples' control over her, with no choice or stability of her own. Victoria, for example, had experienced such chaos in her life that her craving for control took the form of thin, precise lines on her upper arm ("my sergeant stripes").

But another woman may cut or scratch random, erratic marks that crisscross in random arrangement. These injuries are done spontaneously in a whiplash blaze of emotions. Injuries like these tell me of a woman who is desperate and terrified that if she doesn't complete the ritual of self-injury immediately, she will explode. Her cuts are produced by emotions rather than beliefs, and they tend to express anger and self-rejection. These are punishing forms of injuries, in which the body has become a stand-in symbol for her very spirit, which she considers to be shameful and polluted. She is whipping herself with cruel self-talk: "You're so *stupid*! You're such a *slut!* You're *nothing!*" as she marks herself.

But injuries can also be misinterpreted by others. Not everyone has the insight to understand your SI as a form of emotional expression, and negative reactions can compound the feelings of shame and isolation that you may feel. One fact that even some therapists and psychiatrists miss is that self-injury is *not* a form of suicidal behavior. People who use SI are trying to make life manageable; they aren't trying to end it. SI becomes a way to cope with life so it can continue. I am not giving approval for SI behaviors, which are clearly ultimately harmful to both physical and emotional health. But it is impossible to address an issue if we cannot even understand its purpose in someone's life. If all actions are needs which are trying to be met, we ought to inquire what inner needs you are trying to settle with SI.

What even some therapists might misunderstand is that SI is often *precious* to the person who uses it. Unlike a suicidal person, whose thoughts tend to be very rigid ("I must kill myself, because there is no other way out of what I feel"), the mind of a self-injurer tends to be disorganized—a whirlwind of conflict, emotions, and thoughts. SI is used to *force* the mind to become organized and manageable, rather than to escape the simplicity of all-or-none thinking. In fact, persons who self-injure tend to have difficulty thinking of other solutions to anxiety precisely because of their frantic thought processes during stress, which also frequently results in high rates of alcohol use.[3]

Furthermore, a person who attempts suicide usually feels far *worse* afterward; they regard their efforts as a failure, and they feel trapped in a hopeless despair. But for the person who self-injures, the opposite is true: there is a sense of *relief* immediately afterward. But this is also the heart of the addictive nature of SI: it becomes less and less a "coping skill" and more of a chronic, inescapable addiction—"something I have to do or I'll die, like breathing" as one woman put it. Women who use self-injury usually see it as an alternative to suicide, a way to resist suicide.[4]

Consequently, I have seen many self-injuring clients (mis)treated as suicidal patients in hospitals and treatment programs, which is a mistake. Not only does this usually trigger a "suicidal crisis" response by therapists and clinical staff (who exert more control over the person who is already trying to escape a feeling of being powerless), but it diverts us into a misunderstanding what she is *actually* trying to say and do with her actions. Again, therapy cannot be successful if the therapist is approaching the issue from an incorrect set of assumptions. (Therefore, if you perceive that your therapist misunderstands your self-injury, don't remain passive; *speak up* and inform him or her!)

Some self-injurers bristle at the suggestion that SI is done as a form of attention-seeking. To them, it feels like they are being accused of manipulation and insincerity.[5] But I have found that the real answer to the "attention-seeking" controversy is that "it depends." Many women who self-injure do so in very secret, hidden ways: their cuts, scratches, and injuries are tucked under clothing away from view, and they become deeply embarrassed if someone asks about them. Clearly, these women are not seeking attention; they are dreading it!

On the other hand, I have observed others who self-injure in ways that are very publicly conspicuous. Vivid injuries decorate arms and hands, and short sleeves contribute to the display. Websites abound in which young women display their injuries

---

[3] Sinclair, J. M. and Hawton, K. "Reducing Repeated Deliberate Self-Harm." 2002 *Practitioner* 246;1632:164-6, 169-72

[4] Solomon, Y. and Farrand, J. "'Why don't you do it properly?' Young women who self-injure." 1996 J Adolesc 19;2:111-9

[5] Hogg, C. and Burke, M. "Many people think self-injury is just a form of attention-seeking." 1998 *Nursing Times* 94;5:53

like trophies, youtube videos glamorize "cutting" with musical slideshows of blades and injuries, and although they would protest any suggestion they are seeking attention, there is undeniably a sensational aspect to the display. These injuries are done to announce to others, and convince others, that her inner pain is real, and that she indeed *is* different, an outcast, alienated, and impossible to understand. Perhaps this is done to attract attention, but even this is still a representation of inner needs trying to be met. But for this reason I am extremely reluctant to endorse very many online "support" groups for self-injury, because a high number of them are filled with photos, artwork, and descriptions that are triggering, at best, and glamorizing of self-harm at worst, and some attract members who can only be described as having a toxic presence.

The physiology of self-injury

Some amazing research is emerging to show a link between brain function and the urge to self-injure. The act of inflicting harm on the body causes the body to immediately react by initiating the "self-protection and healing" process. One way it does this is to switch off pain receptors in the brain, and switch on the production of the Endogenous Opioid System (EOS), a part of the brain that produces endorphins. Endorphins are natural pain-killers that produce pleasurable sensations; because they resemble opiates they work in a manner similar to drugs like morphine or codeine. Self-injury becomes a way to "trick" the brain into releasing more of these natural drugs. Some self-injurers train their brains so well that they actually begin to feel a numb sense of relief simply by *preparing* to self-injure, when the injury itself has not even happened yet!

There are two theories about why this seems to work to relieve stress in self-injurers.[6] The *pain hypothesis* suggests that the brain's release of opiates causes a dissociative (analgesic) state in which physical pain is diminished or short-circuited completely. The nervous system simply does not feel pain for the moments that the EOS is actively releasing endorphins. The *addictive hypothesis* points out that like morphine and codeine, endorphins are also physically addictive. Self-injury is a method of administering a drug to produce a temporary euphoria ("high") that relieves distress, depression, and frustration. But a physical addiction to these endorphins develops, which drives the self-injurer into more frequent urges to self-harm. Stress and depression become triggers to literal drug abuse *through* self-injury. When I describe this theory to my patients, many women have responded without hesitation, "Oh yes, I am definitely addicted to it!"

Women who self-injure tell me that even making the decision and preparation to self-injure brings about a sense of calm. During the preliminary stress, their heart rates increase and respiration quickens, and even the skin itself contracts. But during and after the act of self-injury, all of these symptoms diminish.[7] Although this sounds like such a positive benefit (it could almost be an advertisement *for* self-injury), the full picture also shows that these benefits not only fade over time, but the person's perceptions of stress,

---

[6] Andrés Martin (2003). *Pediatric Psychopharmacology: Principles and Practice*. Oxford University Press. p358.
[7] Haines, J., Williams, C. L., Brain, K. L., and Wilson, G. V. "The Psychophysiology of Self-Mutilation." 1995 J Abnorm Psychol 104;3:471-89.

physical responses to stress, and ability to problem-solve all become impaired and worsen while SI persists.[8]

What both theories agree on, however, is that the body develops tolerance to the high doses of endorphins in the brain. It takes more severe methods (and frequency) of self-injury to produce the same result. If these artificial sensations of calm and peace have become your automatic habit for coping with trauma, you will likely develop an ever-worsening technique of self-harm, and you are also likely to begin to perceive SI as a "need" you "have to do," and you will depend on it more urgently.

There's more. The brain becomes used to the endorphins and begins to tolerate them rather than switching on the "relief feelings" you once felt. Over time, self-injurers have *lower* than normal levels of endorphins, not higher. As SI's ability to trigger the same numbness or high wears off, your panic and fear at being unable to cope can grow worse. If you are not aware that this is a physical phenomenon like any drug use, your mind may begin to tell you that you are failing to cope because you are *weak*, and this plus your rape trauma combine to convince you that you are a hopeless, helpless, frail woman.

So what's the link?

Okay, so we can see how self-injury has a physical effect on feelings. But what is it about sexual assault that seems particularly linked to self-injury? Studies of self-injurers have found up to 80% have survived sexual abuse or rape, *far* outdistancing any other form of trauma in the background of self-harming behaviors.

One reason these are strongly linked is that sexual trauma, more than *any* other type of trauma, is compounded by the shame and secrecy that the victim feels. Survivors of other types of trauma—combat, tornadoes, car accidents—do not endure the same fear that these issues will be "found out," and don't have to hide them from others for years. Sexual trauma is more deeply internalized than any other trauma because it is locked within the victim as a silent secret. The entire being of the victim herself must become engaged in managing that secret, coping with shame. This alone causes the brain to expend enormous amounts of energy to process thoughts, feelings, and beliefs after the trauma of rape or sexual abuse.

Neuropsychiatrist Dr. Daniel Amen writes that after such trauma, the emotional centers of the brain become inflamed—"hot"—because of disturbances in physical and mental health.[9] This "hotness" in the emotional center of the brain causes a repetitive process of thoughts and feelings as the brain tries to manage the trauma; we call these repetitive processes "depression" and "obsessions and compulsions." Dr. Amen suggests that people who self-injure do so while other psychiatric issues are active at the same time; he names PTSD (and the depression from it) as the most common issue.[10]

Another reason that rape and self-injury are so often linked is that rape teaches its survivor to reject and resent her own physical self. Many women who self-injure do so to punish their bodies from a belief that they "deserve" such punishment, or even that they

---

[8] Sinclair, J. M. and Hawton, K., op cit.
[9] Jershua Clark and Dr. Earl Henslin. *Inside a Cutter's Mind*, p80-83
[10] Ibid., p84.

"deserved" the rape itself. The persistent stuck point of self-blame is *directly* responsible for this form of self-injury, and it is likely to continue as long as you accept the belief—on any level—that you are flawed and deserve punishment.[11]

When I am processing this type of self-injury in therapy with a client, I will often ask what thoughts are going through her head in the moments immediately before the act of injuring. I am often answered with a list of *feelings* instead: "I feel sad, depressed, scared…" But when we begin to examine the actual *thoughts* that precede self-injury, we discover an amazingly-clear set of self-blaming beliefs: "I am bad, I deserve this, my body is ugly, I am a loser, nobody can love me…" If you grew up believing that having certain thoughts and feelings makes you bad, you are more likely to direct the blame for a rape *inward* and conclude, undeservedly, that your own "badness" caused the rape. When you recycle those "bad thoughts" for years afterward, it convinces you further that you truly are bad and need punishment.

Another trait I have observed in many women who self-injure is that they often feel they cannot fit into the values and rigid mannerisms of their family. This deep sense that "I don't belong" or "I don't matter" is extremely common among self-injurers and may be a direct result of rape, or perhaps even a feeling of alienation from the values of her family. Many younger clients of mine are anguished by their belief that their family either disapproves of them outright, or simply upholds a system of rules, morals, or values that she sees as designed to flunk her in her struggle for approval.

Women who self-injure for self-punishment tend to be overly critical of themselves. They will feel crushed and humiliated at even slight disagreements by others ("I always say the wrong things, don't I?" said one client in group when I challenged her beliefs on a very minor matter), and constantly inspect themselves for signs of failure. They fear public judgment, and will often "mind read" others, convinced that people are silently judging and rejecting them. I have found that women who self-harm will simultaneously feel that *everyone* knows thoroughly what her faults and flaws are, including her rape, and yet *nobody* can ever truly know her. She feels shunned but analyzed, ignored but investigated, all at once. One woman even told me that her cuts were a way to satisfy other people in her own mind: "It was my way of saying, 'see? I know I'm as f---ed up as *you* know I am, so I'll do this to show you that I'm not blind to it. This is my way of telling you that I agree with what I think you're thinking about me!'"

One of the hardest truths about SI for me to express to clients is that SI has far more to do with thoughts then feelings. It is easy to link SI with emotions because you *feel* so depressed or upset when you do it. But one of the core principles of cognitive therapy is that *thoughts* precede *feelings*. For example, if I told you to become very sad, you could not simply change your emotions to sadness. You would have to think of something sad first, and then use those thoughts to generate the feelings of sadness. The act of self-injury and the emotions that accompany it are both ways of expressing *thoughts* (or beliefs, if you prefer), that cause them. One client of mine wrote in her journal,

---

[11] Greenspan, G. S. and Samuel, S. E. "Self-Cutting After Rape." 1989. *Am J Psychiatry* 146;6:789-90

> The real reason why I feel ashamed is because I don't want people to see that I am weak, and I can't control everything. Or in other words, I can't handle everything that life gives me. I don't want people to see my pain. I don't really like the person I have become because I am always sad. I am so emotional, I feel like it's making me ugly.

(Notice how she presents these as feelings, but they are really *beliefs* more than emotions. Also, notice the all-or-none wording: "I *can't* handle *everything* life gives me...I am *always* sad..." and her use of the "I should" concept to make herself feel guilty: I should be able to handle everything; if I can't then I am weak.)

If you can discover what your self-injury communicates about your beliefs, rather than simply seeing self-injury as a way to "shut off" emotions, "cope" with distress, or some other motive, then you can begin to deal more directly with the real reasons you use it. When the time comes for you to stop, an essential step will be for you and your therapist to examine the beliefs and thoughts you have that contribute to your urges. I have not seen high rates of success in ending self-injury merely by making promises or signing contracts to stop, by having good intentions of stopping, or by trying to "feel better" or "think positive"; it is absolutely necessary to discover, isolate, and change the *beliefs* about yourself that underlie your self-injury.

JOURNAL: Why do you think self-injurers often hide or deny their cuts and scratches? What reactions or feelings are you trying to avoid by hiding them? OR if you are a person who does *not* hide them, what reactions and feelings are you hoping or expecting to get from others?

JOURNAL: List your self-criticisms. These are all the negative things you think about yourself. This journal entry should include comments about your mind, your body, your spirit, your abilities, your history and childhood, your worth as a person, and things that have happened to you.

JOURNAL: Which experiences have you had that taught you to think those things?

JOURNAL: What other thoughts and feelings lead to your decision to hurt yourself?

Example; one girl wrote to me, *"No one likes me; I hate my body; Nothing ever works out right; No one would ever want to be with me; I'm so stupid; Life sucks; I hate everyone; I can't stand my life; I was abused; I want someone to care about me; Nobody can help me."*

A guy wrote to me: *"I feel like if I have cuts and scratches, people have to take my feelings seriously. It's like I'm saying, 'See? My feelings are real! Stop telling me to just get over it!' I feel like if I have scars, it makes my feelings seem less shallow and more believable."*

What thoughts (not feelings!) are going through your head in the moments right before you hurt yourself?

If your injuries could speak, what would they say and who would they say it to?

Taylor, a young woman I saw in therapy, completed these journal assignments and offered to share her responses. She described the self-talk (thoughts) she has immediately before harming herself. Taylor wrote,

> I can't do anything right; I'm full of errors. My selfish self just has nobody to look up to. I seem to concentrate on the past, when everything was alright. But things change and people move on. Lives are lost never knowing what to do next because some people are so self-centered. They tend to look at the outside instead of the inside. Like me, I'm ugly.
>
> Why do I do this? I am so retarded. Besides, in the morning I'll just be ashamed of myself, yet I'll cut myself again tomorrow. How selfish! There are lots of people dying right now and here I am trying to hurt myself when I should be thinking about someone else.

Notice the themes in Taylor's writings. She labels herself as "selfish" for being hurt or upset, as if she has no right to these emotions. She treats her emotions as privileges she does not deserve, and then compares herself negatively to others. She believes that her own life is so meaningless that to even be upset is arrogant, considering the suffering that others go through. Her "should" thinking ("I should be thinking about someone else") reveals a lot of guilt about being depressed; Taylor saw depression as a form of weakness and punished herself for indulging in such weakness. By punishing herself with cuts, she was outwardly demonstrating her inward beliefs: "You are so selfish for even being depressed! Who are you to feel anything? You're nothing!" The cuts would serve as a form of punishment, but would also cause more shame and more depression. Thus, they continued her cycle of feeling ashamed and depressed, feeling guilty about having feelings, punishing herself, then feeling ashamed and depressed for what she had done!

Taylor's successful effort to end her self-injury began when she accepted that she has the right to feel depressed, angry, and upset because of her rape. She had to really look at the effects of rape on her life, and learn that rape is a life-changing trauma, not a sneeze or a stubbed toe. Taylor had to redefine herself as a worthwhile girl who had been hurt, who had a right to *feel* that hurt. Next, she had to make an agreement with herself that she would *fight* against that hurt, rather than settling into a new role as a needy, defeated, energy-draining person. Just as she had to give up the "who am I to even feel hurt?"-thinking, she also had to reject the temptation to feel privileged as a victim: "I've been hurt, so everyone please take care of me and indulge me!"

(Taylor had a tendency to lash out at others, and then become offended when they confronted her for it, convinced that everyone was merely "picking on her." She could not bear to consider that she actually had some abusive traits of her own and that she had the capacity to hurt others, and had maintained a fantasy that being a victim allowed her to "vent" but nobody had better hold her accountable for it. To her, confrontation felt like being bullied; she would try to excuse her behavior by reciting how abused she'd been, and then withdraw to self-injure.)

Taylor had to find a third option: "My hurt is real, and it matters. Because *I* matter. And that makes it worthwhile for me to face the hurt, accept that it was not my fault, but it *is* my responsibility to fight back against hopelessness."

Finding your way through these three options can be difficult, and it can take a determined therapist to help. It is easy to fall into the rut of thinking "I'm such a nothing, I don't deserve to feel this bad. I should get over my feelings!" And it can be easy to *over*-embrace your hurt as the only defining trait about you. Many of my patients have believed they are "getting in touch with their pain" when they hand me collages and poems heavy with dark, cruel imagery: pictures of torture, cuts, closed eyes, and words that express similar images. When I challenge them to go beyond simply describing their pain to adopting a more empowered, thriving set of images to define themselves, some of them will become disgusted with me, convinced that I "truly just don't get it."

On the contrary, though, I can understand and accept the genuineness of these forms of pain without hesitation. What I am encouraging, however, is a new trajectory for growth away from it. This is not the same as when a well-meaning therapist offers trite advice like "just try to think happy thoughts! Focus on the positive!" This is a bolder, and ultimately more useful, way of raising the standards of what she is willing to accept as the truth of her life. If she is only willing to persist in the unmoving, "stuck" depiction of pain and emptiness as the limit of her life, she is able to do that all without the collaboration of a therapist. It takes less effort to "express" than to *change*. It is when she becomes impatient with these painful images and refuses to let them map the borders of herself, that growth begins. This is why it is important to examine, accept, and name your pain from rape, but not to simply do this and then stop. The necessary next step is to immediately covenant with yourself that you will no longer mold your life to fit within the confines of that pain. Self-injury is an accurate and effective method of expressing pain—I can be honest about that. It is *not*, however, an effective way of overcoming pain or fighting back. *You* must be honest about *that*.

One woman journaled about her frustration at seeing so many of her fellow rape survivors persisting in using bleak, dark, hopeless words and images to describe themselves. Her words carry a powerful "battle call" to all women who are advancing in their own recovery:

> I am at a loss as to how to communicate the importance of choosing life. I hear many of the same emotions, repeated, no matter what specific situation is faced; feelings of worthlessness, hopelessness, exhaustion. These feelings are horrible, no question. Life can be incredibly hard. But it is my absolute conviction that we do not need to allow these feelings to defeat us. They can be overcome with determination.
>
> There needs to be less willingness to give up, to bail out. Many of us are here, offering support, concern, optimism, hope for the future. Make a commitment to get off the ledge, and stay off the ledge. By constantly getting back on the ledge, precious energy is wasted that could be used to improve situations. There are many here who have been out on that ledge before,

climbed back down, committed to life, and will tell you now that their lives are better than they could have ever imagined, as they stood on that ledge. But the commitment must be made…Then, what ever improvement needs to happen in situation, perspective, whatever, that work begins.

With regard to those feelings of worthlessness, they must be exposed for what they are: an absolute LIE that we have accepted as truth. But the truth is that we are all valuable to each other, to ourselves, and most importantly, to God. To accept that ANY of us is worthless is to say that ALL of us survivors are worthless. And we know that is not true. We are all children of God, and have contributions to make to each other and to the world at large. The loss of any one of us diminishes us all. If we choose to disregard the value and contributions we have to make to each other, we cheat ourselves and others of much needed blessings and support. Because it is in loving and supporting others that we are blessed.

Its time we stop devaluing ourselves. It's hurting us, and hurting others. Its time we decide to embrace our purpose on this earth; to share love with others. We all have a piece of this job. Don't walk away from it. We need you.

Many women in therapy have defended their use of self-injury to me by assuring me, "it calms me down." When I ask them to describe the calming effect, I hear very similar replies: "It feels like it releases pressure" and "I can go from upset to numb in a second" and "it just makes me float and forget what I was feeling" and "I just blank out."

So a more accurate statement than "it calms me down" would be that "self-injury *shuts* me down." It grants the brief benefit of relief from thorny emotions, but it does not equip the injurer with any more strength, wisdom, skill, or knowledge to battle back against the sources of those feelings. It is a vampiric behavior: it offers a brief pause of emotional flatness, while sucking emotional strength from you as the price, and then adding more wounds to the burden of shame you carry that will require you to repeat the behavior again. The addiction model of self-injury explains exactly why and how it does this.

Terah, after being raped by her grandfather, began a years-long pattern of self-injury and eating disorders in her frantic effort to shut down her emotions about her rape. She wrote,

How do you handle something like this??? I decided that you don't. I decided to ignore it. That stupid notion that if you ignore it, it will go away…well I tried, but the dam had been broken, and the memories came flooding in. No matter how hard I tried, I couldn't help it. Finally, I just "checked-out" for a while. I needed to be numb. All my filters had been torn down, and I was feeling everything all of the time. I lived life by going through the motions, but not really experiencing any of it. This lasted for a little while and then I started doing bizarre things to see if I was still alive. Things like stabbing myself repeatedly with a fork to see if I could feel it…to see if I would bleed. I would pull my eyelashes out to see what it would feel like. I would scratch at my skin until it bled. I was only about 40% present in my mind at the time…the rest of me was still "checked-out".

I was cutting to reassure myself that I was in fact alive, and the proof was in the blood. I was losing control, though. Then it all changed, and suddenly. The best way I can think to put it is to say that I literally "snapped" back to reality. I think that's when I hit bottom. I didn't have the luxury of the numbness. I felt it quite poignantly, and it was excruciating. I felt as though my whole world was crumbling. I had to deal with a lot more than the memories. I had to deal with the fact that I wasn't a virgin, like I thought I was. I had to deal with the anger about my mother. I had a crisis of faith. I didn't know if I could believe anything I had previously "known", because that was all based on some fundamental lies.

For most of my life, my mother had been my hero, and now, I could hardly believe that she was even human. How does a mother let something like this happen? How does she let it continue once she knows? I couldn't really handle any of this stuff, but I didn't know how to ask for help. I became more fervent with my cutting. I was cutting deeper and more often. I started controlling *what* I ate, and then *when* I ate, and then *if* I ate at all. It made me feel a little better. I started to "crave" feeling hungry, because then I could control the fact that I was wanting food, but not eating. I got a high off of the emptiness. I lost a lot of weight very quickly. Again, don't misunderstand, this wasn't demented dieting, it was *control*. But I am a dancer, and when you drop that kind of weight that quickly, red flashing lights start going off around you. My literature professor started having me over for dinner with his family—and remember that in order to have the control, I needed to not get caught. So I'd go and eat when people were so obviously watching, and purge when they weren't. This went on for quite some time. I'm a good actress.

I like to call this my "denial" phase. I didn't want to deal with the emotions involved with being raped repeatedly throughout my childhood, so I denied it…but I was spiraling down that twisty path of self-loathing and self-destruction. I very quickly arrived at that breaking point. I hadn't talked to *anyone* about it, and it was all just too hard, and I tried to kill myself. I was never a suicidal girl, but at that point in my life, it literally seemed like the only way to make it all stop.

It didn't work.

Are you ready to stop?

It may be apparent to you that self-injury has become an unhealthy way to manage your emotions, and you may be eager to stop the behavior. But self-injury may still have a function in your life, and at times it might suppress an emotional crisis that could otherwise overwhelm you or even tempt you toward suicide. It may sound strange, but I have had many clients whose lives may have been saved by self-injury, because it offered them an option other than suicide to escape crisis. This is not my statement of approval for self-injury; it is my statement of *understanding*.

Ultimately, the choice to end self-injury must be yours, and yours alone. I have not observed lasting success among women who have tried to stop because of pressure or guilt by loved ones, promises to stop, or inducements through rewards and punishments. The most successful reasons to stop are that self-injury no longer works the way it used to, or it is becoming so severe that it is increasingly dangerous, or that you have committed to better emotional and physical health. I have seen the puzzlement across many parents' and husbands' faces when I have bluntly counseled them that nothing they do can *make* you stop self-injuring, especially if it still works the way you want it to.

Again, this is not an excuse for the habit to continue. It would be wrong to point to what I have just written and proclaim, "See? A therapist says right here not to try to make me stop!" I urge you to begin leaving this habit behind as soon as you can because of its highly addictive and strength-diminishing nature. Self-injury causes social alienation because of widespread misunderstanding, and sometimes groups who do accept self-injury often do so because of its shared glamour among members. I have seen groups of self-injurers who mutually support the behavior in one another, even becoming competitive about it, while treating self-injury as an identity-defining trait that elevates the clique to a special status apart from the mainstream. I have not observed successful recovery from self-injury (and indeed, from rape) while remaining attached to any group culture that advocates, sensationalizes, or rationalizes the use of self-injury.

In order to successfully end self-injury, part of your commitment to your own health may mean that you will make difficult choices about entire systems of your lifestyle. This could include changing friendship groups, shunning certain music that you associate with triggers, and adhering to a doctor's prescribed regimen of medications for depression and anxiety. Stopping self-injury is not as simple a choice as deciding to change hair color. It is a difficult, often frustrating process that must be made with a full understanding of how self-injury has served your needs, and what you will begin to do to fulfill those needs without it. It will also force you to become aware of how your use of self-injury has affected your relationships with people close to you, which is often the first insight that motivates a woman to begin to change the behavior.[12]

This book is not meant to serve as a comprehensive guide for treating self-injury. I find that self-injury and sexual trauma are so frequently linked that it is worthwhile to address self-injury here, and I have attempted to treat it with sensitivity, understanding, and accuracy. If you make the decision to include self-injury among the issues you want to resolve as part of your rape recovery, I would like to offer some resources which I have found extremely helpful.

- **The Scarred Soul: Understanding & Ending Self-Inflicted Violence** by Tracy Alderman. I regard this as my personal favorite of all books on the topic of self-injury. Alderman's book is intelligently written, and very sensitive (and sensible) about the topic.
- **Understanding Self-Injury: A Workbook for Adults** by Robin Connors and Kristy Trautmann. This workbook is meant to be used as a part of therapy, rather than a stand-alone "self-help" booklet.

---

[12] Conterio and Lader, *Bodily Harm*, p164.

- **When Your Child Is Cutting: A Parent's Guide to Helping Children Overcome Self-injury** by Merry E. McVey-Noble, Ph.D. A good guide for parents of adolescents who self-injure.

Terah, who previously described her cutting and anorexia, ended her journal with words that are fitting for the end of this chapter. She writes,

> I still have hard times, but I'm a lot better now. I don't cut, and I eat regularly. I'm not avoiding my problems anymore. I still have nightmares, but at least I know that I'm not possessed. I wake up crying and yes, sometimes gagging. But these are just lumped into my category of "bad hours." I've decided that if these are bad hours, then the rest are good hours, and there are a lot more of those. I am who I am because of my experience in life. I am stronger than before, because I know that I came out the other end whole, and that I have the strength to face what's next. I am defined by my own terms now, not by what he did to me or took away from me. That's not to say that I am without scars, but it is my imperfections that make me priceless and beautiful, and my scars are my imperfections.
>
> I am a successful woman who has triumphed over her past. We fought and I won. Every little girl dreams of growing up to be a ballerina, and I get to live that dream every day. I am an educated and well-respected member of my community. I am a leader and a mentor. I'm still young, and I am sure that I have many more years of surprises ahead of me. I'm able to deal with the flash-backs because I can now see that I am no longer that scared little girl. I have an inner strength. I have taken that horrible childhood and learned from it. If I can accomplish one thing by all of this, I hope that it is to let another woman know that she is strong. That she can overcome the pain, the despair, the fear, and she can thrive.

You don't drown by falling in the water.
You drown by staying there.

Why can I work so hard,
and yet sometimes feel like I haven't changed?

Never confuse a single defeat with a final defeat.
--F. Scott Fitzgerald

The process of recovery has never been a single line in any of the hundreds of rape cases I have managed. In every single one, there has been a zigzag pattern of progress, struggle, then more progress. You simply will not be able to succeed at recovery if you are unable to forgive yourself for the occasional mistakes, relapses, and hard times you will pass through, and for the length of time it takes. Recovery from rape never happens on-schedule, and I have observed that the most likely time of regression is when you are feeling pressured—by yourself or others—to "hurry up and get it right."

When I have worked with women young enough to still live with or close to parents, for example, I nearly always get a call from mom similar to this one: "Matt, I'm really concerned about -----. She was doing so well there for a while, and now she's having problems." Then I hear the list: she is argumentative, moody, she's having rages, she's shutting down, and so on. Even when I warn families in advance this will happen, they still call to suggest something expected is happening.

This can be extremely discouraging for you as the survivor, because you might see other women who appear to be doing so well while you struggle and even fail. As you look back on how hard you've worked, it hurts deeply to think that you could have poured your heart and soul into your recovery and yet things can *still* go badly at times. It's painful to think that even your best efforts won't make your life smooth and flawless. So what many women do at that point is to discredit their *therapy*: "Oh, I faked my way through it/I only said what they wanted to hear/The therapy sucked/All therapy did was open me up without teaching me how to put the pieces back again/the therapist was a jerk."

But Rape Trauma Syndrome/PTSD progresses through stages. If you are not familiar with the stages of PTSD, recovery can be very frustrating because you will tend to interpret your difficulties as coming from *personal* flaws. But once you are fluent in the PTSD stages, you can experience an occasional setback without completely devaluing yourself. Instead, you can say to yourself, "I'm having a difficult time right now, but it's because I'm in the Resolution (or Outward Adjustment) stages—it's not happening because I'm failing."

1. <u>The Crisis Stage</u>: This stage occurs *immediately after the assault*. It is temporary, lasting a few days to weeks. During this stage you may:
   - Become agitated, easily frustrated, or frenzied, or you may appear totally numb (because you may be in shock). But emotions are either very strong or very flat, with little middle ground.
   - Have inconsistent memories about the rape, which can mean that the details of the story may change.
   - Have difficulty concentrating, making decisions, and doing simple everyday tasks.
   - Have crying spells and anxiety/panic attacks.

2. <u>The Outward Adjustment Stage</u>: During this stage you resume what appears to be "normal" life. Inside, however, there is considerable conflict which can produce combinations of the following behaviors:
   - Extreme anxiety.
   - Severe mood swings (e.g. happy to angry, etc.). Depression becomes worse.
   - Disruption of activities of daily living, such as skipping work (or working far more hours than usual), falling grades, dropping out of school, substance abuse, starting or increasing smoking,
   - A sense of weakness or helplessness.
   - Hypervigilance, fear, and difficulty trusting others.
   - Physical problems: headaches, stomach aches, muscle pains.
   - Vivid dreams and nightmares, and sleep disorders.
   - Eating disorders, such as vomiting, starving, or compulsive overeating
   - Isolation from friends and relatives. Marriages or dating relationships become jeopardized.
   - Preoccupation with personal safety.
   - Efforts to deny the assault ever took place and/or to minimize its impact, such as trying to convince yourself that you must be mistaken—it couldn't possibly have been rape.
   - Avoidance of places, sounds, images, or other triggers associated with the rape.
   - Fear or disinterest in developing new relationships.
   - Sexual problems, including repulsion of sex with a partner, or sexualized grieving in the form of uninhibited sexual behaviors.

It is during this stage that many victims begin to privately express their inner feelings about the rape, such as through poetry, collecting music that resonates with her emotions, and even joining online discussion forums. I have observed, however, that the poems, artwork, and journals of women in this stage do not suggest that recovery has progressed. The images that most commonly manifest in such creative expressions are those of being broken, dead inside, unknowable to others, hopeless, empty, torn, ugly, worthless, and contaminated. Women who have recovered from rape do not use these same images. If you are continually replaying these words and beliefs about yourself in your mind, it is a sign that you are progressing through the second stage of PTSD. But to enter the stage of survival and recovery, a new lexicon of words and images *must* replace previous self-branding as broken and hopeless.

If you had prior struggles with addictions, compulsive behaviors, or eating disorders, your assault can magnify them during the Outward Adjustment stage. It is during this stage that women are most likely to seek treatment, but usually for reasons other than rape; they are in counseling after suicide attempts and hospitalizations, or for drug problems, or for panic and anxiety, or because of meltdowns at school or work, or for eating disorders. Adolescent and young adult victims have rates of alcoholism, drug addiction, and eating disorders at many times the national average.[1]

It is difficult to move from the second stage of "Outward Adjustment" to the final stage of "Resolution" *without* counseling. It is possible to appear to be okay and even convince ourselves that we are okay. A clear example of this fact would be the countless hundreds of women who have sat in front of me with cuts all over their arms, boyfriends who physically or verbally abuse them, and frequent alcohol and marijuana use to cope with depression and panic, who say "I'm fine."

Because alcohol, drugs, self-injury, and eating disorders are ways to induce emotional numbness in order to avoid more difficult emotions,[2] progress from Outward Adjustment to Resolution *cannot* happen as long as these forms of coping continue. Resolution, by its definition, means that you have confronted your trauma in its entirety and resolved your dysfunctional emotional and behavioral responses to it. When you are blocked from your own feelings and memories by addictions or harmful habits, it is impossible to accurately face the very issues that underlie them. If you are continuing any of those forms of coping, they hold the answer to the question, "Why can I work so hard, and yet sometimes feel like I haven't changed?"

3.   The Resolution Stage: During this stage the rape itself transforms in meaning. It is no longer a continually-threatening wound that remains unhealed, and you do not consider rape to be something that *defines you*. You no longer see your entire

---

[1]   American Psychological Association, 2001, "One Out Of Ten Female Adolescents Experience Date Violence And/Or Rape, Says Study Of Over 80,000 Youths: Victims Report More Suicidal Thoughts And/Or Attempts, Higher Rates Of Eating Disorders And Psychological Problems." http://www.apa.org/releases/dateviolence.html

[2]   Favazza, A. R., DeRosear, L., and Conterio, K. "Self-mutilation and eating disorders." 1989 Suicide Life Threat Behav 19;4:352-61

life as the product of rape. Many women in the Resolution stage also transform their own sense of purpose: not only does she refuse to avoid the issue of rape, but often she becomes fiercely determined to *take it on* through writing, going back to school to learn how to help other women, performing songs, producing art, or engaging in other forms of action for the sake of fellow survivors.

At the Resolution Stage, the woman has transformed from Victim to Survivor (or to "Warrior Women," as author/filmmaker Angela Shelton prefers). She can hear about and discuss rape without shame or avoidance. There is no need to use substances or self-injury to alter her feelings. She develops new patterns of relationships in which she is more powerful and less vulnerable to dangerous partners. She begins to notice and take offense at sexist messages in her environment and media. She no longer describes herself as broken and ugly, but as a valued, strong, passionate person who insists on being strong.

During the Resolution stage, she does *not* forget the assault, nor does she stop having emotions about it. And at times, some of the behaviors and emotions of the second stage may flare up again. If she has prepared herself for this, she will not lose confidence in her recovery, but will recognize it as a critical moment, an opportunity to learn, and will reach out to supporters for help rather than trying to "go it alone" or slipping back into self-damaging thoughts and habits.

I can tell when a woman is beginning her resolution when she connects her rape with her *anger.* I am not talking about the rampaging, hysterical, destructive type of anger that emerges in Stage 2 as tantrums, screaming, and cursing. Nor am I talking about the cheap, superficial anger that pretends to be about the rape when really it is directed inward at one's self. This is the anger that seizes the profound understanding that your rape happened to an *amazing* woman, a *remarkable, powerful* woman, who never deserved to be hurt. It is an anger that finally begins to see the contrast between the meaninglessness of the violence against you versus the *permanent* value you have— still—in spite of it.

My client Leslie struggled with this because during her Stage 2 she still felt she had been contaminated and rendered worthless by her rape. "I can accept that I wasn't raped because I was bad," she said, "but I still think that I'm bad now that I was raped." She was plenty angry about the rape, but her anger was directed at herself because of her inner messages that she should have been "tough enough" to prevent it. Her anger came out as screaming matches at home, insults, snappy comebacks, and curse words hurled at loved ones. She was angry *because* of the rape, but not *at* it.

The best image I can use to explain the way a "recovered" survivor sees herself is that of a crisp, mint condition $100 bill. Anyone would see that it has value. But what if it were seized, crumpled up, thrown to the floor, and stomped on? Would anyone still see it as valuable? When I have actually performed this demonstration in groups (but with a $20 bill—therapists seldom have Hundreds), the group members are baffled: "Well, of course we still want it! It's still worth the same!" I challenge them by asking, "It is? Even though I've abused and mistreated it? Surely it's not important or valuable now!" They protest that the bill, regardless of how I have treated and disrespected it, is still worth exactly what it was created to be worth. A human's value does not diminish either, simply because she has been mistreated or disrespected by another. The value of a person, likewise, is undiminished by another person's mistreatment of her.

This imagery implies that the woman in this stage of recovery will feel some anger toward the person who harmed her, and toward the act and method of that harm. In this stage, you will become increasingly in tune with your anger and you will notice it beginning to change from a disruptive form of unhealthy anger into a sense of motivation and desire to change your inner and outer worlds. It is important for you to let your anger "speak" to you, rather than to stuff it and silence it.[3] Certain threatened interests may not like this new dimension of you, and may react disapprovingly. You have probably noticed that men who are assertive are called "leaders" but women with the same independent determination are called "uppity." But as Laurel Thatcher Ulrich noted in her now-famous quote, "Well-behaved women seldom make history."

Leitha was a child when she was raped. Rape was her first experience with intercourse, and as a child she did not understand what her multiple perpetrators were doing or *saying* to her. During the assault, they mocked her, using vulgarities that she did not yet understand, and the words themselves were etched into her mind. The ultimate humiliation came at the end of the assault: "You are a lousy f*** and this was a waste of an afternoon. I'm gonna have to come back and see if you can't do this better, but here's something to remember me by," and then he urinated on her.

Her rape ended with an incredibly traumatizing action, which even as a child she recognized as an intentional form of degradation. She had not understood what had happened to her, but she knew that at the end of it she had lost her humanity to them.[4] This alone was enough to plant PTSD so deeply within her that it would take years for her to resolve it.

But she explained to me that there was another reason her trauma brought up such anger, again and again. She had not understood the definitions and intent of the words hurled at her during the rape, but with each passing year she began to learn one-by-one what they meant. As the meaning of these insults crystallized, they would horrify her to realize one more dimension of her degradation. She wrote about how "…a child doesn't know what certain terms mean, but as you age you realize piece-by-piece what has been done to you. Its not like you *were* raped, it's like you're *being* raped with each new realization, each new act defined." The heartbreaking by-product of her therapy, then, was that simultaneously with each new positive insight and realization also came clarity into other ways she had been traumatized beyond her child-age understanding.

One can only imagine the insurance company reviewer in a cubicle, considering payment approval for continued therapy, asking questions like, "It's been three weeks in therapy; isn't she over it yet?"

---

[3] Feeny, N. C., et al. "Anger, dissociation, and posttraumatic stress disorder among female assault victims." 2000 J Trauma Stress 13;1:89-100. "Four weeks after sexual assault, anger was predictive of later PTSD severity, and dissociation was predictive of poorer later social functioning." Thus, anger becomes an important issue to resolve, rather than ignore, during therapy.

[4] Of course, a more accurate synopsis is that *they* lost their humanity to *her*, but this story is about her perception at that time rather than about the authentic truth, which Leitha now possesses as a survivor.

I am inspired by Leitha Brogan, who shared so much of her journaling for this book but had always requested "pen names" to hide her identity. And then after she had worked through the trauma of her rape, her entire concept of herself changed:

> I am so happy…Please, please, please, when this book is edited for final printing, please use my real name. It is difficult to explain, but I need to say to the world, "I was raped, these are my feelings, and I am not hiding anymore." Gee, now that it's done I feel sort of like a woman who's just had a baby…you know, that kind of 'wow' moment.

Being able to name, claim and declare yourself as a proud survivor of rape can be difficult if your upbringing taught you that anger is a personal defect, a form of rudeness, or isn't "ladylike."

I am also inspired by the story of Victoria, who endured a series of particularly brutal rapes at a fraternity party. She experienced some of the most vicious violence against her that I have heard during therapy, and the strongest stuck point in her story was that she had stopped fighting back when the weight of her boots had become cumbersome and exhausting. She had worn a pair of heavy black Doc Marten boots to the party, which she had bragged about as her "ass kickers," but the bulk of them had inhibited her efforts to fight, kick, and stomp at her many attackers. For fourteen years she still carried the symbolic weight of her shoes as intense guilt, and she had been angry at herself: "I always thought of these as my ass kickers, but the irony is that it was my own ass getting

kicked." The Doc Marten boots had been discarded, never to be seen again after that.

During therapy, Victoria struggled with excruciating feelings of shame and anger about this, to the point of suffering intense panic attacks and even physical nausea during therapy sessions. Many times I watched her face melt into tears of grief over her memories and shame. She said to me at one point, "I'm scared to give up this pain because it's defined me for so long. I know it's going to kill me if I hold on to it, but I don't know who I'll be without it. What if I lose myself by losing this pain?"

When she had begun to finally defeat her shame and re-find herself, she told us that she had decided to commemorate her success: "this weekend I'm going shoe shopping. It's time to get a new pair of Docs!"

Only another survivor could understand the amazing victory this represents.

Take care of your body.
It's the only place you have to live.

If OB/GYN and dental appointments become triggers
(Medical professionals may benefit from reading this section)

Many women experience a rush of anxiety and even panic about keeping medical appointments because of rape triggers. While OB/GYN care can be triggering for obvious reasons, it is also now known that dental visits can be particularly difficult too. Women have described to me the panic attacks and crying spells that have happened before and even *during* these routine, safe health appointments.

Understanding why these triggers happen is helpful. Dental care, for example, can be laden with amygdala triggers: the position of lying back, the person you see above you, the opened mouth (which can be a specific trigger for oral rape, or a symbolic trigger for the vulnerability of an opened body), the insertion of hands and fingers, and even the passive, dissociative "floating" sensation from the sedative gas. (In fact, even reading that list of triggers may raise your heartbeat, which suggests your amygdala is working very hard to cause you to avoid this information. Don't!)

Self-care of your body is one part of recovery; you cannot heal, love, and respect a body that you do not provide with healing, love, and respect. This creates a difficult paradox: recovery from rape requires total self-care, yet the physical aspects of this self-care can be very difficult at first. Before I continue into any further discussion, I need to assure you right now: it *does* get better. These triggers fade with time, and they fade even faster if you apply the coping skills I will suggest.

Dental and OB/GYN visits

Anxiety about dental and OB/GYN visits is already common (around 80% of adults), even without the complicating issue of sexual abuse or rape. You may not want to disclose to your doctor that you are a rape survivor, and there is no reason she or he must know.[1] If you decide to disclose this to your dentist, the conversation should be done in private and you should ask for a moment together in his/her office to discuss this. But dentists, doctors, and nurses are not psychic, and they may not understand why you are having such difficulty. Even telling them something as unspecific as "I have a dental phobia about gagging or pain" or "I tend to panic during these examinations" can be helpful for them.

If you need more help, the Pandora's Project website has downloadable cards you can print and give to your dentist or doctor that explain that as a survivor of sexual assault, you request certain accommodations (such as a female or male to be present, and to have procedures explained in advance, etc.). They can be found at http://www.pandys.org/quickinfocards.html

Consider too whether you would be more comfortable with a male or female dentist, but keep in mind that most dentists and gynecologists are kind, gentle people who really want to help.

No woman looks forward to gynecological exams. They are uncomfortable and generally mysterious. Gynecological care is important for several reasons, regardless of rape. At a minimum, it is a basic form of self-care. But in rape survivors, it is also a critical aspect of healing, both physically and psychologically. In studies about women's fears of OB/GYN care, a majority of patients felt high levels of anxiety, yet most did not discuss or even disclose those fears with their doctor. And unfortunately, one of the most common reasons women give for not discussing those fears was that they felt their doctor was condescending or patronizing, in the form of either laughing at the fears or merely instructing their patient to "just relax." Adolescents and women from certain cultures and religious traditions often have heightened fears about OB/GYN care.

One study of health communications by Marifran Mattson of Purdue University found that common fears included physical discomfort, the possibility of a cancer diagnosis, or embarrassment. These fears were present, but less intense, when the patients saw a female doctor. Mattson wrote in her study,

> A woman's dignity must be maintained throughout the exam, especially considering the vulnerable position that women are in when they go to the gynecologist. A genuine relationship between a patient and physician is created and maintained through communication. Improved communications may help alleviate the anxiety women experience before, during, and after exams. When a woman knows that her gynecologist cares for her, she feels comfortable expressing herself, and that empowers women to be active in seeking health care and contributing to the decision making in their care.[2]

---

[1] Unless, of course, you are receiving OB/GYN special care immediately after an assault.

[2] http://womenshealth.about.com/cs/gynexam/a/gynfear.htm

Mattson sees this as more than just an issue of patient-doctor conversation, but as a matter of justice and power from a feminist perspective; and she is exactly right. She points out that women's health needs are often marginalized through lack of gender-specific training, under-funding, and even legally-restricted control over women's personal health care decision-making rights.[3]

Try to keep in mind, though, that your doctor examines many women each day, and their purpose is to ensure health and safety, not evaluate you as a person. Even male gynecologists are not viewing you as an "exposed" person; many doctors use the analogy of a mechanic working on a car: they're not assessing the appearance of the car or the personality of the driver, they are ensuring the safe function of its working parts. This is not a graceful or particularly "empowering" analogy, but keeping it in mind is actually helpful for many women.

Rape victims have the highest rate of not showing for OB/GYN and dental care, or not making appointments at all. Here are some things you can pre-arrange with your dentist or gynecologist that can easily reduce your anxiety:

- **Stop Signals.** A raised finger or hand can be used to indicate that you need a brief break to catch your breath. The doctor should withdraw but remain in sight, and offer reassuring feedback: "Okay, you need a break. That's okay. We're going to be fine. I'll continue in a little bit." I train dental hygienists a couple of times a year on treating rape victims, and make a suggested to them that they keep an electric toy game buzzer in their office, which patients can hold. Pressing the buzzer alerts the dentist to stop immediately until the patient becomes calm again.
- **Eye contact and talk.** A doctor who is sensitive to "dental (or OB/GYN) phobia" can, with your permission, put her hand on your shoulder, rub your arm, and with gentle eye contact talk you through any anxiety: "We're going to take deep breaths together. Breathe with me, okay?"
- **Breathing Patterns.** Irregular breathing, shallow breathing, or sudden starts/stops should signal to your dentist that you need a "cooling off" time.
- **Making your own choice about sedation during dentistry.** While being sedated is anxiety-soothing for many, there are some abuse and rape survivors who prefer *not* to be sedated. Sedation may make some feel more vulnerable, rather than calm. If sedation is necessary, you can ask to arrange for a family member or friend to accompany you in the room during the process.
- **If permitted, bring soothing music and headphones.** Relaxation CDs may be helpful as well, and one client of mine brought a home-made CD of nothing but the sounds of her children laughing and playing, which not only lifted her spirits but kept her grounded while re-associating dental care with positive memories!
- **Before dental exams, ask to hold and handle the suction instrument.** This may sound strange, but it is actually quite reassuring to know exactly what it is, what it does, and what it looks like—as opposed to a blurry close-up device making an unusual racket! You may surprise yourself at how small and unthreatening they actually are!

---

[3] Brann, Maria; Mattson, Marifran. "Reframing communication during gynecological exams." *Gender I Applied Communication Contexts*, SAGE Publications, 2004, pp147-168.

- **Breathe deeply when stressed.** Don't gasp for shallow breaths. Take long, full breaths from deep within your lower chest. In your mind, talk to yourself with reassuring encouragements. One possible trigger of panic is an imbalance of carbon dioxide and oxygen in the blood, so deep breathing is the single best method for staving off panic.
- **Reward yourself for success.** A snack, a shopping trip, a dinner, whatever.

Signs your doctor should watch for:

- **Exaggerated startle responses.** The amygdala may trigger your nervous system into "flight" responses, and the urge (or sudden movement) to jump may occur. The doctor should begin using their coping/helping skills. This can happen during the dental or gynecological care itself, or even when the doctor enters the room (if you experienced abuse from an abuser who would enter your room). The dentist should narrate what is happening: "I'm coming in to see you now. Ready?" or "That's Beth. She's bringing me the X-rays."
- **Spontaneous tears**, especially when no crying or sobbing sounds accompany them;
- **Dissociation from eye contact,** or a sudden "fading out" of your attention or responses to cues;
- **Inability for you to talk clearly,** because of breathing patterns or panic;
- **Reluctance or insecurity about answering questions.** Your fear of not answering "correctly" may be a habit learned from abuse. This can include an irrational fear of not being liked by your dentist, and struggling to please her or him with the answers you believe they desire.

Advice to Dentists[4]

(If you are a patient of a doctor and would like her or him to have this information, you may choose to copy this and mail it anonymously! This section was written by a survivor of childhood sexual abuse who chooses to remain anonymous, and it is found at http://www.dentalfearcentral.org/abuse_survivors.html where it is copyrighted, but used here with permission. It is just as applicable to rape survivors.)

> **Talking to your patient.** Abuse survivors are rarely great conversationalists (for a number of reasons - but there is no space here to go into this). Therefore you may find it hard work to keep a conversation going with your patient as you wait for the anesthetic to start working or for the x-rays to come back, and you may feel sorely tempted to do something else or chat with your nurse.
>
> Can I suggest that you persevere? If you ignore your patient, they may start to worry again that you don't like them, wish that they weren't there, are cross with them - you get the idea. So, try out a few topics to see what works - and it'll get easier over time, as your patient gets to know you more. In my case, I don't like

---

[4] http://www.dentalfearcentral.org/abuse_survivors.html used with permission

to talk about family, holidays, hobbies, as this feels too personal. But I can talk quite happily for hours about my job (which I think is terribly interesting and fascinating, but which probably puts others to sleep).

Being empathetic and understanding. As I wrote above, being in the dentist's chair may bring back powerful memories and emotions of the abuse and your patient may slip into their "child-self." Behaving like a small, frightened child, your patient may try to hold onto your hand or even lean against you. (I did this once when my previous dentist had to take impressions.) Understanding this will enable you to be gently reassuring, as you would be with any actual child patient.

Whatever behavior your patient has exhibited, once the treatment session is ended and your patient recovers their "adult self," they may feel very shamed and embarrassed by their previous behavior. This may include feeling that they can't possibly come back for further treatment, because they can't look you and your nurse in the eye again. It can therefore be very helpful if you can be as matter-of-fact and reassuring as possible, and at the end of the session tell your patient that you look forward to seeing them again.

If your patient behaves "oddly" and your response to this is not respectful and understanding, they will feel stupid and shamed. Patients who are abuse survivors still want you to talk to them and discuss their treatment with them.

My previous dentist convinced me that she had to hold patients leaning against her pretty much every day of the week, and this was entirely normal and nothing out of the ordinary. Whilst I did not fully believe this, her matter-of-fact reaction helped me to return for further treatment.

"Quick fix"

If you did all of the above with all of your patients just in case one of them was an abuse survivor, you wouldn't be able to see many patients. Clearly, it isn't possible to do all of the above all of the time.

However, I'd like to think that the following are fairly simple and can be fitted in even if your schedule is very busy:

Asking your patient if they want to sit up or lie down for treatment (and telling them they can change their mind later if they want to...)

Having a soft blanket handy that you can offer to your patient each time before you start treatment is also easy to do. (You can probably imagine how extremely difficult it will be for a patient to tell you that they were sexually abused as a child and now feel naked whenever they sit in the dental chair, and then ask you if they can please have a blanket). Where cross-infection control regulations don't allow this, let your patient know that they can bring a blanket along if they like.

Keeping an eye on your patient's breathing is also fairly simple. Offering reassurance and helping someone to breathe properly again also does not take a great deal of time.

Praising your patient, especially at the end of the session, is also quick and simple, and goes a long way to reassure your patient that you are not cross, annoyed and irritated with them and that they can come back.

Making a difference

If, every now and then, you are able to take a bit more time with a patient when you think you recognize the signs that someone is an abuse survivor, you are likely to make a HUGE difference in someone's life - not just to their oral health but also in contributing to healing the whole person.

At my first appointment with my current dentist, he gave me a special card with his home telephone number on it. He said that knowing how difficult dentist visits are for me, he didn't want me to have to deal with an unfamiliar dentist in an emergency. I was completely amazed at this act of kindness.

My current dentist also cleans my teeth, so that I don't have to see the hygienist, and I greatly appreciate this.

At my previous dentist, I once had to undergo a complicated procedure. When I arrived, the dentist told me that today neither she nor the nurse would be able to hold my hand or touch me in any way because they couldn't risk transferring germs to my mouth. However, she had arranged for a second nurse to be present, whose only job that day was to hold my hands. I was immensely touched that my dentist had clearly thought very hard how to make me comfortable and had gone to so much trouble.

Abuse survivors often feel full of shame, believe that they are dirty and disgusting, and can't imagine that someone would be prepared to bother with them. Coming across someone - you - who genuinely wants to help and is kind, gentle and non-judgmental can make an enormous difference.

Why tell me? I mentioned at the start of this section that your patient is unlikely to disclose that they were sexually abused as a child, but that there may be a few exceptions to this.

If one of your patients does tell you that they were sexually abused, you may not know how to respond and wonder why they are telling you of all people; after all, you barely know them and only see them a few times a year at most.

This may be precisely why they chose you as someone to tell! Many abuse survivors go through life fearful that anyone finds out their secret. As a child, it is likely that their abuser told them never to tell. If they did tell someone, it is likely that they were not believed, and that "telling" had disastrous repercussions. As adults, many abuse survivors feel full of shame, often guilty, believing that the abuse was somehow their fault, and that anyone who finds out will be repulsed. Therefore, those closest to them, such as a spouse, may not know that their partner was abused as a child. Past abuse can affect many aspects of your patient's life today, and they may have made a decision that they want to change that. This may include being (more) open about their past, i.e. talking about it.

If they talk to you about it, they are obviously hoping that you react positively. But they have probably also chosen you, because - no offence - you are not very important. If you react badly to what they are telling you, it is not that difficult to replace you and find another dentist. If they tell someone close to them, and that person reacts badly, that's much harder to deal with. In telling you, they may simply be trying to see what happens if they tell someone now.

You may still be left wondering what to say to your patient in those circumstances. It's probably best not to interrupt while they are speaking. Your patient will be very nervous, and they have probably "practiced" this at home and just want to get to the end of whatever they have decided to say. You may want to respond with something along the lines of: "I am very sorry that happened to you. And I am very glad that you felt able to tell me. Is there any way I can help now?"

I hope this section has answered some of the questions you may have asked yourself about some of your patients. Understanding the particular difficulties and needs of a patient who was abused as a child, and knowing how to respond to these, will make visits to the dentist as comfortable as possible for both patient and dentist.

For more help or information, visit www.dentalfearcentral.org, which offers helpful articles and a support forum.

Advice to Gynecologists (written by an anonymous survivor)

Because of my sexual abuse/rape, the work you have to do is full of possible triggers for me. I know this, and so I begin to feel anxious before I even arrive at the appointment. But you don't know my history, so my reactions may be puzzling to you. I realize you are aware of a certain level of anxiety about OB/GYN care, but unless you know my story you might not understand my strong reactions.

If I ask for time to talk privately with you at first, please do not resent that as "valuable time" lost that you could have used to do your job—this *is* part of your job. Because you went into this field to assist women with our health, it is important that this part of my health be considered too. If I choose to inform you about my sexual abuse, please remember that I am telling you this for information, not for pity; I want you to use that disclosure to help guide your technique.

Even small talk and friendly visiting can help me during the process. It keeps me grounded and comfortable to interact with you, and to know that you see me as a person who needs patience and understanding.

If I do begin to "stress out," please be kind with me. I am so used to people scolding me to "settle down" and "cooperate," and if I could, I would What will help me more than instructions is kindness. Here is what you can do to help me.

Please arrange a "pause" signal with me. For example, if I tap a finger a few times, it means I need a breath-catching break. During that break, don't just sit and watch me; that would make me feel exposed and humiliated. Instead, redirect your eye contact to me—my eyes—and talk with me. Explain what you are doing, and what will happen next, and please use a soothing tone. I may want a reassuring pat on my hand from you, or I may not. But please ask, because for some of us it helps to have human contact.

We feel embarrassed that we react this way. It's as if we "can't handle it" in front of an educated, skilled, stranger. Let us know continually that it's okay, that you understand. Our embarrassment can sometimes keep us from returning, so talk to us in future-tense, such as assuring us that during our next visit we won't feel nearly so anxious, which you know because you've seen this before, and we're not the only ones, and this is common, and you look forward to being able to help us again, etc.

Watch my breathing. If I begin to hyperventilate or take shallow breaths, please stop and talk us through the anxiety. I know it's not your job to be a therapist, and I'm not asking you to be, but it will help your patients immensely to have the emotional comfort as well as your medical skill.

During the exam, keep one point of physical contact with us at all times. It is during the "gaps" where you are not touching us that our anxiety returns because we know that the awkward touching will resume, and we're not sure where, how, or at what point on our bodies. By having one hand or fingertip remain gently on an ankle, foot, or arm, we can mentally "map" where you are, and it doesn't feel as much like a "start-stop-start-stop" process. If hygiene prevents you from doing this, then substitute verbal cues and tell us you're ready to resume touch, and how you will do it.

Offer us a blanket to use to cover our bodies. This can help keep us from feeling so exposed and unguarded.

Explain each part of the process to us. Some of us do not know that the normal routine of this exam is
the external exam;
the speculum exam;
the bimanual exam; and
rectovaginal exam.

Since these are pretty embarrassing to us, go ahead and explain in advance what you are doing. Use matter-of-fact language because anxiety is "contagious" and we want to feel that *you* feel totally comfortable with this process. Random, ambiguous comments like "Hmm." and "uh…*huh*!" during an exam freak us out.

> Praise us frequently! We need supportive feedback! It lets us know you aren't frustrated because of our tension, and encourages us that we *can* do things like this.
>
> Above all, please let us know that our fears are familiar to you, and very normal. We don't want to be "the big dope" who "spazzed out on you." If you can assure us that this is common, and we're just fine, it alleviates a lot of the embarrassment.
>
> Thank you!

One young survivor I know went through these steps and succeeded. She wrote in her journal the words most fitting to end this section:

> I have struggled many years with what happened to me, and sometimes I feel like I have gone nowhere. I have a long way to go, but I believe in the power of the human spirit. While I was still groggy from anesthesia after a colonoscopy, I asked my gastroenterologist if he had seen any of the evidence of what had happened to me. He leaned in and whispered in my ear, "No, you are just fine, the body has an amazing resiliency and you have healed well." Somehow, that was important to me. I believe there are degrees of survival. I want to excel at survival, and I want to bring others with me. I appreciate the opportunity to do anything I can in this journey to healing. God bless *me*!

Come, clad in peace and I will sing the songs
the Creator gave to me when
I and the tree and the stone were one,
Before cynicism was a bloody scar across your brow.
-Maya Angelou

Should I forgive my rapist?

Many readers of earlier editions of this book have told me they were outraged just to *see* a chapter on the topic of forgiveness, because the very notion upset them before they had even read it. I appreciate that outrage, because it shows that my readers are keenly self-protective, and the feedback I've received (once they had read on) has actually been very positive about my approach to the forgiveness issue. I do not love the word "forgive" in the context of rape, and I am not going to persuade survivors to submit to its traditional definitions. I would prefer terms like "purge" or "cleanse" to describe this step of healing, as in "I purge you from my life; I cleanse myself of your effects on me." My understanding of forgiveness steps widely away from the traditional concept of reconciliation and slate-cleaning, and is instead a pro-Survivor one.

In the effort to live up to interpretations of religious and moral beliefs, many survivors (and their ministers, counselors, and families) have the belief that they need to forgive their perpetrators. The message usually goes something like this: "The last step in your recovery is to just *let it go*. You can't move on if you haven't forgiven him. That doesn't mean you have to forget what he did, but you have to move on with your life and release your resentment toward him."

This sounds enlightened and wise. But is it? Frankly, no, not always.

The problem I have with the idea of forgiving a rapist is that the meaning of the word "forgiveness" has become so incredibly warped that it is beyond useless, it is harmful. It softens or removes the offender's consequences and accountability. It bulldozes over the righteous outrage of the victim, forcing a false serenity. It permits epidemics of violence to continue, unopposed. And it suggests that after "forgiveness," you aren't supposed to ever feel any of your former emotions about the trauma, which simply isn't realistic. It may even keep you from completing therapy by making certain feelings out-of-bounds for discussion: after all, you've forgiven him, right? So those feelings are supposed to be gone, right? It has come to describe the act of letting someone else off the hook, wiping the slate clean, cancelling the accountability or consequences deserved by another person, and granting an emotional truce with an offender. I call these the "false serenity" definition of forgiveness.

You owe your rapist none of these things.

I can understand the concern that people have about the dangerous possibility that you will obsess, in dark ways, about your perpetrator. Constantly thinking about him (or using harmful ways to *distract* from thinking about him!), and putting limits on your own life because of his actions, are not healthy ways to live. In that sense, it is wise to overcome your feelings of being vulnerable, blemished, or unworthy. But that is not the same thing as "forgiveness." If forgiveness means letting him off the hook, then what I suggest is something else completely different: letting *yourself* off the hook of the pain he has caused. The final act of grace, then is not done in his behalf, but your own. Marty, a 17-year-old survivor, explained it this way:

> I know that my religion says that I should, but I have a very difficult time with this, because for me there was more than one rape and more than one rapist I don't think that I'll ever be able to. I know people say that I should in order to completely heal and move on, but I think that I'm moving on just fine so far, and maybe one day I'll be able to forgive (I'll never forget). But at this point I don't see that day coming any time soon.

For some women, forgiving their rapist is absolutely not an option. For others, they have found this a necessary step in their recovery. But I have noticed that whenever women have benefited by forgiveness, they have *always* done so with the self-cleansing definition that I am proposing, rather than the "false serenity" definition. Ashley, a 22-year-old survivor, said, "I needed to forgive them in order to move on. It might not be right for everyone but it was for me. I've forgiven those who have hurt me. That doesn't mean I've forgotten. It just means that I'm starting to move on. I just refuse to let it rule my life anymore."

Kara, 24, also made this decision for similar reasons. She said, "He completely consumed my life, I had so much anger built up, it was scary. I couldn't live my life like that anymore. I'm not excusing him in ANY way for what he did, but I had to forgive him to move on. Rapists are all about control, and after forgiving him and releasing him from my life, I feel like I have the power and control back."

Kaye, a 47-year-old survivor, also gave serious consideration to the issue of forgiveness. She journaled,

> I chose to forgive.
>
> We didn't get to choose whether we would be raped or not, but we do get to choose how we respond to it... just like anything else in life. I didn't want to spend my life eaten up with vengeance, hatred and bitterness.
>
> For me and my understanding of forgiveness it was a matter of fully

acknowledging what they did and what it cost me, what it's still costing me today. This places the blame and responsibility exactly where it belongs: on them. As I went over my 'list' of the costs, I took those things and acknowledged that they were now mine to live with and work on, but I gave up my need for vengeance. (I am *not* talking about not pressing charges. This is a legal matter and is what our laws and government are for). I gave up my hatred of them.

What I didn't expect were the benefits. It cut the bond/tie/cord between me and them. The fear began to dissipate and I gained peace. The panic attacks subsided and I was able to leave my house again.

Forgiving did absolutely nothing for them and they still stand accused, but it empowered me and brought me a large measure of peace. It brought me to the place where they were no longer the issue... I was. My healing, my well-being, my life, to do with as I choose.

As far as forgiving AND forgetting. The forgetting part isn't going to happen this side of heaven. That's just life and to think otherwise is pretty much denial of reality.

Jessica, 19, added, "I needed to forgive, because I hated too strongly. The hate I felt towards my attacker consumed my life; so for me, forgiveness had to be part of my process of moving on." Notice that all of these experiences are about purging one's self of dark, toxic emotions, leaving themselves free to live happily. Not one involved any gesture toward their offender; in fact, these acts of forgiveness set the women *farther* apart from their offenders. That liberating disconnection from trauma, after all, is the whole purpose of real forgiveness. It is self-made justice.

Instead of the word "forgive," substitute words like "purge" and "cleanse." When we think of forgiveness as a way of purging someone from our lives, cleansing ourselves of their effects, we're approaching a more useful, healthy, and enlightened concept.

No other person—a therapist, a minister, a parent, a friend—should pressure you with the misguided advice to "forgive him and move on." I have seen that this pressure often creates an even larger emotional wound. I am not suggesting that you persist in feelings of hate and bitterness either; what I am suggesting is that any efforts you make to change your feelings should be done for *your* sake, not his. He, and his well-being, is not the focus of your recovery; *you* are.

Anger is not bad. Anger can be a very positive thing, the thing that moves us beyond the acceptance of evil.
-James Thurber

How can anger help you recover from rape?

From this vantage point, a dot of nothingness in the center of my bed, I understand the vast ocean of work it is to be a woman among men, that universe of effort, futile whimpers against hard stones, and oh God I don't want it.

…I will be able to get up from this bed only if I can get up angry. Can you understand there is no other way? I have to be someone else. Not you, and not even me.

-Barbara Kingsolver

Anger can be a helpful or toxic emotion. The useful form of anger is "anger to…" Anger to move. Anger to act. Anger to refuse to accept. This is different from "anger at…," which is simply an emotion hurled at a target rather than directed into a process of change. "Anger and anxiety are incompatible reactions," says *The Anxiety and Phobia Workbook*. "It's impossible to experience both at the same time…symptoms of anxiety and panic are a stand-in for deeper-lying feelings of anger, frustration, or rage."[1]

Katie was a smart woman in her 30's who had been raised with the belief that "nice girls" don't cause a fuss, and comply with what they are told. She was taught that the appearance of poise and composure was more important than her inner emotional life. In short, her purpose was to be "a good girl." As a result, she was never able to tell her family about sexual abuse as a child because her upbringing forbade emotional upheaval, and anyway deeper emotional survival is less important than the appearance of

---

[1] Bourne, Edmund J. Ph.D. *The Anxiety and Phobia Workbook*, New Harbinger, 2005, p123.

pleasantness. So Katie became exactly what she was trained to become: a perfectly-dressed, polite, cute woman in perfect makeup and a soft voice.

Whenever I would ask Katie a question about her feelings, she would answer in the form of a question back to me: "I feel…good?" I pointed out that her answers were like auditions for approval rather than declarations of herself. She would apologize for taking up group time whenever she spoke, and was afraid to disagree with me, her family, her husband, or anyone. If she ever did speak up about a personal concern, she would later apologize for being so selfish.

But within the outer image of the poised, cosmetically-flawless young woman was a terrified, hurting soul that would drink herself into oblivion and scratch her punishment into her forearms with her fingernails almost nightly. She reminded me of the withering "good girl" of Courtney Martin's book, *Perfect Girls, Starving Daughters:*

> A starving daughter lies at the center of each perfect girl. The face we show to the world is one of beauty, maturity, determination, strength, willpower, and ultimately, accomplishment. But beneath the façade is a daughter—starving for attention and recognition, starving to justify her own existence…
>
> Young women struggle with this duality. The perfect girl in each drives forward, the starving daughter digs in her heels. The perfect girl wants excellence, the starving daughter calm and nurturance. The perfect girl takes on the world, the starving daughter shrinks from it. It is a power struggle between two forces, and at the center, almost every time, is an innocent body.[2]

Katie and I worked for several weeks to improve her assertiveness, and to examine how her childhood roles and lessons contributed to her limited view of her rights as a grown woman. As we progressed, Katie began to face some buried truths about her past, and at one point grasped a peer's hand for strength as she said aloud for the first time, "I'm coming to the point where I can realize that what happened to me…was rape!"

As we progressed through this, Katie would often have difficult nights where her urge to self-injure would reappear, causing her to feel ashamed and her husband to feel stressed and worried for her. We processed her rape and sexual abuse as gently but directly as possible and Katie continued to improve, and eventually made it through an entire week without drinking or self-injuring, and then two weeks.

At this two-week mark, Katie told the group that she had brought letters and photos from her father, who was the perpetrator of her childhood sexual abuse. We encouraged her to read them to us, and she began. As she read, we saw a visible transformation occur in Katie. The letters revealed his very superficial, phony attitude toward her, reeking of platitudes such as "You're my little princess!" and "You're daddy's little girl!" and "I hope you love yourself and have a good life."

As the dripping phoniness of these annoying "I love you's" from the man who had molested her piled up, Katie began to get more and more angry. She would make disgusted faces, roll her eyes, throw the papers into the air as each sheet was read, crumple them up and throw them, and at one point she even flipped off the letter itself with her middle finger! She would read a line—"You're my sweet little baby"—and then

---

[2] Martin, Courtney E., pp20-21.

exclaim, "Hey, *that's* why I hate it when someone calls me 'Baby' to this day!" Katie's anger became positively delightful, and it intoxicated the group with the joyful freedom she was discovering in finally, *finally* being able express an emotion other than sweet, cute, perfect, starving niceness.

At the end of the letters, Katie asked if it would be appropriate to burn them, and the group enthusiastically agreed. We ended group right then, took the elevator down, and gathered in the snow to create a small blaze to destroy the photographs and letters from her incestuous father. Katie, with tears streaming down her face, smiled and described the intense joy and release she was feeling. With one last act of defiance, she stomped out the ashes.

When the purification ceremony was over, we began to gather up the ashes to dispose of them. But in the bottom of the stack, three scraps of paper had survived the fire. Singed on every side with black ash, the three scraps contained only a few words. They said, in sequence,

> *Daughter,*
> *Love yourself*
> *Have a good life.*

"Oh my God!" marveled Katie, as she held them like precious treasures. "Can I keep these?" They had become a new message to her, from something greater and transcending human insight or coincidence. Katie interpreted them as a letter to her from God, revealed through the act of purging and cleansing the worthless tokens of her abusive father. If Katie had not respected and expressed her anger, she never could have found her freedom, or discovered this new way to see herself.

This does not mean that every experience will produce the same kinds of miraculous serendipity. But it *does* mean that your anger is part of your voice, and you will not be able to fully thrive until that voice is given its chance to say some of the things inside you that wait to be said. Rape and sexual abuse teach a woman that the things inside her do not deserve to be brought forth and expressed, that they are dirty, that they are vulnerable, and that you have no right to leave your cave of gloom and isolation. If you continue to silence the voices of your own emotions, you are effectively saying to rape, "I agree with you, Rape—on some level, I really *don't* deserve to be heard and understood." This choice inhibits your growth from victim to survivor to thriver. Only when your full, complex palette of inner life is given voice and expression, can you truly say that you have defeated rape. This is precisely why so many rape survivors use the imagery of overcoming silence as a symbol for victory:

- *"Silent All These Years"* by singer Tori Amos;
- *After Silence: Rape and my Journey Back* by Nancy Venable Raine;
- *Surviving the Silence: Black Women's Stories Of Rape* by Charlotte Pierce-Baker
- *Diary Of A Rape Victim : Breaking the Silence to Break Free* by Phillis Van Godwin;
- *Hours of Torture, Years of Silence : My Soul Was the Scene of the Crime* by Teresa Lauer

Victoria struggled with the question, "Who will I be without my pain?" She began to realize that she was going to succeed, but she had also always defined herself by her pain and the behaviors that pain had led her into:

My greatest struggle in treatment was forgiving myself and learning to see myself as having value. In a very real way, I wasn't angry at the rapists, I was angry at myself. I was a peer sexual health educator in college. I went around to dorms and talked to students about safe sex practices and how to protect themselves on a college campus. Don't walk alone at night, I told them. Don't go to frat parties by yourself, always with a group. Don't drink to excess, especially in an unfamiliar environment. Common sense stuff, right? So what did I do? I went to a frat party alone and drank an obscene amount of alcohol and chased it with pot. What happened? I was gang raped by at least seven members of the fraternity.

I saw what happened to me less as a crime and more of failure on my part -- a failure to practice what I had preached. I saw myself as a worthless hypocrite and failure. I transferred to a different school the following year...I took all the pain, all the trauma, and all the degradation that I had endured and I internalized them.

I turned to the internet and sought out men who would degrade and abuse me -- who would treat me like the filth that I saw myself as. If a man was nice to me, he had to go. Kindness, affection, and respect were a threat to the identity I carved out for myself. If anyone saw me as having worth, they had to be an idiot, not able to see the real me -- the real me the way I saw myself. I carried this self-hatred with me for years and right into Matt's group.

I fought every step of the way to hold on to that self-loathing. I wore it like a suit of armor. If I took it off and set it down, who would I be? I had seen myself as garbage for so long, I was afraid of having to get to know the woman underneath. As hard as I fought, Matt never gave up on me. He saw the person underneath the pain, even when I couldn't. Slowly but surely, I emerged from underneath the pain to find the person full of life and joy...a person I hadn't seen in close to 15 years. The problem: she was a stranger to me.

Thus arose the dilemma. I became a happier and healthier person but I had no idea how to be such a person. This whole world of possibilities opened up to me. I can choose to do something, instead, that doesn't expose me to death and destruction. I can choose to do something that doesn't break my heart every minute of every day. What an amazing gift...to see the world for once as place of limitless possibility rather than one of predetermined suffering. I haven't gotten it all figured out yet, but I'm giddy with anticipation for all the wonderful possibilities that come with living a life without self-hatred and pain. Would I still be willing to make that ultimate sacrifice? Probably so. But the real answer to the riddle is that I can choose not to and still feel just as passionate about what I do and what I've done as before.

One of the most common question I am asked during this painful recovery process is, "Will I ever get to the point where I won't have any sadness about my rape, and I can finally just forget about it?" As usual, the wisest answers come not from me, but from other women in the tribe of survivors. Megan journaled this, and it is worth printing in its entirety:

Today I can say things like, I was assaulted and it was not my fault; but I survived that and I am no longer allowing that person to negatively affect my spirit, nor allowing the event to have any bearing on my current life. I can say this *now*.

But initially, and for a pretty long time, I was ashamed. I believed somehow I must have brought about what happened to me, and I believed that if anyone knew then I would be perceived as dirty and a worthless shell of the human being they thought they knew. So I was too ashamed to tell, and in not telling I was not getting any help. What do you do then, when you are young and you don't k now any better? Pretend it never happened. Take things one day at a time, and even though you wake up daily with the same pain and shame and fears, you hope that each day might be the day that it eases up, or that you forget. It doesn't work.

Time – by itself – does not heal all wounds. Pretending nothing happened only gave me a deep, dark secret. It separated me from people. Finally opening up and sharing the secret gave me sisters I never k new I had. They were out there, waiting for me, with understanding and love. You find that you admire them and are proud of them— then one day it hits you, *why don't I admire myself? Why shouldn't I be proud of myself? Because I am very much like them!*

That's not all, though: you have to face what happened to you head-on and take a hard look at it. "The only way out is through." I was afraid of this because I thought that after so many years—and I was functioning alright, wasn't I?—that this would needlessly open an old wound and plunge me into depression. Again, that's not how it works.

It may have been scary, it may have been difficult work, but it was anything other than depression. You learn amazing things about yourself and in the end it is incredibly worth it.

While I was ashamed and trying to forget, it's like my life was frozen, on hold in many ways. I was a ghost, wandering through the world, going through the motions of life, but not truly living. Recovering and claiming my survivor status started my life up again. Far from being depressing, it has been energizing. The state I was in formerly, while inwardly denying everything, was much closer to depression.

There are those who will say 'The past is in the past' and we need to 'get over' bad things that happen to us and 'move on.' In the case of sexual assault, such advice infuriates me. I do have to acknowledge that rape was a significant event in my life, and while I want nothing more than to 'move on' from the pain, humiliation, and degradation and to be able to be whole and lead a healthy life, *this is now a part of my story* and in recovering from it I discover much about who I am, what I am capable of. There's no forgetting something like that in your life, so don't tell me I should forget. Hell, I tried that, and I'm here to tell you it is impossible.

As for 'moving on'—I think each individual survivor deals with this in her own way and at her own pace and don't you *dare* have the arrogance and condescension to tell someone they'd better 'move on.' I don't believe moving on is linear. For the rest of your life, each time your life changes—marriage, children, menopause—you have moments where you have to stop and deal with the trauma of your past and integrate it into your new present. You'd better believe that's *moving on,* but it does not mean you forget or that your recovery was ever so long ago that it is becoming irrelevant. For the rest of your life, your recovery is very relevant.

When I was younger and the trauma fresh, I wanted desperately for the pain to end, to be happy again and live the life I'd imagined for myself…and now I can say that after facing what happened and properly analyzing it, gaining a better and more truthful perspective on it, each day things *did* get easier and easier, and I *did* find happiness again. I only wish I had started that work right away, and not wasted years in secrecy, shame, pretense, and trying in vain to forget.

Leitha wrote,

[It is important that we] feel the true anger we have every right to feel about our perpetrators, about the losses…about OUR reality. Anger is not the thing we think it is in the usual sense. Righteous anger is a thing that, when expressed in the proper way, releases us, and sets us on a path toward an ingredient some of us have/had issues with…my next word: Forgiveness. We each have differing opinions about this one. I have worked hard to understand HOW to forgive, but I think we have to accomplish many other things before we get to a place where forgiveness is possible.

Deb, at age 34, is a mother of two who is working toward becoming a therapist herself. Recovering from her rape at age 16, Deb wrote to me in her journal,

I broke my self-enforced isolation and gingerly reintegrated back in to the real world. I am more confident and I can trust me again, Taking a risk doesn't equate to getting hurt and I *feel!!!!!!!!!!* Even feeling sad feels good because it is REAL. My relationships have developed, I have taken better advantage of opportunities and things are generally pretty good. When they are not good I am not so quick to assume I could have done anything better. I feel FREE.

Journal activities:

In your family growing up, who was allowed to show anger, and who wasn't?

When anger was shown by others, how did you feel?

Did you believe that anger was a precursor to someone hurting you? Are you frightened to see or feel anger?

What kind of anger was a girl "supposed" to have, and how was it supposed to be different from boys' anger?

Were you given permission or encouragement to express your dislike of an unfair situation?

Do you feel guilty after expressing anger? If so, why?

Are you able to express anger in safe ways, without physical or verbal damage done to yourself or others?

Do you believe you have the right to be angry about your rape? Why?

When someone asks you for your opinion or feelings, do you answer truthfully or do you try to give them the "right" answer that will be politely acceptable?

How has your expression of anger changed since your rape?

How does it *need* to change now to be healthier?

What is your definition of "healthy anger"?

The last thing I want is to be known as "The Girl Who Got Raped."
The big turn-around you make in your head
is from Victim to Survivor.
-Tori Amos

The label of "Survivor"

Among support communities for victims of rape and abuse, there is a sense of reverence toward the term "survivor." As you have learned, a "survivor" is much different than a "victim"; you have experienced victimization, but hopefully this book and your therapy have helped you progress to become a survivor. The term *survivor* can be misleading at times, too, because in some minds it conjures the image of a person who barely scraped through a lethal situation, and while this may be factually true for you, the image of a person just clinging to life may not reflect your status as a thriving woman, full of vitality.

There are some authors and activists who suggest that *victim* be the preferred term, rather than *survivor*. They point out that a woman who has been raped ought to have her trauma validated as real, and receive acknowledgement that she has been harmed—"victimized." The term "victim" is the technical legal term for one who had experienced a crime. Therefore, it is not the fact of her survival (that is, not having been killed) that most characterizes her, but that the assault was egregious and her pain authentic. Thus, in this model, "victim" becomes the term that honors her.[1]

Their point is a good one, and I see how the term "victim" is useful in acknowledging the truth of a person's real experience and real injury from rape. However, I find that the term "victim" describes a role in the actual moment of rape, and in the post-traumatic dysfunction afterward. But it does not also acknowledge the continuation of strength and identity *beyond* the wound; "Survivor," in my opinion, has

---

[1] Martin, Patricia Yancey. *Rape Work*. 2005, Routledge, p5.

acknowledgement of the trauma inherently in it, but with the forward-looking view of the woman as a person of continued strength and identity apart from rape.[2]

Much of the transformation is a matter of choice. I had a young patient who had been in therapy for nearly a month without much improvement. She had survived an attempted rape, which had left her feeling ugly and contaminated. She was not believed and supported by friends and family. When she was at her lowest point, a manipulative abuser named Frank swooped in to console her, initiating a relationship that was marked by physical beatings and verbal abuse. Frank was married but continued an affair with her, and my young patient was afraid to report the abuse because the entire relationship was a secret (and her previous reports of abuse had not been believed anyway).

This is my patient's first collage, which depicts her self-loathing and worthlessness.

During her therapy, my patient was cooperative but not motivated for the first few weeks. But all at once, a remarkable transformation came. She suddenly began bringing in collages and journaling, choosing not to wear makeup to groups (because makeup was her form of hiding under a mask), and she started opening up. I asked her what had changed and she told me that she had gone to a lake, thrown in a ring given to her by Frank, and finally cried. She began systematically expelling all the abusive men in her life who were trying to manipulate her, and she finally stood up to people who hadn't supported her after her sexual assault. She explained to me,

---

[2] There is one exception: when working with the *offender* of a sexual assault, the word "victim" must be used, and *not* the term "survivor," because perpetrators will distort the implications of "survivor" to minimize the damage of their actions. Houston, Julia C. "Sexual Aggression: Research, Theories, and Practice." *The Trauma of Sexual Assault,* 2002, p. 322.

I realized I had been doing all this therapy, but nothing was getting better. And I had to realize that it was because *I* wasn't doing anything to change myself. I had to *choose* that things would be different. It happened when I heard myself saying out loud in group, "I don't deserve a healthy, nurturing relationship." I started to wonder where I had gotten that belief! I mean, that's not who I want to be! I want good relationships! So why was I settling and telling myself I was no good? I had to quit making choices based on my feelings of being worthless, and start making choices as if I already was the woman I want to be.

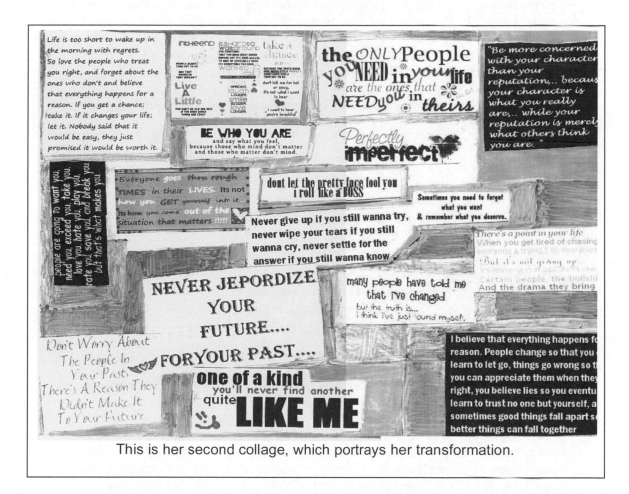

This is her second collage, which portrays her transformation.

Consider this analogy: when wolves were reintroduced to Yellowstone Park as pups, they were air-lifted by helicopter into the park inside a room-sized cage they had been raised in. The cage was placed in a remote area of the park and dismantled, then lifted out again. The wolves were free to roam the entire wilderness. But for two weeks, they remained in one spot, walking an area the same size as the cage they had been raised in. Their experiences in the cage had taught them to accept those boundaries as the limits of their lives—"this far I can go, but no farther"—and they functioned as if those limits were still real. They could see the mountains and forests all around them, but they could not understand that these boundless freedoms were *theirs*; after all, they had learned to limit themselves. Do people do the same thing?

Adopting the term "survivor" for yourself is a significant shift in the type of labels you might use to define who you are. This label transcends the negative, self-rejecting ones like "worthless" and "loser" and "ugly" that so many rape victims have given themselves. Andrea wrote this journal to other survivors:

> I find myself in awe over the fact that we are just an AMAZING TRIBE!
>
> We lift each other up, support one another, give advice, and hope. We help each other process misunderstandings and shed light on something that we may have been blind too. We offer different perspectives. We treat each other with respect, kindness, and love. We will walk with each other along those rough and rocky roads. We share and know that we are safe here. We are proud of each other's accomplishments! We will laugh and give a smile to brighten someone's day.
>
> [Survivorhood] is a sacred place that reaches out and encompasses more with each new day.

But as positive as the term *survivor* is, it must not be *all* of what defines you. Your life's value, and your mission as a woman, is not determined by your relationship to the issue of rape. Rape has changed your life, and today it may even still be the largest influence on your daily habits and feelings, but it must not and can not be the totality of you. Even your triumphant overcoming of trauma is not the core of your worth. The final step in your recovery is to remind yourself (or rediscover) your strengths, personality, and value apart from this recovery process. You are not "a survivor," you are many things *and a survivor also*. Status as a survivor is a quality in addition to all of your other worths, not the fullness of your worth by itself. Leitha, writing about her hope for survivors, offered,

> We all feel fragmented after rape. The 'whole' of my heart is disjointed and disconnected. BUT, then I bury death associated with my rape, and give nourishment to the hope of newness. You, as a therapist see *ability*, but survivors, depending on their level of recovery, may connect more with the limit of ability, displayed either during or after our rape. More than anything else, I want to embody the alive, awake, powerful woman who is able to feel the music of her soul, and allow her heart to overflow with the harmony of a life in tune, synchronized with a renewed spirit. So, I hold out for the hope and promise of a life renewed, and for those who are the strong and empowered survivors.

Now for the tough part. You can fill entire journals with writings, and not yet be transformed into a survivor. You can read every book on rape you can find, and not be a survivor. You can do every activity in this book and not be a survivor. Becoming a survivor is an inner process, not a promotion after doing a certain amount of work. Survivors are not invulnerable, and they are not "cured" (because they were never diseased).

As you transform into a survivor, make sure that there is room inside your definition of that word for bad days and imperfections. Do not convince yourself that a "survivor" is in a superhuman state of evolution and never struggles and never battles doubts. If you fall for that concept, you will become lonely and fearful as you hide your human imperfections in your effort to wear the mask of the fierce, flawless survivor.

Survivorhood (I'm coining that term here and now!) isn't bloodline or birthright. It's something that can only happen in a process.

It's not a badge, it's a role.

It's not a T-shirt slogan, it's a growth of spirit.

It's not a label, it's a call.

It's not a brand name, it's a revelation.

Survivors are also the ones who have rediscovered that beneath the labels and shame and trauma, they are originally a tribe of PEOPLE. They are women who have restored the personhood their Creator has meant for them. Victoria once wrote to me,

> We were not born survivors. Before we become survivors, there must be an intervening trauma. But trauma alone does not a survivor make. It is not our wounds that grant us entry. We must *choose* to be survivors.
>
> But what if we look at the community differently? What if we think of the community not as a tribe into which one must be born, but rather as a tribe (or family) which we join when we're ready? Even though I survived the physical trauma of my rapes, I was not a survivor until I met you and others, and then still not until I recognized the work to be done and then chose to do it. Survival is an act of will...not a birthright.
>
> Just as we choose to survive, there are those who will choose differently. Survivors have all been injured, we have all stared down the pain, and we have all chosen to come out into the light. We are all brave and strong. We all believe in each other's worth. We all love each other. These are the ties that bind us together.

A small group of thoughtful people could change the world.
Indeed, it's the only thing that ever has.
-Margaret Mead

Final work

As you approach the end of this part of your work, there are several difficult rites of passage that you will experience. In my years of work with rape survivors, I have seen these "trials by fire" happen over and over, and yet when I predict them to my patients they usually nod their heads, "yeah, okay," and then still feel set back when they actually happen. So I want to express, as clearly as I possibly can, that there is still one daunting, distressing, challenge experience in your transformation: your transformation will not seem to be noticed by others.

You have worked so hard for so long to rid yourself of the cocoon of "victim" and become a survivor, that you may feel you ought to be glowing, flying, or even have wings! You've shared your story, cried harder than you ever have, relapsed and recovered, suffered, and discovered yourself anew…and then when you go back to your life people greet you with, "Hey, how are you doing? What's for dinner? Oh, you got some bills. I put them on the table…" and so on.

It feels as if your entire resurrection is nothing more than a hiccup in the universe. You'll begin to wonder, "Is it even real? Did I actually change? If I'm so different, why don't other people see it?" If it were a movie, it would end with the scene of an amazing, resurrected woman getting into her car, turning on her blinker, and driving down the road as the scene pulls back until she's just a dot on the earth. This is the final agony of rape recovery: "I should be *luminescent* with power, and yet I feel like I'm just another average speck." Talk about one hell of a stuck point!

But this is exactly how it feels *until* you form connections with other survivors. You will find that the "I'm invisible" feeling is temporary, and that women who need to see the strength you have will recognize it.

For me, the image of a Stradivarius violin is the best description of who you are. Stradivari was a 17th-century master craftsman whose creations still exist, and are so rare that they cost millions of dollars. They are simply the most magnificent instruments ever created.

What makes them so valuable is that the method Stradivari used to create them remains a mystery to this day. Nobody knows how he chose the materials, treated the woods, carved and stained them, and bonded them together, yet they make the richest, most sonorous sounds of any stringed instruments. A musician can go their entire life and not even see a real Stradivari. I grew up playing the cello, and only heard a Stradivarius cello for the first time last year.

This is you. The creator who made you did so in a mysterious way. The materials, the stains, the bonding together, the use of heat and pressure, all work perfectly to make you what you are. To a musician who knows what to recognize, the sound of a Stradivarius is unmistakable and unforgettable. We hear it, and every part of us resonates—*"that's a Stradivarius instrument!"* But to anyone else, it's just a "fiddle," like any other.

When people fail to recognize your transformation, don't turn your insecurities inward. Their blindness to your resurrection has *nothing* to do with whether you really are transformed, or if the work was real. Those who are meant to find you and see your light will, and the rest aren't going to. Consider this a form of protection rather than a form of disappointment: I have found that survivors can locate one another across rooms and feel that bond, whereas the ordinary world continues its clueless ordinary chatter.

The best way to fuel your flickering spark of recovery is to connect with others who share that spark. Your recovery is not meant to turn you into a "normal" or "ordinary" woman, it is meant to imbue you with power. I do not suggest that survivors necessarily start crusades to become therapists and victim's advocates, which can be *extremely* traumatic and disturbing work, but I do believe that becoming a survivor is a process, not an event. Many of the women who finish their work with me commemorate it with a ceremony: a tattoo, cutting hair, etc. But this is not an end of a process; it signals the *start* of a new life.

The final growth of healing is to begin reaching out to others in need who are not yet as far along as you. If survivors of rape are like a tribe, then you are becoming one of the tribe's elders. For too long, women have had to endure the effects of rape alone, which is a shame because there is such a remarkable community of survivors just waiting to become interconnected. While I don't think this means every survivor should feel led into careers as counselors and advocates, I do think there are some amazing opportunities for survivors to pass along hope to victims that they are not alone, and that there is a way out of these feelings.

At the end of therapy when a patient was ready to leave me, I gave one last homework assignment. The final act of grace in a woman's recovery from rape was to reach across to the next wave of women who are victims, and offer support. Nobody should go through this alone, and unfortunately this tribe has too few role models in it; so many people complete their work in solitude and without any further connection with others.

I ask each patient of mine to write a letter to future survivors, and I would like for you to do this as well. I don't tell them what to write, but I give a little guidance: what would have helped you through this if you had known it in advance? What advice would you give?

Many women are hesitant to write these letters because they don't want to sound falsely cheerful or superficial. They reply, "But Matt, this was *hell* for me! It turned out okay, but am I supposed to tell them that this will be easy?" Of course not. In fact, being honest about the pain and heartache in the recovery process can actually be *comforting* to another woman who is wondering whether her own struggles are unique; if she is told that recovery is always pleasant and graceful it will frustrate her all the more when she compares her own upheaval to that kind of saccharine cheerleading.

My patients often reflect back on these last assignments and acknowledge to me, "I wish I'd had these letters to read when I was just starting. I could have used them. But I wonder if I would have even believed them! I might have just skimmed them and set them aside—'yeah, right. These are so phony.'—and missed out. I wonder if writing these letters really benefits younger victims, or if they benefit *us* as we write them."

Perhaps the answer is, "both." But somehow there *has* to be a way for this tribe's elders to reach out to the next victims and pass along inspiration: "I've been in this hole, too, and I know the way out."

I would like to leave you with some examples of actual letters written by my patients, to *you*. These letters are for you, personally. They are not generic statements or made-up platitudes. My patients specifically knew that these would be included in this book, and they wanted you to read them. These letters were all handed to me in the final days of therapy as we hugged goodbye with tears in our eyes. I am so proud and honored to be able to share these with you.

To my precious frien[d]

I have struggled
wanted to find the
and strength. I hope
better for you. I
the perfect words a
tell you is that w
easy, you will find
be fraught with he
when you will w
There are times wh
Please know that
many people who
want to help you
your pain and de
but I can't. Y
won't be easy, bu
stronger than bef
suffered ~~~~~~~~
lost something, or
taken from you.
you'll get it back,
your life has m
can't see it that
feel pain and ang
and doubt. You wi
has happened and i
well up with in
many years, and
wise and dear pers
had to face, he
feelings that fri

To my Precious Friend,

I have struggled writing this letter to you. I wanted to find the perfect words to give you comfort and strength. I hoped that I could make things better for you. I finally realized, however, that the perfect words do not exist. What I can tell you is that while your journey will not be easy, you will find your way.

Your journey will be fraught with heartbreak and there are times when you will wonder if you will make it. There are times when you will feel alone. Please know that you are not alone. There are many people who care about you, love you, and want to help you. I wish that I could take your pain and despair and feel them for you, but I can't. You must face them. It won't be easy, but when you do you will be stronger than before.

The trauma that you have suffered can't be undone. You have lost something; or rather, something has been taken from you. While I can't promise that you'll get it back, what I can promise you is that your life has meaning and value even if you can't see it that way right now. You will feel pain and anger, grief and betrayal, loss and doubt. You will want to hide from what has happened and ignore the feelings that well up within you. Don't. I did for many years, and it almost killed me. A very wise and dear person showed me that I had to face, head-on, the thoughts and feelings that frightened me the most. He never gave up on me and as a result, I was able to not give up on myself.

The work that was and is my survival has been and will always be mine to do. So too is it for you. And although you and I will never meet, please know in your heart that I will never give up on you. We are survivors, you and me, born of the same mother. We are bound together forever by our blood and tears. I will stand beside you always and will love you forever as I have learned to love myself. Peace be with you on the journey ahead.

-Victoria Bailey

To those that are just beginning this journey from being a victim to being a survivor,

I want to tell you that it will be okay. And I want you to believe it with all your heart. No matter how hard the road is at times, it always gets better. Always, as long as you keep walking it through.

It helps me to picture this walk like getting on the interstate. The scenery changes. There are up-hills and down-hills. There are flat expanses of nothingness. Even the sky turns to a bland, empty pallet of nondescript blue. There are forests and deserts to be crossed. There are lakes, torrential rivers and quiet streams. There are sunny days, downpours, blizzards and hurricanes. This is life after trauma. This is life after rape. This is also, just life.

Each step on the journey can be valuable to us as we grow and learn to accept the things that have happened. We integrate the horror into our lives and we enjoy the beauty in this world more... because we lived.

Rape teaches us to stop trusting others, yet in healing we can trust even more strongly as we find those that are trustworthy. We can love more deeply, more passionately, more fiercely because we know how important it is. We know what love means to the human heart and that love is a major definition of who we are as individuals. We've experienced gravest sorrow, pain and fear. But we can also experience joy, freedom and peace.

Don't let rape stop you. Don't let it cause you to curl in on yourself and build walls of protection against pain in your life. It won't work, anyway. You'll only end up costing yourself hope, love and joy. Instead, use it as a catalyst. Accept the pain. Accept the times of nightmares. Accept the losses.... all of them. In learning acceptance of those things, you'll also find that you can accept love and help and peace becomes yours.

There's nothing magical about it. It's a lot of hard, hard work. Some days it's a moment by moment effort that feels like it'll never be better. But keep walking. It's going to be okay. You can find the joy of being you again, a new you that is stronger, wiser, and more compassionate. A new you who finds joy in simple things, is creative, and who is a place of refuge for others. Always remember, we get to determine what kind of people we want to be, even in the face of rape.

I decided to walk the road set before me and discovered that I never had to walk it alone. God is there and He loves us. He loves you. Let me say that again. God loves you. As Corrie Ten Boom said of her experience in the Nazi concentration camp, "There is no pit so deep, that His love is not deeper still." So begin the journey and walk with God. There is no greater companion to be found.

-Kaye

~Dear Future Survivor~

Be brave, beautiful girl. Be very brave. It is time to set yourself free from the nightmares, the shadows, the addictions, the avoidance, the self injury, the sexual grieving, rise above the fear of living without this pain. Its time to the rise from the ashes that were created for you by those that tried to destroy you! Those ashes can no longer hold you, beautiful one: you will not be defeated!

The journey has been long. But you have made it to this intersection in your life. Its time to choose the unfamiliar path, the path opposite of the one that you've been on to make it this far. You know the path I speak about: the path of self loathing, cutting, the path of shame, the path of addiction, the path of having sex just to try and make sense of the pain that was inflicted upon your soul, upon your body. Don't beat yourself up. It was the only thing you knew to do to survive, until today!!! The unfamiliar path awaits you, but you must choose this path you will not be forced down it. If you are forced you will not be truly free. Only you can choose.

You've survived the trauma. It is time to resurrect the girl. She awaits her hero: *you*. Its time to rescue her. She is worthy of healing, REAL love, life, peace, intimacy and purpose!!!

Healing will not be easy. It will hurt like hell. You will feel like your insides are being torn from you! Don't be afraid of this feeling. It will not overtake you. This feeling is necessary. This feeling is saying, "this grossness has to get out of me!!" This feeling is vital to your very existence. Embrace the hurt, let the tears flow freely, grieve, moan, it's ok. You lost something very precious to you, and it is time to feel the sadness of that loss and begin the healing that those that hurt you hoped you would never find.

Throughout this journey you will feel elated that the secret is out, and then within the same moment feel so much fear that you will tremble inside wishing to suck those words back inside of you. You may briefly return to your addictions, to cutting, to sexual self-injury, to avoidance. But get back up, little one. Go one more step, just one more. Trust your words. Do you hear me? I said trust your words, your story. Your story will free you from the prison that your abuser put you in. You have the key to freedom. Now use it. You've been in prison to damn long.

It's time to fight for your wings. Fight!! I said *fight*. It's time to fly! They can no longer hold you down or keep you quiet. Remember, you're not alone. When that feeling comes, close your eyes, breathe and sense the spirits of other survivors all around you. I am right beside you, beautiful girl. I love you!

Don't let your spirit die, for it must live on for the next beautiful survivor. She needs your story. It is time. It is time.

Go one more,
Danée

Dear Friend and Future Survivor,

You do not know me. You can't pick me out of a crowd, or see 'it' in my eyes, but we are connected. What we share binds us as we make our journey through this life.

Somewhere in this world is someone who thinks they have won. Or, gives little to no thought to the crime they committed. But you know. And I know. And they are wrong. We are not beaten, we have not lost!

At first there is wave upon wave of emotion that seems out of your control. Many times there is blame. Know it is NOT yours. Nor is there shame to be shared among us; that belongs to our attackers. Do not allow your mind to drift there. You were not at fault. What binds us is not fault or fear. We are bound by living through the terror.

I have been where you are. I have lain where you lay. I have spent sleepless, terror-filled nights that drag into anxious, dread-laden days. But this will not be forever.
There are feelings you do not believe you will ever feel again, be patient - do not rush. You will know when the time is right to seek and enjoy those feelings.

It is easy to take the wrong path in your thoughts right now. Do not bring guilt, shame, bitterness, hopelessness, or fear on this journey; they belong to the offender Not you. There is no room for those thoughts, because we are on a journey to wholeness.

The path is rough and rocky sometimes, and much is uphill, but thee are many along the path to show where best to step and where not to stay.

You are a person of worth. There is value in surviving. And there is joy in thriving and reaching back to bring others along on this journey. There are many of us, too many.

There is an ability we share, each in our own time, and in our own way. We have the ability and the NEED to trust. But trust is a learned behavior and can only be achieved by wise consideration. There is someone with whom you can entrust your story, and it needs to be told.

There is no magic pill or potion to make this go away. And unfortunately, time does not "Heal all wounds". But time is a tool that allows us to access the recovery we need. Use the time wisely knowing you CAN feel real joy in your life again.

You may not recognize the moment it happens, but there is a day out there, a day you must seek. The day you become a survivor.

Love yourself. Trust yourself, and move forward.

                                        -Leitha Brogan

Dear Sister or broth[...]
    It should go w/o saying
what you've just been through. I
~~Right and at home~~ you nee[d]
you deserve to feel better & be to[...]
loved. Even in your pain, even i[...]
feel worthless and just want to d[...]
out and take my hand and rest i[...]
that other survivors have for yo[u]
in your life still have for you. [...]
of peace & rest in this bubble of [...]
have to say about the road no[w]
    Because believe it or n[ot]
out before you, and you are [...]
of a journey. Maybe you feel [...]
you're thinking the easiest w[...]
end your life, or maybe the [...]
recently, at least. I am tellin[g]
without a shred of doubt: th[...]
this, and a way to a lif[e...]
trust again and life is fun aga[in]

Dear Sister or Brother Survivor,

It should go without saying that I am so deeply sorry about what you've just been through. I am writing to you now because you need to know you are not alone, you deserve to feel better and be treated far better, and you are loved. Even in your pain, even in your darkest hour, if you feel worthless and just want to die, I wish you could reach out and take my hand and rest in the love that I have for you, that other survivors have for you, and that all the *good* people in your life still have for you. I wish you could find a moment of peace and rest in this bubble of love and listen to what I have to say about the road ahead of you.

Because believe it or not, there is a path stretching out before you, and you are about to embark on one hell of a journey. Maybe you feel so horrible right now that you're thinking the easiest way or the only way to cope is to end your life, or maybe the thought has crossed your mind recently, at least. I am telling you firmly, definitely, absolutely, without a shred of doubt: there *is* another way out of this, and a way to a life where you feel again and you trust again and life is fun again. I can't lie, it won't be easy. And it cannot be faked. At least, if you are really going to survive this, you cannot fake your way through recovery.

"Recovery?" Yeah, I know—I used to think that was a clinical term for addicts or something, but no, think about it: if you break a bone, it has to recover; if you suffer from a disease you have to recover from it.

Well, what you have been through has most likely traumatized you. Maybe you're like, "no shit!" or, perhaps, if you are like I was, you are completely unaware that this was traumatic and that you can't heal from it all by yourself. You're going to have to get some aid from professionals who know how to help you weather this storm. And so if you have not already, you must go see a therapist and, best-case scenario, see if you can join group therapy. That may sound horrific and frightening but I cannot stress this enough: if there is a qualified therapist leading the group who knows what he or she is doing, this will not only help you, it will become invaluable to you.

Now. Take a deep breath. Once you have some therapy set up to go to, that's just the beginning. It's like that is the arena, but the rodeo is up to you. If this sounds like a lot of work, it is. If it sounds like it takes a big effort, well, it does. If it sounds exhausting, some days it can be, sure. And I am here, living proof, to tell you it will be worth it.

Every frightening, embarrassing, funny, sad, crazy, confusing, thought-provoking moment will be absolutely worth it in the end. (And often even before it ends.)

But therapy is not 24/7, so you gotta take care of yourself most of the time. And, you may not even feel like you understand yourself anymore. You may have times you feel like you're just going nuts. You may want to hurt yourself sometimes, and sometimes maybe you will. The Number One thing I wish someone had said to me when I was where you are now is: Forgive yourself and be patient with yourself. There's no doubt you blame yourself for something or other, or you feel stupid, or you wonder if you can trust your own judgment anymore. *Forgive* yourself, as you would forgive a friend. And then in the days, months, even years to come, be patient with you.

If you've gone numb, it can take a while to work back up to feeling anything. But don't give up and mistakenly believe this is all there is for you anymore. It's not! You <u>will</u> feel good again. Start by just noticing simple, beautiful things each day. Green trees against blue sky in the sunlight. A bird singing on a wire. A child's smile. A colorful sunset. A piece of art that you like. Anything. Try to find some beauty in each day. That is how I started.

I also read books by Kahlil Gibran and found them helpful, particularly "The Prophet." You may, if you search, also discover books that become meaningful to you and help you get through your days. Same with music. For me, it was Tori Amos's *Little Earthquakes* and Nine Inch Nails' *Pretty Hate Machine* and the Indigo Girls and Aimee Mann (including *Lost in Space* and 'Til Tuesday's *Everything's Different Now*). I realize this dates me, but there is no shortage of music out there from each generation which will speak to you of trauma recovery, of finding yourself, of transcending. Find the music that resonates with you—in a variety: some angry, some with self-pity, some philosophical, some pensive, some hopeful.

Dear Sister or broth[er]
It should go w/o saying
what you've just been through. I
~~[crossed out]~~ you nee[d]
you deserve to feel better & be to[o]
loved. Even in your pain, even i[f]
feel worthless and just want to d[ie]
out and take my hand and rest i[n]
that other survivors have for yo[u]
in your life still have for you. [I]
of peace & rest in this bubble of
have to say about the road no[w]
Because believe it or n[ot]
out before you, and you are a[bout]
of a journey. Maybe you feel
you're thinking the easiest w[ay]
end your life, or maybe the
recently, at least. I am tellin[g]
~~[scribble]~~ without a shred of doubt: t[here is]
this, and ~~[scribble]~~ a way to a li[fe]
trust again and life is fun aga[in]

Dear Sister or Brother Survivor,

It should go without saying that I am so deeply sorry about what you've just been through. I am writing to you now because you need to know you are not alone, you deserve to feel better and be treated far better, and you are loved. Even in your pain, even in your darkest hour, if you feel worthless and just want to die, I wish you could reach out and take my hand and rest in the love that I have for you, that other survivors have for you, and that all the *good* people in your life still have for you. I wish you could find a moment of peace and rest in this bubble of love and listen to what I have to say about the road ahead of you.

Because believe it or not, there is a path stretching out before you, and you are about to embark on one hell of a journey. Maybe you feel so horrible right now that you're thinking the easiest way or the only way to cope is to end your life, or maybe the thought has crossed your mind recently, at least. I am telling you firmly, definitely, absolutely, without a shred of doubt: there *is* another way out of this, and a way to a life where you feel again and you trust again and life is fun again. I can't lie, it won't be easy. And it cannot be faked. At least, if you are <u>really</u> going to survive this, you cannot fake your way through recovery.

"Recovery?" Yeah, I know—I used to think that was a clinical term for addicts or something, but no, think about it: if you break a bone, it has to recover; if you suffer from a disease you have to recover from it.

The final thing that I learned, I cannot believe it took me so long to find out. In telling you this now, it will save you a lot of loneliness and if you act on it, gain you support you cannot even imagine. There is a whole community of survivors out there you can connect with. Some are on the internet, some are literally in your community. There are people who have been through what you're going through, and people going through the same stages as you right now. They are waiting for you with open arms, ready to listen to you, wanting to love you. Find us. Let us help. We're with you.

You may not feel that what has happened has changed you. And I do not advocate that you can change back into the person you used to be before. But you *can* take control of your destiny now and, like the phoenix rising out of the ash, change yourself into whoever you want to be, well and happy and living a full life. It takes a while, it takes facing all your fears, but it will work out. It will, please believe.

I believe in you.
Peace and love,
Megan

Our biggest fear is not that we are inadequate;
Our biggest fear is that we are powerful beyond measure.
We ask ourselves, "who am I to be brilliant, gorgeous, talented, fabulous?"
Actually, who are you not to be?
Your playing small doesn't serve the world –
We are born to make manifest the glory of God that is within us,
And as we let our own light shine,
We unconsciously give other people permission to do the same."
-Marianne Williamson

Where are they now?

Katie came to my office to visit me yesterday. She was smiling broadly, laughing, and telling me, "you know, I'm really doing good! I have a struggle or two with self-injury once in a while, but even that is so much better! I'm really happy with myself." She is remarkable, and is still in the process of discovering that for herself. She is now the mother of two toddlers.

Leslie is happily married and has been drug-free for several months. She has one child.

Suzanne S. spent her adolescence in DHS custody. Suzanne, wherever you are, I pray you are still on this strong path.

Leitha was on the brink of suicide when she first wrote to me. By "brink," I mean she planned to die that day, perhaps minutes later. Instead, she agreed to join a long-term treatment program specializing in PTSD. She writes, "I have just completed the most intensive in-patient trauma based program that is actually one of only a few in the country. I was assigned two extremely talented and caring therapists and a psychiatrist who was gentle and caring. I dug in and worked hard. I was discharged yesterday and I am feeling very strong. I 'made friends' with the inner child I have run from for so long, and I am looking forward to a full life…" In 2008 she wrote this:

I have noticed something that, to me, is astounding. These are things I have noticed over the past couple of months. I think some of this happened when I wasn't paying attention. Maybe I should pay attention more often. Maybe we all should....

I noticed that I was having fewer, and fewer nightmares. Last night, I actually dreamt about a key function on my computer not working. No men, no woman, no pain or evil. Then I tried to remember the last time my husband nudged me awake from the demons....I'm not sure when that was. That is a change I can live with.

I noticed that I cry much less frequently. In fact, I tried to think of when the last time was that I felt the need to "let it out". Other than dealing with the evil in therapy, I have not had that need, in weeks. The last time I did cry was the day I dealt with my anger in therapy. I admit, I cried from that morning, right through the appointment. They were anxious tears, not depressed tears. They turned from anxious, to angry, to relieved tears. Another change I can live with.

Being a person who confronts things head-on, even when I am not fully ready to confront, I tend to allow myself to be consumed with a thing. The topic of rape, and then of rape recovery has been just that, consumption. I have noticed that I am not so consumed with it. It's not like the act has gone away, or that the desire to resolve things has gone away. It's like I am realizing I have conquered some things, some things I don't need to revisit. In *Resurrection After Rape*, I have marked those things with a blue flag. I have red flags on my items I need to work on. I have far fewer red tags than blue.....change, in not so long a time actually.

I noticed I sleep without the aid of sleeping pills. I haven't had to take a sleeping pill in over two weeks now. I sleep soundly, and I haven't "fought off an attack" in weeks. This is change my husband can appreciate.

I feel better physically. I have health issues unrelated to rape. But, I have noticed that I feel like walking, I feel like swimming, I feel like being out of the house, being active. I don't constantly avoid being out. I don't avoid running into old friends in the store, or at a restaurant. I don't "pretend" not to notice them, I am more my old self. I walk right up and start a conversation. I hug. I laugh. I engage. A change BACK to what I have been for so many years.

I accepted employment and will be returning to work toward the end of September. This time, I stated things in my employment interview, like salary requirements. I have always accepted whatever a job paid. This time, I was confident - in me. I told them what I was willing to work for, and what positions I would consider, or not consider. Not only did I get the job, but, I got more than I was asking for, a lot more.

I went for some very painful testing yesterday. I was nervous. I have had the tests done before. They use something similar to a tazer and shock very sensitive areas where nerves run close to the surface. Then, they poke needles in your muscles and expect you to then use the muscle, creating more discomfort. And you have to be exposed, so I was not a happy camper. But, I did it. I didn't have to disclose anything. I not only did the test, the physician who performed it told me what great pain tolerance I exhibited. I did it, and last night, when the nerves in my groin that had been aggravated by the testing were so painful, the pain triggered nothing....no remnants of "that day" invaded.

I have felt things that I haven't wanted to feel, ever. In feeling the emotions attached to rape recovery, I have noticed that it has impacted me on every level, not just in recovery. I mean, being able to feel anger was HUGE for me. A tremendous amount of shame was lifted from me when I was able to access anger - healthy anger, not rage. And, sorrow was possible. True sorrow, not depression, or the blues, but a *sorrow* that helped me realize it was okay to be sad over things I lost to rape. And, in coming out of that sorrow, I have reclaimed some things.

So…change can be good. Change can happen when we aren't planning on it. Change can be gradual, and can settle in and be a "given" if we aren't paying attention. But, for me, taking stock and recognizing the positive changes over the past couple of months has made my skin nicer to live in. A few months ago, I would not have believed those words were possible. I encourage you to look for the changes in yourselves, I know they are there.

Teresa is continuing her recovery from self-injury and eating disorders, and reaching out to other young women. She journals regularly and contributes to support groups with other victims and survivors.

Kaye is married and continues to help other survivors on dailystrength.org. She is an artist, a writer, and a grandmother.

Cassie is sober and is nearly finished with graduate school in psychology.

Taylor found me in a mall a few months ago and brought her best friend over to meet me. Taylor had gone for seven months without cutting herself, and is trying to help other teens overcome the same issue. With tears in her eyes—in the mall!—she showed me her arms, with no cuts, and told me that she still journals. "Thank you for helping me finally talk about this. I am feeling so good!"

Terah went in and out of several abusive relationships for two more years. She watched as her father battered her mother into unconsciousness, and Cassandra developed a methamphetamine habit. As I write this, though, she has just finished one month clean, and is no longer self-injuring.

Ashley emailed me just today to say she has finally reported her perpetrator to the police. I'd like to share her letter with you:

Hey! So after work this morning I got together with the police. I was having a major issue telling them what happened 4 years ago so we took a couple days for me to relax because I flipped out on them saying I couldn't and didn't want to do it anymore. Well, I went back this morning and told them everything I could. It was very, very hard on me. The entire time I never once looked them

in the face; I just sat there looking at the table. When I got done I got brave
and looked up. All I saw was horror in their faces. It made me feel so much
better when they started talking again. They were angry with *him* for hurting
me... THEY BELIEVED ME!! It was like finding out *you* believed me, all over. I
just cried.

Well since he's still been harassing/physically and sexually assaulting me they
are pushing for rape charges for 4 years ago too. They are hoping to arrest
him later this week. I'm so happy, but scared at the same time. It's gonna be a
good day when they pick him up, nice seeing him in handcuffs and shackles. I
just hope I can hold it together when/if this finally does go to court. Gonna
have a while to hold my courage till then. And then I'll have to see him again.

Anyways I just wanted to update you on what's been going on. Thanks again
for everything you've been doing for me, and sticking by my side through all
this. I printed out the message that you sent where you said in the beginning
that I can do it and that you're proud of me for reporting it and I held it the
entire time I was with the Police. I think that might have been where some of
my strength came from. I just imagined it was you sitting there in front of me
and I was telling you what happened again. Believe it or not, it helped.

An update from Ashley:

The police officer told me that the first time they showed my statement to
Andrew he refused to talk and kept saying he was innocent. Then yesterday
he requested to speak to them about my statement. He confessed to
everything. He wanted to speak to me about what happened, but I don't think I
want to. One thing that he told them that I didn't have in the statement was
that he choked me until I almost blacked out at one point. I don't remember
that part but I've had nightmares about it...needless to say, I WON!!

Victoria moved out of state and changed jobs. She said on her graduation day,
"You saved my life in that [group therapy] room more often than you know. I thought
God had brought me here to have a career, but now I know it was so I could be in that
room and do that work…I am finally accepting that I am a good person."

In celebration of her new self, Victoria ceremoniously shaved her head after she
had processed her rape story. She did this in the group, allowing each member to
participate. It symbolized letting go of her past and starting over. Victoria said that if
anyone had described at the beginning the changes she would make, she never would
have believed them. She said to me, with simultaneous tears and a smile, "I've finally left
the abusive relationship I was in with myself!" Victoria wrote:

A while back, Matt asked me to write about the balance/conflict between the pain
of doing the work required in treatment and the benefits that come therefrom. The
pain of the work may seem self-evident, but surely the pain is different for each
person. Just as all of our traumas were unique, so too are the emotional (and
sometimes physical) responses that we have to those traumas. As with many, if
not most, of us, my pain was in full-swing before I even began processing the

traumas. I believe part of what made therapy so painful for me was that I made no connection between the pain of my everyday life and the traumas I had suffered. I hated myself - I saw myself as garbage, but I had no idea why. It may sound strange, but I never hated the rapists or the men who molested me as a child. I don't know why. In some ways, I think it would have been easier to process and work through the trauma if the anger and hatred I felt had been directed outward rather than being internalized.

I hated my soul because I saw myself as wicked. I hated my body because I saw it as an instrument of my suffering - not suffering brought on by rape, but the suffering I inflicted upon myself in the form of self-injury...sexual and otherwise. While I never believed that I deserved to be raped or that I "asked for it," I did (and to some degree still do) believe that I put myself in dangerous situations - situations that I knew then and know now were not safe. I have to accept responsibility for drinking and taking drugs. But did this mean that I deserved to be raped? Of course not. But (and this is still a stuck point for me), I believe that the likelihood of my having been raped would have been decreased if I had made different choices. This seems especially true for me as to the second rape. Shouldn't I have learned my lesson from the frat party? Bottom line -- the source of my pain and despair seemed to be the self-blame I placed upon myself for having made bad choices.

I carried the anger, guilt, and shame with me into therapy. But, to a certain extent, they had been manageable. I was good at my job and had great relationships with my family and friends. Thus, while the pain was there, I had stuffed it down into the far reaches of myself and tried to ignore it the best I could. What was so hard for me about therapy was digging the pain out, pulling it up, tearing it off, and taking a good, hard look at it. This is exactly what I did not want to do. I was making it along ok, right? I was functional. I think part of what I had hoped to get out of therapy was not a way to get rid of the pain, but a way to stuff it done further so I could do a better job of ignoring it. It is one thing to know that, at some level, you are hurting. It is quite another thing to examine the hurt to find from whence it comes.

Therapy, for me, was like looking through a microscope. You look at something with the naked eye and it seems innocuous enough. But when magnified, you can really see the sharp edges, the valleys and caverns, and the barbs. In many ways, examining the pain was more painful than just living with it as it was. Therapy forced me to examine, and thereby challenge, some strongly held beliefs I had about myself. I thought I knew myself - who I was, what I wanted from life, what I valued, etc. What I came to find out was that the real me was the person underneath the pain.

To say that therapy was excruciating might be an understatement. While I do not have any children, I think that the process of childbirth offers a useful analogy. Many women I have talked to who have had children tell me how terrible the pain was. They say it felt like they were being ripped to pieces. When I ask if it was worth it, they look at me with surprise and respond, "of course." Without the pain of childbirth, the new precious life would not be possible. Accordingly, I think that without the pain of therapy, the emergence of one's true self would not be possible either. The question I think we must all ask ourselves is if we are willing to accept and endure the pain of recovery in order to achieve what lies beyond.

> Personally, I have never regretted what I went through - the sleepless nights, the overwhelming sadness, the uncontrollable crying, the fear, the uncertainty, and the doubt. When I was young, I remember my mom telling me something like "nothing good ever comes easily." While I don't think that is an absolute truth, I do believe it to be true in the context of becoming a rape survivor. In the end, when the pain subsides, you find yourself holding your own little bundle of joy. That bundle of joy is you.

I have not heard from her in more than two years; our lives have taken separate paths. I remain immensely proud of the work we did together, and enjoy fond memories of the positive impact I believe we both had on each others' lives.

After three years without contact, Aria found me by chance and she is doing immensely well. She no longer self-injures, she is happy, attends college, and still has her razor-sharp sense of wit. Her parents had also sent me a card to praise her accomplishments since the first time we met.

Danée worked for years for the Department of Human Services in the Child Protection division as part of her vow to protect children. She changed professions out of self-care to prevent emotional burnout. She is also seeking new ways to speak publicly about sexual assault, to share her story and educate communities. Danée has not self-injured in two years at this writing, and she reconciled with her daughters. In fact, she did so well that she was awarded primary custody of her children.

From time to time, Danée visits workshops and college classes to tell her story. She was the featured speaker for a Sexual Assault Month event in Oklahoma, addressing the topic "What survivors need from care professionals." I asked Danée how she felt about being so open with her story now and she told me, "It makes me so proud that I can do this. I don't have panic attacks anymore. I don't feel ashamed anymore. I'm so close to my family now, and we have so much fun, that I know I'm a good person now. I just want to help anyone else who has ever felt the way I did, because for so many years there was nobody speaking out to help me." I asked her how she handles critics, or people who are disinterested and judgmental about her life story. "Honestly?" she replied, "F--- them. Am I allowed to say that? Seriously, though, I have survived so much that I've earned the right to speak. I don't quiver anymore. If someone thinks something nasty about me, I don't wilt anymore. This work is too important, and I feel good about myself now, so I just need to keep trying. I'm no longer defined by a critic's judgment of me. I'm defined by the people who love me, and my love for myself."

Her statement is echoed in the small tattoo on her right wrist: *Loved Survivor.*

Come.

Come, whoever you are,
Wanderer, worshiper, lover of learning,
It doesn't matter.

Ours is not a caravan of despair.
Come, even if you have broken your vows a thousand times.
Come, come yet again.

Come.

-Rumi

Afterword: My letter to Survivors

In Ojibway Indian stories, we are told that the Creator held council with all creatures to announce the imminent creation of humans. The Creator said that humans would be unique among all living things because humans would possess imagination, which would equip us either to build or destroy; pray or prey. The animal beings discussed the importance of hiding the secret Truth of Life so that humans would not discover it prematurely and abuse it. But no idea seemed workable: whether the Truth of Life was hidden in the depths of the oceans, the edges of the prairies, or even on the moon itself, human imagination would devise a way to travel there and seize the secret treasure. It seemed there was no way to prevent humans from imagining new ways to fail, to be cruel, or to miss out on life's truths.

I never intended to grow up and do this work; the work chose me. But here I am, and I love what I do. I love the people I help. They are not "patients and cases" to me, not customers and treatment plans. I love each of you. I love because more than anything, you each need and deserve to be loved, and you are so eager to do good and to be kind to others who are hurt.

Hundreds of times, victims of rape and sexual abuse have told me the worst stories of their pain and trauma, their heads bowed in shame. When they have the courage to look up, they don't see the look of disgust on me that they expect. I can't help but look back at them in respect. It's not pity, and it's not superficial platitudes; I truly feel a genuine sense of reverence. I, too, know what it's like to feel inadequate and to doubt myself, to fail, to falter, to err, and I haven't forgotten when I've felt that way. People who have felt completely valueless have turned over everything in their stories, every secret, in trust. They have trusted me not to shame them. Trusted me to know what to do next after they finally pour out their hidden pain. This is a deeply personal and intensely spiritual act; it's not merely an academic exercise in therapy. It's not something a book can teach you. It's not something you receive like a social work diploma. It's not something you can stuff into a paid hour of time. It's something you have to feel or you can't understand it.

I can't help but bond with some of the very special ones, not that I would resist it if I could. Frankly, without that bond the recovery wouldn't happen. Rape isn't something you can recover from by bouncing ideas off a stoic, detached "expert" in a seat across a room. It's a crime that impacts your soul—your very sense of connection to others—and reconnecting your spirit through an act of trust is more than merely possible, it's essential. Being perfect, being flawless, never failing, never screwing up—those are not the standards we can hold out for. Friendship, care, humor, and loyalty are far more valuable. Never discard the clay-footed friend who cares because you're searching for the spotless healer instead.

My faith tradition teaches me that we encounter God in the stranger, and by keeping that in mind I see resurrection every day. This is not about seeking God down the end of some tunnel, but about realizing that life is the process of God seeking us, and for our lack of attention we miss a million forms of wonder every day. But we also manage to notice a few:

I think of Cassie, the young woman who joined my group feeling invisible and small, but who showed people a new way to be strong. Cassie's intelligence and wisdom seeped through her belligerent disguises, and I watched that tiny slip of a girl transform into a proud, confident woman, head held high, with "SURVIVOR" proudly tattooed after her transformation.

I think of the young woman, so blessed with intelligence and talent, who overdosed right in front of me. I remember holding her hand and ordering her to look me in the eye as she faded from consciousness, while medics scurried about fastening tubes and machines. "You're more than this," my eyes tried to say after the poisons had stolen her hearing. I remember sitting with her in ICU, holding a hand with tape and IV tubes wrapped around it, reading to her during her sickness. This was the one I nearly lost. But I remember her surviving and thanking me for not leaving her, and pledging that she would beat her trauma. And for the next month, she fought back against the darkness that almost took her. She toiled and cried and struggled and screamed...until she succeeded!

And I also think of sadder moments, such as the bright, tragic ones whose anger, disillusionment and hurt made them lash out at compassion. It was a cruel curse of their traumas that they would attack the very things they craved most: acceptance. Friendship. One by one, they've slipped away back into the distant world, hurt, bitter, and alone.

Or the time a teenage girl was assigned to my caseload who did not speak a word of English. In fact, we never did discover what language she did speak. With no way to communicate, and with her dread terror at being in a mental health facility in a foreign country, what was I supposed to do? There was nothing I could do, but abandon all the routine academic training about therapy and simply try to express, You are safe. I will not hurt you. I understand how scared you are.

Or the very gifted and brilliant woman who made powerful gains in her recovery, recovering happiness and pride. When tragedy struck her life again, she called at 4:00 AM. It was no time for a therapist; it was time for a friend. We cried together until dawn.

It's times like these that we put aside textbooks and policies, regardless what it costs us, and just become humans in connection with other humans.

Some of the most priceless treasures I have are the cards and letters that share what it meant for someone to open up and trust again, give themselves over to hope, and to not be pitied or treated as "broken" in return. Those of you who have supportive partners, allies, or therapists, please do not neglect this part of the relationship; s/he needs to hear your thanks more than you know. Never take for granted having an ally or friend who thinks highly of you, supports you, takes time to express what you mean to them, and who would grieve the loss of you. The word "tribe" is the best I know for it.

In Survivors, I see right before my eyes many of the most worthy and respectable people I have ever found. Sometimes you will see others who take this for granted; they drink and cut and kill themselves out of the very tribe that they are meant to be in. Can you see why this is painful for us? You have the right to inclusion in this circle, this interconnected web of powerful people—powerful women—and yet some of you hang your heads down and feel ashamed of who you are. Don't disregard your status as a Survivor. Holocaust Survivor Elie Weisel once wrote, "Just as despair can come to one only from other human beings, hope, too, can be given to one only by other human beings."

Rape recovery is not a curriculum or a business; it is a deeply personal process of bonding, sharing pain, and rediscovering personal strength. It begins with fear, but when done right it ends with friendship. We are all in constant resurrection through this work, me included. That is why interconnection is so vital! Those who see healing as an exchange of pay for routine care in the symptom-management industry will not understand the role of friendship in recovery. One woman wrote to me, "We, all of us (including you), share strong common traits. We have all been injured, we have all stared down the pain, and we have all chosen to come out into the light. We are all brave and strong. We all believe in each other's worth. We all love each other. These are the ties that bind us together. These are the things that make us a tribe."

Do you see why it hurts when this living tribe of Survivors has among it women who are ashamed to even be part of this? Can you be proud of who you are as women surviving rape? Can you proudly belong to what so many others are ashamed to be part of? That pride just might mean holding your head high, opening your mouth, and declaring, "I am a Survivor, and this is my story! I am not ashamed of my story, for it proves me worthy of the strength I carry."

This work has brought me into the lives of many women and men who have felt they had nothing good left inside to give, and yet you have all taught me something: a new way to love. This, to me, is real spirituality: finding and loving God as a Creator that connects us.

In American Indian traditions, an eagle feather is given to certify an honorable achievement. The achievement can be one of bravery, or powerful spiritual accomplishment, or generosity. This work requires all three of those qualities. We don't do this work to gather praise or status, but to give those things to others. If you have no eagle feathers to give as signs of honor to your fellow wounded warriors, can you give hugs or letters, and make sure to let your mentors, inspirations, and life-allies know how much they mean? Every person in this community needs that, like oxygen.

When the Creator and the council of living creatures were trying to solve the riddle of protecting the Truth of Life, it was the hawk who struck upon the solution and found the one hiding place where humans would never look until we were ready to find the secret:

"Hide the Truth of Life inside them."

Do something.
Hope.
Live!

The End.

Suggested Reading:

The Rape Recovery Handbook: Step-By-Step Help for Survivors of Sexual Assault
by Aphrodite Matsakis

Quest for Respect: A Healing Guide for Survivors of Rape
by Linda Braswell

I Can't Get over It: A Handbook for Trauma Survivors
by Aphrodite Matsakis

Post-Traumatic Stress Disorder Sourcebook
by Glenn R. Schiraldi

The Macho Paradox: Why Some Men Hurt Women and How All Men Can Help
by Jackson Katz

The Scarred Soul: Understanding & Ending Self-Inflicted Violence
by Tracy Alderman

"Mom, I Hate My Life!": Becoming Your Daughter's Ally Through the Emotional Ups and Downs of Adolescence
by Sharon Hersh

Reviving Ophelia: Saving the Selves of Adolescent Girls
by Mary Pipher

Searching for Angela Shelton (DVD)

Perfect Girls, Starving Daughters: The Frightening New Normalcy of Hating Your Body
by Courtney E. Martin

The Sexual Healing Journey: A Guide for Survivors of Sexual Abuse
by Wendy Maltz

What About Me? A Guide for Men Helping Female Partners Deal with Childhood Sexual Abuse
by Grant Cameron

Why Does He Do That? Inside the Minds of Angry and Controlling Men
by Lundy Bancroft

Matt Atkinson is a Domestic and Sexual Violence Response Professional. He has worked in crisis services as a staff director, where he developed and implemented programs with women's prisons, university sports teams, churches, and Indian tribes. Matt has also worked with youth at an in-patient treatment hospital, and with adults at an intensive outpatient day treatment group.

In 2004, he became the first male given the National Award for Outstanding Advocacy and Community Work in Ending Sexual Violence by the National Sexual Violence Resource Center.

In 2005 he was awarded "Most Therapeutic" by his professional peers. In 2006 he began to teach college courses on domestic violence and crisis intervention as a university adjunct professor. He regularly presents trainings at workshops and conferences.

Each year since 2008, he and a team of dedicated volunteers run a Spiritual Healing Retreat for Survivors (see www.resurrectionafterrape.org for info). The event draws participants from around the world.

In 2009, a group of his former patients collectively nominated Matt for the "Embrace Award," given to the person who exemplifies the mission of "eliminating racism and empowering women."

In recent years, he has directed a project to develop diverse Sexual Assault Response Teams (SART) by training nurses, therapists, advocates, law enforcement, and program administrators.

In 2011, he produced the book *Letters To Survivors: Words of Comfort for Women Recovering from Rape* to critical acclaim and multiple publishing awards. He continues to speak at conferences and trainings throughout the United States.

Matt is very happily married to the most amazing woman in the world, and has two incredible sons.

He is always writing new material.

Resurrecting

Missing the girl I was –
I miss getting to be her, seeing life through her eyes—
thinking she'd been murdered
and my presence continued merely out of habit,
        a kind of reverse ghost.
Sometimes I wondered if the answer
would be to ditch this useless body,
        the only way to move time forward again?
It turns out, the problem is with the question.
   See, my assumptions, handed to me by others,
came not from my own mind and soul.
Time to unlearn, time to dig deep, time to dive—
I'm afraid, but I will do this to survive.

Now, sing to me of phoenixes
  fiery transformation
  resurrecting the fractured pieces
  rebuilding them into a whole, a whole new—
this time of my own design
      not my mother's, not my father's, not society's
            not men's, hell no—
Letting go, letting go of old props and crutches
I will come forth of my own accord,
and the world had best prepare itself
for I am coming with my voice, I am charging with my words.
Yes, they will hear me, and see me as never before.
And I don't care what they think of it
for I have my girl back—she may be changed
but she is complex now, and beautiful… and faultless.
She brought a few friends with her: Anger, Pride, and Truth,
I welcome them as teachers,
and Hope their headmistress, Love, their muse.

So within I am not alone, nor am I alone without—
you don't have to look far to find
other missing girls
     resurrecting.

Let's sing now of the phoenix!
and reclaim all we deserve,
let's be mad as hell and not take it anymore,
then let's laugh and cry and forgive,
let's set an example for all the world
and then let's go home….and just live.

                    -Tonya N. Atkinson

Letters To Survivors

Words of Comfort for Women Recovering from Rape

The remarkable new book features letters from women who have experienced rape and sexual abuse, written to those who need hope, help, advice, and support.

Crammed with positive messages, *Letters To Survivors* addresses such topics as:

- Coping with suicidal feelings
- How to recognize toxic "helpers"
- Self-injury
- Spirituality after rape
- Isolation and lonliness
- Warnings about what *doesn't* work in recovery
- How to work effectively with your therapist
- Sex and sexuality after rape
- How to feel hopeful again

Presented entirely in full-color beautiful artwork! No triggering or "dark" imagery--just gorgeous, classy, inspirational collages. The entire book is a masterpiece, suitable for gift-giving to readers of all ages.

Actual pages:

WINNER of multiple publishing awards!

Available at BarnesandNoble.com, Amazon.com, and fine bookstores, or at letterstosurvivors.com (in standard paperback and DELUXE editions, with discounts for bulk orders)

"If you work with rape victims, this ought to be the very first resource you put into their hands. It may even save lives." -Jessica, Survivor